Sheffield Archaeological Monographs 9

Series Editor

John R. Collis

Executive Editor

Russell Adams

Sheffield Academic Press

The *Harra* and the *Hamad*

Excavations and Explorations in Eastern Jordan

Volume 1

A.V.G. Betts

and

S. Colledge, L. Martin, C. McCartney,
K. Wright, V. Yagodin

with contributions by

L. Cooke, A.N. Garrard, J. Hather, C. McClintock,
W. Lancaster and D.S. Reese

Sheffield Academic Press

Published by Sheffield Academic Press Ltd
Mansion House
19 Kingfield Road
Sheffield S11 9AS
England
Tel: 44 (0)114 255 4433
Fax: 44 (0)114 255 4626

Copies of this volume and a catalogue of other archaeological
publications can be obtained from the above address or from our home page.

World Wide Web - http://www.shef-ac-press.co.uk

Typeset by Sheffield Academic Press
and printed on acid-free paper in Great Britain
by Bookcraft
Midsomer Norton, Somerset

A catalogue record of this book is available from the British Library

ISBN 1 85075 614 7

Contents

List of Figures

List of Tables

List of Plates

Contributors

A.V.G. Betts   Department of Archaeology
                      University of Sydney
                      Sydney, NSW 2006
                      Australia

S. Colledge   Honorary Fellow
                      Institute of Archaeology
                      University College London
                      31-34 Gordon Square
                      London WC1H 0PY, UK

L. Cooke   4 Lincoln Close
                      Stoke Mandeville
                      Aylesbury HP22 5YS, U.K.

A.N. Garrard   Institute of Archaeology
                      University College London
                      31-34 Gordon Square
                      London WC1H 0PY, UK

J. Hather   Institute of Archaeology
                      University College London
                      31-34 Gordon Square
                      London WC1H 0PY, UK

W. Lancaster   Rysa Lodge
                      Lyness, Orkney
                      U.K.

L. Martin   Institute of Archaeology
                      University College London
                      31-34 Gordon Square
                      London WC1H 0PY, UK

C. McCartney   c/o Lemba Excavation Project,
                      Kissonerga Village
                      Paphos District, Cyprus.

C. McClintock   4 Forthill Road
                      Ballycarry
                      Carrickfergus, Co. Antrim
                      N. Ireland BT38 9JU

D.S. Reese   Field Museum of Natural History
                      Roosevelt Road at Lake Shore Drive
                      Chicago, Illinois 60605- 2496
                      USA

K. Wright   Institute of Archaeology
                      University College London
                      31-34 Gordon Square
                      London WC1H 0PY, UK

V. Yagodin   Institute of History, Archaeology and Ethnology
                      179-A Gorky Street
                      Nukus, Uzbekistan 742000

Preface

It is impossible to thank individually all the people and organisations from whom I have received help during my field research in Eastern Jordan. The reports presented in this volume are selected results of fieldwork carried out over a period from 1979–1990 and each year has seen the list grow. First and foremost I would like to thank the staff of the Department of Antiquities of Jordan: Directors General Dr Ghazi Bisheh, Dr Adnan Hadidi and Dr Safwan Tell; and our Field Representatives, Mr Arif Abu Ghannem (1981–83), Mr Ibrahim Haj Hassan (1986), and Mr Khaled al-Jbour (1988–9).

Work in 1979 was carried out while I was Annual Scholar of the British School of Archaeology in Jerusalem. The Black Desert Survey (1981–3) was sponsored by The British Institute at Amman for Archaeology and History, and was conducted as research for my doctoral thesis while I was a student at the Institute of Archaeology, London University. Fieldwork was supported by grants from the Ashmolean Museum, the British School of Archaeology in Jerusalem, the British Institute at Amman for Archaeology and History, the Central Research Fund (University of London), the City Museums and Art Gallery, Birmingham, the Country Museum, Liverpool, the G.A. Wainwright Fund, the Gordon Childe and Margery Bequest Funds, the Manchester Museum, the Palestine Exploration Fund, and the Pitt-Rivers Museum.

Excavations at Dhuweila (1986) were sponsored by the British Institute at Amman for Archaeology and History, and were supported by the Ashmolean Museum, the British Academy, the British Institute at Amman for Archaeology and History, Birmingham City Museums and Art Gallery, the British School of Archaeology in Jerusalem, the Central Research Fund (University of London), the County Museum, Liverpool, the G.A. Wainwright Fund, the Gordon Childe and Margery Bequest Funds, the Manchester Museum, the Palestine Exploration Fund, the Pitt-Rivers Museum, the Prehistoric Society, and the Society of Antiquaries of London. The Edinburgh University/B.I.A.A.H. Expedition to Burqu'/Ruweishid was sponsored jointly by Edinburgh University, Department of Archaeology and the British Institute at Amman for Archaeology and History. Fieldwork was undertaken while I was a British Academy Post-Doctoral Fellow in the Department of Archaeology, Edinburgh University, and continued while I was Research Fellow at the School of Geosciences, The Queen's University of Belfast. Funding was granted by the British Academy, the British Institute at Amman for Archaeology and History, the Bomford Trust Fund (Ashmolean Museum), the Carnegie Trust for the Universities of Scotland, the Centre of African Studies (Edinburgh University), the Department of Archaeology (Edinburgh University), the G.A. Wainwright Fund, the Munro Fund (Edinburgh University), the Royal Museum of Scotland, the Palestine Exploration Fund, and the Society of Antiquaries of London. This report was started while I was Research Fellow at the Department of Archaeology, Edinburgh University and completed after I became Lecturer in Near Eastern Archaeology at the University of Sydney. This volume was published with financial assistance from the University of Sydney. I am extremely grateful to the staff and funding committees of all these institutions for their support. The last chapter of this volume includes a summary of research carried out by Professor Vadim Yagodin, Head of the Institute of Archaeology, University of Nukus, Uzbekistan. With the aid of a grant from the University of Sydney, I visited Nukus in 1993 at the invitation of Professor Yagodin to see the animal traps which he has been studying for a number of years in the Aralo-Caspian region. The similarities between these and the 'kite' systems of eastern Jordan are remarkable, and I am grateful to Professor Yagodin for allowing me to publish a summary of his work in this volume.

None of this work could have been completed without the help, hard work and forbearance of the in-field staff. To them I owe our results. Staff from all field seasons are listed here collectively: Julia Atkinson, Ali Balcaz, Dominic Best, Alison Bowden, Kirsty Cameron, Alex Creswell, Cliff Denham, Joseph Dortch, Alvarro Figviero, John Grey, Svend Helms, Brian Hitchcock, Evan Jones, Derek Kennet, Fidelity Lancaster, William Lancaster, Alan Lupton, Kirsten Macleod, Louise Martin, Frank Matsaert, Carole McCartney, Cathy Mclaughlin, Lucinda McLintock, Alison McQuitty, Rebecca Montague, Joseph Morgan, Constantine Politis, Anne Porter, Julia Rayner,

Alison Reynolds, Isabelle Ruben, Madelene Sarley, Urs Schupp, Chris Steele, Michael Woods, and Donna Yorkston.

There are many other people to whom I am indebted for advice, guidance, practical assistance and moral support. Among these are the staff of the British Institute at Amman for Archaeology and History, the staff of the American Center for Oriental Research, and colleagues in universities and other institutions in Jordan and elsewhere who share an interest in the history of the Near East. I must also collectively thank the many Jordanians who have offered hospitality and friendship to myself and the field teams. Finally, I would like to thank Svend Helms for years of help, advice and inspiration. It was at his suggestion that I went to the *harra* in the first place.

1. Introduction

A.V.G. Betts

This volume is the first in a series covering fieldwork carried out in eastern Jordan from 1979 to 1991. Up until the 1970s very little was known about the prehistory of eastern Jordan. From then on the area attracted increasing interest, and yet, after almost two decades of fieldwork, our understanding of the region in the prehistoric periods and later is still far from complete.

None the less, considerable progress has been made, not least because much comparative evidence is now available from elsewhere in Jordan and the Near East. The volumes in this series are intended as reference works: the object is to present basic data, together with a summary account of its general significance. Further discussion on the history and prehistory of the study area will appear elsewhere.

The *Harra* and the *Hamad* Today

Land use

Northeastern Jordan is climatically classified as steppe/desert (see Lamb 1972 for Koeppen's classification), a region where the rainfall is too low for effective cultivation of crops, and where the land today is used mainly for grazing. Until recently the region had only one road, the main highway between Amman and Baghdad, and no settlements east of the town of Mafraq, with the exception of small colonies of Circassian and Druze migrants who settled around the springs at Azraq. The area was traditionally used by various bedouin tribes. These included sheep/goat herders who used the western sector and the basalt region (*harra*), and camel herding tribes who, as part of a broader pattern of movement, pastured in the open country (*hamad*) east of the *harra* (Figures 1.1 and 1.2).

Field research has been broadly restricted to the 'panhandle', the northeastern band of Jordanian territory bordering on Syria in the north, Iraq to the east, and Saudi Arabia to the south. Local geology divides the region into two distinct sectors. The western half, the *harra*, is covered by basalts and tuffs, mostly of Miocene/Pliocene origin (Bender 1968). Bedrock in the eastern sector, the *hamad*, is made up of Cretaceous and Tertiary limestones, covered by a deflated crust of chert gravels (Figure 1.3). This has resulted in a broken, rock-strewn landscape in the *harra*; an area which provides shelter, grazing and seasonal water, but which is difficult to cross. The *hamad* is open country, cut in places by broad, shallow wadis; land which has few water sources but which can successfully support sheep/goat herds in wet seasons, and is good camel country in most years. The open gravel plains of the *hamad* are also crossed by a number of ancient routes, both north–south and east–west. These are for the most part 'back door' routes, used to avoid major centres of population closer to the fertile lands.

Both the *harra* and the *hamad* are regions where limited resources are compensated for by personal freedom. The *hamad* lies too far from the settled lands to be effectively under state control. This applies even today where the influence of the sheikhs is as important as that of central government. The *harra*, while lying closer to areas of settlement, is so rough and inhospitable to those who are unfamiliar with it that it has traditionally been a place of refuge, particularly for bandits and brigands. Travellers would try to avoid the edges of the basalt massif for fear of raiders who might sweep down from hiding places among the rocks, and just as rapidly disappear back into the *harra* where pursuit was impossible. However, the *harra* could also be a safe haven for people who would be vulnerable to attack on the open plains of the *hamad*.

In these regions there are great seasonal and annual variations in climate which control the pattern of life to a high degree. In a good year, the first rains come in autumn, late October to November, but even before this, heavy dewfall in September to early October encourages growth of the first winter annual vegetation. The rains continue intermittently until March, often falling as heavy localised storms, flooding wadi systems well beyond the areas of direct rainfall. During the winter, the winds are strong and there is a wide range in diurnal temperature. In spring — late March–early May — the climate is warm and dry. Annual and perennial vegetation growth is still relatively abundant and water lies in rainpools (*ghudran*) along the wadi systems. By

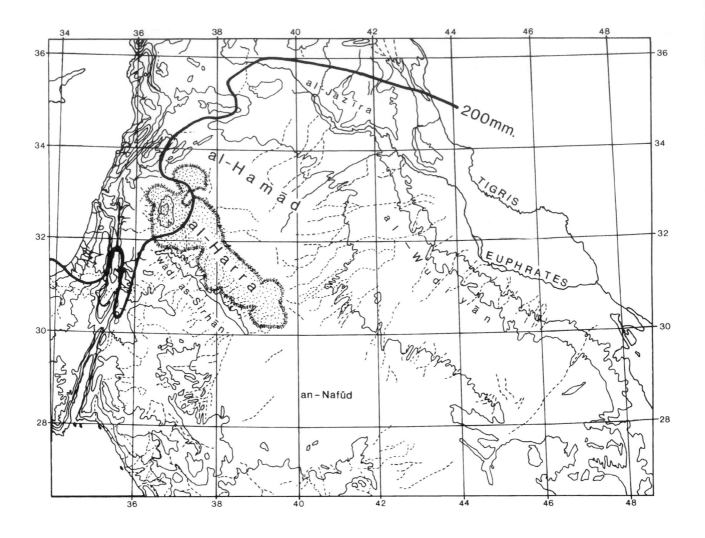

Figure 1.1   The Levant and north Arabia with 200 mm. isohyet

late May, the temperatures begin to approach their summer peaks, annual vegetation has burnt off and most of the *ghudran* are dry. Bedouin traditionally go out into the steppe in early autumn, where they take advantage of the dewfall grazing, but stay close to longterm water sources. As the rains fill the *ghudran*, the bedouin disperse across the steppe, following the rainclouds and the new plant growth. By late spring, they retreat back towards the edge of the settled lands, near to permanent wells and oases.

Environment

Conditions in the *harra* and the *hamad* vary greatly through the seasons. Temperatures, based on readings taken at Azraq (Nelson 1973), fluctuate from 45° C to - 10° C (Figure 1.6), while annual precipitation ranges from over 200 mm. in the northwest to less than 50 mm. in the south and east (Figure 1.7). The climatic zones, according to Koeppen's seminal classification (Lamb 1972) run from BS (steppic grassland) in the north, down into BW (warm desert) in the south (Figure 1.5). Overall precipitation averages 84 mm per year (U.N.D.P. 1966), most of this occurring as erratic winter storms and cloudbursts. The wet season generally lasts from November until March (Figure 1.8).

Perennial springs occur at Azraq, and there is limited groundwater seepage at one or two other places in the *harra*, such as Bir al-Ghusein and Burqu' in the northeast. After storms, some water is absorbed into the ground, but most flows as surface runoff into streambeds (*wudiyan*). Water rises rapidly in the *wudiyan*, creating heavy erosion, and collects in large shallow seasonal lakes (*qi'an*) where it evaporates within a few months. Where the stream channels are deeply incised, water is retained in *ghudran*. These are deeper and less subject to evaporation than the *qi'an*, and in years of good rain, some hold water for several months into the dry season.

Vegetation is largely limited to the *wudiyan* and to the silt deltas on the edges of the *qi'an*. Much vegetation

2

has been lost recently through overgrazing and destruction of bushes and shrubs for fuel. This in turn has affected faunal populations and accelerated the rate of erosion. Even without climatic variation, the region would have been considerably less barren in prehistoric times. Today in spring, the land supports a short season of flowering annuals and grasses. Perennial plants, mostly thorny shrubs and bushes, are varieties suited to dry conditions, and often to saline soils (Figures 1.4, 1.5). Typical vegetation consists of *Haloxylon salicornicum, Artemesia herba-alba, and Achillaea sp.* Where the perennials have been destroyed through overgrazing, ground vegetation is dominated by *Stipa capensis*. There is quite a number of edible species of plant including the seeds of grasses, legumes, chenopods, and roots/ stems of genera such as *Erodium, Orobranche, Ferula, Scorzonera*, and the bulbs of *Iris, Asphodelus* and similar species. In the northwest there

are stands of pistachio (*Pistacia atlantica*) which produce edible fruits, and dwarf bushes of *Prunus arabica* (Zohary 1962; Guest ed. 1966; Garrard *et al.* 1988a: 313).

The fauna of the region today bears very little relation to the great numbers and wide variety of species to be found there only a few hundred years ago. Man as a predator has eliminated the large mammal population almost entirely. As late as the early years of this century, both *harra* and *hamad* were home to hare, gazelle, bustard, partridge, and tortoise, as well as a range of carnivores including wolf, jackal, fox, hyaena, caracal, and cat, while the marsh areas around the springs at Azraq sheltered wild boar. Oryx, onager, ostrich, and large cats were also once common. The seasonal lakes attract large numbers of migrant birds, including raptors, storks, herons, cranes, and also smaller waders and waterfowl. Small mammals — mice, gerbils and jerboas

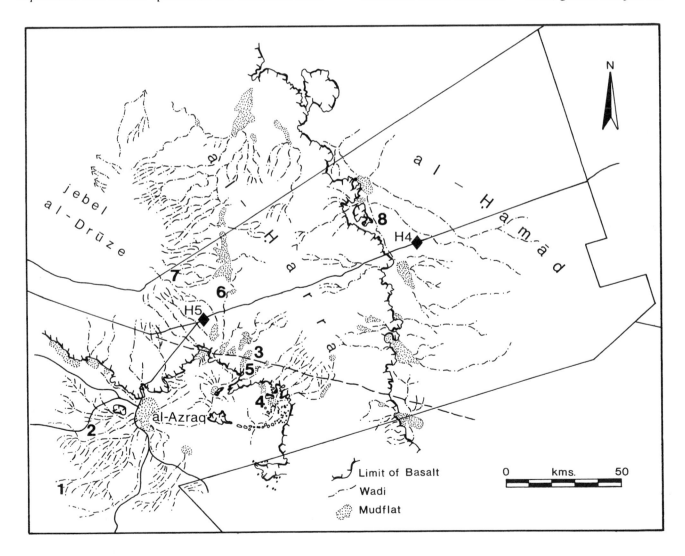

Figure 1.2   Eastern Jordan: 1. Wadi Jilat; 2. Kharaneh; 3. Dhuweila; 4. Jebel Naja; 5. Qa 'al-Ghirqa; 6. Wadi Rajil; 7. Khallat 'Anaza; 8. Qasr Burqu'.

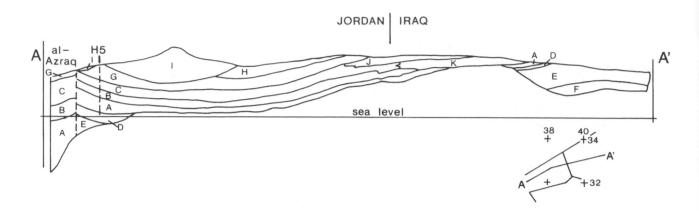

Figure 1.3   East Jordan / west Iraq: schematic geological cross sections (ACSAD Hamad Basin Project, Damascus 1983). A. limestone, marl, sand intercalation; B. chalky limestone, dolomite, chert; C. soft marl and chalk-like limestone, intercalations of chert and phosphate; D. sandstone; E. calcareous, argillaceous and evaporitic deposits; F. sandstone; G. chert, marl, limestone, partly covered with eolian sand; H. chalky and marly limestone; I. basalt; J. marl, limestone; K. limestone, dolomite, marl.

— are still common, as are their predators: snakes, scorpions, and camel spiders.

Basalt apart, rocks and minerals of use to prehistoric man are rare in the *harra*. The most important mineral, chert, occurs in beds within the limestones of the *hamad*. Medium to poor quality grey and brown cherts are most common and can be found eroding out of the limestones on the margins of the *harra*. There are also rare beds of finer green, banded flint in the south of the region, where younger chert beds have been protected from erosion by overlying lavas. These beds also produce fine-grained whitish or creamy flint. In the region of qa' al-Qattafi, the local cherts are a distinctive red colour, sometimes with cream or brown mottling. Black crystalline nodules superficially resembling obsidian were found embedded in the lavas of a volcanic crater in the heart of the *harra* (Betts 1984: 34, 1985: 51) but there was no evidence for the use of this rather fragile substance on prehistoric sites. Small chips of true obsidian have been found occasionally on Neolithic sites in the region, probably imports from Anatolia. Items of ornament found on prehistoric sites are made of various imported materials including sea shells and Dabba 'marble', a greenish-blue stone occurring on the watershed between the Azraq basin and the Jordan valley in fossil springs, where mineralization and thermal activity have coloured and altered the rock.

History of Research

Prior to our initial fieldwork, little was known about the prehistory of the region. Sites in the general area first came to the attention of the public through the reports of RAF pilots who flew across the desert on the airmail route from Cairo to Baghdad in the 1920s (Maitland

1927; Rees 1929). The airmen described walls and corrals visible from the air, and scatters of flints around the desert landing grounds. Later, sites along the airmail route and elsewhere in the *hamad* were examined by Field (1960), and a groundwater survey drew attention to sites around Azraq oasis, some of which were more fully sampled by Kirkbride (Zeuner *et al.* 1957) (Figure 1.2). In the 1930s Waechter and Seton Williams made soundings in two prehistoric sites west of Azraq, near the Wadi Dhobai (Waechter and Seton Williams 1938). In 1966 Helms began survey in the *harra* east of Mafraq, and continued this work in conjunction with excavations at the Bronze Age site of Jawa (Helms 1981; Betts [ed.] 1991). In 1975 Garrard and Stanley Price conducted systematic surveys of the Azraq basin (Garrard *et al.* 1975).

Since 1980 there has been a considerable increase in the number of expeditions to this part of the eastern steppe. Rollefson continued the work of Kirkbride at 'Ain al-Assad (Lion's Spring) (Rollefson 1982) and surveyed sites at Jebel Uweinid, a basalt outcrop west of Azraq (Rollefson and Fröhlich 1982). Copeland, Hours and others began work on Paleolithic sites and wadi terraces around Azraq (Copeland and Hours 1989), and Garrard initiated a major programme of survey and excavation around Azraq and in Wadi Jilat, including the sites previously investigated by Waechter and Seton Williams (Garrard *et al.* 1986, 1987, 1988a, b, 1994; Baird *et al.* 1992). Work was conducted by Muheisen at a large Epipaleolithic site near Kharaneh (1983). The later periods have also been the subject of investigation in recent years. There has been a number of epigraphical surveys of the prolific rock inscriptions in the area (see among others Macdonald 1983) and work has been carried out on Bronze Age sites in the region (Braemer

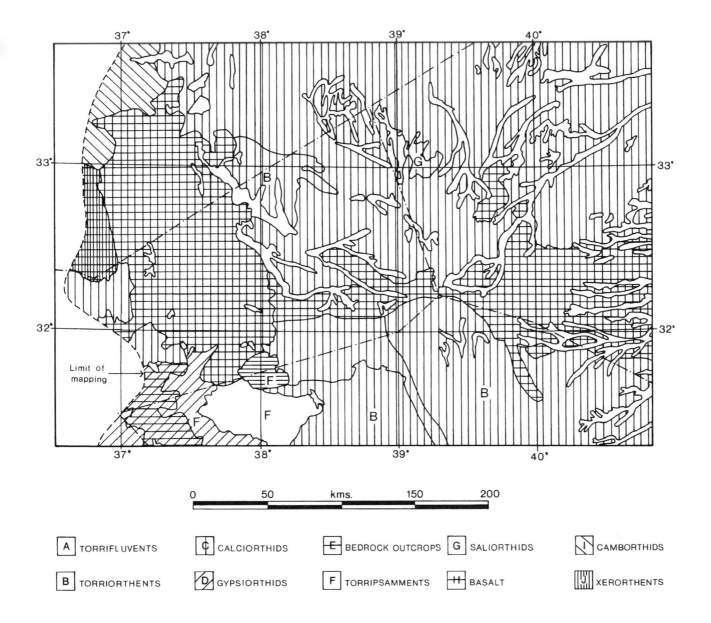

Figure 1.4   Soils of east Jordan and surrounding areas (ACSAD Hamad Basin Project, Damascus 1983).

A	TORRIFLUVENTS	C	CALCIORTHIDS	E	BEDROCK OUTCROPS	G	SALIORTHIDS	N	CAMBORTHIDS
B	TORRIORTHENTS	D	GYPSIORTHIDS	F	TORRIPSAMMENTS	HH	BASALT		XERORTHENTS

1984; Betts *et al.* 1995, 1996), and on sites of the Roman and Islamic periods (see among others King 1982; Bisheh 1982; Desreumaux and Humbert 1982; King *et al.* 1983; de Vries 1981; Kennedy *et al.* 1986; Helms 1990).

The Black Desert Survey

Our fieldwork began in 1979 with a smallscale survey of the lower wadi Rajil (Betts 1982). This was followed by a three year project to study use of the *harra* in the later prehistoric periods (Betts 1983, 1984, 1985). During this programme of research much of the *harra* was surveyed on foot or by vehicle reconnaissance. In the third season soundings were made at four sites: Khallat

'Anaza, a Natufian site on the upper Wadi Rajil, two Pre-Pottery Neolithic B occupation sites (Dhuweila and Ibn al-Ghazi), and one Late Neolithic campsite, the 'burin Neolithic' site of Jebel Naja. The initial soundings at Dhuweila showed that the site was important and needed further investigation. This decision was prompted by the discovery of *in-situ* rock art, a surprising depth of undisturbed occupation deposits, and links between the site and use of the 'kite' systems, complex networks of animal traps found in great numbers in the *harra* (Helms and Betts 1987). In 1986 a full season of excavation was carried out at Dhuweila (Betts 1987a, 1987b, 1988).

The results of survey work began to show a pattern of landuse in the *harra* throughout the later prehistoric

5

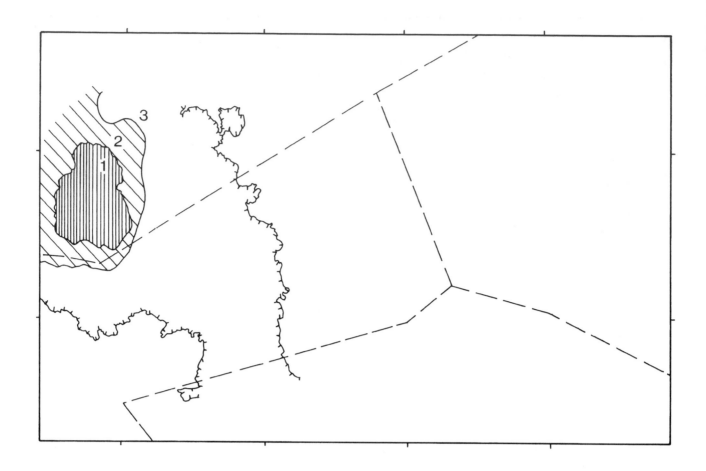

Figure 1.5   Distribution of modern plant geographic zones: 1. Mediterranean; 2. Irano-Turanian; 3. Saharo-Arabian.

periods. A few small camps with artefacts of Geometric Kebaran type were found in areas with good seasonal water supplies. Early Natufian sites were not found in the *harra*, although Garrard has investigated one in the Azraq oasis (Garrard *et al.* 1987: 20). However, Late Natufian sites were found both in the areas of highest rainfall and also eastwards and southwards across to the eastern margins of the *harra*. There was very little evidence for use of the *harra* in the earliest period of the Neolithic, the Pre-Pottery Neolithic A, but in the Pre-Pottery Neolithic B, particularly towards the end of the period, the late 7th millennium BC, the *harra* was used extensively. It was at this time that the 'kite' systems were especially important. The economy of steppic groups using the *harra* was still based on hunting and foraging, despite the presence of large villages on the edges of the steppe by this period.

Our work also showed that major changes seemed to have taken place in the habits of steppic groups around the end of the 7th millennium BC. One of the main achievements of the survey programme was to document and provide preliminary dates for the 'burin sites', flint scatters with high proportions of truncation burins

which, for lack of other diagnostic tools, had remained of uncertain date until soundings at Jebel Naja produced arrowheads of Late Neolithic type in association with concave truncation burins, and a radiocarbon date placing occupation at the site around the mid-sixth millennium BC. At about the same time, similar sites elsewhere were also investigated (Rollefson and Fröhlich 1982; Rollefson *et al.* 1982; Cauvin 1982; Garrard *et al.* 1987; Baird *et al.* 1992; Garrard *et al.* 1994), and it became increasingly clear that the 'burin sites' belonged to a period from around the mid to late PPNB through much of the Late Neolithic period. However, the excavations at Dhuweila had revealed a secondary occupation in the Late Neolithic which was radically different from Jebel Naja, despite radiocarbon dates which showed the two sites to have been used at much the same period. The issue of the Late Neolithic was further complicated by survey findings at a series of sites near qa' al-Ghirqa (Betts and Helms 1987) where the chipped stone industry related to that of Jebel Naja but the choice of location and the presence of formal architecture indicated that these sites were quite different again from the numerous 'burin Neolithic'

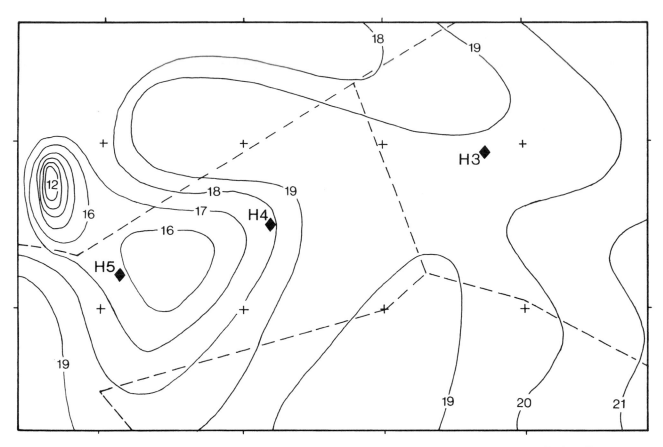

Figure 1.6   Average annual temperature (°C) in east Jordan and surrounding areas (ACSAD Hamad Basin Project, Damascus 1983).

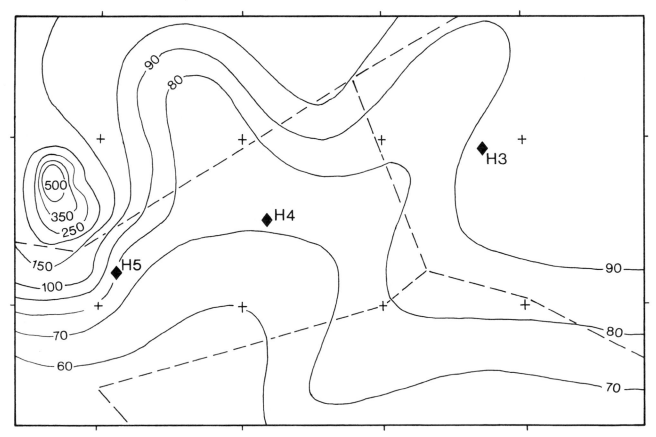

Figure 1.7   Average annual precipitation (mm.) in east Jordan and surrounding areas (ACSAD Hamad Basin Project, Damascus 1983).

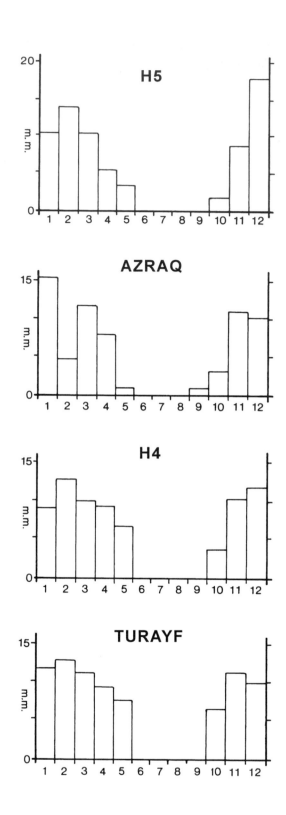

Figure 1.8   Distribution of monthly precipitation (mm.) at H5
(Safawi), Azraq, H4 (Ruweishid) and Turayf
(ACSAD Hamad Basin Project, Damascus 1983).

camp sites of Jebel Naja type found elsewhere in the *harra* and further afield. Unlike Early Neolithic hunting stations such as Dhuweila 1, 'burin Neolithic' camp sites were located in areas selected by bedouin using the *harra* in recent times to herd their flocks of sheep and goat. This choice of location, coupled with a small number of ovi/caprid bones from Jebel Naja, suggested that the 'burin Neolithic' sites might be connected with the introduction of pastoralism to the steppic regions. This idea was corroborated by evidence from Syrian sites where ovi/caprid bones were found in significant numbers on Late Neolithic campsites of similar type (Cauvin 1990). The detailed work of the Wadi Jilat project has now provided substantial evidence for this development (Baird *et al.* 1992; Garrard *et al.* 1994).

These ideas led to the development of a much broader research programme, the Burqu'/Ruweishid Project, designed to investigate archaeological remains in the *hamad* and the eastern edges of the *harra* with particular reference to the study of pastoralism as a component in the multi-resource economies which characterise groups using these environmentally marginal zones (Betts *et al.* 1990, 1991; Betts 1993). Work on the Burqu'/ Ruweishid project involved excavation of a number of sites around the lake near Qasr Burqu', a major *ghadir* with a capacity now enhanced, initially by a dam possibly dated in the 6th/7th centuries AD, and later by a large barrage constructed in the 1950s (for an account of excavations at the Qasr see Helms 1991). Most of the sites around the Burqu' lake were Late Neolithic or later, although there are at least two Early Neolithic sites and some flint scatters with earlier tool types, including epipaleolithic material. Survey in the *hamad* east of Burqu' showed that 'burin Neolithic' sites were common along the wadi systems, but there was little evidence for sites of earlier periods. Faunal remains from Late Neolithic sites at Burqu' contained high proportions of ovi/caprid remains, indicating that pastoralism was a significant component in the economy by that period.

This volume contains the first in a series of reports on the findings of these various research programmes. It is presented in broadly chronological form although further reports on the periods under discussion will appear in later volumes. The first part covers evidence for the Epipaleolithic period, including a report on excavations at the Late Natufian site of Khallat 'Anaza. The second part is a detailed account of excavations at Dhuweila, including a section on the Early Neolithic of the *harra*. The final chapter is a summary of work by Uzbek and Russian scholars on hunting traps and animal migration patterns in Uzbekistan. These Central Asian enclosures are remarkably similar in design and function to the 'kite' systems of eastern Jordan and provide an important comparative research tool for the interpretation of the north Arabian archaeological data on hunting and hunting traps.

2. The Epipaleolithic Periods

A.V.G. Betts

with a contribution by A.N. Garrard

Introduction

The pattern of land-use in the *harra* and the *hamad* during the Epipaleolithic conforms with evidence for these periods elsewhere in the semi-arid regions of the Near East, and, as in all periods, relates closely to the distribution of water and vegetation. Throughout the Badiyat al-Sham, Geometric Kebaran camp sites are found in the major oases including Azraq (Garrard *et al.* 1988a), Palmyra (Hanihara and Akazawa eds. 1979), and al-Kowm (M-C. Cauvin 1981). Beyond the oases, no Kebaran sites are known from the eastern *hamad*, although there are unusually large sites in the wadi systems west of Azraq (Garrard 1991). However, small scatters of microlithic debris, including geometrics and thin backed bladelets, indicate short term camp sites in the *harra*. Geometric Kebaran flint scatters and knapping sites have been found beside the *ghadir* at Burqu', along Wadi Rajil near Jawa, and by Qa' Mejalla (Figure 2.1).

The most extensive use of the *harra* in the Epipaleolithic was in the Late Natufian period. In the Levant, by the Natufian period, resource exploitation strategies changed to include a stronger focus on particular plants and animals (Henry 1989). Increasing sedentism in this period has been linked to collection of seasonal foods which, gathered in bulk, could provide a storeable surplus. The most important of these foods were cereals and nuts, particularly acorns and pistachio. During the early Natufian, sites were concentrated in the Mediterranean vegetation belt, in areas of moderate to high rainfall, but the Late Natufian saw an expansion out into the semi-arid zones (Bar-Yosef 1988: 232). At this time there is evidence for semi-sedentary occupation on the lower slopes of Jebel Druze. On most of the major wadi systems draining south from Jebel Druze there are Natufian sites with structures, bedrock mortars, and heavy grinding equipment. When these sites were occupied, they may have lain closer to the border between steppic (Irano-Turanian) and Mediterranean vegetation zones, with access to supplies of wild cereals, acorns, and pistachio on Jebel Druze, and hunting grounds out into the *harra*. Short term camps for hunting and flint knapping occur across the *harra* and along the western edge of the *hamad* (Figures 2.1, 2.21).

Geometric Kebaran sites

Sites in this broad category are represented by sparse scatters of backed and truncated bladelets, sometimes together with cores and knapping debris (Figure 2.2). Site 1682 near Qa' Mejalla lies on Wadi Rajil, close to the eastern edge of Qa' al-Azraq. Epipaleolithic sites were found by Garrard in a similar location at Uweinid on the western side of the Azraq lake (Garrard *et al.* 1988a; Byrd 1988). The small surface collection from site 1682 includes backed and truncated bladelets and single platform bladelet cores. Scatters of similar backed and truncated bladelets have also been found along Wadi Rajil near Jawa. Here, as in the later Natufian period, a fairly constant supply of water in the wadi bed must have been an important factor in choice of site location. In addition, higher rainfall in the Jawa area would have provided a richer environment than further south and east in the *harra*. There is no evidence so far that the drier areas of the *harra* and the eastern *hamad* were exploited in this period.

Natufian sites

Sixteen Natufian sites have been recorded around Jebel Druze and out into the *harra*. One, Khallat 'Anaza, was excavated in 1983, and at a number of the others (Mugharet al-Jawa, Jebel al-Subhi, Khabrat Abu Hussein, Shubayqa 1), surface collections have produced sufficient evidence to permit limited analysis of the chipped stone artefacts. Khallat 'Anaza and Mugharet al-Jawa are substantial occupation sites on Wadi Rajil near Jawa; Shubayqa 1 is also on Wadi Rajil but downstream, at the point where the wadi debouches into the Shubayqa mudflats. It too is an occupation site with heavy grinding equipment and traces of structures, although the site is disturbed by a recent burial. Jebel al-Subhi and Khabrat Abu Hussein are knapping and short term camp sites in the eastern *harra*. The other sites include more seasonal stations on wadis draining south from Jebel Druze and small knapping floors and ephemeral camps in the *harra* to the east.

Khallat 'Anaza
(BDS 1407 Map Ref. 3454 IV 798188)

Khallat 'Anaza is an occupation site of the Late Natufian period lying on a small outcrop of jagged basalt slabs overlooking a bend in Wadi Rajil (Figure 2.3) (Betts 1983, Betts in Betts Ed. 1991: 181, Betts 1991). A series of plunge pools in the wadi bed below the site acts as *ghudran*, holding water well into the dry season. The

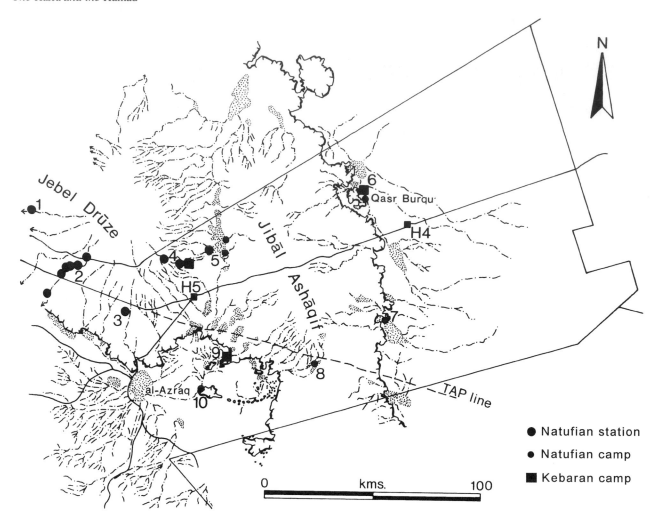

Figure 2.1   Distribution of epipaleolithic sites in the *Harra*. 1 Taibe; 2 Wadi 'Ajib 11, 12, 16, 18, 24; 3 Huwaynit; 4 Mugharet al-Jawa, Khallat 'Anaza, Geometric Kebaran flint scatters, various; 5 Shubayqa 1, 3, BDS 2103; 6 Burqu'; 7 Khabrat Abu Hussein; 8 Jebel Subhi; 9 Qa' Mejalla; 10 Jebel Qurma.

location affords a clear view over the surrounding area on all sides, particularly eastwards and downstream towards the Shubayqa mudflats. The jagged basalt ridge against which the site lies has been joined at either end by a low curving wall to form a small terrace enclosing an area of about 2000 square metres (Figure 2.4). The outcrop has been reinforced by a section of walling in the centre of the ridge where the bedrock is lower. This is briefly interrupted but then continues on from the western end of the outcrop, running out to the lip of the gorge. A second wall runs off northwards, also up to the gorge. These walls belong to the Epipaleolithic phase of occupation at the site and have been robbed out in places for burial cairns of a later period, probably of the Safaitic bedouin (*c.* 2nd century BC – 3rd/4th century AD). There is a thin scatter of chipped stone on and around the terrace. Traces of walls, stone circles and paved areas are visible over much of the terrace, and two mortars are cut into bedrock in the central part of the natural outcrop.

A collection of surface material was made by the random selection of 20 one metre square sample points. This was supplemented by purposive sampling of the whole terrace and the area around it. A twelve metre square sounding was excavated to bedrock. Surface collections were made without sieving of topsoil but all excavated soil was sieved through a 3 millimetre mesh. No suitable samples were obtained for radiocarbon dating. Selected levels were sampled for botanical remains but analysis of these proved inconclusive.

Stratigraphy

For excavation, the sounding was divided into one metre squares. There was little depth of occupation. Jagged ridges of bedrock were found all through the excavated area, in some places breaking through the surface. The cracks in between ridges were filled with ashy occupation deposits, worked flint and bone fragments. The upper level (Level 5) consisted of a layer of windblown sand, small rocks and deflated occupation deposits about 6–8 centimetres in depth containing some flints and fragments of bone. Below this were earlier, and probably also partially deflated occupation deposits (Level 4). These were represented by a layer of light

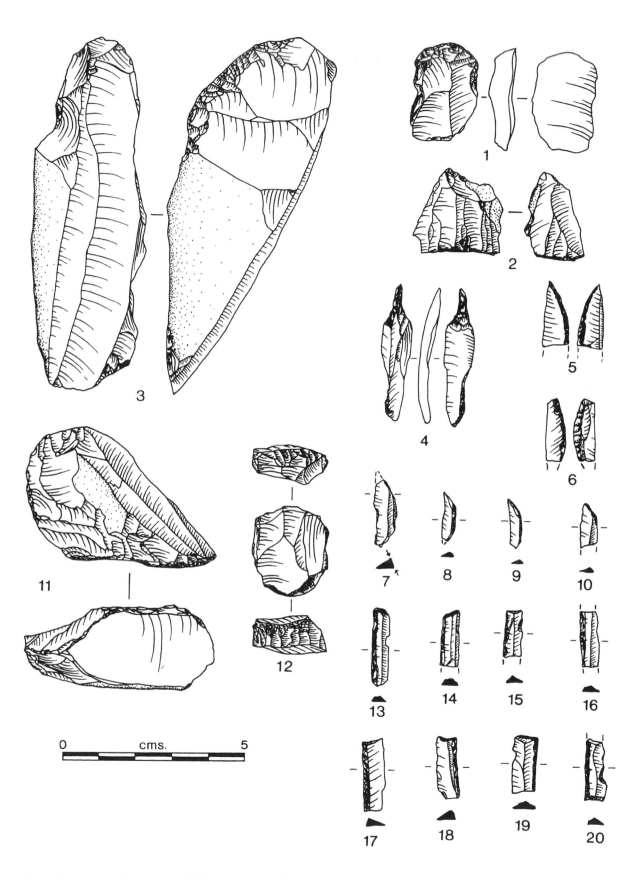

Figure 2.2   Chipped stone from epipaleolithic survey sites. Qaʻ Mejalla [BDS 1682]: 3, 11 bladelet cores, 14, 15, 17–20 backed and truncated bladelets; Jebel Qurma [BDS 1605]: 5, 6 Helwan lunates; Wadi Rajil [BDS 1420]: 1 endscraper; [BDS 1412]: 13 backed bladelet segment; [BDS 1411]: 2, bladelet core, 9 abruptly backed lunate, 10 obliquely truncated bladelet, 16 backed bladelet segment; [BDS 2107]: 7 lunate with abrupt bipolar backing, 12 core tablet worked as scraper; BDS [2204]: 4 borer; Qaʻ Shubayqa [BDS 2103]: 8 abruptly backed lunate.

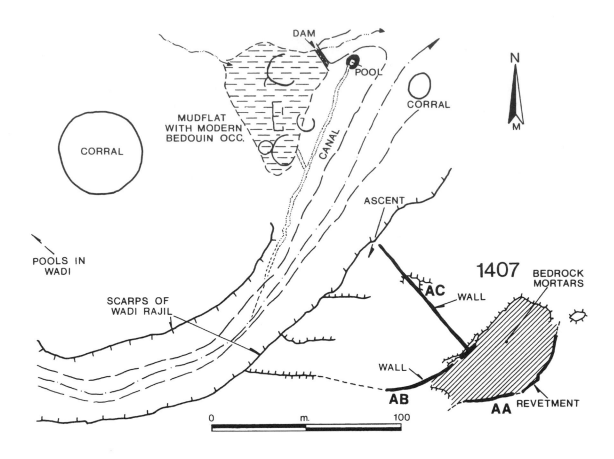

Figure 2.3   Location of Khallat 'Anaza.

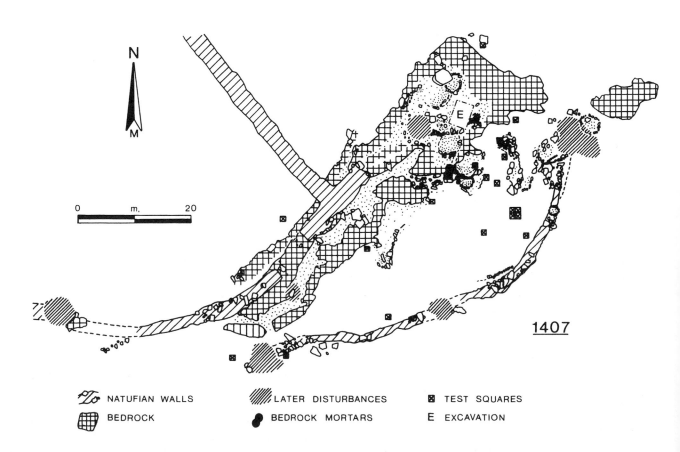

NATUFIAN WALLS   LATER DISTURBANCES   TEST SQUARES

BEDROCK   BEDROCK MORTARS   E EXCAVATION

Figure 2.4   Site plan of Khallat 'Anaza.

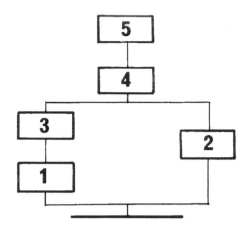

Figure 2.5   Schematic phasing of Khallat 'Anaza.

brown sandy soil with some ashy patches which extended across the whole sounding. This level contained moderate amounts of flint, bone fragments and loose rocks, and its removal revealed part of a circular stone-walled hut (Figure 2.6).

The hut was filled by loose dark grey-brown ashy soil with white flecks (Level 3), partly sealed by tumbled rocks. It contained flints, bone fragments and some ground stone tools and beads. The fill reached a maximum depth of about 35 cms in the centre of the structure where it overlay a compacted 'floor' surface, but in the eastern part of the structure jagged ridges of bedrock came up above the floor level. The hut was constructed partly on bedrock and partly on a thin layer of occupation deposit. A box-like feature consisting of up-ended basalt slabs was found set into the 'floor' deposit within the hut, sealed by Level 3. The 'floor' deposit (Level 1) was a hard-packed layer of dark grey ash with white flecks filling the lowest part of the interior of the structure. It contained some artefacts, and the surface of the layer was level and compacted. A small part of this layer in the western part of the trench was not excavated. External deposits corresponding to the fill of the structure (Level 2) consisted of a layer of light grey ash with sand lying above bedrock and containing flint and fragments of bone. Maximum depth was about fifteen cms.

The two bedrock mortars cut into the ridge of rock above the sounding also contained a fill with Epipaleolithic artefacts (Level X). It was not possible to say if the fill had accumulated during use of the site or if it represented washed occupation debris following abandonment. The fill consisted of ashy sand with a high proportion of flints, some bone and one piece of worked basalt. The relationships between levels are shown in Figure 2.5.

Chipped stone

Raw material

The raw material used for the chipped stone industry is mostly fine-grained grey/brown cherts. Chert of this type can be found around the edges of the *harra* where the limestone beds are exposed on the slopes of the massif created by the more resistant basalts. These cherts vary in quality; those used at Khallat 'Anaza must have been carefully selected for their smooth, fine grained texture. In addition to the grey/brown chert, a smooth creamy translucent stone was also used, particularly for the smaller and more delicate tools. The material is almost glasslike in texture and has a waxy feel to the surface. It is similar to chalcedony, but occurs in nodular form embedded in limestones exposed on the south eastern edge of the *harra* at Tell Hibr and in the southern reaches of Wadi Qattafi. It is likely that small outcrops also occur elsewhere around the edge of the *harra*. There are no chert sources within the *harra* and all raw material must have been brought to the site over a distance of at least thirty to fifty kms, and in the case of the fine creamy stone, perhaps much further.

Technology

A total of 5067 artefacts was recovered from the sounding, of which 845 were retouched pieces, 84 were cores or trimming and preparation elements, 1216 were blanks and the remainder either the by-products of specialised knapping processes such as burin spalls and micro-burins, unclassifiable fragments or waste pieces (Table 2.1). Artefact distribution patterns were difficult to determine because the sounding was shallow and limited in extent. In so far as there was any pattern, it seemed to indicate higher proportions of tools outside the structure and greater proportions of blanks inside. However, this pattern could be illusory.

Forty cores were recovered from the soundings. Most of these were blade/bladelet cores, exhausted or heavily reduced, with a high proportion of crossed or opposed platforms. Flake cores were uncommon and in some cases represented final use of exhausted blade/bladelet cores (Table 2.2). Debitage from initial stages in the reduction sequence was poorly represented. Given the distance from sources of raw material this suggests that much initial core preparation took place away from the site. Low numbers of core trimming elements might also be the result of knapping techniques which rarely produced core trimming elements as a by-product (Byrd 1989a: 35).

Technological characteristics of the Khallat 'Anaza assemblage are typically Natufian. Bar-Yosef, in a summary of the attributes of the Natufian (1983:17, [see also Bar-Yosef 1970:174; Henry 1973, 1981: 422]), describes the chipped stone as predominantly a blade/bladelet industry. Typically, blades and bladelets are short and wide, with blunt tips (as opposed to convergent distal ends). Cores are exploited intensively from more than one striking platform and more than one knapping direction. Specific technological features include use of the microburin technique and Helwan

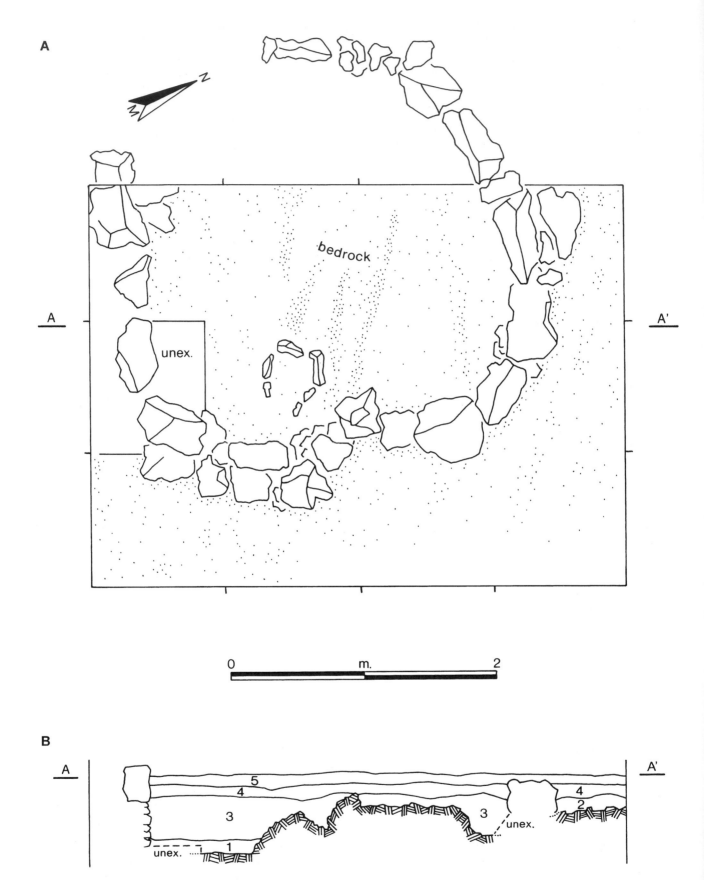

Figure 2.6   Plan (A) and section (B) of excavated area at Khallat 'Anaza.

LEVELS/%	1	%	2	%	3	%	4	%	5	%	total	%
cores	1	0.48	6	2.17	26	2.16	4	0.88	13	2.19	40	1.76
trimming elements	2	0.96	2	0.72	8	1.07	5	1.09	3	0.51	20	0.88
primary flakes	2	0.96	6	2.07	12	1.62	2	0.44	2	0.33	24	1.05
flakes	82	39.42	58	20.94	319	42.99	126	27.57	247	41.65	832	36.40
blade/bladelets	51	24.51	48	17.33	108	14.56	81	17.72	96	16.18	384	16.86
spalls	8	3.85	8	2.89	31	4.18	3	0.66	19	3.20	69	3.03
microburins	16	7.70	7	2.53	14	1.89	4	0.88	6	1.01	47	2.06
splintered pieces	1	0.48	1	0.13	1	0.13	4	0.88	9	1.52	16	0.70
(tools)	45	21.63	141	50.90	233	31.40	228	49.89	198	33.39	845	37.11
SUBTOTAL	208	99.99	277	100.02	742	100.00	457	100.01	593	99.98	2277	99.99
chunks	7	-	15	-	20	-	25	-	18	-	85	
chips	357	-	147	-	963	-	480	-	756	-	2705	
TOTAL	574	-	439	-	1725	-	962		1367	-	5067	

Table 2.1   Khallat 'Anaza major chipped stone categories.

retouch. Henry also notes that quantitative attributes for the industry are markedly uniform from assemblage to assemblage, particularly in respect to the dimensions of bladelets. A sample of measured flakes and bladelets shows that the blanks from Khallat 'Anaza fall only slightly below the mean dimensions given by Henry (Figure 2.7). Byrd (1989a: 39) discusses the issue of whether Natufian assemblages are blade or flake based. He suggests that figures for relative proportions of blades and flakes can vary, depending on the method of analysis and statistical representation. In the case of Khallat 'Anaza, while in the debitage class (Table 2.1) flakes at 36.4% are more numerous than blade/bladelets at 16.86%, blade/bladelets strongly dominate the tool blank class, comprising 78.55% of the total as against 17.37% for flakes (Table 2.3).

Tool types represented in the Khallat 'Anaza assemblage are shown in Tables 2.4 and 2.5. Most tools are made on bladelets or small flakes. There are few large or heavy tools. Notched and denticulated pieces and non-geometric microliths are most common in the general tool classes (Table 2.4), but among specific tool types, borers and lunates feature most importantly (Table 2.5). Discrepancies between tool percentages from surface and excavated contexts can generally be accounted for by differential recovery. Surface collections were not sieved, so that there are relatively

	No.	%
on flake	1	2.5
single platform	5	12.5
bipolar	14	35.0
changed orientation	7	17.5
multiple platforms	6	15.0
broken, roughouts etc.	7	17.5
TOTAL	40	100.00

Table 2.2   Khallat 'Anaza core type.

	No.	%
core trimming elements	10	1.17
primary flakes	25	2.91
flakes	149	17.37
blades	104	12.12
bladelets	570	66.43
TOTAL	858	100.00

Table 2.3   Khallat 'Anaza tool blank types.

higher numbers of larger tools (eg. scrapers) and lower numbers of small tools (eg. geometric microliths).

Scrapers

Scrapers represent 2.45% of the tool assemblage from excavated contexts. This figure is equally divided between two types: single endscrapers and flake scrapers (Figure 2.11: 7–9).

Burins

Burins occur infrequently, representing just over 4% of the excavated tool kit. The most common form is a burin on a break or natural surface (Figure 2.11: 10–14). No dihedral burins were recovered from surface or excavated samples.

Burins

Burins occur infrequently, representing just over 4% of the excavated tool kit. The most common form is a burin on a break or natural surface (Figure 2.11: 10–14). No dihedral burins were recovered from surface or excavated samples.

Borers

Borers constitute nearly 8% of the excavated assemblage. Almost all of these are on bladelets, with a well defined point created by abrupt or semi-abrupt bilateral retouch (Figure 2.9: 15–26).

Backed pieces

Whole or fragmentary backed pieces comprise 9.21% of the excavated sample (Figure 2.10: 27, 28).

Truncations

Truncations occur infrequently, constituting 2.57% of the excavated sample. Truncated blades and flakes occur in roughly equal proportions. Two bitruncated pieces were found in surface contexts (Figure 2.11: 6).

Notch/denticulates

These form an important class, comprising 10.61% of the excavated sample. Single notches on blades or flakes are most common, although there are significant numbers of blade/bladelets with multiple notches, and

LEVELS/%	1	%	2	%	3	%	4	%	5	%	X	%	total	%	surface	%
scrapers	0	0.00	1	0.71	8	3.43	5	2.19	6	3.03	1	7.69	21	2.45	26	5.98
burins	1	2.22	10	7.10	6	2.58	10	4.19	8	4.04	0	0.0	35	4.08	12	2.76
borers	2	4.44	12	8.51	24	10.30	12	5.26	16	8.08	1	7.69	67	7.81	22	5.06
backed blades	2	4.44		10.63	18	7.72	20	8.77	23	11.62	1	7.69	79	9.21	39	8.97
truncations	1	2.22	3	2.13	4	1.72	9	3.94	5	2.53	0	0.0	22	2.57	13	2.99
notch/denticulate	6	13.33	12	8.51	27	11.58	24	10.53	22	11.11	0	0.0		10.61	71	16.32
retouched pieces	6	13.33	22	15.60	27	11.58	24	10.53	19	9.6	1	7.69	99	11.54	41	9.43
non-geometric microliths	9	20.00	18	12.77	34	14.60	42	18.42	23	11.62	1	7.69	127	14.80	47	10.80
geometric microliths	7	15.56	27	19.15	33	14.60	29	12.72	33	16.67	6	46.16	135	15.73	36	8.28
other	4	8.89	2	1.42	6	2.60	3	1.32	5	2.53	0	0.00	20	2.33	10	2.30
miscellaneous retouch	7	15.56	19	13.48	46	19.74	50	21.93	38	19.18	2	15.39	162	18.88	118	27.13
TOTAL	45	99.99	141	100.01	233	100.01	228	100.00	198	100.01	13	100.00	858	100.01	435	100.02

Table 2.4   Khallat 'Anaza tool classes.

	surface	%	excavated	%	total	%
single endscaper	12	2.76	10	1.17	22	1.70
flake scraper	14	3.22	11	1.28	25	1.93
dihedral burin	0	0.00	0	0.00	0	0.00
burin on break	9	2.07	25	2.91	34	2.63
burin on transverse truncation	0	0.00	3	0.35	3	0.23
burin on oblique truncation	0	0.00	1	0.12	1	0.08
burin on concave truncation	0	0.00	5	0.58	5	0.39
multiple mixed burin	3	0.69	0	0.00	3	0.23
borer	22	5.06	64	7.46	86	6.65
multiple borer	0	0.00	3	0.35	3	0.23
naturally backed piece	5	1.15	13	1.52	18	1.39
piece, irregular back	15	3.45	21	2.45	36	2.78
piece, two backed edges	5	1.15	10	1.17	15	1.16
backed fragment	14	3.22	35	4.08	49	3.79
truncated flake	4	0.92	11	1.28	15	1.16
truncated blade	7	1.61	11	1.28	18	1.39
bitruncated piece	2	0.46	0	0.00	2	0.15
retouched notch	22	5.06	42	4.90	64	4.95
blade/bladelet, multiple notches	7	1.61	22	2.56	29	2.24
denticulate	42	9.66	27	3.15	69	5.34
flake, continuous retouch	2	0.46	12	1.40	14	1.08
blade, continuous retouch, one edge	6	1.38	21	2.45	27	2.09
blade, continuous retouch, both edges	8	1.84	18	2.10	26	2.01
strangled blade/flake, wide notch	0	0.00	1	0.12	1	0.08
piece, inverse or alternate retouch	25	5.75	41	4.78	66	5.10
pointed piece	0	0.00	6	0.70	6	0.46
pointed bladelet, fine retouch	3	0.69	22	2.56	25	1.93
bladelet fragment, fine retouch	11	2.53	34	3.96	45	3.48
bladelet, back curved by abrupt retouch	3	0.69	16	1.86	19	1.47
bladelet fragment, abrupt retouch	5	1.15	14	1.63	19	1.47
bladelet, inverse retouch	11	2.53	15	1.75	26	2.01
bladelet, alternate retouch	4	0.92	9	1.05	13	1.01
bladelet, Helwan retouch	6	1.38	7	0.82	13	1.01
truncated bladelet	1	0.23	2	0.23	3	0.23
backed and truncated bladelet	3	0.69	7	0.82	10	0.77
backed bladelet, inverse retouch	0	0.00	1	0.12	1	0.08
triangle	4	0.92	12	1.40	16	1.24
lunate	29	6.67	111	12.94	140	10.83
Helwan lunate	3	0.69	12	1.40	15	1.16
multiple mixed pieces, various	7	1.61	9	1.05	16	1.24
sickle blade/bladelet	1	0.23	5	0.58	6	0.46
other	2	0.46	6	0.70	8	0.62
miscellaneous retouch	118	27.13	162	18.88	280	21.66
TOTAL	435	-	858	-	1293	

Table 2.5   Khallat 'Anaza tool types.

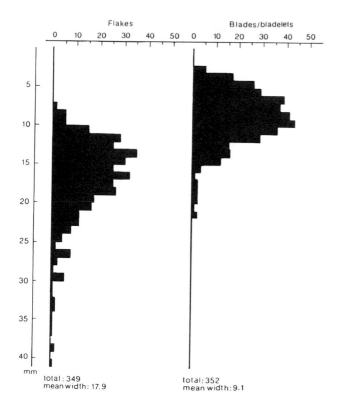

Figure 2.7   Width measurements of blades and flakes from Khallat 'Anaza.

denticulated pieces (Figure 2.10: 33, 34; Figure 2.11: 1, 5, 6).

Retouched pieces

The total number of retouched pieces in the excavated sample is high (11.54%) (Figure 2.10: 37–43; Figure 2.11: 2–4). However, a considerable amount of these pieces are fragmentary, and, if whole, might have been classified as other tool types. Blades (Figure 2.10: 37–43) are worked along one or both edges, with fine semi-abrupt retouch. Inverse retouch is fairly common.

Non-geometric microliths

Non-geometric microliths constitute nearly 15% of the excavated sample. The majority of these are bladelets with fine, sometimes discontinuous retouch (Figure 2.10: 24–26; 29). It is possible that some pieces in the 'backed' category, if complete, could be placed in this group, giving a higher proportion of backed pieces.

Geometric microliths

This is the single most common tool class within the excavated sample and is dominated by lunates shaped by abrupt or bipolar retouch (Figure 2.10: 1–23). Approximately 10% of all lunates were formed by Helwan retouch. Triangles occur in small numbers. Based on the numbers of microburins in the debitage

sample, use of this technique for production of geometric microliths was limited.

Various

This general category includes multiple mixed pieces, pieces with silica gloss (Figure 2.10: 30–32, 35, 36) and miscellaneous tools. Five bladelet fragments with traces of silica gloss were found in excavated contexts. On at least one of these, the cutting edge was markedly rounded and smoothed through use.

Miscellaneous retouch

This category is a catch-all for retouched fragments which cannot be further identified as to tool class.

Relative dating

The Natufian period has been sub-divided temporally into two stages; Early and Late Natufian. Date ranges for the period are generally accepted as falling between 10,300 and 8,500 bc (Bar-Yosef 1983: 13), with the change from the Early to the Late stage occurring around 9,000 bc. The two stages are marked by differences in the stone tool assemblages, particularly in the form of lunates. In the Early Natufian, lunates are relatively large and most are formed by Helwan retouch. In the later stages lunates are smaller and mostly shaped by abrupt backing. The proportion of Helwan lunates in the Khallat 'Anaza assemblage suggests a date in the Late Natufian for the assemblage (Figure 2.20) (see also Summary below).

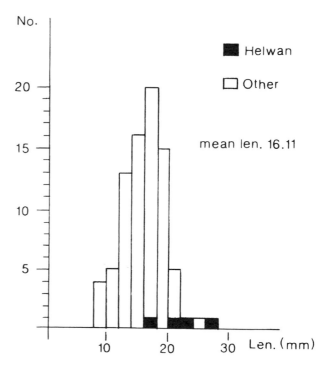

Figure 2.8   Length measurements of lunates from Khallat 'Anaza.

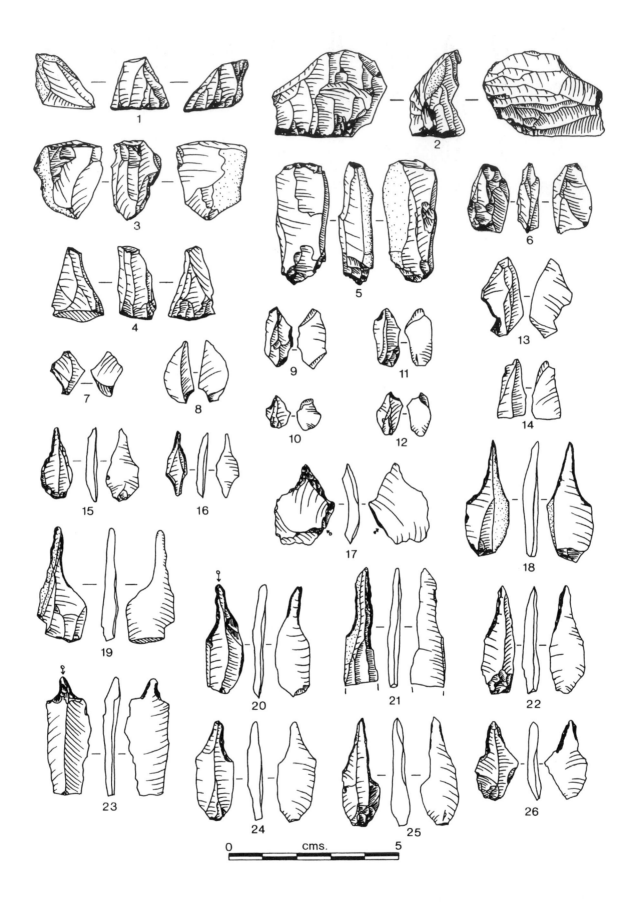

Figure 2.9   Chipped stone from Khallat 'Anaza. 1–4 bladelet cores; 5, 6 splintered pieces; 7–14 microburins; 15–26 borers.

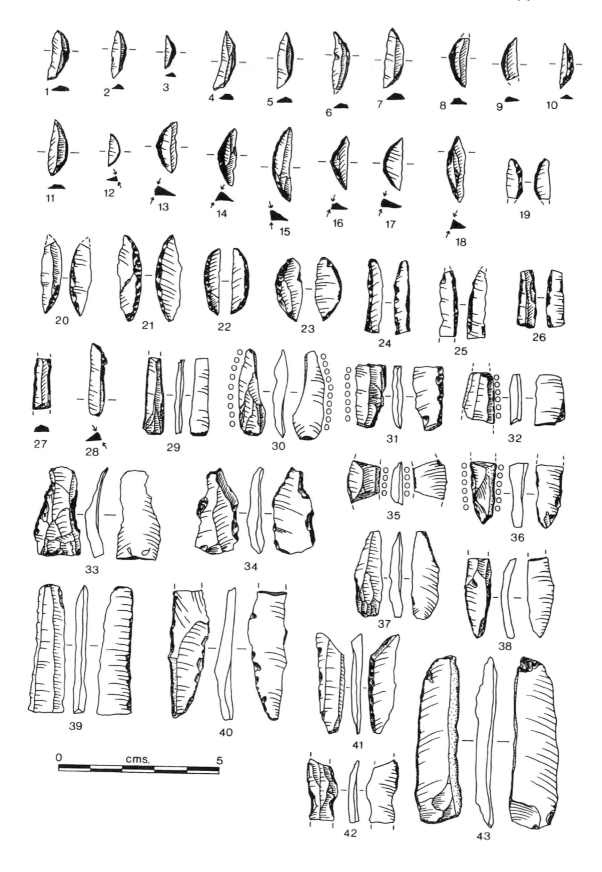

Figure 2.10   Chipped stone from Khallat 'Anaza. 1–11 abruptly backed lunates; 12– 18 lunates with abrupt bipolar backing; 19–23 Helwan lunates; 24–26 bladelets with Helwan retouch; 27 bilaterally backed bladelet segment; 28 bladelet with abrupt bipolar backing; 29 bladelet with fine bilateral retouch; 30–32, 35, 36 pieces with silica gloss; 33, 34 notched pieces; 37–43 retouched blade/bladelets.

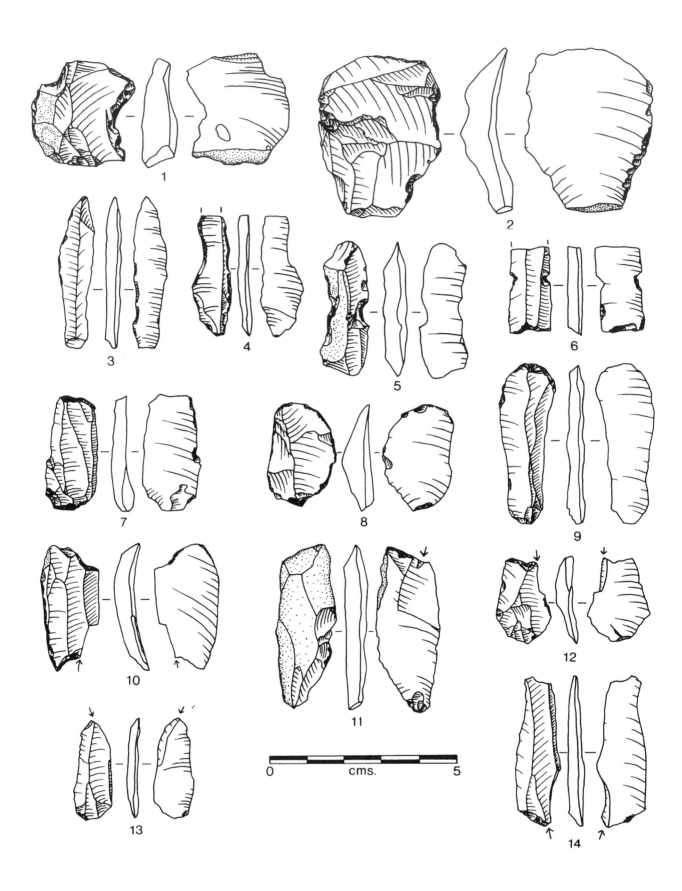

Figure 2.11   Chipped stone from Khallat 'Anaza. 1 notched flake; 2 retouched trimming element; 3, 4 retouched blade/bladelets; 5 notched blade; 6 notched and truncated blade; 7–9 scrapers; 10–14 burins.

The animal bones

A. N. Garrard

A small number of animal bones was recovered from the soundings. A basic analysis of these is given below.

Gazella sp. : 7 fragments were found, all of which belong to the limb extremities — metapodials, tarsals and phalanges. Limb extremities often form a high proportion in bone assemblages on prehistoric sites and it seems likely that this is due to butchering practices. It is common when skinning an animal to peel off the hide as far as the metapodials, and then to cut through the skin and bone of the distal metapodials, discarding the non-fleshy limb extremities.

Ovis/Capra sp.: 18 fragments were found, including scapula, pelvis, femur, tibia, metapodial and phalange fragments and a maxillary tooth. A phalange and a humerus fragment are characteristic of *Capra sp.*. From the morphology it is impossible to say if these were domesticated animals, but it is likely that wild goat/ibex inhabited the craggy areas adjacent to the site.

Equus sp.: 2 fragments were recovered, one from a scapula and the other an astragalus. The astragalus, which comes from the surface deposits, has a hole bored through it.

Canis cf. aureus.: 1 fragment of phalange 1 was found.

Lepus cf. capensis.: A humerus, a pelvis and a tibia fragment were recovered.

Surface	*Gazella sp.*	metapodial	1
	Equus sp.	astragalus	1 (bored)
Level 5	*Gazella sp.*	metatarsal	1
	Canid cf. aureus	phalange 1	1
	Capra/Ovis	phalange 2	1
	Ovis/Capra	metacarpal	1
	Ovis/Capra	metapodial	1
Level 4	*Lepus cf. capensis*	humerus	1
	Lepus cf. capensis	pelvis	1
	Lepus cf. capensis	tibia	1
Level 3	*Gazella sp.*	phalange 2	1
	cf. Capra sp.	phalange 1	1
	Gazella sp.	phalange 1	1
	Ovis/Capra sp.	scapula	1
	Ovis/Capra sp.	pelvis	1
	Ovis/Capra sp.	pelvis	1
	Ovis/Capra sp.	phalange 3	1
	cf. Capra sp.	humerus	1
	Capra/Ovis sp.	phalange 1	1
Level 2	*Gazella sp.*	metacarpal	1
	Ovis/Capra sp.	phalange 2	1
	Ovis/Capra sp.	tibia	1
	Ovis/Capra sp.	phalange 1	2
	Ovis/Capra sp.	phalange 2	3
	Ovis/Capra sp.	astragalus	1
	Ovis/Capra sp.	calcaneum	1
	Ovis/Capra sp.	maxillary tooth	1
Level 1	*Gazella sp.*	naviculo-cuboid	1
	Ovis/Capra sp.	femur	1
	Equus sp.	scapula	1

Table 2.6   Khallat 'Anaza faunal remains.

Surface	worked basalt pebble, hollowed on one side, broken
Level 5	marine shell, irregularly pierced: *Arcularia gibbosula*, of Mediterranean origin
	worked basalt pebble, oval with one flattened and slightly smoothed surface
	broken basalt pebble, smoothed on one surface and slightly battered
	basalt hammerstone, elongated with chipped end
	bead blank, 'Dabba marble'
	broken basalt block, smoothed on one side
Level 4	marine shell, broken: *Cerastoderma* fragments, probably of Mediterranean origin
	shell bead (unidentified)
	worked basalt pebble, oval with one flattened and slightly smoothed surface
Level 3	rectangular bead, 'Dabba marble'
	basalt pebble fragment, smoothed on one face
	basalt mortar
	basalt pebble hammerstone
	basalt pebble hammerstone
	basalt pebble hammerstone
Level 2	basalt pebble fragment, smoothed on one face
Level X	round basalt pebble, slightly battered

(I am grateful to David Reese for identification of the shells)

Table 2.7   Khallat 'Anaza special finds.

The species found at the site are typical of a craggy steppe/desert environment similar to that of today. The range of animals represented suggests that the inhabitants of the site were exploiting all the main herbivores then available in the area

Special finds

During the Natufian period heavy ground stone tools were first used extensively at prehistoric sites in the Near East. The ground stone pounders, mortars and hammerstones from Khallat 'Anaza are typical of the period, and by their weight and lack of portability indicate a degree of continuity in occupation of the site (Figures 2.12, 2.13). Greenstone beads and marine shells indicate exchange networks or contact beyond the *harra*. Marine shells and exotic stone have been found on a number of Natufian sites (Bar-Yosef 1983: 22; Rees 1991a) and it seems that exchange systems were well established by this period (Bar-Yosef 1988: 232).

The same systems may also have functioned for the movement of more utilitarian goods such as foodstuffs or skins which have left no trace in the archaeological record. Although green stones worked as beads occur quite widely in the Natufian period, the type of raw material may vary to include phosphorite and malachite. The 'greenstone' or 'Dabba marble' found at Khallat 'Anaza is a form of apatitic limestone found only around fossil springs on the watershed at the head of Wadi Dabba, southeast of Amman (Figure 2.21). This green stone was widely traded throughout the east Jordanian steppe in later periods, particularly in the Neolithic (Baird *et al.* 1992:24).

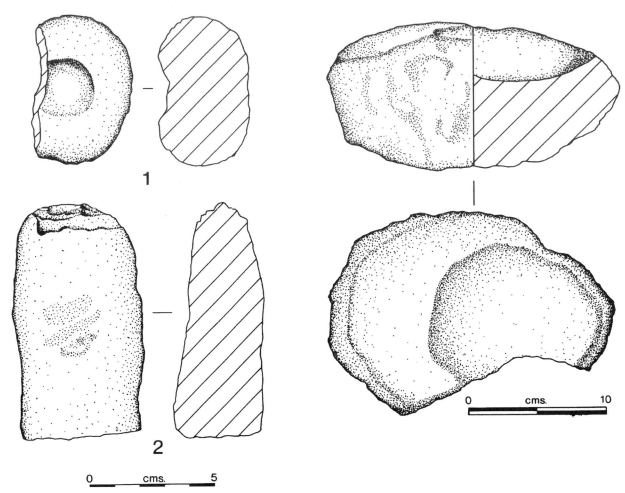

Figure 2.12 Ground stone from Khallat 'Anaza. 1 hollowed pebble; 2 rubber/pounder.

Figure 2.13 Basalt mortar from Khallat 'Anaza.

Summary

The evidence suggests that Khallat 'Anaza was a fairly substantial settlement occupied during winter and spring. The hut revealed by the excavations is probably one of several similar structures, the outlines of which can be roughly distinguished across the terrace. Small circular or sub-circular structures with stone footings are known from other Natufian sites, and bedrock mortars are also a typical Natufian phenomenon (Bar-Yosef 1983, Byrd 1989b). The only unusual aspects of the site are the enclosure walls. The main terrace wall (Figure 2.3 AA) linking both ends of the bedrock outcrop presumably functioned as a simple perimeter fence, possibly to discourage wild animals from approaching the camp. Even today, hyena dens are common in the caves around Jawa, and in the 9th millennium bc there would have been other large predators including large cats and wolves. Walls AB and AC leading off to the gorge are harder to account for. One explanation is that they functioned as a simple form of animal trap, a precursor to the more elaborate 'kite' systems of the Neolithic and later periods (Helms and Betts 1987). Khallat 'Anaza lies above the mouth of the Wadi Rajil gorge. Just below the site the wadi opens up and a tributary stream enters from the northwest. It would be relatively simple for a small group of people to drive animals up the wadi, block off the mouth of the gorge and turn the herd up the scree slope into the area enclosed by walls AB and AC. The steep climb up the side of the wadi would tire the animals and they could be quite easily dispatched by hunters on the hilltop (see also Cope 1991).

Khallat 'Anaza is one of several Natufian sites on the lower slopes of Jebel Druze, some way into the steppe (Figure 2.21). These sites, including Taibe in southern Syria (M.-C.Cauvin 1974), all lie on high ground, next to deeply incised wadis and *ghudran*. They show signs of regular, if not permanent use, with structures, groundstone and bedrock mortars. Although it might have been possible to stay at these sites all year round if the water supply was sufficient, it is perhaps more likely that they were used in winter/spring when the area would have been most abundant in natural resources. It is possible that Khallat 'Anaza and other sites were low-lying winter camps for groups who moved up onto the higher slopes of Jebel Druze in the summer months.

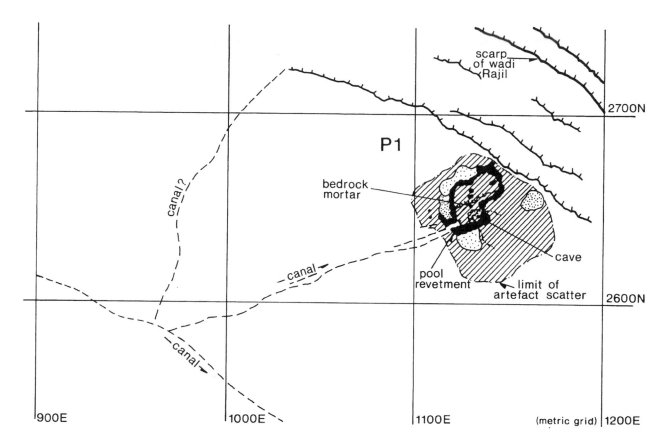

Figure 2.14   Location of Mugharet al-Jawa.

'Dabba marble' and seashells found on these sites show that the people who used the area were in contact with groups to the south and west.

The faunal remains from Khallat 'Anaza indicate that the inhabitants were hunting locally available game (see Garrard above). Despite flotation of soil from the site, no identifiable botanical remains were recovered. This

	No.	%
on flake	0	0.00
single platform	7	23.33
bipolar	5	16.66
changed orientation	3	10.00
multiple platforms	6	20.00
broken, roughouts etc.	9	30.00
TOTAL	30	99.99

Table 2.8   Mugharet al-Jawa core types.

	No.	%
scrapers	67	8.17
burins	9	1.99
borers	2	0.44
backed blades	32	7.06
truncations	11	2.43
notch/denticulate	56	12.36
retouched pieces	93	20.53
non-geometric microliths	70	15.45
geometric microliths	40	8.83
other	8	1.77
miscellaneous retouch	95	20.97
TOTAL	453	100.00

Table 2.9   Mugharet al-Jawa tool classes.

was due in part to the small size of the sample, and also to poor preservation of botanical material in the loose sandy soil of the *harra*. However, blades with silica sheen, basalt grinding and pounding tools, and bedrock mortars, all imply processing of plant foods. At the time of occupation, Khallat 'Anaza may have lain close to the fringes of the oak-pistachio forest of Jebel Druze. Cereals and nuts may not have been available in abundance, but as Bar-Yosef points out (1988: 232), a subsistence strategy which involved exploitation of a broad spectrum of resources common to both Mediterranean and Irano-Turanian belts would have enabled semi-sedentary groups to survive in marginal, although not arid zones. The success of such economic strategies would have been improved by the facility to store seasonally available foods; this in itself requiring some degree of sedentarization.

Mugharet al-Jawa BDS 1422

Map Ref. 3354 I 803111

Mugharet al-Jawa is a second Late Natufian site in the Jawa area (Betts in Betts ed. 1991: 181, Betts 1991). It lies on the west bank of the wadi north of the ancient settlement at Jawa. The site presently consists of a heavily disturbed flint scatter around the mouth of and inside a lava flow cave (Figure 2.14). Although the cave has been used as a cistern with resulting disruption to

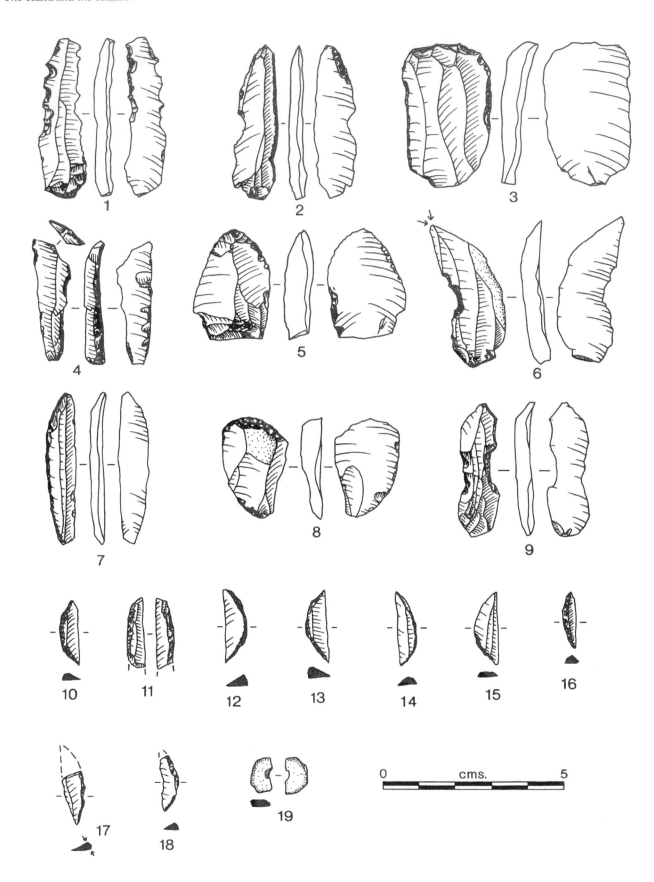

Figure 2.15   Chipped stone: Mugharet al-Jawa. 1, 6, 9 notched blades; 2, 7 backed blades; 3, 5, 8 scrapers; 4 backed and truncated
blade; 10, 13–16 abruptly backed lunates; 11 bladelet segment with Helwan retouch; 12 lunate with abrupt bipolar
backing; Huwaynit. 17 lunate with abrupt bipolar backing; 18 abruptly backed lunate; 19 'greenstone' bead ('Dabba
marble').

	No.	%
single endscraper	22	4.86
flake scraper	15	3.31
dihedral burin	3	0.66
burin on break	5	1.10
burin on concave truncation	1	0.22
borer	1	0.22
multiple borer	1	0.22
naturally backed piece	11	2.43
piece, irregular back	11	2.43
piece, two backed edges	3	0.66
backed fragment	7	1.55
truncated flake	2	0.44
truncated blade	8	1.77
bitruncated piece	1	0.22
retouched notch	25	5.52
blade/bladelet, multiple notches	25	5.52
denticulate	6	1.32
flake, continuous retouch	19	4.19
blade, continuous retouch, one edge	23	5.08
blade, continuous retouch, both edges	11	2.43
strangled blade/flake, wide notch	8	1.77
piece, inverse or alternate retouch	25	5.52
pointed piece	7	1.55
pointed bladelet, fine retouch	4	0.88
bladelet fragment, fine retouch	17	3.75
bladelet, back curved by abrupt retouch	23	5.08
bladelet fragment, abrupt retouch	7	1.55
bladelet, inverse retouch	5	1.10
bladelet, alternate retouch	2	0.44
bladelet, Helwan retouch	3	0.66
truncated bladelet	2	0.44
backed and truncated bladelet	6	1.32
backed bladelet, inverse retouch	1	0.22
triangle	1	0.22
lunate	37	8.17
Helwan lunate	2	0.44
multiple mixed pieces, various	1	0.22
sickle blade/bladelet	4	0.88
other	3	0.66
miscellaneous retouch	95	20.97
TOTAL	453	99.97

Table 2.10   Mugharet al-Jawa tool types.

the occupational deposits, the site must once have been fairly extensive, probably similar to Khallat 'Anaza. Like Khallat 'Anaza, it is located on a bedrock outcrop above the Wadi Rajil gorge. Water would have been available for most of the year from pools in the wadi bed below the site.

Groundstone artefacts — pounders and mortars — were found along with chipped stone and faunal remains in the spoil thrown up by clearance of the cistern. A circular mortar was also cut into bedrock immediately in front of the cave. The cave is low with several small passages, the longest of which appears to stretch several metres underground. Inside, two or more stone columns form supports for the fractured rock of the cave roof. Artefacts were collected from surface deposits in and around the cistern. No soil was sieved.

Chipped stone

Because the assemblage is represented only by surface collections from disturbed contexts, the analysis is restricted to core types and retouched pieces.

Raw material

Raw material used at Mugharet al-Jawa consists mostly of the fine grained grey/brown flint found also at Khallat 'Anaza. Less use was made of the smooth creamy flint, although it occurs in small quantities.

Tools and technology

The Mugharet al-Jawa assemblage is similar to that from Khallat 'Anaza. Cores are heavily reduced, and frequently turned and re-used. Most of the cores are of grey/brown flint. Borers are common at Khallat 'Anaza but rare at Mugharet al-Jawa, while scrapers form a significantly higher proportion of the tool kit. Helwan retouch is rare and most of the lunates are shaped by abrupt uni- or bipolar backing. Limited use was made of the microburin technique. As with Khallat 'Anaza, the Mugharet al-Jawa assemblage seems to represent the kind of generalised tool kit which might be expected on an occupation site in regular use (Table 2.9, Figure 2.15: 1–16).

Summary

Mugharet al-Jawa is similar to Khallat 'Anaza and the lithic assemblage suggests that the two sites must be broadly contemporary. However, Khallat 'Anaza is an open air site with structures while Mugharet al-Jawa appears to be a rockshelter occupation with limited use of exterior areas and no obvious traces of structures. Both lie on rock outcrops above the Wadi Rajil gorge, with a seasonal water supply nearby and clear views from the site out across the surrounding landscape. The amount and nature of the disturbed deposits from Mugharet al-Jawa suggest that, like Khallat 'Anaza, it may have been used regularly for prolonged periods, most probably on a seasonal basis.

Shubayqa 1

Map Ref. 3454 IV 332871

Qa' Shubayqa is a large area of mudflats on the eastern side of Jebel Druze (Figures 2.1, 2.21). Wadi Rajil runs into the southwestern end of the playa and drains out southwards from the southeastern end. During rescue survey work in 1994 several new Epipaleolithic sites were located. Two of these were fairly substantial Natufian sites with extensive flint scatters, traces of walls, heavy grinding equipment and bedrock mortars. Shubayqa 1 is a Natufian campsite at the southern edge of Qa' Shubayqa near to the point where Wadi Rajil debouches into the mudflat. Thick layers of ash with bone and flint were exposed by a recent burial, and several basalt mortars were found around the grave. Traces of earlier structures could also be distinguished which might be associated with the Natufian seasonal camp. These sub-circular stone walls are similar to the structures at Khallat 'Anaza and Mugharet al-Jawa.

Chipped stone

The assemblage is represented only by surface collections from disturbed contexts.

Raw material

The raw material for the chipped stone assemblage consists predominantly of fine-grained grey/brown flint. Smooth creamy chalcedonic flint is rare.

Tools and technology

Scrapers form a relatively high proportion of the tools but otherwise the tool kit is similar to that at Mugharet al-Jawa (Tables 2.11–2.12).

	No.	%
scrapers	17	17.89
burins	2	2.11
borers	4	4.21
backed pieces	2	2.11
truncations	5	5.26
notch/denticulate	9	9.47
retouched pieces	25	26.32
non-geometric microliths	14	14.74
geometric microliths	9	9.47
miscellaneous retouch	8	8.42
TOTAL	96	100.00

Table 2.11   Shubayqa 1 tool classes.

	No.	%
single endscraper	12	12.5
double endscraper	2	2.0
flake scraper	3	3.1
dihedral burin	1	1.0
burin on break	1	1.0
borer	4	4.1
piece, irregular back	2	2.0
truncated flake	2	2.0
truncated blade	3	3.1
retouched notch	4	4.1
blade/bladelet, multiple notches	3	3.1
denticulate	2	2.0
flake, continuous retouch	9	9.3
blade, continuous retouch one edge	11	11.4
blade, continuous retouch both edges	1	1.0
piece, inverse or alternate retouch	4	4.1
bladelet, back curved by abrupt retouch	1	1.0
bladelet fragment, abrupt retouch	2	2.0
bladelet, inverse retouch	3	3.1
bladelet, alternate retouch	4	4.1
bladelet, Helwan retouch	2	2.0
backed and truncated bladelet	2	2.0
lunate	5	5.2
Helwan lunate	4	4.1
multiple mixed pieces, various	1	1.0
miscellaneous retouch	8	8.3
TOTAL	96	100.0

Table 2.12   Shubayqa 1 tool types.

Shubayqa 3

Map Ref. 3454 I 360843

Shubayqa 3 lies on the southeastern side of the mudflats close to where Wadi Rajil drains southwards. It is a Natufian site, apparently used for intensive processing, possibly of plant material. It is located on a low rise and consists of an extensive flint scatter around a small cairn. Below the cairn are several areas of flat rock which are pitted with large numbers of bedrock mortars of varying depths. A basalt pestle was found lying near the bedrock mortars.

Shubayqa 3 was visited only briefly during a duststorm and collections from the site are limited. Preliminary analysis suggests that the tool kit is similar to the other Wadi Rajil sites but the extensive number of bedrock mortars might suggest a specialist site and it is possible that a more detailed study of chipped stone from the site might reflect this.

BDS 2103

Map Ref. 3454 I 370915

BDS 2103 is a small knapping site on one of the volcanic cones of Qitar al-Abd. The site is on the summit of the hill overlooking the Shubayqa mudflats. A small scatter of knapping waste and artefacts included two abruptly retouched lunates.

Huwaynit BDS 0201

Map Ref. 3354 III 822608

Huwaynit is a Natufian site on the lower slopes of Jebel Druze (Figures 2.1, 2.21). It lies above Wadi Jilad, a deeply incised drainage system running southwards just west of the volcanic peak of Jebel Aritayn. The Natufian camp consists of a scatter of lithics and traces of walls on and around a bedrock outcrop. The location is on a hilltop with clear views over a long distance in all directions. The strategic value of the site was recognised in the historical periods when a Roman watchtower was built on the same hillock. In both periods, the location was chosen for its panorama and for access to water. In the wadi below, the flood waters have cut into a lava flow cave which functions as a cistern. In addition, the wadi bed is rocky and impermeable, with many pools.

Huwaynit was found unexpectedly during field survey for later water systems and only a limited surface collection was made. The site appears to be comparable in size to Mugharet al-Jawa. There are traces of sub-circular structures and the lithics suggest that it represents a Late Natufian occupation similar to Khallat 'Anaza and Mugharet al-Jawa (Figure 2.15: 17, 18). One interesting aspect of the site is the high proportion of 'Dabba marble' fragments, together with broken and partially worked beads (Figure 2.15: 19). 'Dabba marble' beads and worked fragments were also found at Khallat 'Anaza, although in smaller quantities. Such evidence suggests either established exchange systems in exotic materials within and beyond the *harra*, or resource exploitation over a wide area. Local resources such as 'Dabba marble' and chalcedony may have been collected by parties from Jebel Druze but marine shells must have been traded into the area.

Wadi 'Ajib 11 (Khirbet al-Khan)

Map Ref. 3354 IV 690802

Khirbet al-Khan is one of several Natufian sites located during a survey of the Wadi 'Ajib in 1992 (Betts *et al.* 1995. Wadi 'Ajib is another wadi system draining off Jebel Druze, running southwards into the mudflats near Qasr Hallabat. Like the other sites, the Natufian camps on Wadi 'Ajib are typically sited on bedrock outcrops near to a *ghadir* in the wadi bed. Khirbet al-Khan is fairly large, with traces of structures and some bedrock mortars. It lies on the west side of the wadi with good views of the surrounding landscape. The chipped stone collection included a few micro-burins.

Wadi 'Ajib 12 (Rujum Sawwan)

Map Ref. 3254 II 520635

The Rujum al-Sawwan are limestone hills with chert beds exposed on the upper slopes. Below the hills is a large *ghadir* with many inscriptions and rock carvings. On the eastern side of the wadi above the pool is an extensive area of multi-period prehistoric occupation including material from the Natufian, PPNA and PPNB periods. Among the Natufian finds were abruptly retouched lunates and fragments of worked 'Dabba marble'.

Wadi 'Ajib 16

Map Ref. 3354 IV 680799

Wadi 'Ajib 16 is a disturbed Natufian site on a hill overlooking the wadi, with good views both up and downstream. The site has been extensively re-used in later periods up until modern times.

Wadi 'Ajib 18

Map Ref. 3354 IV 677798

Site 18 is one with multi-period occupation above a fairly large *ghadir*. Natufian artefacts were mixed with Middle Bronze Age and Roman material. Two bedrock mortars were found in the wadi below the site.

Wadi 'Ajib 24

Map Ref. 3254 I 593768

Site 24 is a large Natufian site on a hill above a massive *ghadir* cut within a short deep gorge. The site has traces of an enclosing wall and sub-circular stone structures. The chipped stone collections included abruptly backed lunates, microburins and worked 'Dabba marble'.

Jebel Subhi BDS 3114

Map Ref. 3553 IV 304799

Jebel Subhi is a small site about eighty kms southwest of Jawa (Figures 2.1, 2.21). Local rainfall is appreciably lower than in the Jawa area and although the site overlooks an extensive, seasonally flooded, mudflat, there are no *ghudran* in the immediate vicinity. The site lies on the summit of a low basalt promontory at the edge of a long mudflat which provides a route from the heart of the *harra* out into more open country. There is a scatter of flint artefacts around a small cairn, covering an area of about thirty square metres. Around the cairn are a number of low walls and hut circles but it is not clear if any of them are associated with the Epipaleolithic occupation. Surface collections were made over the extent of the artefact scatter. Surface soil was not sieved.

Chipped stone

The assemblage consists of surface collections from disturbed contexts and some mixing must be assumed.

Raw material

Raw material used for the chipped stone industry includes a high proportion of smooth cream, ivory or translucent chalcedonic flint similar to that found in small quantities at Khallat 'Anaza and Mugharet al-

	No.	%
cores	94	10.11
core trimming elements	7	0.75
primary flakes	24	2.58
flakes	485	52.15
blade/bladelets	123	13.23
spalls	4	0.43
microburins	4	0.43
splintered pieces	14	1.51
(tools)	175	18.82
total	930	100.01

Table 2.13   Jebel Subhi major chipped stone categories.

	No.	%
scrapers	25	14.29
burins	22	12.57
borers	10	5.71
backed pieces	11	6.29
truncations	7	4.00
notch/denticulate	10	5.71
retouched pieces	29	16.57
non-geometric microliths	24	13.71
geometric microliths	9	5.14
other	2	1.14
misc. retouch	26	14.86
total	175	99.99

Table 2.14   Jebel Subhi tool classes.

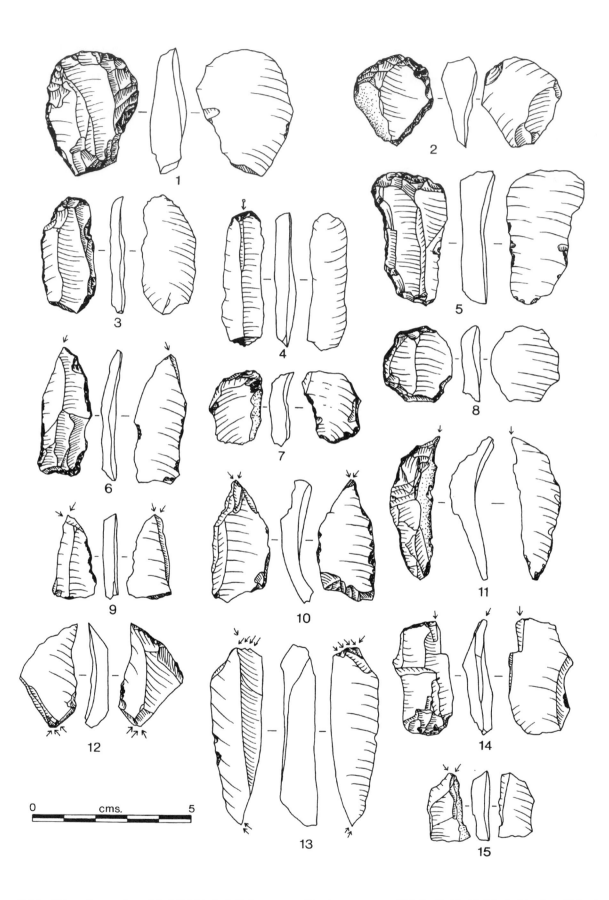

Figure 2.16   Chipped stone from Jebel Subhi. 1–5, 7, 8 scrapers; 6 burin on truncated blade; 9, 10, 15 dihedral burins; 11 burin on break; 12, 13 multiple dihedral burins; 14 truncation burin.

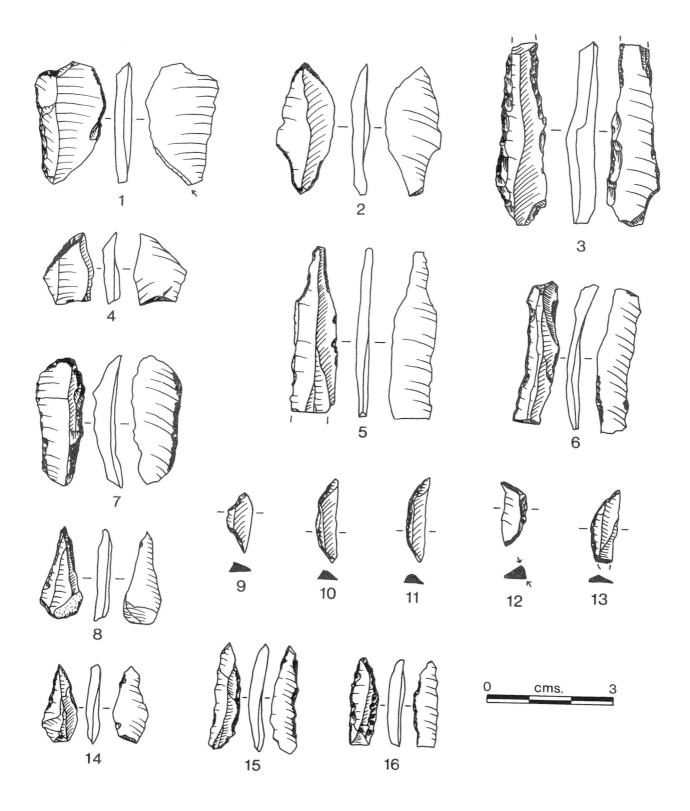

Figure 2.17   Chipped stone from Jebel Subhi. 1. burin on striking platform; 2, 3, 7 retouched blades; 6, 15, 16 retouched bladelets; 5, 8, 14 borers; 9 –11, 13 abruptly backed lunates; 12 lunate with abrupt bipolar backing.

	No.	%
single endscraper	18	10.29
flake scraper	7	4.00
dihedral burin	2	1.14
multiple dihedral burin	5	2.86
burin on break	7	4.00
burin on transverse truncation	2	1.14
burin on oblique truncation	2	1.14
burin on concave truncation	3	0.57
borer	10	5.71
naturally backed piece	2	1.14
piece, irregular back	5	2.86
piece, two backed edges	2	1.14
backed fragment	2	1.14
truncated flake	2	1.14
truncated blade	4	2.29
bitruncated piece	1	0.57
retouched notch	7	4.00
blade/bladelet, multiple notches	3	1.72
flake, continuous retouch	5	2.86
blade, continuous retouch, one edge	8	4.57
blade, continuous retouch, both edges	7	4.00
piece, inverse or alternate retouch	7	4.00
pointed piece	2	1.14
pointed bladelet, fine retouch	1	0.57
bladelet frag., fine retouch	5	2.86
bladelet frag., curved, abrupt retouch	6	3.43
bladelet frag., abrupt retouch	6	3.43
bladelet, inverse retouch	1	0.57
bladelet, alternate retouch	4	2.29
backed bladelet, inverse retouch	1	0.57
triangle	2	1.14
lunate, abrupt retouch	7	4.00
other	2	1.14
miscellaneous retouch	26	14.85
total	175	100.00

Table 2.15   Jebel Subhi tool types.

Jawa. Jebel Subhi is considerably closer to known sources of this stone which may account for its regular use at the site. Medium grained grey/brown chert was also used in smaller quantities. Both types of raw material could be obtained within twenty to thirty kms of the site (Figure 2.21).

Tools and technology

A high number of cores were found at the site, most of them heavily used or exhausted, but there
were few primary elements, suggesting that the raw material received preliminary treatment at source before being carried to the site. Flakes form a higher proportion of blanks than at the sites in the Jawa area (Table 2.13). This may be partly the result of greater use of the creamy flints which occur as small nodules, normally worked as flake cores, producing thin, slightly elongated blanks. There are low frequencies of geometrics, none with Helwan retouch (Tables 2.14, 2.15). There is evidence for some use of the microburin technique. Among the rest of the tool kit scrapers, burins and borers are all relatively common. Notched pieces occur in moderate numbers. Knapping techniques and tool typology are generally consistent with Late Natufian industries elsewhere (Figures 2.16, 2.17).

Summary

Jebel Subhi appears to be a short term camp site, although the amount of flint in the vicinity suggests that the site was re-used on more than one occasion. Since it lies so far into the steppe, it must have been visited mainly in winter and spring, and the tool kit, with less variety than the sites in the Jawa area, suggests that a more limited range of activities was carried out there. It may have been a short term camp used by small groups from Jebel Druze, who came out into the steppe to hunt and to collect chalcedony. Chalcedony cores are very rare on the Jebel Druze sites which suggests that knapping took place close to the source of the raw material. The evidence from Jebel Subhi indicates that some knapping took place at camps in the vicinity of the chalcedony outcrops, as part of a varied exploitation of the dry steppe.

Khabrat Abu Hussein BDS 4101
Map Ref. 3654 III 119515

The Natufian site at Khabrat Abu Hussein is in a similar location to Jebel Subhi, on a hill overlooking an extensive mudflat. Just below the site is a narrow gulley which channels floodwater from a second mudflat enclosed within the *harra* to the west. The gulley fills with water in the rainy season and holds its contents into late spring/early summer, depending on the volume of the winter rains. Abu Hussein is represented by an extensive flint scatter in and around low walls of uncertain date. The site lies at the eastern edge of the *harra* and looks out to the east over the open plains of the limestone *hamad*. To the west lie a chain of volcanic peaks linked by a string of elongated mudflats which form a convenient route into the centre of the *harra*, up to the central watershed of the Ashaqif range.

The small surface collection made at the site includes abruptly backed lunates and triangles, borers, notched and retouched bladelets and a limited range of other tools of similar type to the Jebel Subhi collection (Tables 2.16, 2.17). Much use is made of fine yellow and cream chalcedony, possibly because of easy access to sources across the open *hamad*. The assemblage is more limited in range than those from the sites on Jebel Druze, which suggests that the range of activities carried out at the site was similarly limited. Given the location of the site so far out into the dry steppe, it seems likely that it was used as a short term camp in winter/spring by hunter/forager bands coming out into the more marginal areas, possibly to exploit local resources such as the chalcedonic flint outcropping in the area.

Qasr Burqu'
Map Ref. 3555 II 027086

Small scatters of microlithic debris and Epipaleolithic

	No.	%
scrapers	9	7.63
burins	2	1.70
borers	3	2.54
backed pieces	3	2.54
truncations	4	3.39
notch/denticulate	10	8.48
retouched pieces	48	40.68
non-geometric microliths	17	14.41
geometric microliths	11	9.32
other	1	0.85
misc. retouch	10	8.48
TOTAL	118	100.02

Table 2.16   Khabrat Abu Hussein tool classes.

	No.	%
single endscraper	6	5.08
flake scraper	3	2.54
burin on break	2	1.70
borer	3	2.54
naturally backed piece	1	0.85
backed piece	2	1.70
truncated blade	4	3.39
retouched notch	5	4.24
blade/bladelet, multiple notches	4	3.39
denticulate	1	0.85
flake, continuous retouch	10	8.48
flake, discontinuous retouch	8	6.78
blade, continuous retouch, one edge	4	3.39
blade, continuous retouch, both edges	2	1.70
blade, fine discontinuous retouch	8	6.78
piece, inverse or alternate retouch	15	12.71
pointed piece	1	0.85
bladelet, fine retouch	4	3.39
bladelet, curved, abrupt retouch	1	0.85
bladelet, inverse retouch	2	1.70
backed bladelet,	2	1.70
truncated bladelet	3	2.54
backed and truncated bladelet	5	4.24
triangle	5	4.24
lunate, abrupt retouch	6	5.08
other	1	0.85
miscellaneous retouch	10	8.48
TOTAL	118	100.04

Table 2.17   Khabrat Abu Hussein tool types.

artefacts were found at various spots around the *ghadir* at Burqu' (Figures 2.1, 2.21). No extensive spreads were identified. Finds included two abruptly backed lunates, scrapers, borers and retouched bladelets.

BDS 1605

Map Ref. 3453 IV 205259

This is a large multi-period knapping site on a basalt capped peak overlooking Wadi Rajil just east of Jebel Qurma (Figures 2.1, 2.21). The site is an excellent lookout spot and was used from the Epipaleolithic through the Neolithic periods. The collection included two Helwan lunates and some unretouched bladelets (Betts 1983:4).

The Natufian in the *harra*

In eastern Jordan during the Natufian period, changes in land-use through time closely follow those observed

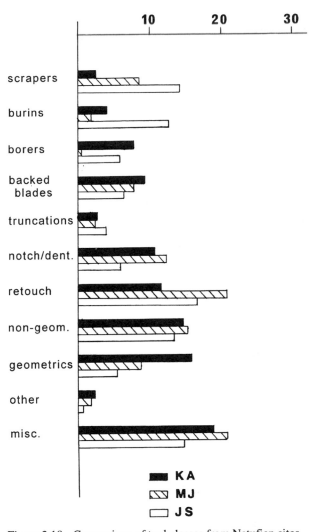

Figure 2.18   Comparison of tool classes from Natufian sites.

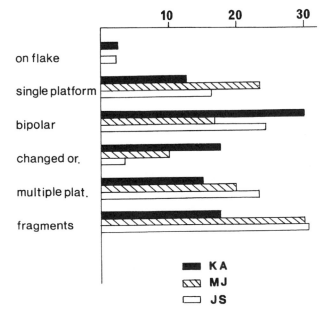

Figure 2.19   Comparison of core types from Natufian sites.

33

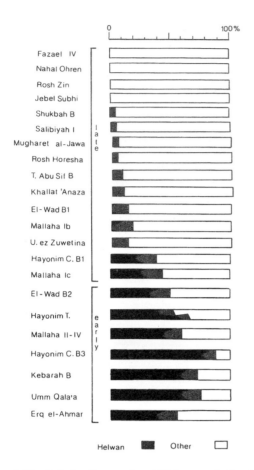

Figure 2.20   Relative frequencies of Helwan and other lunates from Natufian sites in the *harra* and elsewhere (after Bar Yosef 1981a, fig. 8).

elsewhere in the Levant where Early Natufian sites are located well within the Mediterranean vegetation zone, while in the Late Natufian sites extended into more marginal areas within the Irano-Turanian vegetation belt (Bar-Yosef 1988: 232). Although there are no radiocarbon dates for Natufian sites in eastern Jordan, a pattern of occupation and landuse can be constructed on the basis of relative chronology using lithic assemblages. Ain Saratan is the only Early Natufian site so far identified in the area (Garrard *et al.* 1988a [Azraq 18]; Byrd 1989b: Table II; Garrard 1991). Although the site is within the Irano-Turanian vegetation zone, it lies beside a permanent spring in the resource-rich environment of the Azraq marshes.

On the basis of the chipped stone assemblages, sites on Jebel Druze appear to have been established in the Late Neolithic. Taibe in Syria (M.-C. Cauvin 1974) (Figure 2.1: 1) has low proportions of Helwan lunates in the geometric microlith class. Bar-Yosef, in his analysis of Natufian sites (Bar-Yosef 1981a: Figure 8) classes the site as Late Natufian. Relative proportions of Helwan and other lunates at Mugharet al-Jawa and Khallat 'Anaza indicate that both sites are of Late Natufian date (Figure 2.20), while the other Natufian sites known from the slopes of Jebel Druze can probably also be classed as Late Natufian. There is clearly a pattern where semi-permanent sites were established on the lower slopes of Jebel Druze on the modern boundary between the Irano-Turanian and Saharo-Arabian vegetation zones, but also close to the 'island' of Mediterranean vegetation on the summit of Jebel Druze.

There is still debate over climatic conditions in the Natufian, and some apparent discrepancies in the available evidence remain as yet unresolved (Byrd

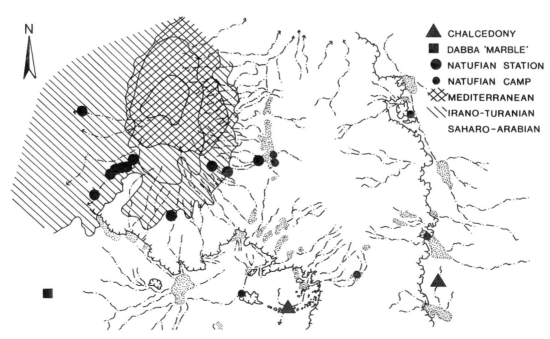

Figure 2.21   Distribution of Natufian sites in the *Harra*, and raw material sources in eastern Jordan.

1989b: 168; Baruch and Bottema 1991; Leroi-Gourhan and Darmon 1991). However, throughout the Levant there is evidence for an expansion of landuse in the Late Natufian beyond the core Mediterranean climatic zone into the steppic areas (Goring-Morris 1987:23; Bar-Yosef and Belfer-Cohen 1992:31). The upper slopes of Jebel Druze form an 'island' zone of Mediterranean vegetation. It is possible that in the Natufian period this was more extensive. The archaeological evidence indicates the establishment of semi-permanent stations in what is at present a zone of Irano-Turanian climatic conditions (Figure 2.21). Most of the sites in the area which today lies in the Saharo-Arabian vegetation zone are small short-term camps such as Jebel Subhi and Khabrat Abu Hussein or knapping sites and small flint scatters such as those at Burqu' and Jebel Qurma.

Analyses by Byrd (1989b) and Olzewski (1986) show evidence of overall similarity in tool typology between the *harra* sites and other sites in steppe and desert locations. Byrd has argued that the steppe/desert sites fall into two clusters. Of these, Khallat 'Anaza and Jebel Subhi belong with Cluster 2, characterised by relatively high percentages of notches and denticulates, scrapers

and miscellaneous retouched pieces (Byrd 1989b:179). Byrd suggests that a tool kit of this type may indicate a focus on processing of animal carcasses. However, at a more detailed level of comparison, there are differences in the tool kits of the *harra* sites (Figure 2.18). Those from Khallat 'Anaza and Mugharet al-Jawa are fairly similar, although there are variations in the numbers of borers, scrapers and geometrics. There are slightly greater differences between the Jebel Druze sites and camp sites in the dry steppe, which, at the latter, probably reflects the more specialised nature of tool kits from short-term occupation sites. Of the three clusters identified by Byrd, two are associated with steppe/desert environments. Of these, Cluster 2 including Khallat 'Anaza and Jebel Subhi, appears to be characterised by a broader range of activities than the other steppe/desert cluster (No. 3) which seems to be associated with a more specialised emphasis on hunting (Byrd 1989b: 181). This suggests that Late Natufian camp sites in the dry steppe were not exclusively hunting stations, and that use of the area may have been fairly extensive, although length of occupation at sites beyond Jebel Druze was restricted by limited water supply.

3. Dhuweila: Stratigraphy and Construction

A.V.G. Betts

The Dhuweila area

Dhuweila (Figure 3.1) is a small rock-strewn mound lying at an elevation of 635 metres above sea level. It is located on rising ground overlooking a large open area of silts and mudflat (Figure 3.2). Immediately to the north is a well incised wadi system, and to the south is a shallower system with a seasonally flooding *qa'*. In the northern wadi — Wadi Dhuweila — runoff water collects in a series of small *ghudran*. The basalt forms a low ridge along the eastern side of the main *qa'*, which consists of two parts: *marabb dhuweila* (silts with salt tolerant perennial vegetation), and *qa' dhuweila* to the south (sterile mudflat).

Dhuweila saw two episodes of use. It was first constructed in the late seventh millennium bc as a camp for hunters using the 'kites' in the area. Abandoned some time around the turn of the millennium, the main structures were cleared out and re-used in the later sixth millennium bc, again by hunting groups making use of the 'kites'. The site continued to see occasional use as a camp site up until recent times. These later occupations left traces in the form of artefacts, carvings and a cairn on the top of the mound which caused slight disturbance to the upper levels of the Late Neolithic structures. The site is built on a series of interconnecting 'kite' walls, and is one of several such camps in the immediate area. A chain of 'kites' runs north and south along the ridge, the 'kite' enclosures lying just over the break of slope, on the side facing the *qa'*. Two smaller Early Neolithic hunting camps, Abu Masiyad al-Gharbi and al-Sharqi, are built against 'kite' walls northeast of Dhuweila,

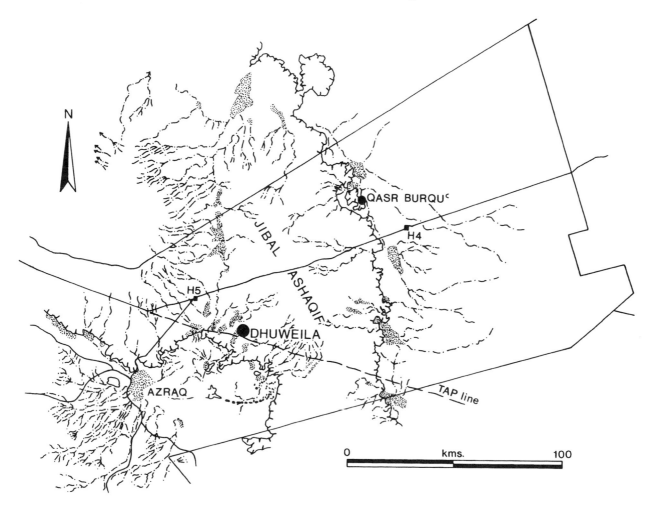

Figure 3.1   Location of Dhuweila.

37

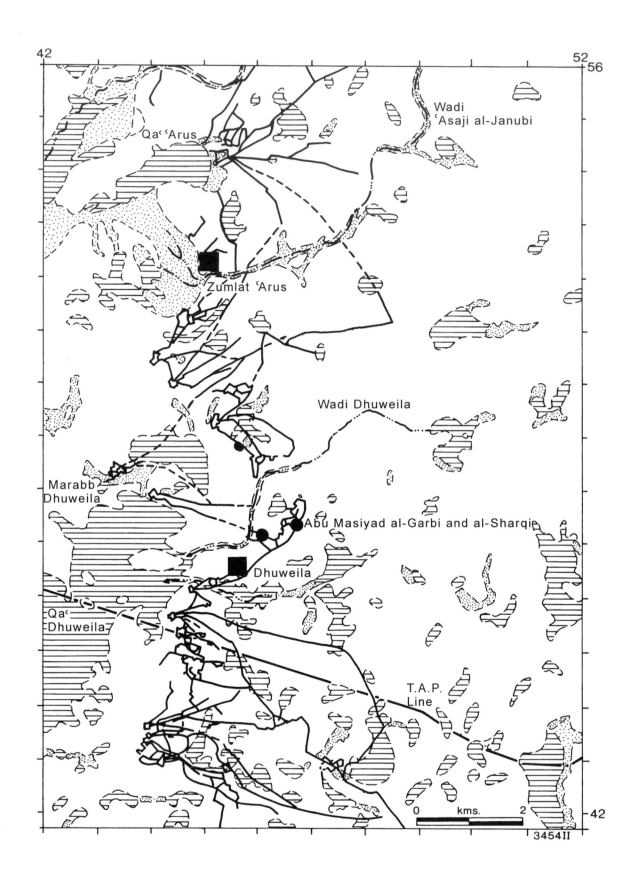

Figure 3.2   Sites in the Dhuweila survey area.

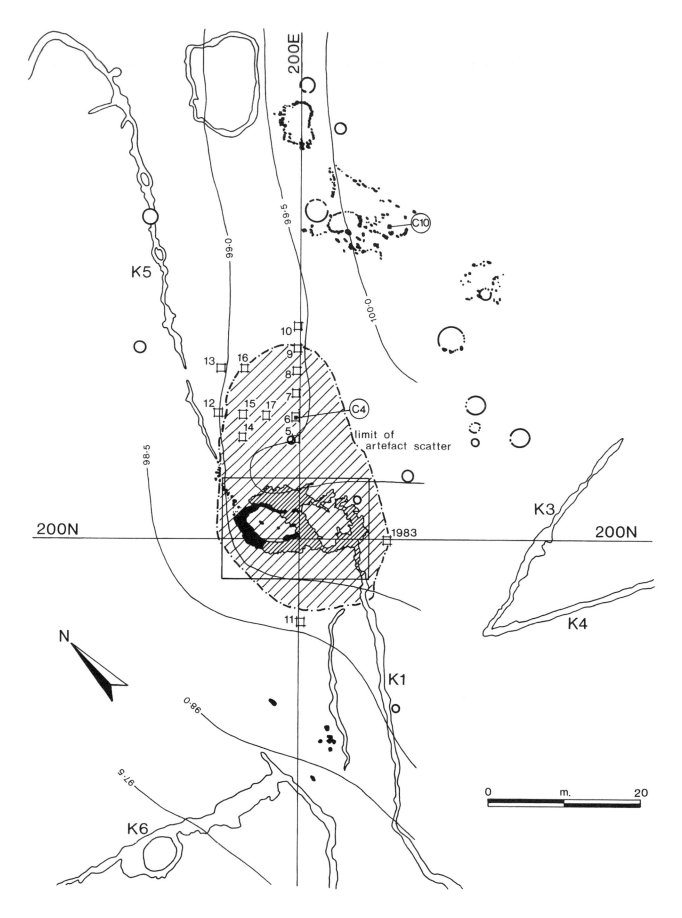

Figure 3.3   Dhuweila: site plan.

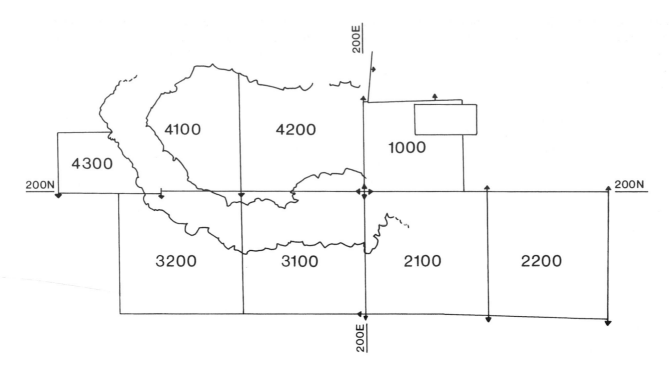

Figure 3.4   Dhuweila: schematic plan of trenches.

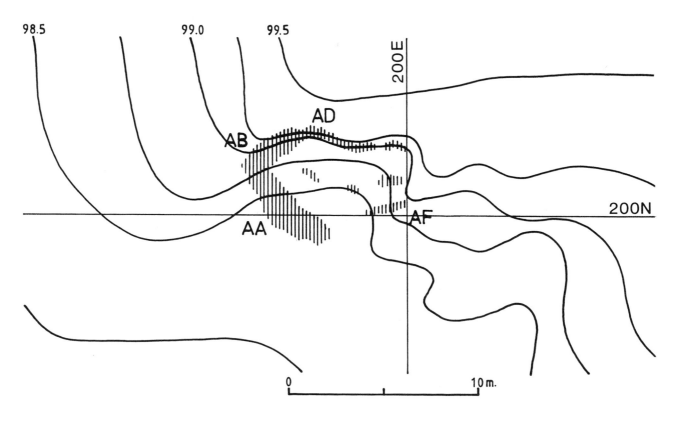

Figure 3.5   Dhuweila: site contours.

close to the *ghudran* in the wadi. Further north again the main ridge is cut by a larger wadi, Wadi 'Asaji al-Janubi. This wadi has several large *ghudran* in the streambed, and on the hill above is another Neolithic site, Zumlat 'Arus. Like Dhuweila, Zumlat 'Arus was first used in the Pre-Pottery Neolithic B period, and then re-occupied in the Late Neolithic period. Broken arrowheads, of both Early and Late Neolithic types, have been found in and around 'kite' enclosures of the Dhuweila chain, and some of the small hillocks along the main ridge have knapping debris on their summits where hunters may have prepared their arrowheads while watching for game.

Scattered in and around these Neolithic sites are carved rocks, with fine engravings of animals, abstract designs, and occasionally human figures. Dating of rock art is a difficult task. Many of the abundant Arabian rock carvings can only loosely be dated (Betts n.d.). Art of the Dhuweila style is unique in that several carvings have been found during excavation, on stones built into structures and sealed by dated occupation levels. The carvings are associated with the first stage of use at Dhuweila, the late 7th millennium bc.

All the Neolithic sites in the Dhuweila area are located in relation to the 'kite' systems. The ideal situation is behind (downwind of) the 'kite' enclosures, on high ground with good visibility but slightly below the exposed summits, and near a source of water. All the sites conform broadly to this pattern. The eastern side of the Dhuweila mudflats is particularly suited to 'kite' construction. 'Kite' guiding walls usually begin in an area of grazing, in this case the wadis draining into the mudflat from the east. In almost every case, the walls run roughly westward up a long, gentle slope leading to a ridge overlooking open ground or, less frequently, a wadi system. The enclosure will be placed just over the break of slope, invisible to animals running up the hill until the last minute.

Stratigraphy

Introduction

The site consists of a low rubble mound lying along the ridge just below the crest (Figure 3.5). 'Kite' walls run up to the site (Figure 3.3: K1-6). K1 is built into the enclosure wall relating to the final phases of Stage 2, while K5 has been robbed out at some point, probably to provide building material for the structures. A surface

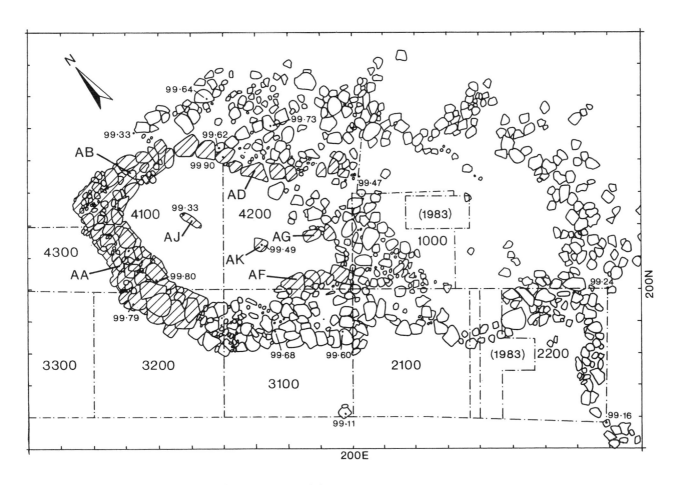

Figure 3.6   Dhuweila: major structural features and trench layout.

scatter of artefacts extends for some way beyond the mound (Figure 3.3: hatched area). The main structures at Dhuweila date from the first occupation at the site, Early Neolithic Stage 1 (Phases 1–5). When the site was re-occupied in Stage 2 (Phases 6–9), much of the site was disturbed as the new occupants cleared out the structures at the western end of the mound. However, there is considerable depth of occupation debris which has been protected from serious erosion and deflation by the solid walls of the main structures. It seems reasonable to assume that the site was only used sporadically. Certainly in its second stage of use, and probably from time to time in the earlier stage as well, some of the structures were cleared out, and the fill distributed outside the walls. The structures themselves were partitioned, and occasionally partially or totally rebuilt. This has resulted in a certain mixing of artefacts in the second stage, and makes it difficult to determine the architectural sequence. However, much of the Stage 1 deposits were clearly undisturbed, and the interior of the main structure preserved intact occupation levels of Stage 2. A series of radiocarbon dates linked to secure deposits provides a useful indication of the basic integrity of the sequence.

Following abandonment of the site at the end of Stage 2, Dhuweila saw sporadic use (Stage 3: Phase 10). The upper parts of the walls were disturbed to build a cairn or tomb, and later artefacts indicate use of the site for temporary camps or lookout posts.

Radiocarbon Chronology

Eight dates have been obtained for the Dhuweila sequence, two for Stage 1, three for Stage 2, and three for Stage 3. Because of its steppic location, there is no tree charcoal at Dhuweila. Dating material from Stages 1 and 2 is derived from short-lived shrubs and grasses. The Neolithic dates (uncalibrated) range from mid to late 7th millennium bc for Stage 1, and from mid to late 6th millennium bc for Stage 2. The dates also coincide chronologically with the phases within each stage. However, the samples chosen for analysis had to be taken from well stratified deposits, and thus fairly low in the occupation sequence. Lack of suitable samples in the upper levels meant that dated samples for Stage 2 came from the earlier phases. It is possible that a date for the upper phases might have extended the time range.

The three dates for Stage 3 were obtained from carbonised fabric preserved on small chunks of plaster in the uppermost levels. The fabric remains are discussed further below. The dates, which range from the mid third millennium to the mid second millennium bc, indicate that the site saw a brief period of re-use at the beginning of the Early Bronze Age.

OxA-1637 was obtained from a sample collected in the fill of P8, a pit cut into bedrock on the edge of the site, in an external working area. The pit forms part of a complex of holes cut one into another, all associated with the early phases of the site. BM-2349 was a sample collected during the first soundings at the site in 1983 from an internal fire pit in phase 3 of Stage 1, well sealed by later Early Neolithic occupation levels. While the relative ages of the two samples must be taken only as a general indication of date, the later date is clearly from a later context.

Samples OxA-1728 and OxA-1729 came from P18, a pit cut through the lower pavement inside the main excavated structure. OxA-1728 was taken from above the floor level, and OxA-1729 from below it. It is possible that the pit was recut at some stage, but this was difficult to determine during excavation as the fill was soft and loose. OxA-1636 was a sample taken from higher in the fill of the same structure, in an area of ashy deposits sealed by further occupation levels within the building.

Samples UtC 2028, 2029 and 2030 all came from the uppermost levels and were not apparently associated with any structures or identifiable occupation deposits. They were dispersed across the site. One fragment was found in sand/loam deposits by Wall AD, and the other dated pieces came from the lower slope of the mound in the open area beyond the main structure.

Excavation Strategy

The main site consists of an oval pile of tumbled rocks about 20 m long and 12 m wide. In 1983 two soundings were laid out on the southeastern side of the mound (Betts 1985). By 1986, these trenches had suffered heavy erosion and it was not possible to reconstruct the original grid, so a new grid was laid out on a similar alignment. The site was divided into quadrants about a central point, and each quadrant was subdivided into squares of 4 x 4 m. (Figures 3.4, 3.6). In addition to the main site, one square metre test pits were cut around the periphery to check the extent of occupation (Figure 3.3). All soil was sieved through 5 mm mesh. Positions of carved stones around the site were also recorded (Numbers prefixed by C: Figure 3.3). All levels are relative to Site Datum.

The site straddles a series of 'kite' walls (Figure 3.3) which follow the contours of the slope on which

Stage	Lab Ref.	Phase	Material	Age(bp)	Date(bc)
1	OxA-1637	1	charcoal	8350±100	6400
1	BM-2349	3	charcoal	8190±60	6240
2	OxA-1729	6	charcoal	7450±90	5500
2	OxA-1728	6	charcoal	7140±90	5190
2	OxA-1636	8	charcoal	7030±90	5080
3	UtC-2030	10	fibre	5510±60	3560
3	UtC-2028	10	fibre	5010±80	3060
3	UtC-2029	10	fibre	4440±90	2490

Table 3.1   List of radiocarbon dated samples.

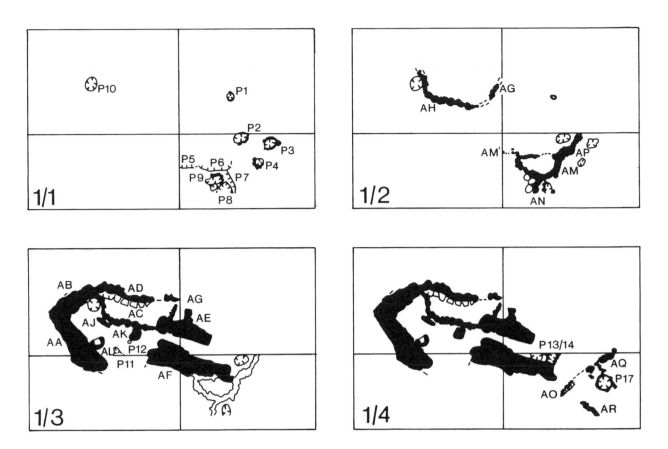

Figure 3.7   Dhuweila: general plan of features in Stage 1, phases 1–4.

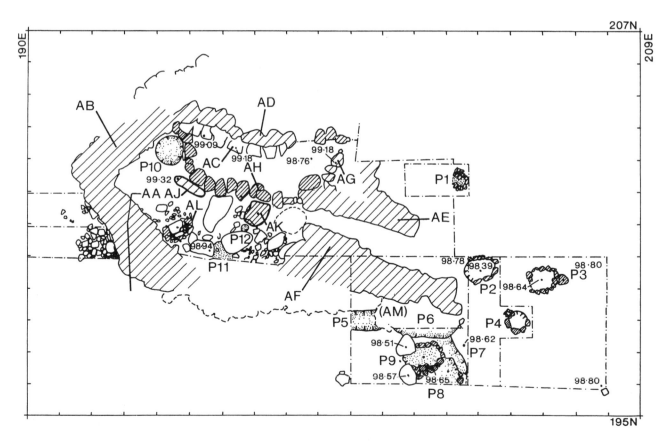

Figure 3.8   Dhuweila: detailed plan of major features in Stage 1.

Dhuweila lies. Apart from the main structural complex, there are also some subsidiary stone circles and enclosures on the flat ground to the northeast. These are relatively insubstantial, but some may relate to use of the main site in one or both stages of occupation. Surface collections were made in and around these structures, but no excavation was carried out.

Stratigraphic Sequence

Stage 1

Phase 1

The first phase consists of a series of pits (P1;P2;P3;P4;P8; P9; P10) and scoops (P5; P6; P7) cut into the natural ground surface (Figure 3.7 1/1; Figure 3.8). Bedrock beneath the site is made up of solid basalt occurring in smooth rounded surfaces, and weathered rock appearing as compact orange grit. The pits are stone-lined at the rim, roughly circular in plan, and of varying depths. Most were filled with ashy sand containing charcoal and some fragments of flint and bone. The scoops may have been living hollows, protected on the downslope side by low walls which were lost in subsequent rebuilding. The lowest occupation levels over the excavated area are associated with this phase Plate 1.

Phase 2

Phase 2 is closely related to the initial phase, and may simply represent inter-seasonal reconstruction. Some thin walls are preserved, built against the downslope side of the hill (Figure 3.7. 1/2: AH, AM, AN, AP; Figure 3.8: AH; Figure 3.9: AM, AN, AP; Plate 3). Similar walls may have been associated with Phase 1, and some of the pits of Phase 1 may still have been in use in Phase 2. The walls are low, constructed of basalt cobbles, laid side by side in irregular curves. They are placed as if functioning as the base for windbreaks, perhaps of brushwood or skins. Two carved stones were found in levels of this phase. Carvings C1 and C2 were on stones incorporated into wall AM (Figure 3.9). The stones had been used apparently with little regard for the carvings. In both cases the carved surfaces were partly exposed, with the figures at irregular angles.

Phase 3

This is the major building phase at the site (Figure 3.7. 1/3). A massive new wall (AA, AB) was built against the prevailing wind at the western end of the site (Figure 3.8). The wall is rough on the outside but carefully faced with smooth flat stones to the interior. Two other thick walls (AE, AF) lie parallel to one another along the middle of the mound. Wall AF has been interrupted at the southeastern end and the northwestern end is unexcavated, but surface clearance in squares 3200 and 3100 (Figure 3.6) indicate that wall AF was linked to wall AB at some period in the life of the site, although

not necessarily in Stage 1. Wall AE has been truncated at the southeastern end. It may join on to another wall running off northeastwards (Figure 3.8). At the eastern end, wall AB is abutted by a more irregular wall (AD). There are two distinct construction techniques; Walls AA, AB, AF, and AG are of well laid drystone walling, usually three or four stones thick. Wall AD is made of single upright slabs or large boulders, held in place by the stones of AC at the base. Similarly, Wall AH was rebuilt, and used as the support for uprights AJ and AK. Wall AO, an external structure set against AM, was a short length of low uprights supported by flat stones at the base, a smaller version of the construction techniques used in AD. An internal fitting, a small box of upright basalt slabs (AL), was set close to the main wall (Figure 3.8; Plate 4). Four internal pits (Figure 3.7: 1/3; Figure 3.8: P11, P12; Figure 3.9: P13, P14) also belong to this phase. P11 was thickly lined with plaster containing small chunks of charcoal. P12 was an amorphous ashy hollow within the occupation deposits. P13 and P14 were plaster lined features, partially ringed by small rocks. In addition, the external pits were recut (Figure 3.9: P15, P16). Several carved stones were associated with this phase. C6 (Figure 3.9) was on a stone forming part of the surround for P14. The stone was placed with the carving upside down, facing the inside of the pit. Both stone and carving were heavily fire damaged. C8 was carved on an upright slab forming part of wall AO (Figure 3.9). The area enclosed by wall AM was partly covered over by a rough section of paving (AS), and two carved stones (C5, C9) were found on stones forming part of AS. Again, the stones seemed to have been used with little regard for the carvings.

Phase 4

This phase saw the construction of further small, irregular walls (Figure 3.10). AQ and AR were thin rows of basalt cobbles similar to those of Phase 2. P17 was a shallow stone ringed pit or hearth similar to those in Phase 1. Pits 13 and 14 were sealed by a plaster surface which ran up against Wall AF.

Phase 5

Phase 5 is represented by a heavy buildup of occupation levels in the external areas; south and east of Wall AF. This debris consists of a sloping bank of dark ashy soil filled with broken angular pebbles and a dense concentration of discarded bone and flint (Plate 2). The only new structural element in this phase is a rough pavement (Figure 3.11: AT) set against the eastern extent of Wall AF. A carved stone (C7) was set into the pavement, design upwards. The presentation of the decorated surface may have been incidental, as the carved face was the only flat surface of the stone suitable for a paving slab. Occupation levels of this stage covered over most of the earlier external features

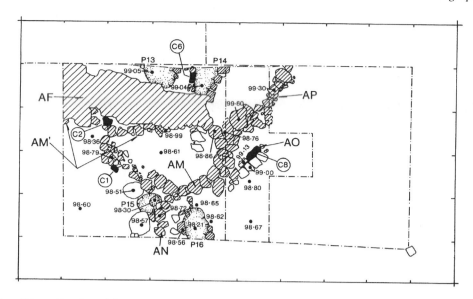

Figure 3.9   Dhuweila: plan of features in squares 2100 and 2200, Stage 1, phases 1–3.

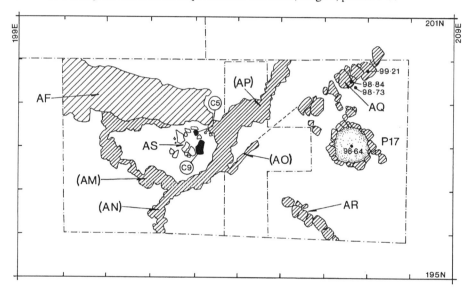

Figure 3.10   Dhuweila: plan of features in squares 2100 and 2200, Stage 1, phases 3–4.

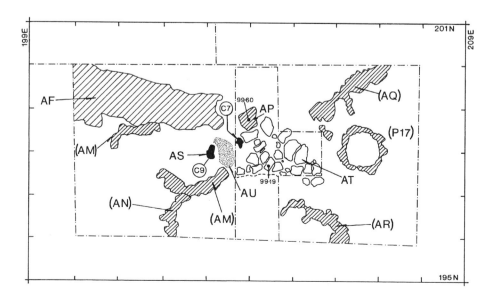

Figure 3.11   Dhuweila: plan of features in squares 2100 and 2200, Stage 1, phases 4–5.

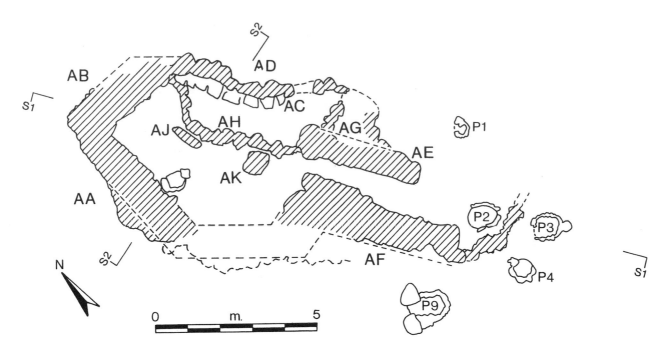

Figure 3.12   Dhuweila: general plan of major features in Stage 1, showing cross-sections of schematic reconstructions (Figures 3.13, 3.14).

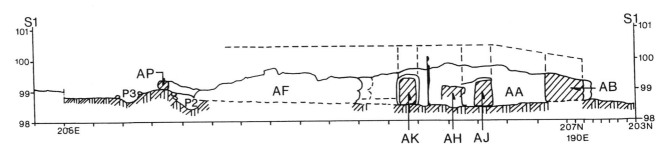

Figure 3.13   Dhuweila: Stage 1, schematic cross-section.

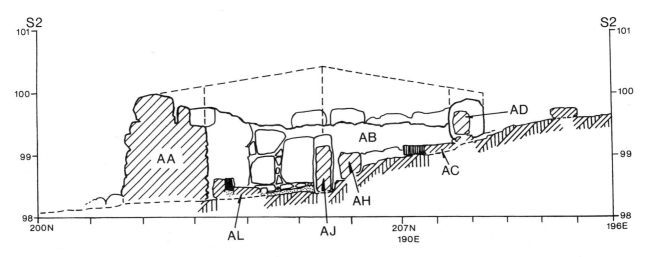

Figure 3.14   Dhuweila: Stage 1, schematic cross-section.

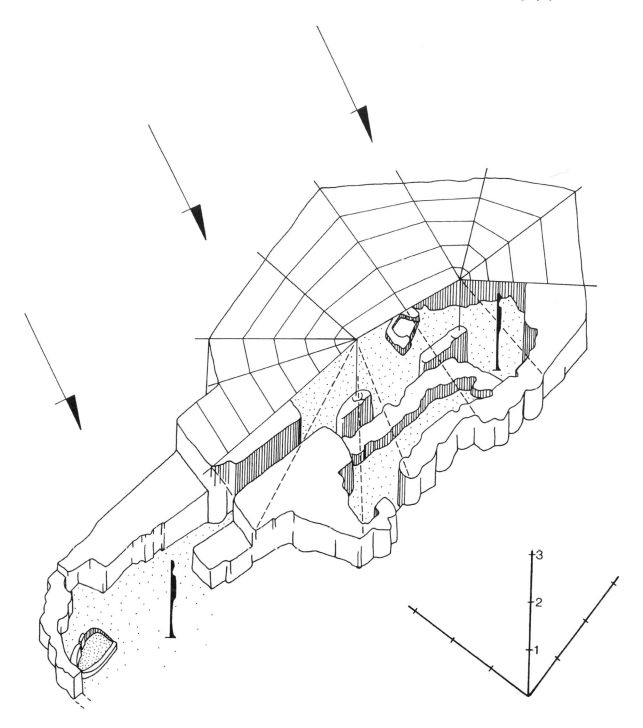

Figure 3.15   Dhuweila: Stage 1, suggested reconstruction.

in Squares 2100 and 2200, with the exception of wall AF. It is likely that the main structure continued in use, and the change in external deposits shows either a change in activities, or a change in the location of certain areas of activity.

Summary

The occupation levels in Stage 1 are ashy, with a high concentration of faunal and chipped stone waste. Burnt and fire-cracked stones occur in large quantities throughout all phases (dark ashy deposits are shown as close oblique hatching on sections). Figure 3.20 shows scoop P5 and pit P8 cut into bedrock. P5 goes out of use and is sealed by external occupation deposits (Figure 3.20a), while P8 is recut as P16, and re-lined with stones around the upper edge. In the final phase (5) of Stage 1, the pits are sealed by a layer of dark ashy soil filled with broken angular pebbles (Figure 3.20b: 13). Figure 3.21 shows P2 cut into bedrock, and sealed by stones and occupation deposits. Later pits P13 and P14 are shown set into earlier occupation deposits. P13 is lined with mud-plaster. In phase 5, the pits are sealed over by a rough mud-plaster surface (Figure 3.21b: 19) overlaid with a thin occupation layer (Figure 3.21b: 20, 21). Levels of Stage 1 preserved within the main structure can be seen in Figure 3.23 (3.23b: 1–6) where P11 is truncated and sealed by levels of Stage 2. Stones relating to occupation in Stage 1 were incorporated into the earliest Stage 2 pavement within the structure (Figure 3.23: BB/C).

The structures at Dhuweila are designed as windbreaks. The walls are set against the wind, facing onto the gentle slope of the hill, just below level ground (Figure 3.5). It is hard to distinguish a clear pattern to the structures, and the original plan of the main walls has been lost in a series of rebuildings and expedient alteration. Figure 3.12 suggests a reconstruction of the basic structural plan in Stage 1. A cross-section (Figure 3.14) shows the way in which the walls are set against the slope, and the differing construction techniques. Figure 3.13 illustrates how the upright slabs AJ and AK may have been used as the basis for roof supports, and Figure 3.15 gives an example of how the structure may have been covered, using short poles covered with brushwood or skins. At present, there are no trees or large shrubs in the vicinity of the site, but acacia and pistachio can still be found in some of the wadi beds close to the Azraq lake. Selected branches could have been transported to the site for use as tent poles. Local supplies of wood seem unlikely, given the lack of wood charcoal at the site.

Firepits or hearths are a special feature of Stage 1. The most common design is a rounded pit of varying depth, ringed at the top by stones, and filled, in most cases, by loose ashy soil. These pits are mainly external features. Internal plaster-lined features form a second class. These may perhaps have been intended for storage or as work surfaces. They are normally irregular and fairly small. Isolated ashy patches without stone surrounds may have been *ad hoc* hearths.

Stage 2

Phase 6

When the site was re-occupied in Stage 2, no major rebuilding was carried out. The main walls must still have been visible, partially covered with weathered occupation deposits from the previous stage. The main structure, defined by walls AA, AB AD, AE, AF and AG, may have been partially cleared out, but not down to bedrock. Instead, a pavement of flat basalt slabs and cobbles (Figure 3.16: BA, BB, BC, BD) was laid out inside the southwestern part between Walls AA, AB and AH, overlying the remaining occupation deposits from Stage 1 (Plate 5). The pavement was carried right across and a set of steps led up into the passage formed by Walls AE and AF. The floor of the passage was also roughly paved. A circular grinding stone with a central

depression (BA) was set into the pavement, surrounded by a rough ring of cobbles, and several other stones in the pavement also showed signs of wear (Figure 3.16: stippled stones; see also Chapter 5, No. 24 below). A pit (P18) was cut into the floor of the structure. Later, this was partially covered by further paving slabs. The occupation deposits immediately above the pavement contained a number of worked basalt tools.

External deposits from this phase, and later phases of Stage 2, consist of loose sandy soil with some artefacts. There are no indications of specific work areas.

Phase 7

Levels relating to Phase 7 consist of occupation deposits above the pavement within the structure. The soil was loose, soft, and brown, and there was a high proportion of intact artefacts including flint tools and worked basalt.

Phase 8

In this phase, a second, less extensive and more irregular pavement was laid out at the northwestern end of the interior of the main structure (Figure 3.17: BF). The circular grinding stone embedded in the lower pavement continued in use for a time, and was then covered over by further crude paving (Figure 3.18: BG). In the sector east of Wall AH, a semi-circular platform was laid against Wall AD (Figure 3.17: BE).

Phase 9

This is the latest definable phase in Stage 2. The pavement was covered by further occupation deposits and a new grinding stone with a central depression was built into a semi-circular platform against the northern end of Wall AF (Figure 3.19: BH, Plate 6). In the latest part of the phase, this platform was covered over with a thin layer of occupation debris. The main structure was largely filled in by this time, and a wall was built in Square 1000, blocking off the end of the passage, which must have gone out of use. This wall forms the western side of a sub-circular enclosure which links onto 'kite' wall K1 at the southeast end of the site (Figures 3.3; 3.6).

Summary

Stage 2 at Dhuweila is markedly different from Stage 1. There is no buildup of fire-cracked stones and ash and little evidence of external processing area. Most activity seems to have been carried out within the main structure. There is particular evidence for work involving grinding or rubbing. During the Late Neolithic period the site saw several phases of occupation and internal rebuilding, probably indicative of intermittent occupation. Evidence of successive occupation levels can be seen in Figure 3.23. Figure 3.24 shows the paving within the entrance, and the subsequent blocking in the later phases. Figure 3.22 shows buildup of rubble

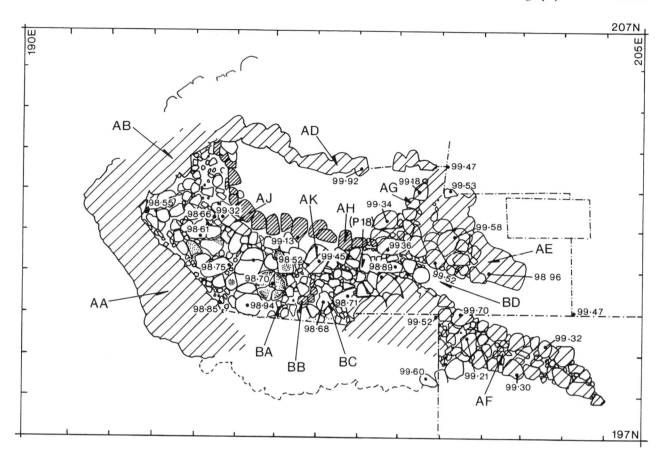

Figure 3.16   Dhuweila: Stage 2, phases 6, 7.

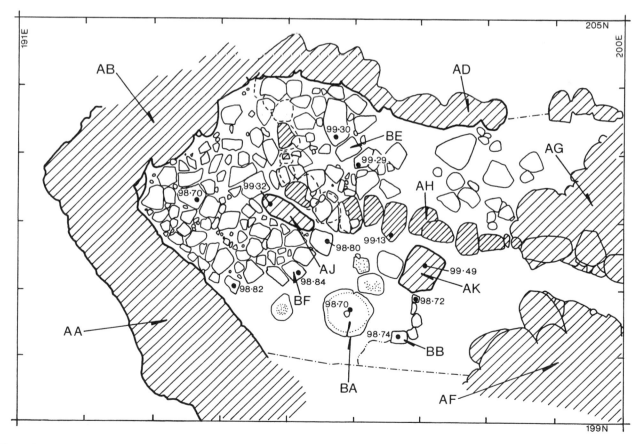

Figure 3.17   Dhuweila: Stage 2, phase 8.

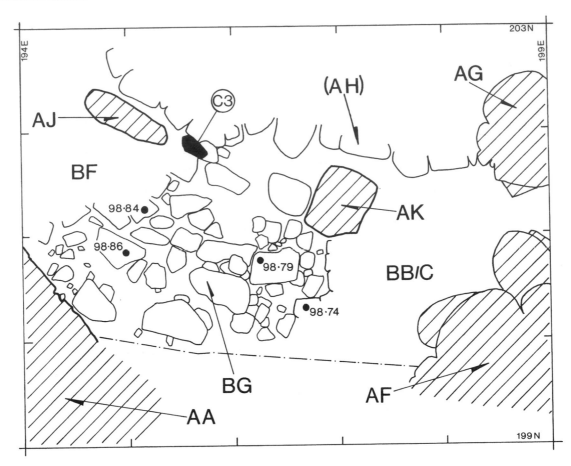

Figure 3.18   Dhuweila: Stage 2, phase 8.

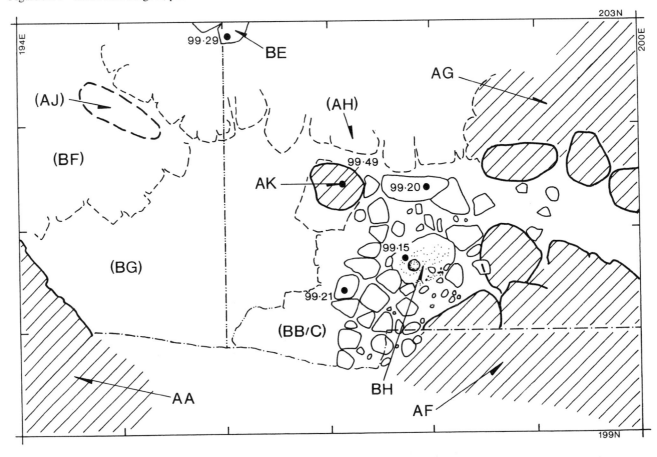

Figure 3.19   Dhuweila: Stage 2, phase 9.

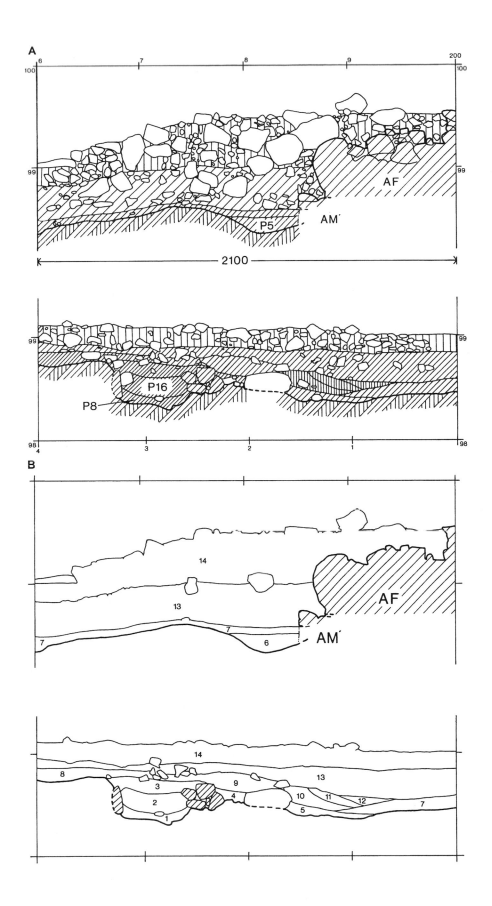

Figure 3.20   Dhuweila: square 2100, west and south sections.

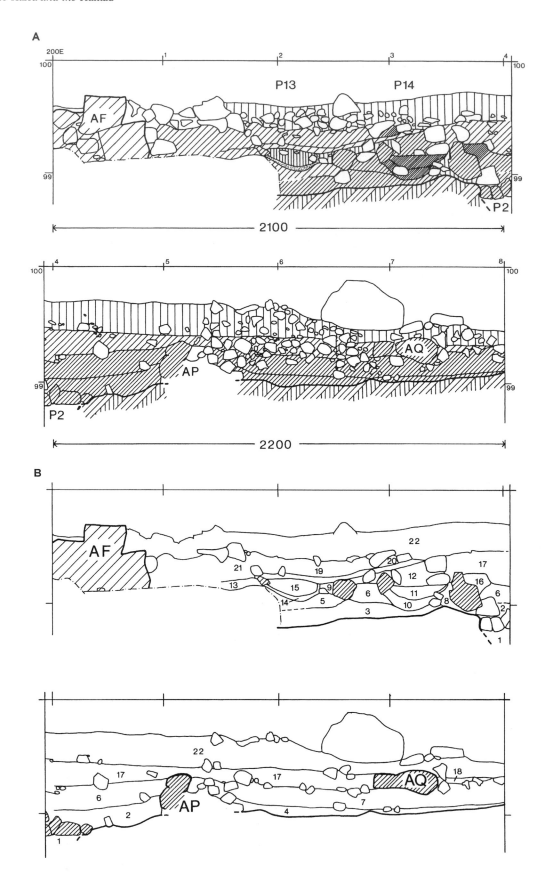

Figure 3.21   Dhuweila: squares 2100, 2200, north sections.

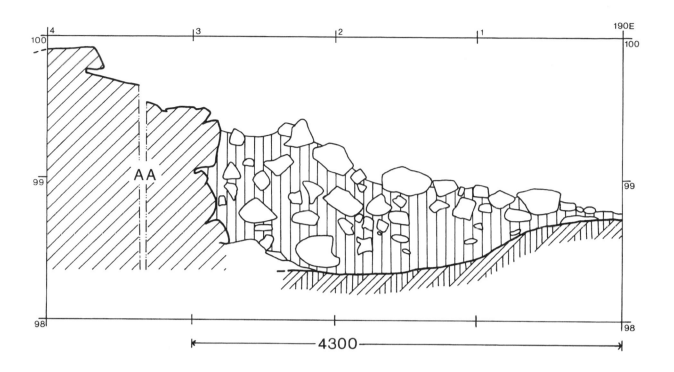

Figure 3.22   Dhuweila: square 4300, south section.

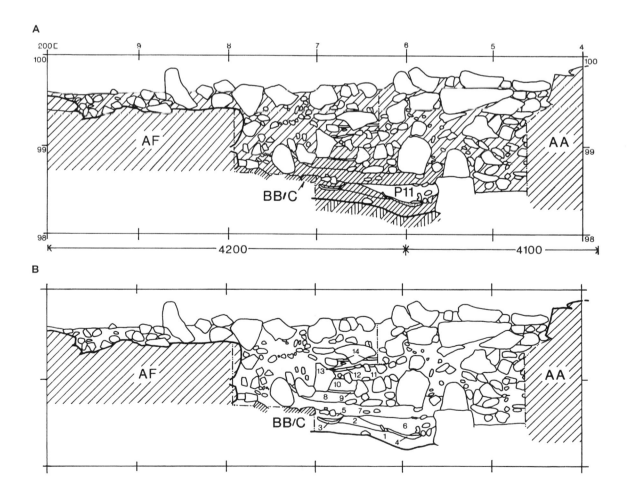

Figure 3.23   Dhuweila: squares 4100, 4200, south section.

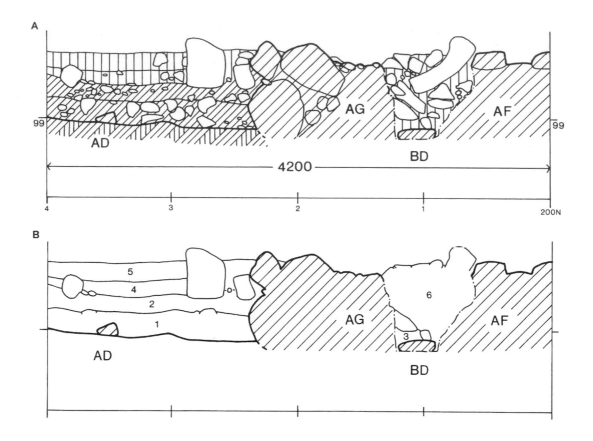

Figure 3.24   Dhuweila: square 4200, east section.

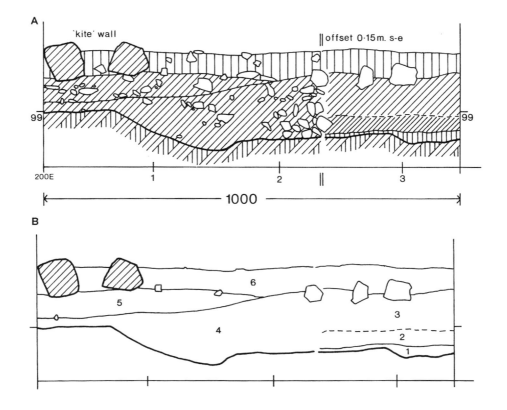

Figure 3.25   Dhuweila: square 1000, north section.

outside the main structure during Stage 2. The soil matrix containing the rubble was largely sterile. The buildup may have been caused by partial collapse of the main wall AA, together with intermittent rubble clearance from the interior. At this point wall AA is set against the prevailing wind, and the loose rubble trapped windblown sand blowing up against the structure.

Stage 3

Phase 10

The third and final stage at the site consists only of topsoil and deflated occupation deposits. No stratigraphic sequence is preserved. Disturbed stones, Safaitic carvings, fragments of fabric impressed plaster and a few post-Neolithic potsherds indicate that the site was visited sporadically between the sixth millennium B.C. and the twentieth century. A rough cairn was put up at some time, using rubble from the main structure. This may once have contained a burial, or was perhaps simply a landmark.

Test Squares

Fourteen metre squares were excavated around the site to test the extent of occupation beyond the main complex. Test square 11 and the test area sounded in 1983 were beyond the maximum extent of occupation, but those on the level ground to the north of the mound had traces of occupation and use relating to Stage 1 at the site. In most cases this took the form of a very thin scatter of artefacts, but evidence from test square 5 and 6 was somewhat more substantial. Test square 5 contained ashy deposits and a stone ringed hearth similar to P17. Test square 6 also contained a thin layer of ashy occupation deposits and small stones. One of the stones had the figure of an animal carved on it (C4).

Stratigraphic Concordance

Each layer as excavated was given a four digit number. The first two digits refer to the square in which the layer was located, and the second two digits are the individual layer numbers within each square. Thus, for example, 1008 denotes level 08 in square 1000. In the lowest phase with which any layer is associated the number is given without brackets. If the layer was associated with more than one phase, as for example in a deflated external area where sub-divisions could not be identified, it is listed in subsequent phases surrounded by a bracket.

Stage 1

Phase 1

1008	2133	2217	4119	4233	4305	5003	6003
	2132	2216	4117	4224		5002	
	2131			4223			
	2130						
	2129						
	2128						
	2124						
	2122						
	2121						

Phase 2

(1008)	2127	(2216)	(4119)	(4233)	(4305)	(5002)	6002
	2126	2214	(4117)	(4224)			
	2125	2213		(4223)			
	2119	2212					

Phase 3

(1008)	(2126)	2215	4120	(4233)	(4305)	(5002)	(6002)
	2120	2211	(4119)	(4224)			
	2118	2210	(4117)	(4223)			
				4232			
				4230			

Phase 4

(1008)	2123	2209	(4119)	(4233)	(4305)	(5002)	(6002)
	2117	2208	(4117)	(4224)			
	2115	2207	(4223)				
	2114	2206					
	2113						
	2111						

Phase 5

(1008)	2116	2205	(4119)	(4233)	(4305)	(5002)	(6002)
	2112	2204	(4117)	(4224)			
	2110	2203	(4223)				
	2109						
	2108						
	2107						
	2106						
	2105						

Stage 2

Phase 6

1007	2104	2202	4118	4231	4304
1006	2103		4114	4229	
1005	2102			4228	
				4227	
				4225	
				4221	

Phase 7

1004	(2104)	(2202)	4116	4226	(4304)
1003	(2103)		4115	4220	
	(2102)		(4114)		
			4113		

Phase 8

(1004)	(2104)	(2202)	(4114)	4222	(4304)
(1003)	(2103)		4112	4219	
(2102)			4111	4218	
			4110	4217	
			4109	4216	
			4108	4215	
				4214	
				4213	
				4210	

Phase 9

1002	(2104)	(2202)	4107	4212	(4304)
	(2103)		4106	4211	
	(2102)		4105	(4210)	
			4104	4209	
				4208	
				4207	
				4206	
				4205	
				4204	
				4203	

Stage 3

Phase 10

1009	2101	2201	3102	3202	3301	4103	4202	4303	5001	6001
1001			3101	3201		4102	4201	4302		
						4101		4301		

Contexts

Square 1000

1001	loose sand, rocks and windblown deposits, surface.
1002	ashy occupation deposits.
1003	as 1002.
1004	light brown compacted soil, small stones.
1005	grey ash and stones, LN clearance of EN deposits.
1006	wall.
1007	as 1005.
1008	ashy occupation deposits, interior, mixed.
1009	as 1001.

Square 2100

2101	loose sand, rocks and windblown deposits, surface.
2102	rocky, compacted sandy matrix, exterior.
2103	as 2102.
2104	as 2102.
2105	dark ash and stones, LN clearance.
2106	loose grey ash and stones, LN clearance.
2107	loose dark ash and stones, LN clearance.
2108	grey/yellow sandy, some ash, mixed exterior/LN clearance.
2109	dark ash and stones, LN clearance.
2110	grey/yellow sandy, some ash and rocks, mixed exterior/LN clearance.
2111	loose brown ashy, much flint, interior.
2112	ashy sand and stones, LN clearance.
2113	as 2110.
2114	plaster surface, interior.
2115	fine sandy, loose fill of wall.
2116	ash and larger stones, LN clearance.
2117	large stones in brown silty matrix, under 2114, interior, includes fill of P13.
2118	dark brown ashy, fill of stone lined pit, interior, upper fill of P14.
2119	dark ashy, below 2118, fill of pit, interior, lower fill of P14.
2120	grey/brown occupation deposits, interior.
2121	fine loose black fill, external pit, fill of P8.
2122	loose black fill, orange grits and small stones, external pit, fill of P9.
2123	red mud plaster with grits, some finer lime plaster, charcoal.
2124	brown fill, exterior pit, fill of P8.
2125	grey ashy occupation deposit, interior, below 2123.
2126	dark ashy occupation deposits, exterior.
2127	pavement, ashy matrix with orange grit, exterior.
2128	loose brown soil on bedrock, exterior.
2129	fill of pit, exterior fill, of P5.
2130	fill of pit, exterior fill, of P6.
2131	fill of pit, exterior fill, of P6.
2132	occupation deposits on bedrock, interior.
2133	fill of pit, much charcoal, exterior fill of P8.

Square 2200

2201	loose sand, rocks and windblown deposits, surface.
2202	brownish grey ashy soil, exterior.
2203	sand and ash with loose stones, exterior.
2204	brown sandy soil with ash and loose stones, exterior, LN clearance.
2205	light grey ash, interior.
2206	brownish silty soil with loose stones, exterior.
2207	fill of hearth, soft greyish ashy soil, some stones, exterior, fill of P17.
2208	ash and loose stones, exterior, occupation deposits.
2209	fill of hearth, below 2207, soft dark grey ash, fill of P17.
2210	removal of hearthstones, P17.
2211	ashy grey soil, exterior.
2212	soft dark loose ash, interior.
2213	darkish soft slightly ashy soil, exterior.
2214	ashy soil, small stones, exterior.
2215	concentration of bone and flint in ashy matrix, exterior.
2216	compact ashy soil, some small stones, exterior.
2217	fill of hearth, brown ash, exterior, fill of P3.

Square 3100

3101	loose sand, rocks and windblown deposits, surface.
3102	loose sand, rocks and windblown deposits, surface.

Square 4100

4101	loose sand, rocks and windblown deposits, surface.
4102	soft loose brown sandy soil, loose stones, fill of tumbled LN structure.
4103	as 4102.
4104	loose brown soil, loose stones, interior.
4105	loose brown soil, some ashy patches, interior.
4106	as 4105.
4107	as 4105.
4108	loose brown earth, occupation deposit on floor.
4109	as 4108.
4110	compacted dark brown soil, occupation deposit, interior.
4111	loose dark brown soil, pit fill, interior fill of P12.
4112	as 4111.
4113	fine loose brown loamy soil, occupation deposit above floor.
4114	stone platform, internal.
4115	fine loose loamy soil, occupation deposit above floor.
4116	as 4114.
4117	loose brown soil, occupation deposit above bedrock, internal.
4118	pit fill, loose soft ashy soil, interior, fill of P18.
4119	pit fill, fill of P11.
4120	stone feature, interior.

Square 4200

4201	loose sand, rocks and windblown deposits, surface.
4202	as 4201.
4203	loose brown soil, some ashy patches, interior.
4204	as 4203.
4205	loose dark brown ashy soil.

4206   as 4205.

4207   loose brown soil, some ashy patches, interior.

4208   soft sandy soil, loose stones, interior.

4209   soft sandy soil, some occupation deposits, interior.

4210   loose brown earth, occupation deposits.

4211   soft grey/brown loose fill, interior.

4212   stone platform, greyish brown sandy soil.

4213   hard compact grey occupation deposits around stone platform.

4214   compact grey ashy occupation deposits on floor in corridor.

4215   soft fine grey ashy soils, occupation deposits, interior.

4216   greyish brown sandy soil.

4217   dark ashy patch, internal.

4218   collapsed wall, mixed grey ash and brown soil.

4219   dividing wall, soft brown soil.

4220   soft grey brown soil, occupation deposits, interior.

4221   soft ashy soil, occupation deposits, internal.

4222   soft grey ash in corridor.

4223   loose brown soil, occupation deposit above bedrock, interior.

4224   compact brown soil, stony, above bedrock.

4225   soft ash with charcoal, pit fill, interior, fill of P18.

4226   soft brown occupation deposit above floor.

4227   soft ash with charcoal, pit fill, interior, fill of P18.

4228   soft brown occupation deposit above floor.

4229   rich red brown loamy soil, occupation deposit.

4230   fill of pit, interior, fill of P11.

4231   grey ash and occupation deposit.

4232   plaster lining of P11.

4233   compacted occupation surface.

Square 4300

4301   loose sand, rocks and windblown deposits, exterior, surface.

4302   soft brown sandy soil and loose stones, exterior.

4303   soft brown sandy soil and loose stones, exterior.

4304   brown sandy soil, exterior.

4305   compact gritty brown soil above bedrock, exterior.

Square 5000

5001   loose stones, compacted silt.

5002   loose grey ashy soil, occupation deposit, exterior.

503   ashy soil, loose stones, occupation deposit, exterior.

Square 6000

6001   loose stones, compacted silt.

6002   sandy ash and loose stones, occupation deposit, exterior.

4. Dhuweila: Chipped Stone

C. McCartney and A.V.G. Betts[1]

Lithic technology

Introduction

The following report considers the reduction methods and techniques employed during the two major occupation stages at Dhuweila, and the relationship between stages 1 and 2 as demonstrated by the debitage assemblage. Much of the information discussed in this report was originally documented in 1989 to fulfil the requirements of an M.A. degree at the University of Edinburgh (McCartney 1989). Substantial revisions and additional analysis have been made to that original reporting. Readjustment to the site phasing has significantly altered the original debitage category proportions, eliminating a bulk of residual material. A larger sample of blanks was analysed in order to consider a selection of attributes in relation to blank type. In addition, a sample of tools was evaluated to understand relationships between blanks produced by the generalised reduction strategy and the selection of particular blanks for the production of various tool classes. Finally, an extended consideration was made of the Dhuweila naviform (*sensu lato*) reduction strategy.

The results of debitage analysis correlate well with the placement of the Stage 1 sample in the Late PPNB and that of Stage 2 in the Late Neolithic. Though changes can be detected in reduction strategy and technique associated with the transition from the PPNB to the Late Neolithic, a considerable degree of continuity between Stages 1 and 2 is also readily apparent. The evolution of the Stage 2 debitage assemblage towards a flake based industry is clear. However, a combination of attributes including the presence of naviform cores (*sensu lato*) also demonstrate that this change is a gradual one.

Procedures

Introduction

In 1989 an analysis was made of all cores, core elements, blanks and waste material (McCartney 1989). At the outset, the assemblage was partially incomplete as some waste was discarded following excavation in order to facilitate storage of the material. Impoverished values for the chip and chunk categories have resulted. All excavated material was sieved through a 5 mm mesh. The Stage 2 occupants of the site cleared Early Neolithic material from part of the main structure, creating the possibility of residual material in the later debitage sample.

All measurements, given in millimetres, were taken with standard callipers. Both 10x and 20x hand lenses were used for the identification of attribute detail. Core platform angles were measured with the aid of a mason's depth gauge in degrees 1–180, while blank platform angles were measured using the method described by Kobayashi (Kobayashi 1975: fig 2; see also McCartney 1989: 31).

Core measurement

Core platform angles were measured between the core platform and the main core face (e.g. Callahan 1984: fig. 12). Where relatively strong angle deviations occurred across the core platform edge, an average angle was taken. This often coincided with the midpoint of the core platform edge. In the initial analysis of the Dhuweila assemblage blank platform angles were measured between the ventral face and the platform surface. Unfortunately, time limitations did not permit exterior platform angle measurement during the later targeted analysis additions. No sophisticated method of platform angle calculation (core or blank) was utilised (e.g. Dibble and Whittaker 1981: 286; Sollberger in Callahan 1984: 86–87). Thus, platform angle values presented in this report should be considered as averages. With respect to the blank platform angles, it should be noted that the restricted nature of the bulbs belonging to both blades and bladelets did not significantly affect angle measurement, although flake platform angles may be expected to show a greater degree of subjective variation.

Blank measurement

Blank length is defined as the maximum distance, end to end, parallel to the axis of propagation. The width measurement is the maximum distance between the lateral edges perpendicular to that of length. Blank thickness is defined as the maximum distance between

---

[1] C.McCartney studied the debitage ('lithic technology') and A. Betts the retouched pieces ('lithic typology').

the ventral and dorsal surfaces (including the bulb) perpendicular to the blank width. Platform width is taken as the maximum distance between the lateral edges on the platform surface. The maximum distance on the platform surface perpendicular to the width measurement is defined as the platform thickness. While it is acknowledged that problems exist with the use of the dimensional parameters outlined above, they provide a quick, representative method for accessing blank size and relative blank shape (Baulmer n.d.). Core dimensions were recorded in a similar manner. Core length represents the maximum distance, end to end, along the longest axis, and core thickness is the maximum distance perpendicular to the core length. Parallel measurements were made of the maximum length and width of the core face in the case of the naviform core (*sensu lato*) sample. The face width variable can be considered equivalent to a 'maximum' core width measure in the case of the Dhuweila naviform cores.

Definitions

The term blank is used throughout this analysis to indicate any unretouched/unutilised flake, blade, bladelet or spall. Blades are defined as any blank with a length at least two times the width of the artefact. Bladelets, forming a sub-group of the blade category, are those pieces less than 40 mm long and 12 mm wide. Chips are any blank less than 10 mm^2. Comprehensive discussions of blank type definitions may be found in Baird (1993: 148–151) and Nishiaki (1992: 79–82). In general, the definitions utilised in this analysis are the same as those used by Baird, permitting direct correlation between the Dhuweila samples and contemporary assemblages from Jilat and Azraq. The possibility of a production continuum between blades and bladelets is accepted (Baird 1993: 150; Kaufman 1986). Indeed, the consistency of the evidence presented for the Stage 2 sample suggests an increased continuum effect in Late Neolithic lamellar production. However, evidence provided by some technical attributes supports the distinction between blades and bladelets, suggesting differences in terms of reduction strategy. The blade/bladelet differentiation has been retained for comparative purposes in this analysis.

For the purpose of this analysis, cores are considered as debitage in the broad sense of the term, because they embody the end result of reduction strategies applied to various sorts of raw material (Inizan, Roche and Tixier 1992: 84). Detailed consideration of cores and reduction strategies in the present report deals primarily with naviform related material. Naviform cores are referred to generally with the sub-script *sensu lato*, while the alternative sub-script, *sensu stricto*, is reserved for reference to the classic naviform reduction method (after Rollefson 1989: 172). Core types representing non-

naviform reduction strategies are discussed more generally, following McCartney (1989). Core type definitions are incorporated within the text below. Detail on other classifications may be found in McCartney (1989).

Debitage: relative proportions

Debitage category counts and proportions are presented in Tables 4.1 to 4.5, with a summary of generalised debitage groups and the proportions of each blank type presented in Table 4.6. Tables 4.3 and 4.4 document extended phase configurations in which individual contexts of less discrete character were assigned to consecutive phases. In the total site phasing, thus expanded, individual artefacts were counted more than once in phase and total assemblage tabulations. It is significant to note that the assignation of single contexts to multiple phases does not cut across the division between the two main occupation stages at the site. These poorly defined contexts, therefore, do not

Stage 1 PPNB						
Phase	*1*	*2*	*3*	*4*	*5*	*Total*
Cortical Blades	4	13	3	4	4	28
Partly Cortical Blades	71	141	85	60	82	439
Non-cortical Blades	144	248	138	109	178	817
Cortical Bladelets	1	4	0	1	1	7
Partly Cortical Bladelets	28	70	19	23	38	178
Non-cortical Bladelets	139	252	84	113	148	736
Cortical Flakes	27	51	22	13	22	135
Partly Cortical Flakes	93	317	117	98	146	771
Non-cortical Flakes	221	448	175	153	241	1238
Spalls	62	81	25	13	32	213
Chips	0	22	0	7	2	31
Chunks	3	24	2	6	0	35
Blank Fragments	159	562	153	216	285	1375
Cores	22	24	8	7	64	125
Core Fragments	0	0	1	2	16	19
Crested Pieces	31	72	31	34	58	226
Platform Rejuvenations	8	14	7	4	10	43
Overshots	7	8	4	6	12	37
Tool Resharpenings	14	14	4	11	26	69
Total	1034	2365	878	880	1365	6522

Stage 2 Late Neolithic					
Phase	*6*	*7*	*8*	*9*	*Total*
Cortical Blades	8	4	2	5	19
Partly Cortical Blades	181	43	105	112	441
Non-cortical Blades	235	92	114	148	589
Cortical Bladelets	0	1	0	2	3
Partly Cortical Bladelets	194	50	50	35	329
Non-cortical Bladelets	94	158	95	123	570
Cortical Flakes	49	27	28	45	149
Partly Cortical Flakes	382	222	256	308	1168
Non-cortical Flakes	711	395	388	490	1984
Spalls	61	40	33	30	164
Chips	47	182	1	26	256
Chunks	19	54	11	9	93
Blank Fragments	600	571	330	509	2010
Cores	169	26	80	110	385
Core Fragments	12	3	6	15	36
Crested Pieces	69	28	36	35	168
Platform Rejuvenations	23	14	20	12	69
Overshots	19	7	20	16	62
Tool Resharpenings	72	36	100	67	275
Total	3045	1953	1675	2097	8770

Table 4.1   Debitage: absolute counts by phase.

	Stage 1 PPNB					
Phase	*1*	*2*	*3*	*4*	*5*	*Total*
Cortical Blades	0.39	0.55	0.34	0.45	0.29	0.43
Partly Cortical Blades	6.87	5.96	9.68	6.82	6.01	6.73
Non-cortical Blades	13.93	10.49	15.72	12.39	13.04	12.53
Cortical Bladelets	0.10	0.17	0.00	0.11	0.07	0.11
Partly Cortical Bladelets	2.71	2.96	2.16	2.61	2.78	2.73
Non-cortical Bladelets	13.44	10.66	9.57	12.84	10.84	11.28
Cortical Flakes	2.61	2.16	2.51	1.48	1.61	2.07
Partly Cortical Flakes	8.99	13.40	13.33	11.14	10.70	11.82
Non-Cortical Flakes	21.37	18.94	19.93	17.39	17.66	18.98
Spalls	5.99	3.42	2.85	1.48	2.34	3.27
Chips	0.00	0.93	0.00	0.80	0.15	0.48
Chunks	0.29	1.01	0.22	0.68	0.00	0.54
Blank Fragments	15.36	23.76	17.43	24.55	20.88	21.08
Cores	2.22	1.01	0.91	0.80	4.69	1.92
Core Fragments	0.00	0.00	0.11	0.23	1.17	0.29
Crested Pieces	2.99	3.04	3.53	3.86	4.25	3.47
Platform Rejuvenations	0.77	0.59	0.80	0.45	0.73	0.66
Overshots	0.67	0.34	0.46	0.68	0.88	0.57
Tool Resharpenings	1.35	0.59	0.46	1.25	1.90	1.06
Total	100.00	99.98	100.01	100.01	99.98	100.02

	Stage 2 Late Neolithic				
Phase	*6*	*7*	*8*	*9*	*Total*
Cortical Blades	0.26	0.20	0.12	0.24	0.22
Partly Cortical Blades	5.94	2.20	6.27	5.34	5.03
Non-cortical Blades	7.72	4.71	6.81	7.06	6.72
Cortical Bladelets	0.00	0.05	0.00	0.10	0.03
Partly Cortical Bladelets	6.37	2.56	2.99	1.67	3.75
Non-cortical Bladelets	6.37	8.09	5.67	5.87	6.50
Cortical Flakes	1.61	1.38	1.67	2.15	1.70
Partly Cortical Flakes	12.55	11.37	15.28	14.69	13.32
Non-cortical Flakes	23.35	20.23	23.16	23.37	22.63
Spalls	2.00	2.05	1.97	1.43	1.87
Chips	1.54	9.32	0.06	1.24	2.92
Chunks	0.62	2.76	0.66	0.43	1.06
Blank Fragments	19.70	29.24	19.70	24.27	22.92
Cores	5.55	1.33	4.78	5.25	4.39
Core Fragments	0.39	0.15	0.36	0.72	0.41
Crested Pieces	2.27	1.43	2.15	1.67	1.92
Platform Rejuvenations	0.76	0.72	1.19	0.57	0.79
Overshots	0.62	0 36	1.19	0.76	0.71
Tool Resharpenings	2.36	1.84	5.97	3.20	3.14
Total	99.98	99.99	100.00	100.03	100.03

Table 4.2 Debitage: relative counts by phase.

generate any mixing of Stage 1 and Stage 2 materials. Comparison of Tables 4.1 to 4.4 demonstrates virtually no variation in debitage category proportions within either the absolute or the relative phase totals. For the sake of numerical simplicity only the totals for materials from individual units counted once in the phase they appeared first will be considered for detailed discussion, and have been used to generate the proportions represented in Table 4.6. Table 4.5 shows the debitage category values calculated for the Stage 3 sample. The Stage 3 (phase 10) sample was too small to be statistically useful in the detailed discussions that follow. In general, Stage 3 debitage proportions suggest a broad similarity between Stages 2 and 3. In particular, the high concentration of flakes belonging to Stage 3 indicates a continued expansion of the flake based industry seen to begin within the Late Neolithic sample.

All phases of Dhuweila Stage 1 (Late PPNB) may be described as lamellar, with blades and bladelets combined representing 47–54% of the total number of

blanks produced in each phase (Table 4.7, Figure 4.12). In all Early Neolithic phases blade production (26–35%) exceeds bladelet production (16–23%). The combined blade/bladelet proportions (34–42%) in Late Neolithic phases (6–9) show a strong, though decreased, desire for lamellar products during Stage 2 (Figure 4.13; Betts 1987a: 125). Overall, only a 10% decrease in each of the blade and bladelet categories is demonstrated in the Dhuweila assemblage between Stages 1 and 2. Despite a dip in blade production during phase 7 (perhaps the result of a high proportion of indeterminate blank fragments in this phase), all Stage 2 phases demonstrate a relatively high proportion (20–21%) of blade products in terms of the total number of blanks produced. Significant bladelet production (20–21%) during the Late Neolithic phases 6 and 7 continues to parallel the bladelet proportions from the earlier PPNB phases. A decrease in the proportion of bladelets in subsequent phases 8 and 9 is marked. Bladelets comprise only 12–14% of the total number of blanks produced. Flake proportions increase slightly during phase 6,

	Stage 1 PPNB					
Phase	*1*	*2*	*3*	*4*	*5*	*Total*
Cortical Blades	4	14	6	5	5	34
Partly Cortical Blades	71	177	134	83	105	570
Non-cortical Blades	144	317	227	159	228	1075
Cortical Bladelets	1	5	3	2	2	13
Partly Cortical Bladelets	28	85	38	34	49	234
Non-cortical Bladelets	139	325	172	158	193	987
Cortical Flakes	27	71	49	32	41	220
Partly Cortical Flakes	93	368	189	133	181	964
Non-cortical Flakes	221	580	332	249	337	1719
Spalls	62	106	66	28	47	309
Chips	0	22	10	7	?	41
Chunks	3	25	2	6	0	36
Blank Fragments	159	659	284	286	355	1743
Cores	22	46	30	25	82	205
Core fragments	0	0	1	2	16	19
Crested Pieces	31	85	53	40	64	273
Platform Rejuvenations	8	19	13	7	13	60
Overshots	7	11	10	9	15	52
Tool resharpenings	14	22	15	18	33	102
Total	1034	2937	1634	1283	1768	8656

	Stage 2 Late Neolithic				
Phase	*6*	*7*	*8*	*9*	*Total*
Cortical Blades	8	10	8	9	35
Partly Cortical Blades	181	149	211	216	757
Non-cortical Blades	235	230	252	283	1000
Cortical Bladelets	0	1	0	2	3
Partly Cortical Bladelets	194	92	92	76	454
Non-cortical Bladelets	194	296	233	250	973
Cortical Flakes	49	60	61	71	241
Partly Cortical Flakes	382	461	495	536	1874
Non-cortical Flakes	711	795	788	861	3155
Spalls	61	73	66	67	267
Chips	47	205	24	42	318
Chunks	19	58	15	13	105
Blank Fragments	600	960	719	880	3159
Cores	169	125	179	207	680
Core Fragments	12	6	9	18	45
Crested Pieces	69	75	83	82	309
Platform Rejuvenations	23	28	34	20	105
Overshots	19	16	29	32	96
Tool Resharpenings	72	77	141	121	411
Total	3045	3717	3439	3786	13987

Table 4.3 Debitage: extended counts by phase.

Stage 1 PPNB

Phase	1	2	3	4	5	Total
Cortical Blades	0.39	0.48	0.37	0.39	0.28	0.39
Partly Cortical Blades	6.87	6.03	8.20	6.47	5.94	6.59
Non-cortical Blades	13.93	10.80	13.89	12.39	12.90	12.42
Cortical Bladelets	0.10	0.17	0.18	0.16	0.11	0.15
Partly Cortical Bladelets	2.71	2.89	2.35	2.65	2.77	2.70
Non-cortical Bladelets	13.44	11.07	10.53	12.31	10.92	11.40
Cortical Flakes	2.61	2.42	3.00	2.49	2.32	2.54
Partly Cortical Flakes	8.99	12.53	11.57	10.37	10.24	11.14
Non-cortical Flakes	21.37	19.75	20.32	19.41	19.06	19.86
Spalls	6.00	3.61	4.04	2.18	2.66	3.57
Chips	0.0	0.75	0.61	0.55	0.11	0.47
Chunks	0.29	0.85	0.12	0.47	0.00	0.42
Blank Fragments	15.38	22.44	17.38	22.29	20.08	20.14
Cores	2.13	1.57	1.84	1.95	4.64	2.37
Core Fragments	0.00	0.00	0.06	0.16	0.90	0.22
Crested Pieces	3.00	2.89	3.24	3.12	3.62	3.15
Platform Rejuvenations	0.77	0.65	0.80	0.55	0.74	0.69
Overshots	0.68	0.37	0.61	0.70	0.85	0.60
Tool Resharpenings	1.35	0.75	0.92	1.40	1.87	1.18
Total	100.00	100.02	100.03	100.01	100.01	100.00

Stage 2 Late Neolithic

Phase	6	7	8	9	Total
Cortical Blades	0.26	0.27	0.23	0.24	0.25
Partly Cortical Blades	5.94	4.01	6.14	5.71	5.41
Non-cortical Blades	7.72	6.19	7.33	7.47	7.15
Cortical Bladelets	0.00	0.03	0.00	0.05	0.02
Partly Cortical Bladelets	6.37	2.48	2.68	2.01	3.25
Non-cortical Bladelets	6.37	7.96	6.78	6.60	6.96
Cortical Flakes	1.61	1.61	1.77	1.88	1.72
Partly Cortical Flakes	12.55	12.40	14.39	14.16	13.40
Non-cortical Flakes	23.35	21.39	22.91	22.74	22.56
Spalls	2.00	1.96	1.92	1.77	1.91
Chips	1.54	5.52	0.70	1.11	2.27
Chunks	0.62	1.56	0.44	0.34	0.75
Blank Fragments	19.70	25.83	20.91	23.24	22.59
Cores	5.55	3.36	5.21	5.47	4.86
Core Fragments	0.39	0.16	0.26	0.48	0.32
Crested Pieces	2.27	2.02	2.41	2.17	2.21
Platform Rejuvenations	0.76	0.75	0.99	0.53	0.75
Overshots	0.62	0.43	0.84	0.85	0.69
Tool Resharpenings	2.36	2.07	4.10	3.20	2.94
Total	99.98	100.00	100.01	100.01	100.01

Table 4.4   Debitage: extended relative counts by phase.

demonstrating the gradual nature of the shift from lamellar to flake dominated blank production at the site. A more heavily flake dominated assemblage appears in phase 7 (65% of all blanks produced) and continues thereafter, showing a 20% increase relative to the Early Neolithic phases, parallel to the decreases in both lamellar products noted above. Spall production, highest in phase 1 (6%), is somewhat greater overall in the Early Neolithic occupation stage (3.2% on average), with a lower (1.8%) average in Stage 2.

In Stage 1 the focus of lamellar blank production was on non-cortical pieces (Table 4.2). However, the ratio (*c.* 2:1) between non-cortical and partly-cortical blades is less exaggerated than the non-cortical/partly-cortical bladelet ratio at nearly 5:1. Comparison of the two production ratios suggests either that bladelet manufacture may have continued on individual cores after blade removal was no longer possible or that bladelet core preparation entailed more extensive cortex

removal. The first possibility is in keeping with the overall diminutive nature of the Dhuweila cores, but the probability of different reduction strategies being employed is increased with consideration of additional blank and core variables (see below). A shift in the ratio of partly-cortical and non-cortical blank production occurs with the advent of the Late Neolithic. In contrast to the preceding Early Neolithic pattern, during all phases of Stage 2 (except the anomalous phase 7), production of both partly-cortical and non-cortical blades was approximately 1:1. Late Neolithic bladelet production shows a similar increase in the number of partly-cortical examples, with a fluctuating ratio (2:1 to 3:1), though non-cortical bladelets continue to dominate. Non-cortical flake products dominate partly-cortical examples (*c.*1.6:1) in both Stages 1 and 2.

The proportion of blade and bladelet blanks in the Dhuweila Early Neolithic sample is low in comparison with the closest contemporary sites. Late PPNB site assemblages in the Wadi Jilat and Azraq (Site 31) possess blade/bladelet proportions of between 62–66% (Baird 1993: 251, Baird *et al.* 1992: 7; Garrard *et al.* 1994b). The combined blade and bladelet proportions of the Dhuweila PPNB phases are most closely parallelled at the early Late Neolithic site of Jilat 13 which shows 57% lamellar debitage (Baird 1993: 251). However, the lower (47–54%) PPNB lamellar figures at Dhuweila are in line with similar blade/bladelet proportions at both 'Ain Ghazal (Rollefson *et al.* 1989: tabs. 1–3) and Wadi Shueib (Simmons *et al.* 1989: tabs. 1–3). While differences in blade/bladelet definitions may reduce the significance of the latter correlations, the extreme lamellar proportions of the Jilat and Azraq PPNB assemblages may be somewhat unique.

The proportion of bladelets in lithic samples from both 'Ain Ghazal and Wadi Shueib decreases over time, but with numbers rising again slightly in the

Stage 3

	no.	%
Cortical Blades	1	0.96
Partly Cortical Blades	5	4.80
Non-cortical Blades	8	7.69
Cortical Bladelets	0	0.00
Partly Cortical Bladelets	1	0.96
Non-cortical Bladelets	9	8.65
Cortical Flakes	2	1.92
Partly Cortical Flakes	12	11.54
Non-cortical Flakes	30	28.85
Spalls	0	0.00
Chips	0	0.00
Chunks	1	0.96
Blank Fragments	20	19.23
Cores	3	2.88
Core Fragments	1	0.96
Crested Pieces	7	6.73
Platform Rejuvenations	2	1.92
Overshots	0	0.00
Tool Resharpenings	2	1.92
Totals	104	99.97

Table 4.5   Debitage: Stage 3 – absolute and relative counts by phase.

Phase	1	2	3	4	5	6	7	8	9	(10)
Blades	219	402	226	173	264	424	139	221	265	(14)
Bladelets	168	326	103	137	187	388	209	145	160	(10)
Flakes	341	816	314	264	409	1142	644	672	843	(44)
Waste	162	608	155	229	287	666	807	342	544	(21)
Spalls	62	81	25	13	32	61	40	33	30	(0)
Core Elements	68	118	51	53	160	292	78	162	188	(13)
Tool Elements	14	14	4	11	26	72	36	100	67	(2)
Total	1034	2365	878	880	1365	3045	1953	1675	2097	(104)
					Percent					
Phase	1	2	3	4	5	6	7	8	9	(10)
Blades	21.18	17.00	25.74	19.66	19.34	13.9	27.12	13.19	12.64	(13.46)
Bladelets	16.25	13.78	11.73	15.57	13.70	12.74	10.70	8.66	7.63	(9.62)
Flakes	32.98	34.50	35.76	30.00	29.96	37.50	32.97	40.12	40.20	(42.31)
Waste	15.67	25.71	17.65	26.02	21.03	21.87	41.32	20.42	25.94	(20.19)
Spalls	6.00	3.42	2.85	1.48	2.34	2.00	2.05	1.97	1.43	(0.00)
Core Elements	6.58	4.99	5.81	6.02	11.72	9.59	3.99	9.67	8.97	(12.50)
Tool Elements	1.35	0.59	0.46	1.25	1.90	2.36	1.84	5.97	3.20	(1.92)

Table 4.6   Debitage: summary of total assemblage (non-extended).

Yarmoukian (Rollefson *et al.* 1989: 11; Simmons *et al.* 1989: 31). Baird, however, has noted a preference for narrow lamellar blanks at both Azraq 31 and most

Phase	1	2	3	4	5	6	7	8	9
Blades	30.08	26.04	35.15	30.14	30.70	21.70	14.01	21.29	20.90
Bladelets	23.08	21.11	16.02	23.87	21.74	19.86	21.07	13.97	12.62
Flakes	46.84	52.85	48.83	46.00	47.56	58.44	64.92	64.74	66.48
Total No.	728	1544	643	574	860	1954	992	1038	1268

Table 4.7   Blank types: relative counts by phase.

		B-3	B-2	BL-3	BL-2	F-3	F-2	Frg.	Chunks
				PPNB Sample					
Burins	No.	25	12	2	0	6	2	6	3
	%	44.64	21.43	3.57	0.0	10.71	3.57	10.71	5.36
Borer/Drill	No.	7	5	5	1	3	1	1	0
	%	30.43	21.74	21.74	4.35	13.04	4.35	4.35	0.00
Bifaces	No.	0	0	0	0	0	0	0	0
	%	0.00	0.00	0.00	0.00	0.00	0.00	0.00	0.00
Arrows	No.	9	0	3	2	0	0	1	0
	%	60.00	0.00	20.00	13.33	0.00	0.00	6.67	0.00
Notches	No.	4	2	2	1	4	0	4	0
	%	23.53	17.65	11.76	0.00	23.53	0.00	23.53	0.00
Retouched	No.	3	0	2	0	0	1	0	0
	%	50.00	0.00	33.33	0.00	0.00	16.67	0.00	0.00
Utilised	No.	2	2	1	0	1	0	0	0
	%	33.33	33.33	16.67	0.00	16.67	0.00	0.00	0.00
Scrapers	No.	0	1	0	0	1	2	1	0
	%	0.00	20.00	0.00	0.00	20.00	40.00	20.00	0.00
				LN Samples					
Burins	No.	9	2	0	1	2	1	8	2
	%	36.00	8.00	0.00	4.00	8.00	4.00	32.00	8.00
Borer/Drill	No.	5	3	6	0	1	0	0	0
	%	33.33	20.00	40.00	0.00	6.67	0.00	0.00	0.00
Bifaces	No.	2	0	0	0	1	0	3	5
	%	18.18	0.00	0.00	0.00	9.09	0.00	27.27	45.45
Arrows	No.	10	0	4	0	3	0	10	0
	%	37.04	0.00	14.81	0.00	11.11	0.00	37.04	0.00
Notches	No.	6	2	5	0	7	4	4	1
	%	20.69	6.90	17.24	0.00	24.14	13.79	13.79	3.45
Retouched	No.	6	5	1	0	1	1	2	0
	%	37.50	31.25	6.25	0.00	6.25	6.25	12.50	0.00
Utilised	No.	3	1	0	1	1	1	3	0
	%	30.00	10.00	0.00	10.00	10.00	10.00	30.00	0.00
Scrapers	No.	1	1	0	0	1	1	1	0
	%	20.00	20.00	0.00	0.00	20.00	20.00	20.00	0.00

Table 4.8   Tool Blank types.

Neolithic sites in the Wadi Jilat (Baird *et al.* 1992: 7). The Dhuweila assemblage shows a decrease in the total proportion of bladelets in Stage 2, yet there is relative continuity in bladelet production during the first two Late Neolithic phases. The high number of bladelets in phases 6 and 7 at Dhuweila links the early part of the Stage 2 occupation more closely with the 7th and early 6th millennium pattern described by Baird, while the lower bladelet proportions of phases 8 and 9 correlate with the decrease in bladelet production described by Rollefson. Typological change in the arrowhead class showing an increasing selection of bladelet sized blanks at the end of the PPNB suggests a reason for the continued production of significant numbers of bladelets in the initial Late Neolithic occupation of a hunting station like Dhuweila (Gopher 1989: 52; Bar-Yosef 1981b: 561).

Table 4.8 shows the blank types used for each tool class within the sample of tools considered during this analysis (for total assemblage proportions see the tool analysis by Betts this volume, see also Betts 1986, 1987a, 1988a, 1988b). Though some flakes were used in every tool class (except the arrowheads), it is apparent that blade and bladelet blanks were favoured for PPNB tool production. The preferred blade or bladelet blank was non-cortical, an attribute which was clearly demonstrated by the blank production proportions belonging to Stage 1. The flake dominated tool classes showed a higher number of incomplete examples than the blade and bladelet dominated tool classes.

The distribution of blank type utilisation in the different tool classes demonstrates a more varied picture in the Late Neolithic sample. A high proportion of incomplete tools in the Late Neolithic sample, however, skews the information somewhat. Burins, though more often fragmentary, are most frequently made on non-cortical blade blanks. Continuity in the utilisation of blades for burin production has been demonstrated in the 'Ain Ghazal assemblage from the PPNB through the

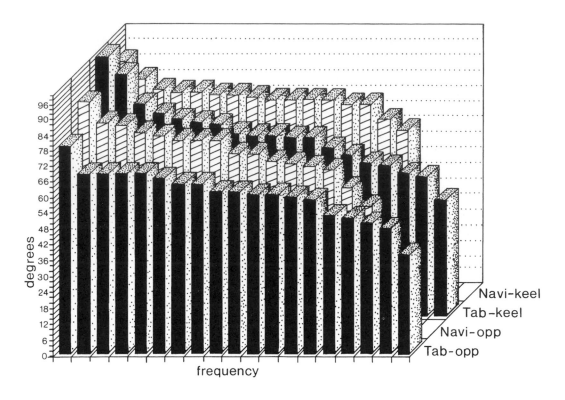

Figure 4.1   Chipped stone: naviform core platform angles.

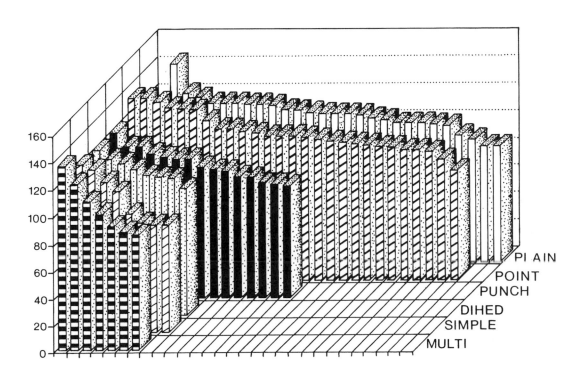

Figure 4.2   Chipped stone: Stage 1, platform angles/types.

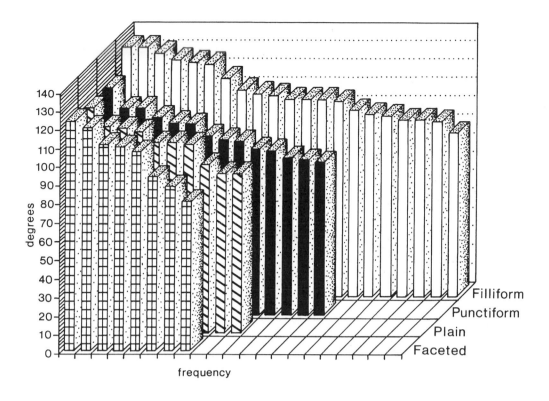

Figure 4.3   Chipped stone: Stage 1, blade/bladelet platform angles.

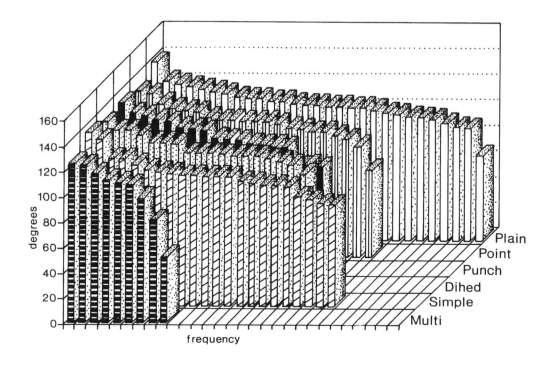

Figure 4.4   Chipped stone: Stage 2, platform angles/types.

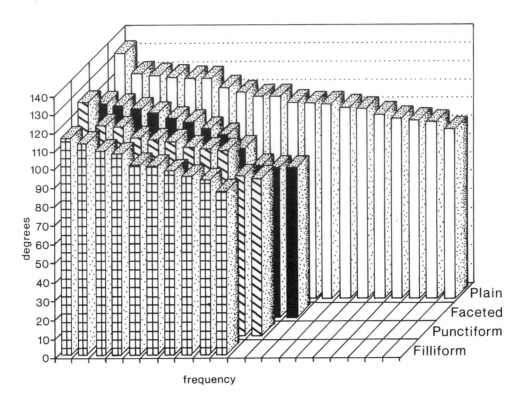

Figure 4.5   Chipped stone: Stage 2, blade/bladelet platform angles.

Yarmoukian periods (Rollefson 1988: 441, tab. 2). Tools in the borer/drill class of Stage 2 were made almost exclusively from lamellar products, including a high proportion of non-cortical bladelets and spalls. Retouched, utilised and scraper classes all demonstrate a continued selection of blade blanks with increased proportions of partly-cortical examples in the retouched and scraper classes. The arrowhead class illustrates perhaps the most obvious change between the two occupation stages. While many of the Late Neolithic arrowheads in the sample were incomplete (most made from probable bladelets), the decrease in the relative proportion of blade blanks is readily apparent. The increase in the proportion of flakes utilised in the Stage 2 arrowhead class can be accounted for by the presence of transverse arrowheads. Only the notch class demonstrates a significant increase in the proportion of flake blanks, many partly cortical. Bifaces show a mixture of blank types. However, this tool class is limited to the Late Neolithic and so choice of blank type cannot be compared across the two stages. In general, the Dhuweila Late Neolithic tool sample shows a relatively high proportion of blade blanks which corresponds with the continuity in blade production discussed above. While bladelet blanks were deliberately selected for in the borer/drill and arrowhead tool classes, a broad decrease in the number of bladelets used for tool manufacture coincides with decreased production of bladelet blanks. Flake blanks do not dominate the Stage 2 tool sample, but were used in a greater variety of tool classes.

Relative proportions of core elements are broadly similar in both stages. Crested core preparation and re-preparation products decrease slightly in Stage 2, but platform rejuvenation pieces and overshots occur in low, yet relatively constant, proportions in all phases. The most obvious difference between the two stages is in terms of the higher number of cores in the later occupation stage; a circumstance noted within other contemporary assemblages, (McCartney 1992: 50; Rollefson *et al.* 1989: 11–12; Simmons *et al.* 1989: 32). The Early Neolithic phases 2–4 show lower numbers of cores and core fragments, possibly related to the fact that the Stage 2 occupants of the site cleared away PPNB material during rebuilding activities (see 'stratigraphy' above). Phase 5 shows a total proportion of cores which compares well with the subsequent Stage 2 phases, suggesting that the mechanisms accounting for the Late Neolithic core increase may have had antecedents in the later PPNB occupation.

Core preparation and re-preparation elements were relatively numerous in the Stage 1 sample. As expected, a major proportion of the PPNB core elements (twice as many as in Stage 2) were either bicrested or unicrested blades and blade fragments (Figure 4.10). Crested blades have long been considered one of the most diagnostic elements of the naviform reduction strategy (*sensu stricto*) (Baird 1993: 189; Nishiaki 1992: 123–124; Calley 1986b: 52–54; Crowfoot Payne 1983: 669–670). The majority of the examples were primary bicrested pieces, indicating that naviform cores in the early stages of reduction, perhaps biface preforms, were

	PPNB Sample											
	10	*20*	*30*	*40*	*50*	*60*	*70*	*80*	*90*	*100*	*110*	*120*
Crested	2	4	7	16	15	12	7		2			
Platform				1	2	6	6	7	3			
Over							3	2		1		3
Tablet					2			2	1	1		

	LN Sample											
	10	*20*	*30*	*40*	*50*	*60*	*70*	*80*	*90*	*100*	*110*	*120*
Crested	1	2	6	2	6	4	2					
Platform							1	5	9	8	4	1
Over								1	5	1	2	1
Tablet									1			

Table 4.9   Core Elements: dorsal ridge angles

carried to the site for reduction. Though not classified separately in this analysis, the presence of secondary cresting examples, upsilon blades and a variety of more irregular crested pieces demonstrate the developed nature of the Dhuweila naviform (*sensu lato*) reduction strategy (Calley 1986b: 57–59, fig. 4). The numbers of crested blades in the Stage 1 sample suggests that the numbers of naviform cores (*sensu stricto*) was originally much higher, even if the recresting of these cores was frequent. In addition, the longest crested blades demonstrate the once greater size of the classic naviform cores. A few tabular unicrested examples represent core preparation or repreparation pieces (Figure 9: a–c; Baird 1993: 148).

In the Stage 1 sample there were relatively few core tablets, with a slightly higher number of overshots (including distinctive blade core examples) (Figures 4.9: g–i, 4.10: i–k). The small number of classic core tablets suggests that little initial preparation of naviform core (*sensu lato*) platforms occurred on site, but the frequent presence of irregular, often diminutive, flakes displaying core tablet characteristics shows a high proportion of more restricted platform re-adjustments (Figure 4.9: d).

The presence of significant numbers of completely cortical flakes shows that at least some core preparation took place on site in all Early Neolithic and Late Neolithic phases (Rollefson 1990: 121; Betts 1987a: 123, 125). However, the paucity of preparatory core elements shown above suggests that naviform core preparation (*sensu stricto*) took place off site, as with the association elsewhere between desert hunting stations and the reduction of cores at quarries or specialised knapping sites (Nishiaki 1992: 121, 146; Cauvin 1982; Calley 1986b, see below). Initial preforming of classic naviform cores may have taken place at knapping stations like those near Qa'a Mejalla *c.* 20 km distant from Dhuweila (Betts 1982). It is significant that despite the presence of cortical flakes in all Early Neolithic phases, only one flake similar to the Cxf-1 type was identified (Figure 4.9: f; Baird 1993: 260–261). Nearly half of the naviform cores (*sensu lato*) employed at Dhuweila, those with a simplified reduction strategy which did not require the development of an elaborate crest, may have been worked entirely on site (see the discussion of the naviform cores below). A

dichotomy between naviform (*sensu stricto*) and the non-classic naviform and non-naviform reduction strategies is thus created, and the shift away from the logistically expensive naviform (*sensu stricto*) reduction strategy towards more on-site production is understandable.

A significant number of core trimming elements was present in the Stage 2 sample (*contra* Betts 1987a: 125). However, unlike the PPNB sample, the majority of crested pieces and other core trimming elements from the Late Neolithic phases were produced on flakes (Figure 4.11). A low number of crested blades or bladelets occurred in the Stage 2 sample, presumably relating to the presence of the few naviform cores (*sensu lato*) assigned to Late Neolithic contexts (Figure 4.11: b). Though some crested pieces belonging to Stage 2 represented coarser examples of core preparation, they more often exhibited characteristics suggestive of core rejuvenation (Figure 4.11: a and d). Based on a sample of 167 core elements (105 from Stage 1 and 62 from Stage 2) (Table 4.9), measurements of dorsal ridge angles on the various crested pieces suggest that classic naviform crests were most successfully produced at between 40–70 degrees. Crested pieces with dorsal ridge angles higher than 70 degrees exhibited characteristics suggestive of removals struck for purposes of platform rejuvenation. The majority of Stage 2 'crested' examples fell into the latter category. Overshots, core tablets and the coarser 'crested' pieces form a cluster demonstrating a significant amount of attention given to core (primarily platform) maintenance during Stage 2. The frequency of core rejuvenation at Dhuweila agrees with evidence from other Late Neolithic assemblages in the Levant (e.g., Nishiaki 1992: 262).

Raw Material

In general, the raw materials used at Dhuweila were the same in Stages 1 and 2. The assemblage is characterised by variety in raw material type during both stages, an attribute which increased during the Late Neolithic occupation. Most raw material consisted of medium to fine grained chert showing variety in colour. Moderate proportions of fine grained chalcedony (in the wider sense) were used, particularly within the Late Neolithic sample. The most extensively reduced cores are mostly of chalcedony, suggesting that it was prized and/or most useful for small blank production (Betts 1988b: 379, 1987a: 125). It is significant that these finer quality materials were consistently numbered among the core types most regularly used for flake production: splintered pieces, cores-on-flakes, discoidal cores. Obsidian was not found in the debitage collections of the site.

Colour distinctions are provided with corresponding Munsell colour chart coordinates. While the subjectivity associated with the use of colour as a diagnostic attribute is acknowledged, it does provide a scale for considering possible variation in raw material use. Brown chert (10yr 5/3,5/2; 7.5yr 5/2 and 2.5yr 5/2) was the most common of all colour varieties in both stages. Other shades of brown ranged from light grey-brown (10yr 6/2, 5yr 4/1) through pale and yellow brown (10yr 7/6, 6/3, 5/6 8/3 and 5/4). Dark brown and mixtures of darker brown with red (7.5yr 5/4, 4/2, 4/5; 5yr 6/4, 6/3 and 10yr 3/3) were also present in both Stages 1 and 2 and describe some chalcedony varieties. Shades of red form the most diverse colour group (10yr 4/6, 4/3; 10R 4/4, 4/2, 3/4, 3/1 and 2.5R 4/2), which was particularly dominant with the chalcedony and possibly heat treated materials. Grey chert was also relatively common in the following varieties (10yr 7/2, 7/6; 5yr 5/1, 5/2, and 6/1), as was pink coloured chert (10yr 6/3; 2.5yr 4/6; 5yr 8/3 and 7/4). Grey and pink were some times mottled or banded, corresponding to Munsell coordinates (5yr 4/2, 7/2, 6/2, 6/1; 7.5yr 6/2, and 6/4). The dominance of brown and grey chert, particularly with respect to the production of naviform cores (*sensu lato*), has been noted at other sites in the region: Azraq 31, the Jilat sites and several burin sites in the region (Baird 1993: 170–172; Rollefson and Abu Ghanima 1983: 465–6; Garrard *et al.* 1975).

The Munsell chart was not used during the initial analysis, but was applied with the extended analysis of the assemblage. Standardization provided by the Munsell chart alters the previous conclusion which suggested differences in the chert types used in each of the two major occupation stages (McCartney 1989: 70–71). Some cores described earlier as 'grey' are in fact categorised as varieties of brown by the Munsell colour system. Baird (1993: 171) has suggested that many of the cherts found within the Wadi Jilat region show a brown 'patina' on the exterior surface of essentially grey chert, but also that much of the local chert was grey-brown in colour. A light 'desert patina' was apparent on a few of the Dhuweila cores, but milky white and pale yellow patinas were more common.

Chalcedonic materials were present in a variety of colours ranging from reds and pinks to greys, yellows, pale and dark brown, as well as the odd vivid green. The fact that these materials often occur as small, irregularly shaped pebbles, sometimes containing inclusions, made them well suited for the production of flakes and perhaps little else. The greater frequency with which these materials occurred at Dhuweila, particularly in the Late Neolithic sample, suggests a different procurement pattern from neighbouring sites in the Jilat area which have demonstrated a dearth of exotic materials following the Early PPNB (Baird 1993: 179; Nishiaki 1992: 346–347, 349; Garrard *et al.* 1994a).

Tabular raw materials have been discussed at length with respect to their procurement and use in the production of naviform cores (*sensu lato*) (Baird 1993: 183, 202–203; Betts 1988b: 9; Garrard *et al.* 1994a;

Baird 1995). The overall shape of tabular raw materials provided for and helped with the maintenance of the correct naviform core shape and platform angles, as well as providing for a relatively flat core removal surface (Baird 1993: 232; Baird 1995). It would seem from the small sample of naviform cores (*sensu lato*) in the Dhuweila assemblage (in cases where cortex remained on the core to provide conclusive evidence) that the same preference for tabular material was practised. In the Late Neolithic, tabular materials were found more widely within various core types, in a few cases demonstrating a reutilization of exhausted naviform cores. The naviform cores (*sensu lato*) belonging to Stage 2 show an exaggerated tabular raw material and naviform core correlation (see below).

Heat treatment is suggested by chert materials, sometimes banded, which exhibited a medium lustre less brilliant and silky than the microcrystalline chalcedony. Diagnostic colour differences between exterior and interior core surfaces were not evident to confirm this characteristic since these core examples were, perhaps understandably, heavily reduced. Heat treatment has been described as one of the hallmarks of the PPNB and may have occurred within the Jilat area sites (Bar-Yosef 1981b: 562; Baird 1993: 246). Heat treatment would have been useful for the production of fine bifacial, pressure retouched Late Neolithic arrowheads, but was perhaps no longer required since the fine grained chalcedony was available (Betts 1988a: 379).

No raw material sources are known to exist within the immediate vicinity of the site, deep within the *harra* (Betts 1988a: 370, fig. 1). The closest possible sources are at a distance of some 20 km from the site at locations along the interface between the *harra* and *hammada* where chert occurs in limestone outcrops (Betts 1987a: 125, 1982). A particular source of rose-pink chert (less common among the Dhuweila colour varieties) has been found outcropping near Qattafi Wells (Betts 1986: 191). Chert is also widely available in the form of weathered cobbles from the surface flint carpet of the *hammada* used extensively from the beginning of the 6th millennium bc (Betts 1993a: 10; McCartney 1992; see also Garrard *et al.* 1994a). The existence of cores exhibiting a relatively thick pitted cortex suggests that some Dhuweila material may have been collected from such sources. The finer grained chalcedonic material may have been collected or imported from farther afield. This type of material occurs in isolated exposures on the southeastern edges of the Jordanian *harra* (Figure 2.21).

Given the location of the site deep within the basalt *harra*, raw material was apparently always at a premium at Dhuweila. The diminutive nature of the Dhuweila cores in both occupation stages amplifies the negative correlation between raw material sources and the site location. Azraq 31, the most directly comparable site in logistic terms, may have had some local resources available, yet shows a similar raw material deficit relative to the sites of Wadi Jilat (Baird *et al.* 1992: 6). The suggestion that raw material was more widely available during the PPNB than the subsequent Late Neolithic is not supported by the Dhuweila assemblage (Rollefson 1990: 122–123). Considering the plentiful (though non-local) availability of good chert in the landscape today and the volume of material belonging to the Stage 2 sample, it is clear that the Late Neolithic knappers had good access to suitable raw materials. Two large unworked tabular slabs (both over 220 mm long) belonging to the Stage 2 sample demonstrate the availability of tabular raw materials similar to those used during the preceding PPNB occupation (McCartney 1989: 34). Considering the amount and variety of chalcedony materials used during Stage 2, the sources exploited by the Dhuweila Late Neolithic knappers were, if anything, more extensive than those of their PPNB counterparts.

Raw material procurement at Dhuweila must have been 'logistic' during all occupation phases, though the site itself may have formed a limited source during the post-PPNB occupations (Torrence ed. 1989; Edmonds 1987). Changes in the selection of raw materials made by the Late Neolithic knappers at Dhuweila (like concurrent changes in reduction strategy and tool type) appear to have developed as deliberate choices rather than impositions forced upon the inhabitants by necessity (Nishiaki 1992: 350–351; Baird 1995). The fact that the Stage 2 occupants re-used some 'local' Stage 1 materials does reflect a line of procurement organisation not available to the Early Neolithic knappers. The increase in the proportion of chalcedony in the Stage 2 sample also demonstrates an increased variety of procurement patterns (Nishiaki 1992: 349). The fact that Dhuweila could form a limited raw material procurement site itself, as well as having raw materials which were acquired from much farther afield, suggests that the inhabitants of the site knew their territory well and ranged perhaps more widely during the Late Neolithic. Extensive trade or exchange networks may have provided some raw materials, but the seasonal nature of the desert sites argues against the possibility of fixed trade mechanisms fulfilling all raw material requirements.

Discussion

Cores

Table 4.10 shows the total number and proportions of each core type for Stages 1 and 2. The core sample from the Early Neolithic (Stage 1) assemblage consists of 125 examples compared to a total of 385 for the Late Neolithic (Stage 2) sample. Only three cores were assigned to the post-Neolithic contexts (Stage 3). These were similar to the amorphous cores from Stage 2 but

because of the small sample size they have not been analysed in detail.

As Table 4.10 clearly demonstrates, the Early Neolithic sample showed an expected preference (20% in total) for naviform cores (*sensu lato*). The following Stage 2 sample shows a low number of naviform cores in all phases, but the overall proportion of this core type is very low (2.6% of the total Stage 2 sample). The presence of naviform cores in Stage 2 was initially considered fortuitous, because of the presence of other residual material and the limited re-use of PPNB core material during Stage 2 (McCartney 1989: 53). The naviform cores assigned to Late Neolithic contexts are evenly distributed across phases 6–9, and do not show signs of additional reduction as might be expected if these cores were simply extracted from PPNB contexts

PPNB Core Types							
Phase		1	2	3	4	5	Total
Naviform	No.	1	12	3	0	9	25
	%	4.55	50.00	37.50	0.00	14.06	20.00
Opposed Platform	No.	1	3	1	0	4	9
	%	4.55	12.50	12.50	0.00	6.25	7.20
Single Platform	No.	5	1	0	1	10	17
	%	22.73	4.17	0.00	14.28	5.62	13.60
Crossed Platform	No.	5	3	0	2	9	19
	%	22.73	12.50	0.00	28.57	14.06	15.20
Amorphous	No.	1	1	2	1	9	14
	%	4.55	4.17	25.00	14.28	14.06	11.20
Discoidal	No.	2	1	0	0	5	8
	%	9.09	4.17	0.00	0.00	7.81	6.40
Alternate Platform	No.	0	0	0	0	1	1
	%	0.00	0.00	0.00	0.00	1.56	0.80
On-Flake	No.	2	1	1	0	5	9
	%	9.09	4.17	12.50	0.00	7.81	7.20
Splintered Pieces	No.	5	2	1	3	12	23
	%	22.73	8.33	12.50	42.85	18.75	18.40
Split Pebble	No.	0	0	0	0	0	0
	%	0.00	0.00	0.00	0.00	0.00	0.00
Total	No.	22	24	8	7	64	125

LN Core Types						
Phase		6	7	8	9	Total
Naviform	No.	3	4	2	1	10
	%	1.78	15.38	2.50	0.91	2.60
Opposed Platform	No.	10	1	8	9	28
	%	5.92	3.84	10.00	8.18	7.27
Single Platform	No.	17	3	7	11	38
	%	10.06	11.53	8.75	10.00	9.87
Crossed Platform	No.	21	3	11	14	49
	%	12.43	11.53	13.75	12.73	12.73
Amorphous	No.	22	2	9	18	51
	%	13.02	7.69	11.25	16.36	13.25
Discoidal	No.	15	1	2	7	25
	%	8.88	3.84	2.50	6.36	6.49
Alternate Platform	No.	8	0	0	2	10
	%	4.73	0.00	0.00	1.82	2.60
On-Flake	No.	17	3	7	12	39
	%	10.06	11.53	8.75	10.91	10.13
Splintered Pieces	No.	53	9	34	36	132
	%	31.36	34.61	42.50	32.73	34.29
Split Pebble	No.	3	0	0	0	3
	%	1.78	0.00	0.00	0.00	0.78
Total	No.	169	26	80	10	385

Table 4.10 Core Types: absolute and relative counts by phase (Naviform = *sensu lato*).

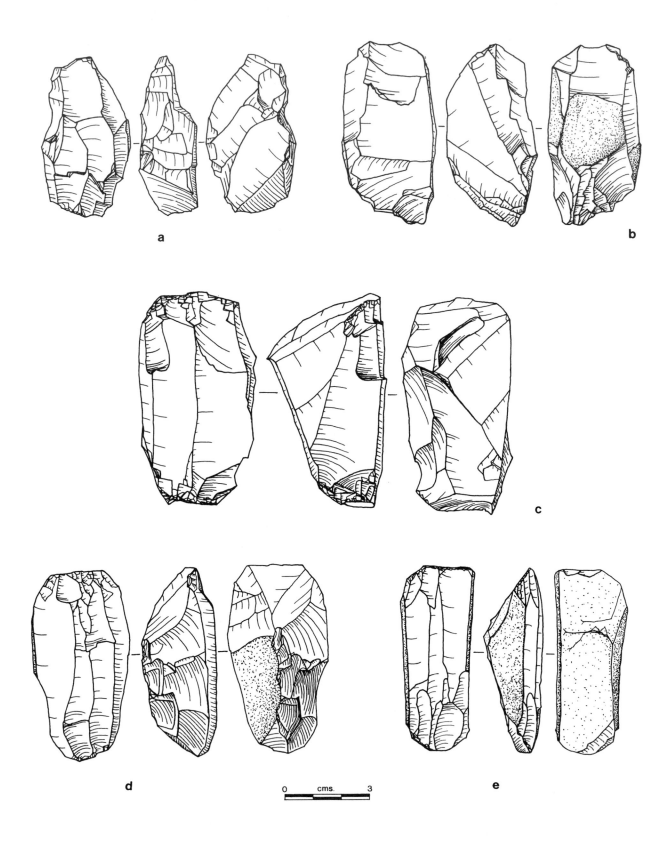

Figure 4.6   Chipped stone: naviform cores - a, c naviform (*sensu stricto*); b, d, e naviform tabular.

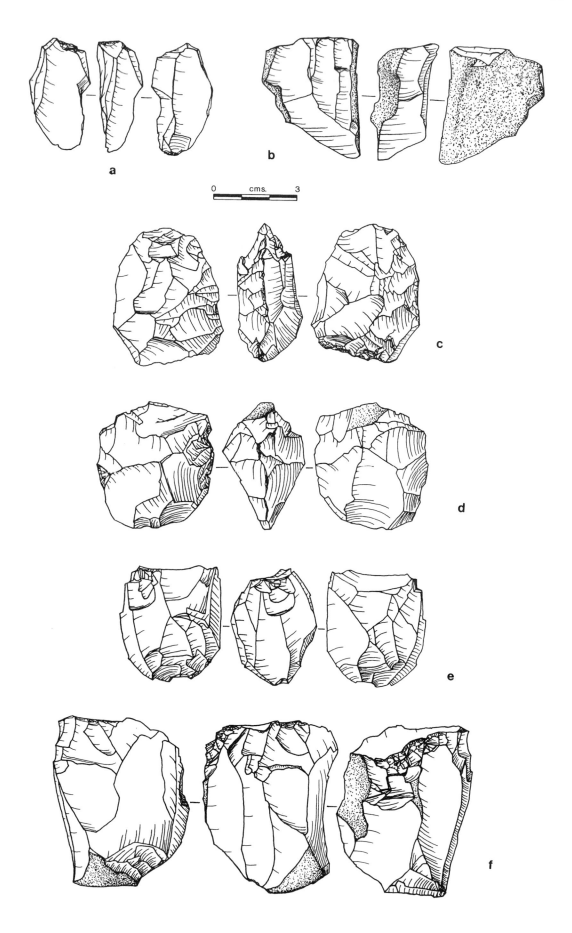

Figure 4.7   Chipped stone: Stage 1, non-naviform cores - a splintered piece; b single platform; c, d discoidal; e opposed platform; f crossed platform.

71

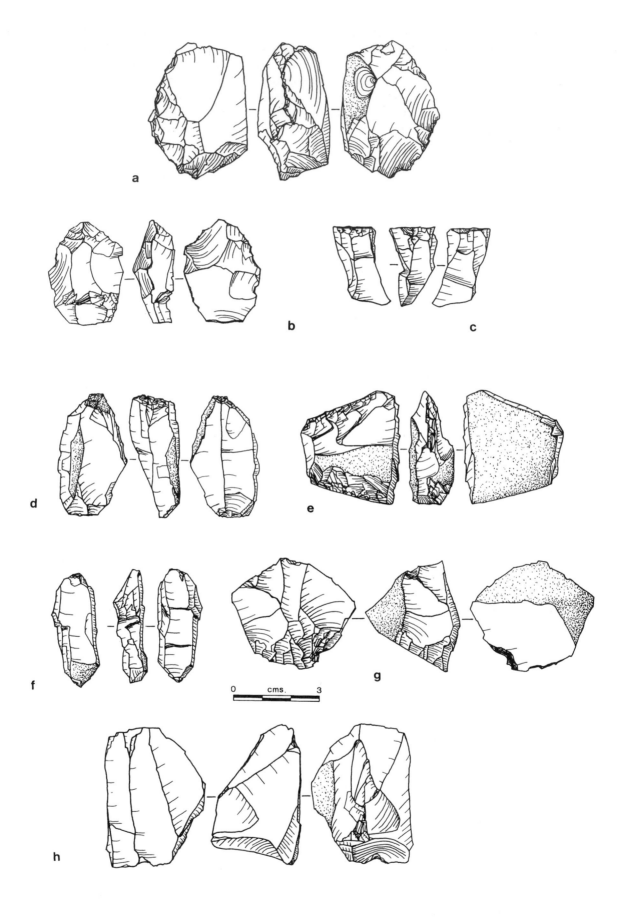

Figure 4.8   Chipped stone: Stage 2, non-naviform cores - a alternate platform; b core on flake; c single platform; d, f splintered pieces; e, g opposed platform; h reused naviform (*sensu stricto*).

for reutilization. Differences in the reduction strategies of naviform cores from Stages 1 and 2 also distinguish the two samples (see below). The rather high proportion of this core type in phase 7 seems anomalous (due to sample size) since the number of naviform cores in this phase corresponds well with that of the other Late Neolithic phases. A nominal presence of naviform cores in all Stage 2 phases, together with other assemblage characteristics considered above and below, argue for the acceptance of a low proportion of naviform (*sensu lato*) core reduction during the Late Neolithic occupation. Evidence of the continued utilisation of the naviform reduction strategy into the Late Neolithic period has become frequent enough that the presence of this typically PPNB characteristic in Late Neolithic assemblages may be considered as more than simply residual (Baird 1993: table 6.6; Baird *et al.* 1992: 7; Nishiaki 1992: 352; Bar-Yosef 1981b: 564).

The term naviform (*sensu lato*) in this analysis refers to all cores with two opposed platforms oriented on a single removal face (Figure 4.6). These cores all exhibit some form of 'keeled' or 'd-shaped' profile generally considered diagnostic of the naviform reduction strategy (Baird 1993: 165; Nishiaki 1992: 116; Calley 1986b: 54; Crowfoot-Payne 1983: 667). A few examples no longer possess true opposition of the striking platforms, but the 'keeled' profile is so distinctive that they have been included within the naviform core type. The naviform cores from Dhuweila represent only late stage morphological forms which characterise this core type (Nishiaki 1992: 119–120; Calley 1986b: 54). No preforms or partly reduced naviform core types are present in the assemblage. Opposed platform cores differ from the naviform core group in terms of reduction strategy. The twin platforms on opposed platform cores are often located on opposite or adjacent core faces, and they lack any evidence of the platform and crest preparations so distinctive of the naviform reduction strategy. Opposed platform cores are better considered with other core-turning varieties (Figure 4.8: e and g, see below).

Beyond the naviform type, other cores in the assemblage represent reduction strategies unified by their lack of extensive striking platform or core shape preparation. These non-naviform reduction variants (including the opposed platform type) are referred to as 'core turning' reduction strategies in the present context, since the different shapes and scar patterns of these core types have resulted from varying methods of core rotation during blank removal. The single platform, crossed platform, and amorphous core varieties were numerous in the Early Neolithic sample (see Table 4.10, Figure 4.7: b and f). The proportions of these core types vary erratically from phase to phase during Stage 1, but appear to be more stable in the subsequent Late Neolithic. The proportions of single platform and crossed platform cores decrease somewhat in the Late

Neolithic stage, while amorphous and alternate cores show slightly higher frequencies. Opposed platform and discoidal cores both show similar proportions in Stages 1 and 2, demonstrating the relatively low priority but consistent use of these reduction varieties. The presence of distal battering on a few cores (particularly single platform examples) suggests the occasional use of an anvil support during core reduction.

Single platform cores are rather poorly distinguished in the Dhuweila assemblage and seem best related to other core-turning types in many cases. While some Stage 2 examples have more pyramidal (conical) or prismatic forms showing signs of bladelet production (Figure 4.8: c), the Stage 1 single platform cores are an ill-defined group. Baird (1993: 221) has noted the poor definition of single platform and 'change of orientation' cores during the seventh millennium bc at Azraq 31 and sites in the Wadi Jilat. The intensity of reduction in all core-turning types at Dhuweila means that little comparative diagnostic information has survived. The large sample of core-turning examples belonging to the Stage 2 sample allows the possibility of extracting greater information about non-naviform reduction strategies in future analysis. It is possible that a better understanding of the Stage 2 core-turning reduction patterns will aid in analysing the smaller Stage 1 sample.

Crossed platform cores and amorphous cores were both generated by rotation of the core to exploit multiple platforms during the reduction process. Crossed platform cores have two or more platforms oriented perpendicularly on the same, opposite, or adjacent core faces; cores of this type often exhibit a prismatic core morphology. Amorphous cores may have 'crossed' platforms, but generally also possess bifacial platforms alternating across the core face. These usually have the greatest number of platform orientations and show intensive utilisation of the raw material. Such cores are termed amorphous in this analysis because they cannot be consistently oriented along any dominant axis of reduction.

The discoidal and alternate platform core types represent related strategies with removals struck alternately from the edge of a relatively flat pebble or tabular material fragment. Alternate platform cores possess one or two bifacial platform edges (Figure 4.8: a). They may represent partially completed discoidal cores where, when complete, removals radiate around the entire core circumference (Figure 4.7: c–d). One exception to the bifacial majority is a small group of cores which have a radial scar pattern on only one face. Due to their flat profile, radiating flake scar pattern and raw material similarities, these cores were included within the discoidal core type. Although they are technically single platform cores, the poor definition of most single platform cores contrasts with this clearly distinguishable discoidal sub-group. The presence of discoidal cores within the PPNB core repertoire indicates a deliberate reduction strategy aimed at the production of flakes (Figure 4.7: d). These diminutive cores would not (unless originally much larger) have been useful for the production of blades, but do consistently exhibit more bladelet removals than their Stage 2 counter-parts (Figure 4.7: c).

The Stage 2 core sample was more heavily dominated by cores used for the production of small flakes. Discoidal cores, cores made on flakes and, most frequently, the splintered pieces, were all used for flake production during Stage 2. The diminutive nature of these three core types demonstrates a unified strategy often aimed at the extensive exploitation of valued, exotic raw materials by various reduction techniques (e.g. Baird 1993: 215). The need for such a strategy is clear from the numerous small arrowhead types in the Late Neolithic tool assemblage (Betts 1988a, b, 1987a, see also Betts this volume). The use of small flakes has been the subject of discussion in analyses of many later prehistoric assemblages in the context of more expedient core reduction strategies (Teltser 1991; Torrence ed. 1989; Johnson and Morrow 1987; Patterson 1987). Theories employed to help describe the shift away from naviform related blade production during the PPNB to an increasing flake dominated production in Late Neolithic assemblages have included suggestions of a change towards increasingly expedient raw material exploitation (Nishiaki 1992: 349–351; Baird 1995). However, little mention has been made of the nature of this new strategy. Perhaps the most salient characteristic of an expedient core technology is the concentrated production of small flakes. The following discussion of both the core-on-flake and splintered piece types (included with the cores in this analysis) provides examples of such 'expedient' flake production.

The core-on-flake distinction was made to designate flakes which have had smaller flakes removed from their surfaces (Figure 4.8: b). This type represents one of the most difficult categories in classification, similar to that of the splintered pieces discussed below. Within the context of this analysis these 'flaked-flakes' are defined as cores. The use of larger blanks for the subsequent production of smaller flakes has been a reduction strategy employed by knappers from great antiquity (Ashton *et al.* 1991; Goren-Inbar 1988). In Neolithic contexts, Baird (1993: 164) has included flakes from which other flakes were removed within his core shape categories, while Nishiaki (1992: 74–75) has removed such flaked-flakes from the core repertoire. Nishiaki (1992) described several parameters which might prevent the categorisation of such pieces as cores rather than tools. The core-on-flake type in the Dhuweila assemblage represents a recognisable group of artefacts which are either diagnostic parts of larger blanks (mainly flakes) or pieces with relatively few removals. Subsequent flake removals, albeit often quite small, were deliberately struck from the ventral or dorsal

surfaces of these flakes. Perhaps most importantly, no subsequent signs of use-damage were present along the edge between the negative scars and the striking platform. In addition, distinct (often protruding) arris ridges creating exaggerated concavities between removals would have made such pieces unsuitable for use in most tool types. These pieces appear to have functioned as blanks from which small flakes were struck. There are no signs that they were used as tools and so it seems appropriate to consider them with the other core categories.

As Table 4.10 clearly demonstrates, the most marked core type, particularly during Stage 2, was the splintered piece (Figure 4.7: a, Figure 4.8: d and f). By comparison with other contemporary assemblages in the area (Baird 1993: 438–439; McCartney 1992: 50), the abundance of this type is apparently unique at Dhuweila. Nishiaki, while suggesting that splintered pieces should tentatively be assigned to a tool category (Nishiaki 1992: 74), still describes splintered pieces from the Pottery Neolithic site Tell Damishilyya as cores for the production of flakes from fine grained raw materials (Nishiaki 1992: 193). Splintered pieces have been the focus of a debate similar to that regarding the core-on-flake category. They have been described as either cores or tools and assigned a variety of names (Callahan 1987: 12–13; Hayden 1980; Broadbent 1979: 71, 108–109; White 1968). The splintered pieces in the Dhuweila assemblage were primarily made on chunks, and to a lesser degree on blanks. Nearly all examples show multiple opposite removals from two or more surfaces and are bounded on either end by heavily stepped and battered platforms diagnostic of the bipolar anvil technique associated with this reduction type (Crabtree 1972: 10–11). The presence in the assemblage of a significant number of flakes, small bladelets and

		Max-Length	Max-Thick
PPNB Sample	Max	62.30	44.40
21	Median	47.00	21.70
	Min	28.70	07.50
	Avg	47.10	21.40
	Vars	00.59	00.56
	Stds	00.76	00.75
LN Sample	Max	69.20	40.70
82	Median	41.80	18.80
	Min	27.10	07.20
	Avg	43.20	19.10
	Vars	01.10	00.45
	Stds	01.05	00.74
Total Sample	Max	69.20	44.40
103	Median	43.20	19.10
	Min	27.10	07.20
	Avg	44.00	19.60
	Vars	01.02	00.47
	Stds	01.01	00.69

Table 4.11 Non-Naviform Core Dimensions: measurements in mm.

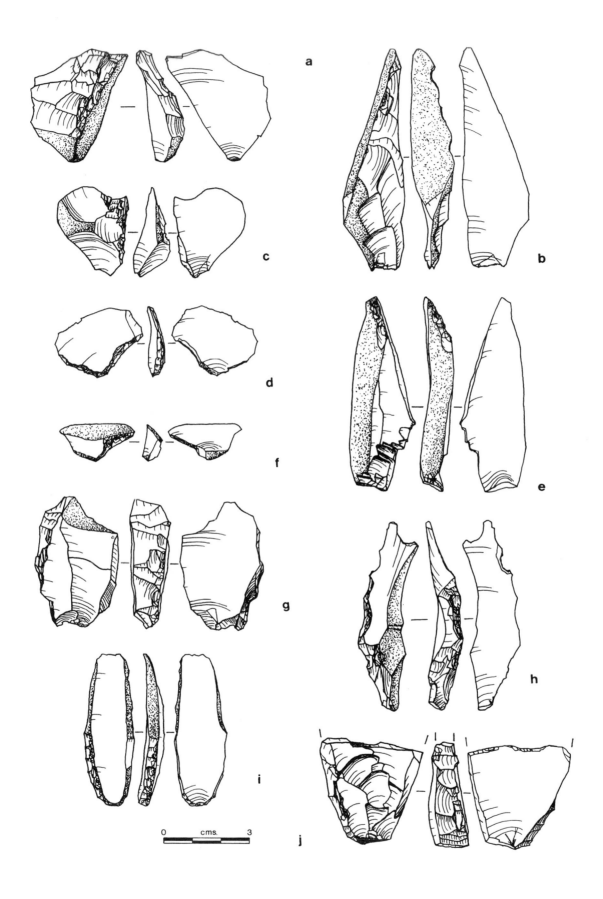

Figure 4.9   Chipped stone: Stage 1, core platform preparation and rejuvenation pieces - a, b, c, d, h platform
preparation/rejuvenation pieces; e, f crested pieces; g, i, j core tablets.

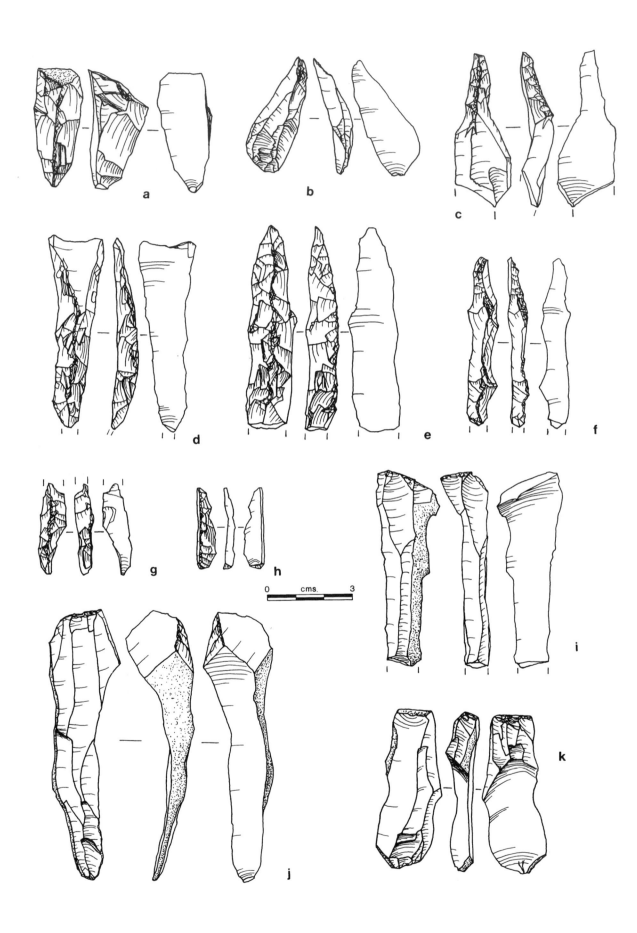

Figure 4.10   Chipped stone: Stage 1, crested pieces and overshoots - a - g crested pieces; h platform rejuvenation; i - k overshots.

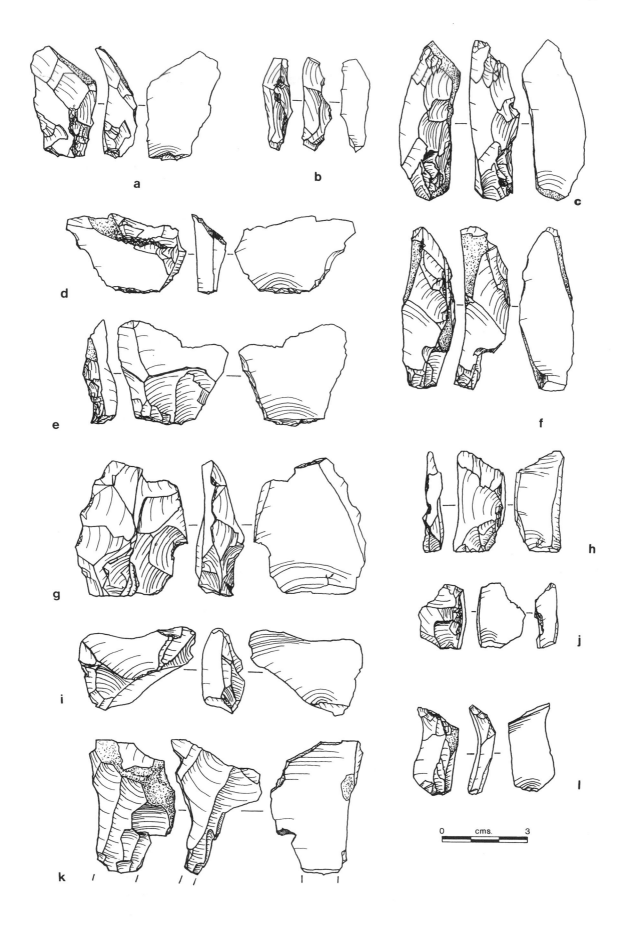

Figure 4.11   Chipped stone: Stage 2, core preparation and rejuvenation pieces - a, b, d, f crested pieces; c, g, h, i platform rejuvenations; e core tablet; k, l overshots.

		Max-Length	Max-Thick
PPNB Sample 9	Max.	53.40	12.50
	Median	39.20	10.00
	Min	33.80	01.00
	Avg	40.80	09.20
	Vars	00.44	00.12
	Stds	00.66	00.34
LN Sample 63	Max.	49.30	22.40
	Median	30.70	10.20
	Min	14.20	03.80
	Avg	32.10	10.80
	Vars	00.43	00.18
	Stds	00.66	00.43
Total Sample 72	Max.	53.40	22.40
	Median	32.50	10.20
	Min	14.20	01.00
	Avg	33.20	10.60
	Vars	00.51	00.18
	Stds	00.71	00.42

Table 4.12 Splintered Piece Dimensions: measurements in mm.

spalls with battered or crushed proximal and/or distal ends supports the definition of these artefacts as cores. Judging from the high number of spall scars on these pieces, the production of spalls may well have been an important aspect of the splintered piece reduction strategy, forming a related strategy to the use of concave truncation burins as spall cores (Finlayson and Betts 1990: 20). Some of the splintered pieces, those made on regular flakes or blades, might be considered as 'pièces esquilleés' (Hayden 1980: 2–3; Brézillon 1983: 288). These more regular examples, however, generally had extensive removal scarring across the 'core' faces, rather than scarring limited to 'working' edges, as might be expected if these pieces were created for tool use. Because these regular examples merged with the more distinctly core-like group in terms of technique and the extent of reduction, they were retained within a single category. The high proportion of splintered pieces in both stages at Dhuweila may be somewhat illusory as multiple pieces may represent the debitage of a single pebble reduced with the bipolar anvil technique (Knight 1991; Broadbent 1979: 111–116; Callahan 1987: 31–34). The application of this material-wasteful technique supports the suggestion that the Stage 2 knappers at Dhuweila had little trouble finding suitable (though perhaps diminutive) raw materials, as well as the techniques with which to exploit them.

The relatively small size of the majority of the Dhuweila cores reflects the intensive use of raw materials at the site (Tables 4.11–4.13). Measurement of the core-turning types shows an average size range of 44 mm in maximum length and *c.* 20 mm maximum thickness (Table 4.11). The average core-turning core size was slightly larger in the Early Neolithic sample than during the Late Neolithic, but the degree of variation was also greater in the earlier stage. The Stage 2 cores appear to have been produced more regularly on narrower pieces of raw material. The smaller average dimensions of the splintered pieces demonstrate a clear distinction between this group and the various core-turning core types (Table 4.12). The size difference is explained by use of the bipolar anvil technique which typically results in the production of diminutive core debitage as described above. The naviform cores (*sensu lato*) are also distinguished in terms of core size, being dominated by examples consistently larger than all other core types in the Dhuweila assemblage (62 mm in maximum length, 35 mm wide and 25 mm thick) (Table 4.13). The average naviform core size does not differ significantly between the Early Neolithic and Late Neolithic stage samples. Size differences between two naviform sub-types are discussed in detail below.

The small average size of the Dhuweila cores compares well with core dimensions given for contemporary sites in the steppe. This suggests that the core-turning and splintered core types were not regularly employed in the production of blades, at least during the latter stages of use (Baird 1993: 178). At Tell Damishilyya, Tell Nebi Mend and Azraq 31, core lengths range between 20–60 mm. These cores are also narrow and thin (Baird 1993: 216; Nishiaki 1992: 175–176, 219, 227). In the Jilat sites, Baird (1993: 215) demonstrates the greater size of most Jilat non-naviform cores (>50 mm long and between 50–70 mm in width), though a second smaller width range (15–35 mm) is more comparable with the Dhuweila material. Baird (1993: 218) has suggested that the core size difference between the Jilat sites and Azraq 31 correlates with relative distance from raw material sources. The Dhuweila assemblage clearly supports such a correlation. At sites (regardless of occupation period) where material had to be carried significant distances to the site, core reduction was continued to an extent perhaps considered extreme elsewhere. The constant exception to the more heavily reduced core-turning core types is the naviform core group; an exception directly related to the desired end product (see below).

Blade, bladelet and flake scars were commonly found on the same core during both stages (McCartney 1989: 56). While the discoidal and core-on-flake varieties were used more exclusively for the production of flakes, the single platform, crossed platform, opposed platform, amorphous and splintered piece categories showed a wider range of removal types. Naviform cores (*sensu lato*) were uniquely dominated by blade removals, yet exhibited bladelet and flake scars which were possibly failed attempts either to rejuvenate the core or to extract further material from the core block. Effective blade production placed a lower limit on naviform core size, after which reduction of the naviform core was halted and, unless re-employed with non-naviform strategy, these cores were discarded, preserving their final naviform morphology. Nishiaki has noted that most cores he examined were dominated by flake production during later reduction stages, particularly in the Late Neolithic samples such as Tell Nebi Mend (Nishiaki 1992: 226; see also Baird 1993: 212–222). For all core types, the large proportion of examples representing mixed or more heavily flake based strategies in the Stage 2 sample at Dhuweila is in keeping with evidence from other broadly contemporary sites.

Most Dhuweila cores had little surface or platform cortex (McCartney 1989: 59–60). Cores from both Stages 1 and 2 exhibited very little core platform cortex (6% in Stage 1 and 8% in Stage 2), suggesting that a degree of core platform preparation was probable in all reduction strategies, though the lack of cortex is consistent with the heavily reduced nature of the core sample. A greater number of cores had cortex on the sides of the core body (37% in Stage 1 and 54% in Stage 2). Cortex found on the sides of the core was more frequent and represented by slightly higher proportions during the Late Neolithic, though the majority (31% in Stage 1 and 42% in Stage 2) in both stages had only 25% or less surface cortex. Naviform cores (*sensu stricto*) never exhibited platform cortex, though cortex was present on the sides of some naviform cores (*sensu lato*) (see below). The disposition of cortex on the sides of the tabular naviform cores in the Dhuweila assemblage is the most distinct variation in core cortex location relating to reduction strategy. The near absence of core platform cortex in both stages is at odds with the relative frequency of blanks with cortical platforms (see below). The general lack of cortex in the Dhuweila core sample suggests that the removal of blanks with dorsal or platform cortex must have occurred during the earlier stages of core reduction. Evidence from contemporary sites suggests that the paucity of core cortex at Dhuweila is somewhat unique. Extensive platform cortex, particularly within the single platform type, has been demonstrated for the Jilat sites (Baird 1993: 194). Baird (1993: 195, 201) documents a higher degree of cortex cover on the sides of non-naviform core types. Cortical core platforms were also noted by Nishiaki at Tell Damishilyya (*c.* 30%) and Tell Nebi Mend (c. 18%) within the coarser grained core examples (Nishiaki 1992: 177, 224).

The 35 naviform cores (*sensu lato*) in the Dhuweila assemblage (Stages 1 and 2) are considered in greater detail below. The presence of non-classic naviform examples, the small size, and heavily reduced nature of this core sample meant that a broad definition was employed to designate the group (see Baird 1993 and Nishiaki 1992 for detailed discussions on the development of naviform core research and comprehensive subtype classifications). The keeled profile (mentioned above) was considered to be the most diagnostic criterion within the heavily reduced Dhuweila sample. The resulting core shape showed a trapezoidal section and side-plan view which clearly distinguished these cores from the rest of the Dhuweila core assemblage

(Baird 1993: 188–189; Nishiaki 1992: 120; Crowfoot-Payne 1983: 667). A second primary characteristic, though not without exception, was the presence of two parallel platforms opposed at each end of a primary, flat removal surface (*ibid.*). The presence of a dorsal crest lying opposite to the main removal face was variable. While in part the poorly recognisable character of a dorsal surface crest demonstrates the heavily reduced nature of the sample, in some cases the lack of a crest preparation helps to distinguish between two naviform reduction methods employed at the site.

The heavily reduced, variable nature of the Dhuweila naviform core sample (*sensu lato*) posed serious difficulties to the construction of a systematic classification. Two examples with only a single platform remaining were included in the sample because other morphological characteristics suggested that they were recognisable, though more heavily reduced, examples of the basic naviform reduction strategy. Both of them

	Max-Length	Face-Length	Face-Width	Max-Thick
Total Sample Count =35				
Max	80.50	78.70	50.40	44.50
Median	63.80	61.00	38.20	23.10
Min	41.00	41.00	18.90	10.90
Avg	62.20	61.10	35.40	25.30
Vars	01.06	00.99	00.70	00.52
Stds	01.03	00.99	00.84	00.72
PPNB Sample Count =25				
Max	80.50	78.70	50.40	44.50
Median	63.80	60.30	37.10	22.50
Min	41.00	41.00	20.10	10.90
Avg	61.40	60.20	35.20	25.30
Vars	01.18	01.10	00.66	00.71
Stds	01.08	01.05	00.81	00.84
LN Sample Count =10				
Max	76.20	76.10	47.50	30.50
Median	64.10	62.50	38.80	24.00
Min	50.20	49.20	18.90	21.50
Avg	64.10	63.20	36.00	25.50
Vars	00.80	00.75	00.88	00.09
Stds	00.89	00.86	00.94	00.31
Naviform Sample (*sensu stricto*) Count =16				
Max	80.50	78.70	46.20	44.50
Median	61.50	60.90	33.00	24.50
Min	42.10	41.00	20.10	16.90
Avg	62.80	61.90	33.70	26.70
Vars	01.37	01.30	00.50	00.79
Stds	01.17	01.14	00.71	00.89
Tabular Naviform Sample Count = 19				
Max	76.20	76.10	50.40	36.80
Median	64.40	61.20	39.70	23.10
Min	41.00	42.10	18.90	10.90
Avg	61.60	60.40	36.80	24.20
Vars	00.85	00.78	00.87	00.30
Stds	00.92	00.88	00.93	00.55

Table 4.13 Naviform Core Dimensions: measurements in mm.

were included in the tabular naviform sub-type (see below). Two exceptions, worked bifacially as double opposed platform cores (demonstrating more lenticular morphologies than the other examples), were also included in the sample because their broadly 'keeled' profile suggested a naviform reduction origin. The two bifacial examples were included in the naviform (*sensu stricto*) sub-group (defined below) because of their heavily reduced state and greater resemblance to other members of this group. The dorsal core face of the one example, however, may have resulted from a simple non-crested platform preparation similar to the majority of the tabular naviform sub-type.

A few examples were partly re-worked after they could no longer be usefully manipulated with the naviform strategy for which they were originally intended. These examples have been included in the naviform core sample because the form of the original naviform core had not been unrecognisably altered (Betts 1986: 121). One method of re-working used the core in a discoidal fashion, generating radial removals which partly truncated the original naviform core face. A second method showed flake scars removed perpendicularly from the main core face, much in the manner of the crossed platform core type described above. These partly re-used cores (found most commonly in the naviform [*sensu stricto*] sub-type) demonstrate the value of raw material, even during the Early Neolithic occupation, which has resulted in the impoverished naviform core sample (*sensu lato*) belonging to the site. Overly reduced examples were not included in the sample when they deviated too far from the primary criteria stated above and were more likely to produce inaccurate measurement results. The sample discussed below must be considered to represent a minimum number of the total possible naviform cores once used at the site.

Two generalised sub-types, utilised for comparison, demonstrate the presence of two distinct naviform reduction methods in the assemblage. The first sub-group represents heavily reduced naviform cores (*sensu stricto*). These examples all showed signs of a remnant crest preparation on the dorsal core surface and exhibited very little, if any, cortex to indicate the original nature of the raw material from which they were produced (Figure 4.6: a and c). The dorsal crest stubs were variable; the majority were directly parallel with the blank removal surface, but a few examples were skewed at a more acute angle to the main core face. In addition to small core size, the core face (judging from the majority of examples) had become too convex to permit further blade removals. In morphological terms the Dhuweila naviform cores (*sensu stricto*) are anything but classic; their heavily reduced nature makes the resulting morphologies quite variable. It is the remnant core shaping on the dorsal surface (allowing these cores to be specifically identified as end products of bifacial

preform reduction) which distinguishes the naviform (*sensu stricto*) group. The dorsal scar morphology of the naviform (*sensu stricto*) cores in conjunction with the high proportion of diagnostic core elements in the assemblage confirms the presence of classic naviform reduction strategy in the Dhuweila assemblage (Baird 1993: 168; Nishiaki 1992: 117; Calley 1986a: 169, 1986b; Crowfoot Payne 1983: 667). A second 'tabular naviform' sub-group was used to distinguish those cores made on recognisable blocks of tabular raw material, which in general failed to show signs of a dorsal crest preparation (Figure 4.6: b, d–e). Though it is likely that the naviform (*sensu stricto*) group also derived from tabular raw material, the cores in this group were prepared and reduced in such a way that the distinctive form and tabular cortex of the parent material was generally obliterated. The tabular naviform sub-group, in contrast, was reduced in a manner which more directly utilised the tabular form of the selected raw material. The dorsal surface of one example was curved, suggesting that the original core material was a flat elongated cobble rather than a tabular slab.

While the naviform (*sensu stricto*) and tabular naviform sub-types utilised in this analysis are not without exceptions, these classifications broadly define two different naviform reduction methods used at the site. A similar distinction for a wider range of Black Desert naviform (*sensu lato*) core material was made earlier by Betts between bipolar cores with a flat back or transverse ridge replacing the naviform 'keel' (equivalent to the tabular naviform designation used here) and more classically 'keeled' naviform cores (*sensu stricto*) (Betts 1986: 121, 1982: 27). Betts suggested that both groups were produced on tabular raw materials, and noted that one group seemed somewhat longer than the other (see below, *ibid.*). The fact that the two parallel sub-groupings used in this analysis were arrived at independently of the above analysis helps to demonstrate the validity of the categorisation within the Dhuweila assemblage.

Of the cores identified as naviform (*sensu lato*) in this assemblage, only eight (23%) had any extant dorsal crest which made them more readily recognisable as naviform products. Of these eight, only four (two naviform [*sensu stricto*] and two tabular naviform) had alternating, bifacial crests. The naviform (*sensu stricto*) examples (both from phase 2) were heavily reduced and oriented at a skewed angle to the core removal surface (Figure 4.6: a). Two examples included in the tabular naviform sub-type (one belonging to phase 3 and the other to phase 7) did possess alternating crests opposite the main core face. Both examples were produced on narrow tabular slabs and demonstrated no extensive shaping of the core sides still predominantly covered with cortex. These two crested examples were included in the Dhuweila tabular naviform sub-type because of the high proportion of lateral cortex. They broadly parallel the 'naviform-tabular' sub-type defined by Baird (1993: 166, figs. 6.7, 6.8). The remaining four cores with 'crests' were all examples of unidirectional preparations. This type of 'crest' was formed on the dorsal face using a natural cortical surface as a platform; the core was then rotated so that this cortical surface subsequently formed the alternate side of the 'crest' (Figure 4.6: d). This type of preparation shows less care taken with the initial core form, using instead natural contours of the raw material worked. All examples with this type of dorsal preparation belong to the tabular naviform sub-group.

The tabular naviform sub-type represents a more simplistic reduction method in comparison with the classic biface preform naviform strategy. The unidirectional dorsal 'crest' preparation discussed above demonstrates the desire to imitate the 'keeled' morphology of more classic crested examples. Like the two bifacial crested examples described above, the unicrested method of preparation shows a degree of overlap between the two naviform reduction methods. Most of the tabular naviform examples, however, possessed no crest at all. These uncrested examples show dorsal surfaces with often little more than a few opposing scars oriented to generate the appropriate acute angled platform configuration (Figure 4.4: b). One core was completely unprepared, employing a weathered tabular corner oriented at the correct angle for the establishment of the opposed platforms (Figure 4.6: e).

Variability in the presence or absence of a dorsal crest in the Dhuweila naviform core sample defines the distinction of two naviform core reduction methods One (resulting in heavily reduced remnant cores) employed a bifacial preform, subsequent preparation of core platforms and establishment of the main core face by the removal of one or more crested blades; the second type lacked the extensive core shaping and platform preparation of the former, using instead natural contours and surfaces provided by the tabular raw material with only limited additional adjustment. Unlike the conclusion reached for assemblages studied by Nishiaki, the two naviform reduction methods at Dhuweila do appear to represent different reduction sequences, though both could be said to belong to the same overall reduction strategy (Nishiaki 1992: 120). It remains only to note the high proportion of crested blades assigned to phases 1–5 (Stage 1) and the fact that the majority of the naviform (*sensu stricto*) sub-type examples (thirteen out of sixteen) belong to the PPNB period sample. In contrast, the majority of the naviform cores belonging to Stage 2 (seven out of ten) were tabular naviform core examples. The differences in the proportions of each naviform core sub-type indicate that while the devolved tabular naviform category formed a significant part of Late PPNB naviform core (*sensu lato*) reduction, the naviform reduction method (*sensu stricto*) was all but

replaced by the more simplistic method during the Stage 2 occupation.

Similar examples of heavily reduced naviform cores (*sensu stricto*) or cores lacking the distinctive dorsal core preparation have been documented elsewhere. The naviform (*sensu stricto*) sub-type used in the Dhuweila analysis is represented by heavily reduced examples of the classic naviform reduction strategy discussed in related assemblages (Baird 1993: 165; Nishiaki 1992: 120). Calley (1986a: 169) refers to examples with rudimentary dorsal crests as 'primitive'. Betts (1988a: 376) also describes the naviform cores from the PPNB site Ibn al-Ghazzi as heavily reduced, demonstrating a general pattern of extremely evolved naviform cores at desert occupation sites, in particular where raw material sources were non-local (Calley 1986b). Baird distinguishes naviform cores (*sensu lato*) without dorsal crests or little initial core preparation as 'sub-naviform', a term broadly parallel to the type 5 category used by Nishiaki (Baird 1993: 165–166; Nishiaki 1992: 120). Baird has also described the 'sub-naviform' type belonging to the Jilat and Azraq assemblages as a continuation of the naviform strategy essentially limited to the early 6th millennium (Baird 1993: 165–166, 284). The tabular naviform sub-type defined for the Dhuweila assemblage seems to correlate well with the 'sub-naviform' type described by Baird, though the two crested examples find better parallels in the 'naviform-tabular' type used in the Jilat/Azraq analyses as noted above. The presence of many tabular naviform sub-type examples in the Dhuweila Stage 1 sample suggests that this reduction method was regularly employed perhaps somewhat earlier at Dhuweila than in the neighbouring wadi Jilat sites.

Table 4.13 lists the core sizes for the total naviform sample compared with sub-sets from each of Stages 1 and 2 as well as between the naviform (*sensu stricto*) and tabular naviform sub-types. Core face length is broadly equivalent to the maximum core length, thus indicating the exacting use of available raw material. Core width in the table is represented by the term 'face width', as the maximum width of the Dhuweila naviform cores is the same as the breadth of the primary removal surface. The naviform (*sensu stricto*) and tabular naviform cores are similar in average length (62.8 mm and 61.6 mm respectively), although the median values for this attribute suggest a greater proportion of somewhat longer examples in the tabular naviform sub-type. The naviform (*sensu stricto*) cores are somewhat narrower (33.7 mm versus 36.83 mm), yet slightly thicker (26.7 mm compared to 24.2 mm) than the tabular naviform examples. The closeness of the dimensions between the two Dhuweila naviform sub-types suggests that a general standard was observed during the reduction of all naviform cores (McCartney 1989: 64). The slightly greater width in the tabular naviform group is perhaps indicative of the lack of core shaping, which in the naviform (*sensu stricto*) sub-type altered the original size of the raw material employed. The broadly parallel core lengths from each sub-type (and general agreement between the dimensional variables for both sub-types) demonstrates the degree to which the more opportunistic tabular naviform strategy could be used to mimic the classic prepared core reduction method. Naviform cores (*sensu lato*) from the Late Neolithic sample were slightly longer and broader relative to those from Stage 1, reflecting the greater proportion of tabular naviform examples in this sample.

Dimension ranges listed by Baird (1993: 192) for both the classic naviform and 'sub-naviform' cores in the Jilat/Azraq assemblages (50–90 mm long, 59–76 mm wide and 27–37 mm thick) correlate well with the statistics provided in Table 4.13. The Jilat cores show greater dimensional ranges (particularly in the length and width variables) than the Dhuweila sample, but are more broadly similar in average dimensions (67 mm x 31 mm x 33 mm) (Baird 1993: 440). Naviforms (*sensu stricto*) in the Jilat assemblages were significantly narrower (20–45 mm) than the 'sub-naviform' examples (42–62 mm), demonstrating a more exaggerated size dichotomy related to the two parallel sub-types as defined in the Dhuweila assemblage. The greater range of size variation in the Jilat samples is probably related to the immediate availability of tabular raw materials. In comparison with the Azraq 31 sample, the Dhuweila cores are, on average, longer, but similar in average width and thickness variables (54 mm x 31 mm x 26 mm) (Baird 1993: 440).

The suggestion of a size threshold in the reduction of naviform cores (*sensu lato*) has been well demonstrated by Baird (1993: 192, 213). Though a greater degree of variation is apparent with regard to minimum acceptable length, the tight correlation between the Dhuweila and Azraq 31 samples suggests more exact minimum width and thickness thresholds. Despite the obvious need to exploit transported raw materials to their fullest extent in both the Dhuweila and Azraq 31 assemblages (relative to Jilat examples), naviform core reduction (*sensu lato*) was maintained within the minimum acceptable core dimensions. Baird (1993: 440) has discussed the more diminutive nature of naviform cores (*sensu lato*) from steppic sites in relation to those of the verdant zone (see also Crowfoot Payne 1983: 667). It seems probable that the small Dhuweila and Azraq 31 average naviform core dimensions represent the extreme testing of size thresholds in environments of high material cost.

The distinction between the naviform (*sensu stricto*) and tabular naviform sub-types is again demonstrated by the core platform angles. Both platforms of each core were measured (excluding the two examples with only one remaining platform). The angle located nearest to the keel apex on the dorsal surface of the core was labelled as the 'keeled' angle and the platform angle at the other end of the core was noted as the 'opposite' angle (Figure 4.1). A clear distinction between the naviform (*sensu stricto*) and the tabular naviform sub-types was demonstrated. The platform angles belonging to the tabular naviform examples are clearly lower than those of the naviform (*sensu stricto*) sub-type. The higher 'keeled end' average value (69.2 degrees) given for the tabular naviform sub-type is nearly parallel with

PPNB Sample	B-3	B-2	BL-3	BL-2	F-3	F-2
Count	100	100	80	80	100	100
Max	96.00	104.90	39.90	41.00	62.70	64.20
Median	45.60	47.90	27.20	29.50	27.20	31.50
Min	24.90	29.20	12.60	18.80	11.70	15.40
Avg	46.90	51.00	27.50	29.90	28.20	32.40
Vars	2.21	2.16	0.24	0.33	0.64	1.13
Stds	1.48	1.47	0.49	0.58	0.80	1.06
LN Sample	B-3	B-2	BL-3	BL-2	F-3	F-2
Count	100	100	80	80	100	100
Max	77.90	83.30	39.90	40.30	66.10	64.20
Median	43.10	45.90	27.80	29.90	23.20	27.20
Min	25.50	28.30	19.00	17.00	12.60	14.10
Avg	44.50	48.00	28.40	30.20	25.60	28.70
Vars	1.02	1.24	0.30	0.38	0.88	1.02
Stds	1.01	1.11	0.55	0.62	0.93	1.01

Table 4.14 Blank Length: measurements in mm.

PPNB Sample	B-3	B-2	BL-3	BL-2	F-3	F-2
Count	100	100	80	80	100	100
Max	29.50	39.80	14.20	13.30	54.50	57.20
Median	14.80	16.70	9.70	9.70	22.80	26.00
Min	6.80	7.70	4.80	0.90	8.60	13.90
Avg	15.60	18.20	9.30	9.50	24.70	28.60
Vars	0.16	0.34	0.03	0.04	0.64	0.86
Stds	0.40	0.58	0.18	0.20	0.80	0.93
LN Sample	B-3	B-2	BL-3	BL-2	F-3	F-2
Count	100	100	80	80	100	100
Max	32.80	39.70	12.90	12.90	76.30	55.80
Median	16.50	17.40	9.30	10.70	23.90	24.90
Min	9.60	11.00	2.50	4.80	9.30	12.50
Avg	17.30	18.10	9.50	10.20	24.00	25.80
Vars	0.18	0.19	0.03	0.04	0.85	0.63
Stds	0.43	0.43	0.19	0.20	0.92	0.72

Table 4.15 Blank Width: measurements in mm.

	PPNB Sample					
	B-3	B-2	BL-3	BL-2	F-3	F-2
Count	100	100	80	80	100	100
Max	15.30	19.50	8.80	10.00	17.20	14.80
Median	4.50	6.80	2.90	3.80	4.80	5.90
Min	2.20	1.60	1.30	1.50	1.00	2.20
Avg	4.90	7.20	3.30	4.00	5.60	6.80
Vars	0.04	0.10	0.02	0.02	0.06	0.08
Stds	0.20	0.32	0.15	0.15	0.25	0.29
	LN Sample					
Count	100	100	80	80	100	100
Max	18.90	17.20	9.30	10.30	22.00	24.10
Median	6.40	7.00	3.50	4.30	5.50	6.20
Min	2.10	1.10	1.50	1.80	1.70	1.70
Avg	6.60	7.50	3.80	4.60	6.10	7.10
Vars	0.07	0.09	0.02	0.02	0.09	0.13
Stds	0.27	0.30	0.15	0.16	0.31	0.36

Table 4.16 Blank Thickness: measurements in mm.

the lower (opposite end) average measurement (70.4) belonging to the naviform (*sensu stricto*) group. The 'opposite end' average angle measure for tabular naviform examples (60.0 degrees) is even more acute than the parallel naviform (*sensu stricto*) measurement. In contrast, the 'keeled end' naviform (*sensu stricto*) average angle (76.9 degrees) represents the most obtuse naviform platform angle range in the sample. In addition, as Figure 4.1 demonstrates, the range of angle measurements representing the naviform (*sensu stricto*) sample is less variable across both core ends than the corresponding tabular naviform platform angle measurements. The wider acceptable range of variation in the tabular naviform variant suggests less control, possibly in terms of platform preparation, was exercised in maintaining the core striking platform angle (Baird 1993: 230; Callahan 1984: 95). The Dhuweila naviform (*sensu lato*) core platform angles are somewhat high in relation to examples documented for the Levant which show a lower general average of *c.* 60–62 degrees (Nishiaki 1992: 124; Crowfoot Payne 1983: 667). Naviform core platform angles from the neighbouring Jilat sites, however, demonstrate a closer parallel with the higher Dhuweila values, showing two core platform angle groups (between 73–93 degrees). Interestingly, core platform angles for the 'sub-naviform' type in the Azraq 31 and Jilat assemblages show lower average angles than the naviform cores (*sensu stricto*) (Baird 1993: 180, 193, figs. 6.45, 6.46).

Blanks

Blank size

A sample of 560 blades, bladelets and flakes was measured with a limited number of attributes to look more closely at individual blank types poorly represented in the smaller blank sample analysed for the preliminary reporting of the assemblage (McCartney 1989). Blank dimensions, platform types and dimensions, as well as the proportion of blanks showing dorsal edge platform preparation, were recorded with the larger blank sample (Tables 4.14–4.16). The sample includes 100 blanks each from the non-cortical and partly-cortical blade and flake categories. The more fragmentary nature of the bladelet blank type allowed for samples of only 80 examples for each of the non-cortical and partly-cortical categories. However, the smaller sample presented for the bladelet category is representative and of comparative value with the larger blank samples.

Platforms

The proportions of each platform type in both Stages 1 and 2 are shown in Table 4.17, and the platform type proportions relative to each blank type are shown in Table 4.18. The plain platform type represents any platform with a single facet. The punctiform and

filliform platform types represent specialised types of single faceted platforms showing intensive preparation on the dorsal platform edge. The punctiform type was also defined metrically in this analysis, relating to diminutive platforms equal to or less than 2 mm squared (± a few hundredths of a mm) (Calley 1986a: 44, 264, fig. 4). Filliform platforms (not distinguished in the original analysis) appear to be larger, elongated examples of the more classic punctiform type since dorsal edge trimming (though coarser than punctiform examples at times) was again the diagnostic criterion of this type (Baird 1993: 268, Calley 1986a: 45). The filliform type was defined metrically (between 2–6 mm wide and 0–2 mm thick) in order to standardised the division between the punctiform and filliform types. Other platform definitions represent commonly used terms and are defined in the original analysis (McCartney 1989).

Several differences between the total Early Neolithic and Late Neolithic samples are apparent (Table 4.17). Plain and punctiform platforms dominate the PPNB platform sample, comprising more than half of all blank platforms analysed. Filliform and cortical platforms also represent significant proportions of the Stage 1 sample; faceted types occur in relatively low frequencies. In total, the punctiform and filliform platform types show a high concentration (*c.* 40%) in the Stage 1 sample. The Late Neolithic sample, in contrast, shows significant increases in the proportions of both plain and cortical platforms and a corresponding decrease in the number of punctiform platforms. The presence of the filliform platform type remains constant between the two stages, but a significant decrease in the total proportion of prepared platform types (*c.* 24%) is evident in the Stage 2 sample. The decrease in Stage 2 of the number of compressed/crushed and snapped platforms is perhaps related to the decreased proportion of punctiform platforms (Calley 1986a: 116, fig. 61.1; Rollefson and Abu Ghaneima 1983: 462). Faceted platform types show essentially unchanged proportions between the Early Neolithic and Late Neolithic samples. In general, the values shown in Table 4.17 demonstrate a relatively stereotypic shift from the extensive use of prepared platform types in the Early Neolithic sample to the unprepared types generally associated with the Late

	PPNB	PPNB%	LN	LN%
Plain	150	26.79	216	38.57
Filliform	80	14.29	80	14.29
Punctiform	146	26.07	53	9.46
Dihedral	19	3.39	30	5.36
Simple-Facet	54	9.64	51	9.11
Multi-Facet	14	2.50	17	3.04
Cortex	73	13.04	103	18.39
Compress\Crush	7	1.25	5	0.89
Snapped	17	3.04	5	0.89
Total	560	100.00	560	100.00

Table 4.17 Platform Types: counts and percentages.

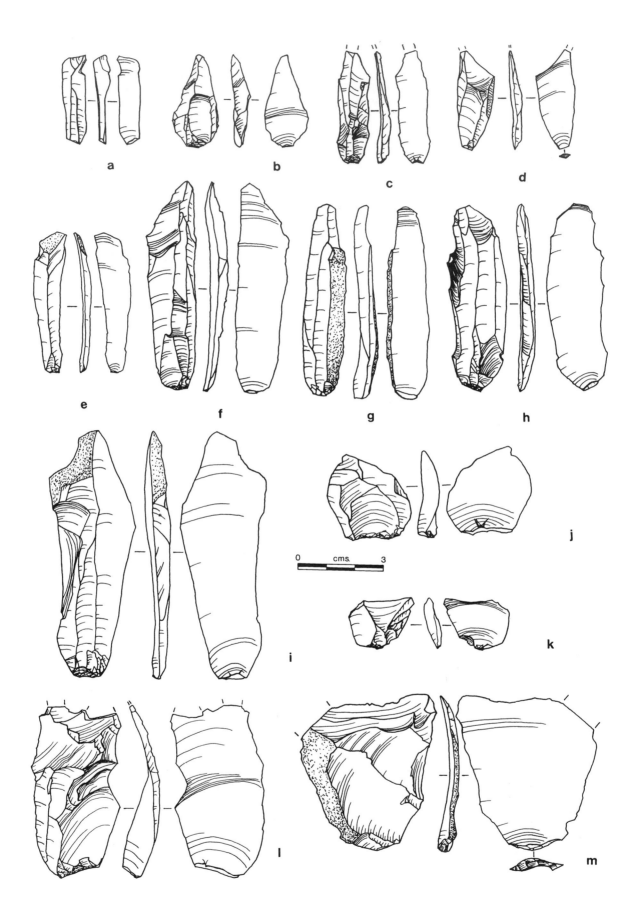

Figure 4.12   Chipped stone: Stage 1, blanks - a - e bladelets; f - i blades; j - m flakes.

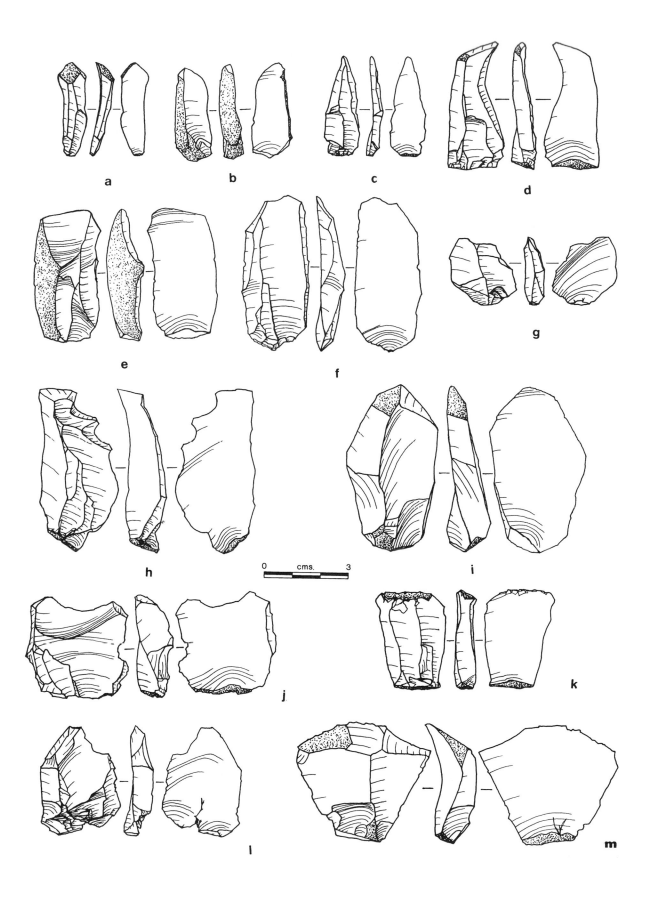

Figure 4.13   Chipped stone: Stage 2, blanks - a - c bladelets; d - f, h blades; g, i - m flakes.

Neolithic (Nishiaki 1992: 217, 225; Rollefson 1990: 121, 1988: 443; Rollefson and Simmons 1988b: 399; see below). The continued significance of the punctiform and filliform platform types in the Stage 2 sample, however, suggests an on-going practice (though more limited in scale) of prepared core reduction.

General changes in proportions of the various platform types are clarified when considered according to blank type (Table 4.18). In the Early Neolithic sample 53% of the non-cortical blades were produced with either punctiform or filliform platforms, showing nearly equal proportions of each platform type. The high proportion of plain platforms (26%) in the non-cortical blade sample and the greater dominance of this platform type in the partly-cortical blade category (36%) of Stage 1 suggests that a considerable part of total blade production was executed without extensive core edge preparation. It is possible that high numbers of plain platforms, particularly in the partly-cortical blade group, may be associated with earlier core reduction stages, suggesting that intensive dorsal edge preparation was not equally necessary in all episodes of blade removal. However, the consistency of platform preparation with the naviform (*sensu lato*) reduction method makes the use of different reduction methods equally likely, though the residual state of the Dhuweila core sample makes any direct correlation impossible (Baird 1993: 199, 224; Nishiaki 1992: 124). Late Neolithic blade platforms demonstrate a shift towards greater production of blades with plain and cortical platforms, indicating an increase in unprepared core reduction methods for blade production. The suggestion that plain platforms are linked with a desire for thicker blades correlates well with the increased blade thickness and plain platforms

found in Stage 2 (Rollefson and Abu Ghanima 1983: 462). Moderate proportions of punctiform and filliform platforms on Stage 2 blades suggest that the low proportion of naviform cores (*sensu lato*) in this sample is not residual, but that a limited proportion of naviform related blades were still being produced during the Late Neolithic at Dhuweila (Baird 1993: 223). The high number of cortical platforms in the Stage 2 sample would seem to relate to early core reduction stages or non-naviform reduction methods, but direct correlation with reduction strategy must remain speculative as the near absence of cores with platform cortex in the assemblage demonstrates.

Seventy-five percent of the bladelets from the PPNB stage were produced with punctiform and filliform platforms, the vast majority (62.5%) with clearly punctiform type platforms. As with the partly-cortical blades, partly-cortical bladelets show a greater number of examples with cortical platforms. Bladelet platforms in the Late Neolithic sample demonstrate a dichotomy between blade and bladelet production during Stage 2 in the punctiform and filliform platform types. A high proportion of the punctiform (26.25%) and filliform (46.25%) platforms in the Stage 2 sample belong to the bladelet categories and relatively little difference is noted between the non-cortical and partly-cortical bladelets in this respect. While the proportion of punctiform platforms associated with blade production (24%) is nearly equal to that seen in bladelet production, filliform platforms represent a lower proportion (25%) of blade production relative to the dominance of this type (46.25%) in the bladelet category. Late Neolithic bladelets do show higher numbers of both plain and cortical platforms relative to their Early Neolithic counter-parts, but unlike the blades belonging to Stage 2 show a greater degree of continuity in the utilisation of prepared core reduction strategies.

The general pattern showing punctiform platforms in association with the production of blades, particularly within PPNB assemblages, has been reported frequently elsewhere (Baird *et al.* 1992: 7; Nishiaki 1992: 124; Rollefson 1990: 121, tab. 2; Gebel *et al.* 1988: 122; Calley 1986a: 118). However, the high proportions of punctiform and filliform platforms represented in the Dhuweila assemblage exceed that of the neighbouring Jilat and Azraq sites. The Azraq 31 filliform platform proportions (21–25% of the blade/bladelet platforms are represented by filliform platforms) demonstrate the closest parallel with the Dhuweila PPNB proportion of this platform type (Baird 1993: 268, tab. 6.12). The punctiform platforms at Azraq 31, however, were significantly lower in number (between *c.* 12–14%) than in the Dhuweila assemblage. The Azraq 31 and Dhuweila assemblages share more features in common than with the assemblages in the wadi Jilat. Contemporary PPNB samples in Jilat 7 and Jilat 32 show between 12–16% filliform platforms, yet only *c.*

PPNB Platforms by Blank Type

	B-3	B-2	BL-3	BL-2	F-3	F-2
Plain	26.00	36.00	13.75	10.00	30.00	39.00
Filliform	26.00	15.00	12.50	20.00	8.00	5.00
Punctiform	27.00	19.00	62.50	38.75	14.00	5.00
Dihedral	4.00	1.00	1.00	1.00	6.00	6.00
Simple Facet	6.00	6.00	3.75	5.00	18.00	17.00
Multi Facet	0.00	2.00	0.00	0.00	7.00	5.00
Cortex	9.00	17.00	1.25	11.25	16.00	21.00
Compress\Crush	0.00	0.00	2.50	5.00	0.00	1.00
Snapped	2.00	4.00	2.5	8.75	1.00	1.00

LN Platforms by Blank Type

	B-3	B-2	BL-3	BL-2	F-3	F-2
Plain	35.00	33.00	30.00	26.25	55.00	48.00
Filliform	17.00	8.00	25.00	21.25	9.00	9.00
Punctiform	12.00	12.00	15.00	11.25	3.00	5.00
Dihedral	3.00	3.00	5.00	3.75	9.00	9.00
Simple Facet	4.00	9.00	6.25	7.50	13.00	14.00
Multi Facet	1.00	4.00	1.25	2.50	4.00	5.00
Cortex	27.00	27.00	16.25	26.25	5.00	10.00
Compress\Crushed	1.00	2.00	1.25	0.00	1.00	0.00
Snapped	0.00	2.00	0.00	1.25	1.00	1.00

Table 4.18 Platform type percentages for each blank type.

9% and *c.* 5% respectively show punctiform proportions. Early Late Neolithic Jilat 13 shows a decrease in the number of filliform platforms (*c.* 8–11%) and a low proportion (*c.* 6–3%) for the punctiform platform type. In general, a broad parallel exists between the Azraq and Jilat assemblages and that of Dhuweila in proportions demonstrated for the filliform platform type. However, the high proportion of punctiform platforms in the Dhuweila assemblage and the relatively low proportion of naviform cores (*sensu lato*), contrasts with reverse proportions in the Jilat/Azraq assemblages (Baird 1993: 205, tab. 6.6). It seems likely, therefore, that other prepared core reduction methods (perhaps single platform) may have added to the high proportion of punctiform platforms indicated by the Dhuweila Stage 1 bladelets in particular.

The increasing importance of plain and cortical platforms shown by the Dhuweila Late Neolithic sample has also been documented at other broadly contemporary sites (Nishiaki 1992: 217, 225; Rollefson 1990: 121; Rollefson 1988: 443, tabs. 2 and 3; Rollefson and Abu Ghanima 1983: 462). Rollefson also shows increases in both the plain and cortical platform proportions in the PPNC and Yarmoukian phases at 'Ain Ghazal to be concentrated in the blade categories rather than with the bladelet groups as at Dhuweila (Rollefson 1990: 5–7, tabs. 2–4). The high proportions of plain platforms represented for the Azraq 31 assemblages (between *c.* 40–50%) are greater than the proportion of this type in the Dhuweila assemblage, and do not demonstrate the degree of change indicated between Stages 1 and 2 at Dhuweila (Baird 1993: 269, tab. 6.12, 1992: 7). The increase in the number of cortical platforms between Stages 1 and 2 at Dhuweila is also more exaggerated than that apparent in the majority of the Jilat and Azraq 31 samples (*ibid.*). Plain platforms appear to dominate Syrian assemblages in both the PPNB and early Late Neolithic samples more strongly than is the case with the Dhuweila assemblage (Nishiaki 1992: 217, 225; Calley 1986a: 117–118).

The flake samples from both stages at Dhuweila showed the greatest proportions of faceted platforms. The high proportion of faceted platforms on flake blanks suggests that in both stages a greater proportion of flake production was related to non-naviform reduction strategies (Nishiaki 1992: 225; Rollefson 1990: 121, tab. 2; Calley 1986a: 118). The decrease in the number of flakes with punctiform and cortical platforms in the Dhuweila Stage 2 sample may partly relate to a reduced proportion of flakes associated with core preparation (Rollefson 1990: 121; Rollefson and Abu Ghanima 1983: 462; Betts 1986: 122). During both stages at Dhuweila the majority of flakes had plain platforms. The significant increase in the number of flakes with plain platforms in the Stage 2 sample is in keeping with the increase of this platform type in the Late Neolithic period generally (*ibid.*).

PPNB Sample

	B-3	B-2	BL-3	BL-2	F-3	F-2
Count	100	100	80	80	100	100
Max	23.30	33.10	11.70	16.30	46.30	36.00
Median	5.20	7.30	3.20	3.30	11.00	13.30
Min	1.40	1.10	0.50	1.10	2.10	0.80
Avg	6.10	8.40	4.00	3.90	12.90	14.60
Vars	0.15	0.25	0.04	0.06	0.62	0.60
Stds	0.39	0.50	0.21	0.24	0.79	0.77

LN Sample

	B-3	B-2	BL-3	BL-2	F-3	F-2
Count	100	100	80	80	100	100
Max	23.80	44.80	19.80	14.60	68.60	36.90
Median	8.20	7.60	4.90	5.10	10.60	11.50
Min	0.30	0.50	0.60	0.60	0.90	1.70
Avg	8.60	8.30	5.50	5.30	13.00	12.8
Vars	0.25	0.32	0.11	0.08	0.94	0.52
Stds	0.50	0.57	0.33	0.28	0.97	0.72

Table 4.19 Platform Width: measurements in mm.

LN Sample

	B-3	B-2	BL-3	BL-2	F-3	F-2
Count	100	100	80	80	100	100
Max	26.20	25.10	7.20	5.80	17.30	13.50
Median	2.10	2.50	1.20	1.30	3.60	4.40
Min	0.50	0.60	0.30	0.50	0.70	0.70
Avg	2.70	3.50	1.60	1.60	4.20	4.90
Vars	0.09	0.10	0.01	0.01	0.08	0.08
Stds	0.30	0.32	0.12	0.10	0.28	0.29

LN Sample

	B-3	B-2	BL-3	BL-2	F-3	F-2
Count	100	100	80	80	100	100
Max	14.90	11.50	6.20	7.80	22.70	17.70
Median	2.70	2.80	2.00	2.20	3.70	4.30
Min	0.40	0.40	0.40	0.40	0.40	0.30
Avg	3.80	3.50	2.20	2.50	4.40	4.60
Vars	0.08	0.05	0.02	0.02	0.10	0.08
Stds	0.29	0.23	0.15	0.16	0.32	0.29

Table 4.20 Platform Thickness: measurements in mm.

Platform size

Platform widths demonstrate a greater disparity between Stages 1 and 2 than is evident in the blank width measurements (Table 4.19). In all cases but that of the partly-cortical flakes, the Late Neolithic blanks were equal to or wider than those of the Early Neolithic occupation stage. The near equality of the Late Neolithic non-cortical and partly-cortical blade categories shows more homogeneous blade production strategy relative to the Stage 1 sample. In contrast platform width evidence again demonstrates a more polarised difference between the non-cortical and partly-cortical blades of the Early Neolithic sample. Bladelet platforms belonging to the Stage 2 sample are significantly larger than those of the Early Neolithic sample, though little disparity between the non-cortical and partly-cortical categories is shown in both stages of occupation. Unusually, the non-cortical bladelets widths in both stages are slightly larger than partly-cortical examples, reversing the pattern of the blank measurements shown for these categories. Flake platform widths demonstrate relative continuity between occupation stages, yet again the larger size of the Early Neolithic partly-cortical flakes is distinct.

Platform thickness, like blank thickness, demonstrates a very low amount of sample variation (Table 4.20). Platform thickness is generally considered to demonstrate a degree of control exercised over blank length and blank thickness (Dibble and Whittaker 1981: 293; Speth 1981: 17). Dibble and Whittaker have qualified the relationship between these variables by including platform angle, which in both stages at Dhuweila would help to explain the greater platform thickness variation in the blade categories relative to the bladelet groups (see platform angle discussion below). The platform thickness values reflecting non-cortical blades of the Early Neolithic sample show the greatest effort in the production of consistent thin blades, while the Late Neolithic samples again demonstrate greater homogeneity in the production of relatively thicker blade blanks in both the non-cortical and partly-cortical blade categories. Bladelet production in both stages is highly consistent in terms of the degree of variation, with Stage 2 bladelets (like their blade counter-parts) demonstrating a desire for relatively thicker bladelet products.

The platform dimensions shown above are somewhat larger than evident in the neighbouring Jilat and Azraq site assemblages. At Azraq 31 the platform sizes are relatively small (<5 mm wide and 2.5 mm thick), a fact which reflects the heavily bladelet based nature of the assemblage (Baird *et al.* 1992: 7, fig. 13). The Azraq 31 platform sizes, while significantly smaller than the Dhuweila blade platforms, are closely parallel with figures provided for the bladelet categories from both Stages 1 and 2. Average platform width and thickness values from the Jilat sites are also smaller than the corresponding Dhuweila values (4.5 mm wide and 1–1.5 mm thick) (Baird 1993: 271). The Jilat values, like those of Azraq 31, correlate more closely with the Dhuweila bladelet figures, especially those within the Stage 1 sample. Baird suggests that the diminutive Jilat average platform size reflects the PPNB character of the majority of the sites studied. A wider range which shows variation parameters for platform size in the Jilat sites (4.5–6 mm wide and 1.5–3 mm thick) correlates well with the majority of the Dhuweila Early Neolithic non-cortical blade sample (Baird 1993: 272). The distinction in the Jilat 13 assemblage of two platform width groups (3–6 mm and 7.5–9 mm) fits well with the differentiation between the Dhuweila blade and bladelet platforms, particularly those of Stage 2 (Baird 1993: 271).

Platform angles

Figures 4.2–4.5 demonstrate platform angle variation relative to each platform type. The figures are based on interior platform angles measured during the original analysis of the assemblage (McCartney 1989: tab. 12). Interior platform angles are perhaps a more direct measurement of knapping events rather than reduction strategy. Dibble and Whittaker have suggested that interior and exterior platform angles are correlated, despite the fact that they considered interior platform angles to be a relatively poor independent measure (Dibble and Whittaker 1981: 287). In spite of the problems associated with the measurement of interior platform angles, the data generated by this variable in the present analysis demonstrates relationships worth consideration. The sample sizes (95 blanks for Stage 1 and 208 blanks for Stage 2) are large enough to be statistically significant for each stage in general, but individual blank types are not equally represented within each sample. Over half of the Stage 1 sample angles (55: 40) are from blades and bladelets. The Stage 1 sample is, however, heavily weighted towards the flake categories (150: 58). The blade and bladelet platform angles are shown in Figures 4.3 and 4.5. While the samples used to produce Figures 4.3 and 4.5 are small, these figures give a better indication of the role of platform type and angle in the blade and bladelet categories without the 'background noise' provided by the flakes in each sample.

The distribution of platform angles in the Stage 1 sample shows two relatively distinct clusters across all blank types (Figure 4.2). Separation between the punctiform and filliform platform types seems to contradict generalised correlations between these two platform types and reduction technique (Baird 1993: 274; Calley 1986a: 44–45). The association of both punctiform and filliform platform types with 'soft hammer' technique, however, may represent knapping conditions including indirect punch and direct soft stone hammer techniques of reduction (Baird 1993: 262–274; personal observation). The greater size of the filliform and plain platforms and an association with direct percussion might require a more acute holding position of the core in order to effect blank removal. The higher filliform platform angles relative to those of the punctiform platforms may demonstrate a link between the more acute angled tabular naviform cores and the obtuse angled naviform (*sensu stricto*) cores respectively (see above). The reasons for the correlation between the plain and filliform platform angles versus the punctiform and faceted platform types may be complex, but the dichotomy illustrated in Figure 4.2 clearly demonstrates the technical variety seen within the Early Neolithic occupation stage. Figure 4.3, which shows the PPNB blade and bladelet platform angles without the flake examples, suggests the filliform

PPNB Sample

	B-3	B-2	Bl-3	Bl-2	F-3	F-2	% Total
Plain	50.00	50.00	54.54	25.00	43.33	35.89	44.00
Filliform	80.76	46.66	50.00	43.75	75.00	40.00	60.00
Punctiform	62.96	68.42	62.00	32.25	57.14	100.00	57.53
Simple Facet	66.66	83.33	0.00	50.00	33.33	29.41	40.74
Multi Facet	0.00	100.00	0.00	0.00	85.71	60.00	78.57
Cortex	11.11	17.64	100.00	11.11	25.00	23.81	20.54
Compress\Crush	0.00	0.00	0.00	50.00	0.00	0.00	28.57
Snapped	0.00	0.00	0.00	14.28	0.00	0.00	05.88

LN Sample

	B-3	B-2	Bl-3	Bl-2	F-3	F-2	% Total
Plain	37.14	30.30	37.50	4.76	61.81	50.00	41.13
Filliform	52.94	62.50	60.00	35.29	66.66	33.33	51.25
Punctiform	50.00	58.33	33.33	55.55	66.66	60.00	50.94
Simple Facet	50.00	22.22	20.00	16.66	61.53	35.71	37.25
Multi Facet	0.00	100.00	100.00	50.00	75.00	60.00	70.58
Cortex	14.81	14.81	30.76	23.81	20.00	10.00	18.44
Compress\Crush	0.00	0.00	100.00	0.00	0.00	0.00	20.00
Snapped	0.00	0.00	0.00	0.00	100.00	0.00	20.00

Table 4.21 Presence of platform preparation.

platform angles deviate most strongly in blade and bladelet production during Stage 1.

In contrast, the platform angles belonging to the total Late Neolithic sample (Figure 4.4) demonstrate a more homogeneous distribution between the different platform types. The lack of a distinction in the platform angles for Stage 2 is in keeping with other attributes, suggesting a greater homogeneity in reduction strategy during the Late Neolithic at Dhuweila. Figure 4.5, however, demonstrates a difference within the blade and bladelet platform angles when the large number of flake data are removed from the sample. In contrast to the above PPNB example, Stage 2 blade and bladelet platform angles show a greater disparity within the plain platform type. The closeness of the filliform platform angles to those of the punctiform type during Stage 2 suggests continuity in prepared core reduction for blade and bladelet production during Stage 2. In contrast, the uniqueness of blade and bladelet plain platform angles belonging to Stage 2 demonstrates an increased distinction between lamellar blanks produced with prepared versus unprepared reduction methods.

Platform preparation

Platform preparation was measured for the extended blank sample in order to consider initial analysis results against possible variation in blank type (McCartney 1989: 83–84). With the augmented platform preparation data, distinct differences between Stages 1 and 2 become apparent. Platform preparation was defined broadly, indicating any additional dorsal edge modification applied to the platform for the purpose of facilitating blank removal. Both abrasion and edge

faceting are included under a single preparation category, and no distinction is made between degrees of fine or coarse preparation (e.g. Baird 1993: 268–270 table 6.13; Nishiaki 1992: 124–125). Because of the generalised platform preparation term used in this analysis, detailed comparison with contemporary assemblages has not been carried out.

Table 4.21 illustrates the proportions of platform preparation for each platform type in relation to blank type during Stages 1 and 2. The high overall proportions of platform preparation are due (at least in part) to the broad definition of the platform preparation variable as applied in this analysis. In all cases the frequency of preparation in the Late Neolithic sample was lower than that of the Early Neolithic sample. A decrease in the amount of preparation and core platform faceting has been noted by Baird for broadly contemporary Jilat sites Jilat 13 and Azraq 31, in particular association with the presence of 'sub-naviform' cores in these assemblages (Baird 1993: 225). The high proportions of preparation indicated for the plain, simple faceted and multifaceted platform types relates primarily to the presence of faceting along the dorsal platform edge. Faceting preparation in the above platform types was relatively consistent during both Stages 1 and 2. The proportions of platform preparation for the punctiform and filliform platform types were consistently the highest in each occupation stage. Platform preparation in the punctiform and filliform platform types was (by definition) dominated by abrasion, often combined with fine dorsal edge faceting.

More significant differences in preparation frequency between the Early Neolithic and Late Neolithic samples is shown by the blank type designations (Table 4.21, see also Table 4.22). Blade categories belonging to the Late Neolithic sample show less platform preparation overall than their Early Neolithic counter-parts. Early Neolithic plain platforms on blades were consistently prepared (50%), compared to 30–37% in the Stage 2 sample. The highest amounts of platform preparation, as expected, belong to the punctiform and filliform platforms in both stages. An average of 65% of the Stage 1 blades with filliform and punctiform platform types were heavily prepared. Blades belonging to the Stage 2 sample show a reduced number of examples (56% on average) with platform preparation for the same two platform types. Preparation of bladelet platforms for the filliform and punctiform platform types show equal proportions between the two occupation stages (47% during Stage 1 and 46% in Stage 2). The higher proportions of platform preparation on blades and bladelets in each stage is consistent with these blanks being produced with prepared core reduction methods such as the naviform (*sensu lato*) strategy (Nishiaki 1992: 124; Calley 1986a: 125–6). High proportions of preparation shown for the faceted platform types are exaggerated by the small sample sizes representing these platform types in each

blanks measured above. Partly cortical bladelets belonging to the Late Neolithic sample, however, are unusually thick, greater even than some of the blades belonging to the Stage 2 sample. The latter may be anomalous, but the parallel median value suggests that the large thickness of this blank category in the Stage 2 sample is correct.

The use of shorter blades and longer bladelets in the Stage 2 sample is probably partly linked to changes in the types of arrowheads produced in the Late Neolithic period (Betts 1988b: figs. 5–6; Cauvin 1977: 34; Bar-Yosef 1981b: 564). Rollefson has also suggested that burins became shorter, wider and thicker over time at 'Ain Ghazal (Rollefson 1988: 443; see also Betts 1988a: fig. 13, 1987a: fig. 4). This pattern of blade size decrease is generally followed at Dhuweila, though relatively high proportions of lamellar tools and the consistency of the width measurements in particular, suggests a measure of continuity between the two stages. The Late Neolithic sample shows the use of a greater proportion of diminutive flakes, reflecting their use in the production of small bifaces and transverse arrowheads (Betts 1988a: 125, fig. 4, 1988c: fig. 13).

Comparison between Tables 4.23–4.25 and 4.26–4.28 shows tool class dimension values in relation to the tool blank type dimension given above. Major blank type changes in the tool sample are correlated with differences in tool class size, though the tool classes demonstrate smaller average sizes, in general, due to the variety of blank types utilised in the production of each tool class (see Table 4.8). PPNB tool class sizes are all relatively long with the burin, retouched and utilised classes suggesting a consistent use of the longest blades available. The greater size of these tool classes may be accounted for in part by the less heavily reduced nature of the morphology of these tool classes relative to other tool classes like the arrowheads. Tool class lengths representing the Late Neolithic sample demonstrate greater consistency. The Stage 2 arrowheads are significantly shorter, showing the greatest change relative to their Early Neolithic counter-parts, while the notch and utilised tool classes also demonstrate size decreases in the Late Neolithic sample.

Tool class average widths in the Early Neolithic sample tend to mirror the tool class length relationships with the notch and scraper classes dominating the rest of the stage 1 sample. Stage 2 tool classes, except the arrowheads and borers, demonstrate greater widths than those of Stage 1. In particular the biface, notch and scraper class widths clearly illustrate the higher proportion of flake blanks used in the production of these tools during the Late Neolithic occupation.

Tool class thickness means indicate chunkier proportions in the Late Neolithic sample. Burins in both stages show the greatest thickness values, second only to the thick scrapers belonging to Stage 2. The arrowhead class of the Late Neolithic sample indicates a unique

PPNB Sample

	Count	Max	Median	Min	Avg	Vars	Stds
Burins	56	82.95	41.9	23.4	43.6	1.59	1.26
Borers	23	77.6	41.8	6.6	40.7	2.69	1.64
Bifaces	0	0.0	0.0	0.0	0.0	0.00	0.00
Arrows	15	61.1	39.0	17.2	36.9	1.49	1.22
Notches	17	62.5	37.8	22.8	40.4	1.78	1.33
Retouched	6	62.0	43.4	23.4	43.3	2.62	1.62
Utilized	6	78.3	47.0	21.0	46.8	4.79	2.19
Scrapers	5	50.8	35.9	25.1	36.1	1.08	1.04

LN Sample

	Count	Max	Median	Min	Avg	Vars	Stds
Burins	25	63.6	42.3	22.9	41.6	1.02	1.01
Borers	15	98.0	39.1	18.5	41.6	3.49	1.86
Bifaces	11	50.3	38.8	21.7	37.0	0.65	0.80
Arrows	27	42.2	20.3	11.0	28.0	0.59	0.77
Notches	29	53.6	34.7	14.7	34.0	0.76	0.87
Retouched	16	61.7	41.2	24.3	41.1	0.93	0.96
Utilized	10	49.8	31.5	21.3	34.5	0.96	0.98
Scrapers	5	60.7	48.0	22.6	41.6	2.51	1.58

Table 4.26 Tool Class Length: measurements in mm.

PPNB Sample

	Count	Max	Median	Min	Avg	Vars	Stds
Burins	56	34.0	17.3	8.0	18.2	0.20	0.44
Borers	23	63.3	13.7	15.9	15.8	1.29	0.20
Bifaces	0	0.0	0.0	0.0	0.0	0.0	0.0
Arrows	15	17.3	12.0	8.8	12.8	0.07	0.26
Notches	17	29.0	18.9	8.2	19.4	0.38	0.04
Retouched	6	36.3	14.5	8.9	17.4	0.93	0.97
Utilized	6	25.3	17.8	11.5	17.9	0.33	0.58
Scrapers	5	38.1	33.2	14.9	27.9	1.17	1.08

LN Sample

	Count	Max	Median	Min	Avg	Vars	Stds
Burins	25	36.0	17.8	13.1	19.0	0.25	0.50
Borers	15	48.3	12.9	5.9	14.7	1.00	1.00
Bifaces	11	37.3	21.9	13.7	23.4	0.77	0.87
Arrows	27	19.4	9.0	6.6	12.7	0.10	0.33
Notches	29	43.3	20.5	9.7	20.9	0.74	0.86
Retouched	16	36.1	17.9	11.5	19.9	0.43	0.65
Utilized	10	27.1	16.3	11.2	18.0	0.28	0.52
Scrapers	5	44.8	27.5	17.5	30.6	1.11	1.05

Table 4.27 Tool Class Width: measurements in mm.

PPNB Sample

	Count	Max	Median	Min	Avg	Vars	Stds
Burins	56	18.8	6.8	3.5	7.3	0.06	0.26
Borers	23	9.6	5.3	2.3	5.6	0.04	0.20
Bifaces	0	0.0	0.0	0.0	0.0	0.0	0.0
Arrows	15	6.3	4.0	2.6	4.1	0.01	0.09
Notches	17	10.8	4.9	2.8	5.3	0.04	0.20
Retouched	6	7.5	4.8	2.6	4.8	0.04	0.19
Utilized	6	11.1	5.0	3.6	6.0	0.08	0.28
Scrapers	5	7.5	6.8	5.3	6.7	0.01	0.08

LN Sample

	Count	Max	Median	Min	Avg	Vars	Stds
Burins	25	19.1	8.8	4.3	9.9	0.17	0.42
Borers	15	12.1	5.1	2.5	5.8	0.09	0.30
Bifaces	11	13.3	5.1	3.6	6.6	0.06	0.26
Arrows	27	5.9	2.5	2.0	3.9	0.01	0.10
Notches	29	13.3	5.9	0.4	6.1	0.07	0.27
Retouched	16	10.9	6.6	3.4	6.1	0.06	0.26
Utilized	10	10.0	6.3	3.4	6.4	0.04	0.20
Scrapers	5	15.0	11.1	4.6	10.1	0.16	0.40

Table 4.28 Tool Class Thickness: measurements in mm.

preference for thin blanks while the remaining tool classes are significantly thicker than their Early Neolithic counter-parts.

Broadly speaking, the shorter, chunkier dimensions shown above for the Stage 2 blanks are supported by changes in the production of specific tool classes. Early Neolithic tools are somewhat shorter than expected (in part resulting from the inclusion of broken tools in the sample measured) but other tool dimensions illustrate the use of finer blanks for tool production during Stage 1. The more varied nature of the Stage 2 tool class sizes reflects a more regular use of different blank types within single tool classes during the Late Neolithic occupation.

Summary

The Dhuweila Stage 1 sample is typical of a Late PPNB desert hunting station, showing a concentrated use of naviform (*sensu lato*) core reduction for which initial preparation stages are rare or absent from the site. The Late Neolithic sample from Dhuweila is important for the transitional features and gradual nature of the trend away from lamellar production with naviform (*sensu lato*) core reduction demonstrated by the Stage 2 sample. The low proportion of naviform (*sensu lato*) cores in conjunction with the presence of naviform related core trimming elements and significant proportions of filliform and punctiform platforms in the Stage 2 sample require the acceptance of this typically PPNB reduction strategy within the Late Neolithic at Dhuweila. The presence of naviform cores (*sensu lato*) in Late Neolithic assemblages elsewhere in the Levant suggests a normal transitional pattern of limited naviform core reduction particularly related to the tabular naviform sub-type as used in this analysis. The greater proportion of tabular naviform cores in the Stage 2 sample (a reduction method with its origins in the PPNB) demonstrates a decreased investment in core preforming and suggests a decreased necessity for the close relationship between hunting stations and knapping sites demonstrated by the Stage 1 sample. The more homogeneous production of thicker, shorter blade products may technically be a result of such a decrease in attention to core preparation, yet the tool samples

measured in this analysis (as well as increased pastoral activities associated with the Late Neolithic) suggest that the long thin blades so typical of the PPNB were perhaps no longer so exclusively required.

Decreases in the numbers of lamellar blanks, particularly bladelets, in the Stage 2 sample were met with an increase in the number of flake products suggesting broad similarity with other Levantine Late Neolithic sites. Bladelet production, however, remained parallel with that of the PPNB stage during the first two Late Neolithic phases at the site. Bladelet attributes suggest a great degree of continuity between both occupation stages in terms of the reduction strategies employed for bladelet production. The relatively high proportions of prepared platform types assigned to the Stage 2 bladelets demonstrates the continued use of prepared core reduction strategies, but the heavily reduced nature of the Dhuweila core sample suggests only that both naviform (*sensu lato*) and single platform reduction methods may have been employed. Clearly, the Late Neolithic knappers of Dhuweila did not simply lose the ability to use prepared core reduction strategies, rather the decrease in the proportion of prepared core reduction, particularly associated with the production of blades, was made by deliberate selection processes.

Comparison with the neighbouring Jilat sites demonstrates a relatively lower proportion of lamellar products and consistently smaller blank and core dimensions, illustrating the later chronological position of the Dhuweila assemblage relative to the majority of the Jilat assemblages, as well as the lack of local material resources at Dhuweila. Greater correspondence between Dhuweila debitage and core dimensions with the assemblage of Azraq 31 shows the temporal and logistic similarities between the two sites, though more significant proportions of platform preparation at Dhuweila, in particular, demonstrates technical differences between Dhuweila and neighbouring sites. The debitage types with blank and core attributes demonstrate a unified cultural tradition in north-east Jordan, as well as the continuous nature of the transition between PPNB and Late Neolithic assemblages seen in the technology employed for the production of chipped stone tools.

Lithic Typology

Introduction

The typological analysis of the Dhuweila assemblage is based as far as possible on recognised type groupings commonly used for southern Levantine, and particularly Trans-Jordanian, industries (eg. Rollefson and Simmons 1988b; Rollefson *et al.* 1991; Baird *et al.* 1992: 11 ff., 1995). Much work has recently been dedicated to reaching a common standard in research techniques for Near Eastern Neolithic chipped stone industries (Gebel and Kozlowski eds 1994). Part of this effort has focussed on creating a common tool type list for the Neolithic (cf. Bar-Yosef 1994: 8). Bar-Yosef suggests a three-level analysis where well-defined forms are included in the first list, the second list "reports the less well-defined forms, such as retouched or nibbled blades, denticulates and notches", and the third list deals with debitage products. For analysis of the Dhuweila chipped stone a modified version is used where notches and denticulates are included in the first group while the second is restricted to atypical retouched blanks. Debitage products are dealt with separately (see 'lithic technology' above).

For the purposes of classification, the definitions used below follow generally accepted standard groupings widely used in analysis of Levantine Neolithic industries. Where possible, use has been made of Baird's (1993) analysis of the Azraq/Jilat material which, in terms of the location of the sites, is the closest to Dhuweila both in physical distance and in environmental conditions. There are problems in dealing with the 'less well-defined forms', particularly where they constitute a relatively high proportion of the retouched pieces (cf. Bar-Yosef 1994: 8; Baird 1993: Sect. 8.1). Despite their limited or irregular secondary retouch, some might still represent discrete tool types. In addition, some consistent method of quantifying them must be attempted if the analysis of the assemblage as a whole is to be usefully compared with other assemblages. Here they have been classified according to the general nature, location and extent of retouch (for metric analysis of blanks see 'lithic technology' above). The assemblage is presented here as a complete group, without particular reference to intra-site variability which will be the subject of a separate study.

Comparative Proportions of Major Tool Groups

A number of features distinguish the Dhuweila assemblage from those of contemporary sites, almost certainly reflecting the specialised nature of the site. Proportions of major tool types are broadly similar over all three stages, dominated in all cases by arrowheads and burins (Tables 4.29–4.30). Proportions of arrowheads average around 20% of the total tool counts

Tools	1	2	3	4	5	6	7	8	9	10
arrow	66	88	32	35	117	112	50	175	89	90
burin	73	118	54	45	149	110	32	99	77	99
scraper	6	6	3	5	14	19	15	27	54	29
biface	0	3	0	1	1	3	3	5	2	3
tile knife	3	1	4	4	6	23	8	12	16	19
borer	2	12	2	1	12	12	9	16	11	6
drill	0	2	1	0	2	3	0	0	4	2
sickle	1	4	0	2	2	0	1	1	2	2
denticulate	3	1	0	0	7	11	9	6	19	10
notch	0	1	2	1	5	4	2	2	3	3
truncation	0	1	2	2	4	3	1	4	8	7
hammer stone	0	0	0	0	0	0	0	0	1	0
mixed piece	0	0	0	0	1	2	0	0	0	0
Retouched pieces										
blade	79	94	61	42	145	173	73	174	130	122
bladelet	0	0	0	0	0	0	2	0	2	1
flake	8	20	14	7	40	49	34	80	89	44
chip	11	9	4	5	16	26	12	40	18	16
chunk	4	0	1	0	2	5	2	5	4	4
core element	1	0	0	0	6	0	3	3	1	0
spall	4	1	3	1	5	2	0	5	2	1
miscellaneous	0	1	2	0	3	1	7	3	9	2

Table 4.29 Major Tool Groups: absolute counts by phase.

Tools	Stage 1 No.	Stage 1 %	Stage 2 No.	Stage 2 %	Stage 3 No.	Stage 3 %	Total No.	Total %
arrow	338	22.59	426	21.1	90	19.57	854	21.48
burin	439	29.34	318	15.75	99	21.52	856	21.53
scraper	34	2.27	115	5.69	29	6.30	178	4.48
biface	5	0.33	13	0.64	3	0.65	21	0.53
tile knife	18	1.20	59	2.92	19	4.13	96	2.42
borer	29	1.94	48	2.38	6	1.30	83	2.09
drill	5	0.33	7	0.35	2	0.43	14	0.35
sickle	9	0.60	4	0.20	2	0.43	15	0.38
denticulate	11	0.74	45	2.23	10	2.17	66	1.66
notch	9	0.60	11	0.55	3	0.65	23	0.58
truncation	9	0.60	16	0.79	7	1.52	32	0.80
hammer stone	0	0.00	1	0.05	0	0.00	1	0.02
mixed piece	1	0.07	2	0.10	0	0.00	3	0.07
Retouched pieces								
blade	421	28.14	550	27.24	122	26.52	1093	27.5
bladelet	0	0.00	4	0.20	1	0.22	5	0.13
flake	89	5.95	252	12.48	44	9.57	385	9.68
chip	45	3.00	96	4.75	16	3.48	157	3.95
chunk	7	0.47	16	0.79	4	0.87	27	0.68
core element	7	0.47	7	0.35	0	0.00	14	0.35
spall	14	0.94	9	0.45	1	0.22	24	0.60
miscellaneous	6	0.40	20	0.99	2	0.43	28	0.70
Total	1496	99.98	2019	100.00	460	99.98	3975	99.98

Table 4.30 Major Tool Groups: absolute and relative tools counts by stage.

and are significantly higher than on sites in the more fertile regions. At 'Ain Ghazal, for example (Rollefson *et al.* 1992: 455), arrowheads average less than 1% of the PPNB assemblages, rising to around 3% in the PPNC and Yarmoukian stages. At the earlier PPNB site of Kfar Horesh in Lower Galilee (Goring Morris 1994) arrowheads number around 10% of the tool total. On the Wadi Jilat sites, arrowhead proportions are also lower with points occurring in variable quantities in the Neolithic assemblages in numbers ranging from 4% at Jilat 26 to 16% on Jilat 13 (Baird 1993: Sect. 8.10). At the site of Azraq 31 the figures for the PPNB and the Late Neolithic are 17% and 9% respectively (Baird *et al.* 1992: fig. 14). The closest assemblage in terms of arrowhead proportions is from the Late PPNB site of Nahal Issaron in the semi-arid zone where figures vary from around 14 % to 26%, averaging around 20% (Gopher *et al.* 1994: 481). The high proportions of arrowheads in all stages at Dhuweila clearly reflects the specialised nature of the site, with its particular emphasis on hunting.

On the other hand, burins are a dominant feature of Transjordanian Neolithic assemblages, regardless of site location. However, burins may not be as task-specific as arrowheads and the types of burins vary significantly both regionally and chronologically throughout the Neolithic period (Betts 1987c; Rollefson 1988; Garrard *et al.* 1994b: 90). The combined burin class represents 29% of the assemblage in Dhuweila Stage 1. This figure compares closely with the figure of 27% for the Late PPNB at 'Ain Ghazal while the figure of 15% for Dhuweila Stage 2 is lower than the relative proportions for 'Ain Ghazal with 26% for the PPNC and 29% for the Yarmoukian (Rollefson *et al.* 1992: tab. 4). The wadi Jilat sites show a temporal trend in burin numbers with figures of 10–14% in the early PPNB levels of Jilat 7 rising to 28–37% in the later PPNB and Late Neolithic levels on the Jilat sites and Azraq 31 (Garrard *et al.* 1994b: 90). The lower relative proportion of burins in Dhuweila Stage 2 may be a reflection of differences in occurrence and function of certain burin types (see 'burins' below).

All other tools occur only in relatively low proportions. With the introduction of tabular scrapers and knives in the Late Neolithic industry, knives and scrapers are more common in Stage 2 than in Stage 1. Truncations are also more common in Stage 2, reflecting a trend towards truncated pieces in the later Late Neolithic (Betts 1993b: 52–3; fig. 6, Nos. 7, 8). Sickles occur in very low numbers throughout. Figures for Stage 3 probably reflect a mixing of Late Neolithic with later material and are so somewhat ill-defined. The overall similarity in tool proportions throughout the three stages is likely to be the result of similar economic activities in all phases, with a strong emphasis on hunting and meat processing.

Arrows

Of all the major tool classes, arrowheads are the most chronologically sensitive and, as a result, are one of the most useful tools with which to construct relative sequences for the Neolithic periods in the Levant (cf. Baird 1993; Bar-Yosef 1981b: 559 ff.; Gopher 1994). Arrowhead typology for the Neolithic industries of the Levant has been well documented by a number of scholars (cf. Gopher 1994: 30 ff.; Baird: 1993: Sect. 4.2.1). Within the Dhuweila assemblage most arrowhead types can be clearly assigned to recognised classes (Tables 4.31–4.33), but there are still some areas where

classification has proved problematical. Two difficulties arose with the analysis of the Dhuweila arrowheads. One is the problem of assigning broken pieces to specific classes. Pieces with characteristics such as tangs or retouched tips which could not be more closely defined were listed in the 'broken' class. It is likely that some pieces in the 'broken blades' class also come from arrowheads, particularly the less diagnostic mid-sections. Study of breakage can also yield useful information on curation of tools and arrow shafts. Analysis of the broken arrowheads (Table 4.33) shows that higher proportions of intact arrowheads occur in the later two stages. Of the broken pieces, most are from the base of the point. A good many of these exhibited impact fracture. This suggests that the damaged arrows were being brought back to the base camp where the broken points were discarded, presumably to be replaced by new points. In an area such as Dhuweila where reeds or wood for shafts would be in short supply, re-use of shafts would not be surprising. A number of tips with impact fracture were also recovered. These may have been brought back to camp in the carcases and discarded during the meat processing. The higher numbers of intact pieces in Stages 2 and 3 may be simply due to the smaller average size of Late Neolithic arrowheads.

The other problem relates to classification within the Byblos point class, where there is a sub-type sufficiently distinct to be put in a class of its own (Figure 4.14). These points are made on wide pointed blades, usually with retouch only around the tang. The point is normally formed only by the natural tip of the blade. The tang is shaped by alternate or inverse retouch. Pieces of this type have been found elsewhere in the steppe including Um Dabaghiya (Mortensen 1983: fig. 3, a–d). Because they are so distinctive and may be a type peculiar to the steppe, it is proposed to give them the name Badia points.

Because of clearance and disturbance during the re-occupation of Dhuweila in Stage 2, some mixing of the assemblage is inevitable. The problem of mixing in multi-period Neolithic sites is not confined to Dhuweila (Bar-Yosef 1994: 10).The presence of small numbers of Late Neolithic forms in the PPNB levels indicate a degree of mixing, but overall, the proportions conform to PPNB and Late Neolithic typology (eg. Baird *et al.* 1992: 15). Byblos points dominate in Stage 1, along with a smaller but significant number of Amuq points occurring throughout all PPNB phases. The small numbers of Nizzanim, Herzliyah and transverse arrowheads in Stage 1 are probably intrusive. Most occur in phase 5, in the uppermost levels of Stage 1. Byblos points continue into Stage 2 but are reduced from almost 40% in Stage 1 to just over 15% in Stage 2, while Amuq points fall from just over 15% to just over 10%. Almost 25% of the Late Neolithic group is Nizzanim points. The phase by phase analysis indicates

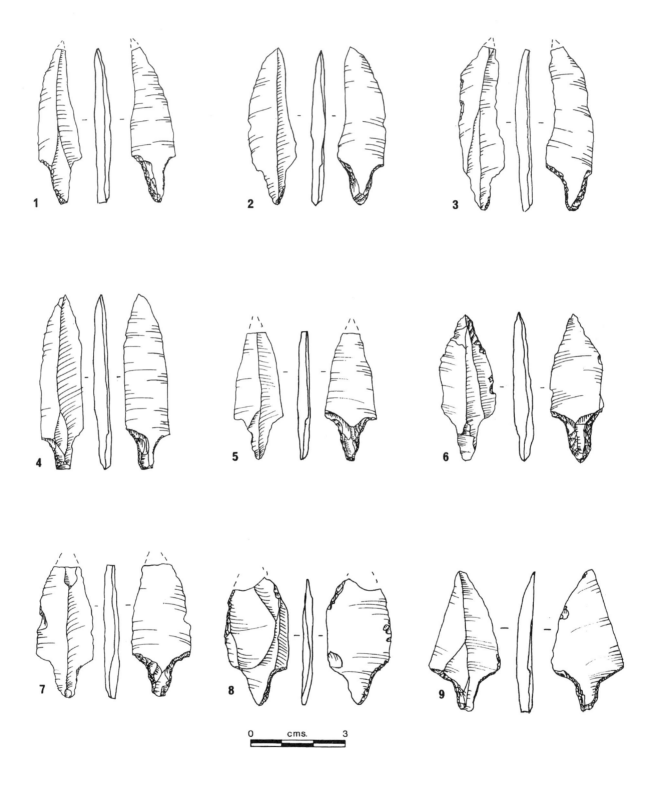

Figure 4.14 Chipped stone: Badia points, 1-7 Stage 2; 8, 9 +.

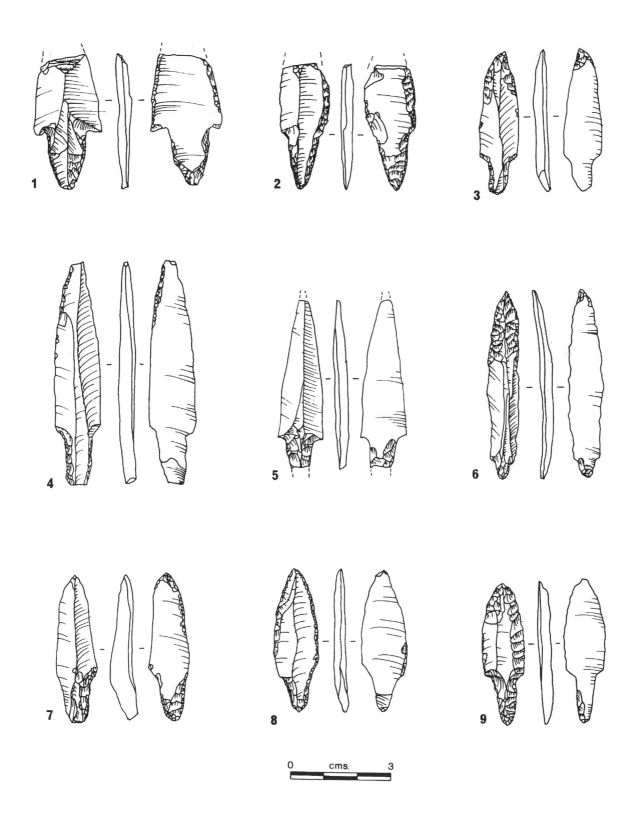

Figure 4.15   Chipped stone: Byblos points, 1, 2, 5, 6, 9 +; 3, 4, 7, 8 Stage 1.

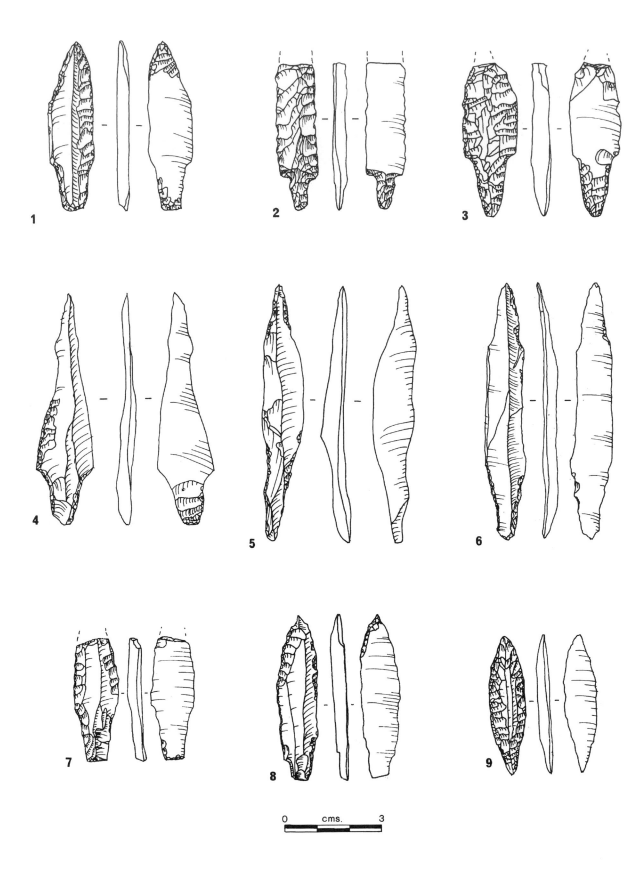

Figure 4.16   Chipped stone: Byblos points, 1, 3 -5, 7, 8 Stage 1; 2, 6 +; Amuq Point, 9 Stage 2.

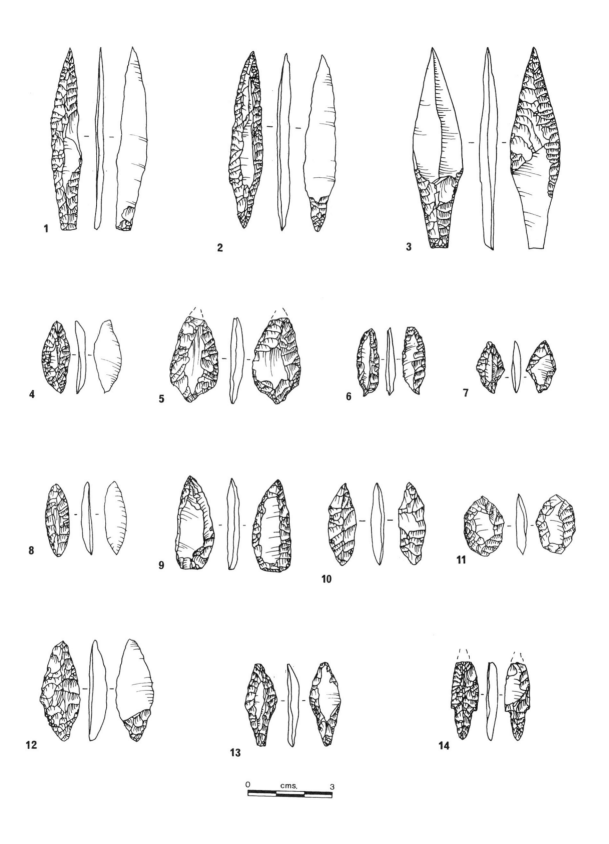

Figure 4.17   Chipped stone: Amuq points, 1-3 +; Herzliyah points, 4-7, 9, 12, 13 +; 8, 10, 11 Stage 2; Nizzanim point, 14 Stage 2.

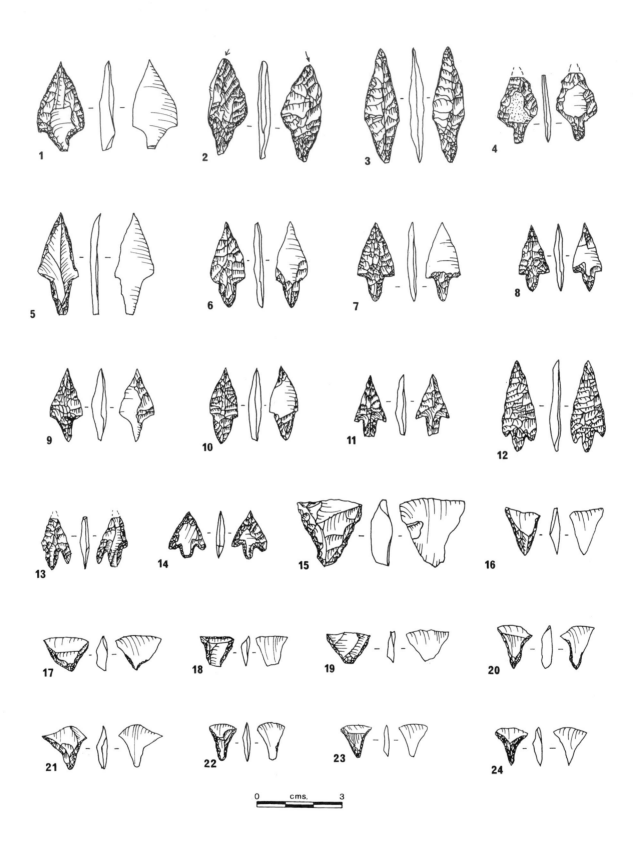

Figure 4.18   Chipped stone: Nizzanim points, 2-5 +; 1, 6-10 Stage 2; Haparsa points, 11-14 Stage 2; Transverse arrowheads, 21, 22 +; 15-20, 23-24 Stage 2.

Type	Phase									
	1	2	3	4	5	6	7	8	9	10
Amuq	8	10	8	4	26	10	8	22	10	6
Byblos	27	39	9	13	44	21	11	27	10	25
Jericho	2	0	0	0	1	0	1	1	0	0
Badia	1	0	0	1	3	1	2	5	2	3
Nizzanim	5	1	0	0	4	18	12	53	19	14
Herzliyah	0	0	1	0	1	5	2	24	16	10
Haparsa	0	0	0	0	0	0	0	2	1	1
Transverse	0	0	0	1	2	8	2	13	10	4
Other	0	0	0	0	0	1	0	0	0	2
Broken	23	38	14	16	36	48	12	28	21	25

Table 4.31 Arrows: absolute counts by phase.

	Stage 1		Stage 2		Stage 3		Total	
	No.	%	No.	%	No.	%	No.	%
Amuq	56	16.57	50	11.74	6	6.67	112	13.11
Byblos	132	39.05	69	16.2	25	27.78	226	26.46
Jericho	3	0.89	2	0.47	0	0	5	0.58
Badia	5	1.48	10	2.35	3	3.33	18	2.11
Nizzanim	10	2.96	102	23.94	14	15.56	126	14.75
Herzliyah	2	0.59	47	11.03	10	11.11	59	6.91
Haparsa	0	0	3	0.7	1	1.11	4	0.47
Transverse	3	0.89	33	7.75	4	4.44	40	4.68
Other	0	0	1	0.23	2	2.22	3	0.35
Broken	127	37.57	109	25.59	25	27.78	261	30.6
Total	338	100.00	426	100.00	90	100.00	854	100.02

Table 4.32 Arrows: absolute and relative counts by stage.

	Stage 1		Stage 2		Stage 3		Total	
Portion	No.	%	No.	%	No.	%	No.	%
Complete	85	25.15	234	54.93	43	47.78	362	42.39
Base	162	47.93	79	18.54	21	23.33	262	30.68
Base/mid	35	10.35	43	10.09	19	21.11	97	11.36
Mid	37	10.95	36	8.45	6	6.67	79	9.25
Tip	19	5.62	34	7.98	1	1.11	54	6.32
Total	338	100.00	426	99.99	90	100.00	854	100.00

Table 4.33 Arrows: Portion Preserved, absolute and relative counts by stage.

that Herzliyah, Haparsa and transverse arrowheads occur in greater numbers mid-way through the Late Neolithic, suggesting some chronological development through Stage 2, with a change occurring roughly between Phases 7 and 8.

This pattern closely conforms to that documented for Azraq 31 (Baird *et al.* 1992: 15–6; Garrard *et al.* 1994b: 88). Gopher (1994: 265) has shown that transverse arrowheads appear late in the Late Neolithic. At Dhuweila their appearance in significant numbers in phase 8 coincides with that of Herzliyah and Haparsa points. In the more fertile regions of the southern Levant, Nizzanim, Herzliyah and Haparsa points appear together from the beginning of the Late Neolithic. The Dhuweila Late Neolithic arrowhead class is clearly dominated by Nizzanim points, with lower numbers of Herzliyah points and very few Haparsa pieces. The Badia point appears predominantly in the Late Neolithic. This is consistent with evidence from Burqu' 27 (McCartney 1992: 44) where they occur in the earliest two phases (here referred to as a 'Byblos point, triangular form'), which are dated broadly in the first

half of the sixth millennium BC (McCartney 1992: 37). They appear together with Nizzanim, Herzliyah and transverse arrowheads.

Burins

Overall, there are higher proportions of burins in the PPNB levels of Stage 1 (*c.* 30%) than in the Late Neolithic of Stage 2 (*c.* 15%), although the proportions climb again to roughly 20% in Stage 3 (Tables 4.19–4.30). The burin types vary significantly from stage to stage, although not obviously from phase to phase (Tables 4.34–4.35). In Stage 1, dihedral forms account for almost 45% of all burins, followed by burins on a break at 18% and truncation burins at only 10%. In Stage 2, numbers of dihedral burins are still relatively high at 27%, burins on a break account for 25% and truncation burins about 15%. The dominance of dihedral burins is surprising, given a general trend towards a predominance of truncation burins in the Late Neolithic steppic industries. Baird in his studies of the Azraq/Jilat sites has shown that burin types and relative proportions vary considerably from site to site. It seems that burins are an important indicator of variety in site function, and also perhaps of cultural variation (Baird in Garrard *et al.* 1994b: 90–1). The Dhuweila pattern of burin numbers is markedly different from that of the Jilat/Azraq sequence where dihedral burins commonly comprise less than 10% of the total burin count. The Azraq/Jilat sites are dominated by truncation burins and burins on a break from the mid-PPNB onward (Garrard *et al.* 1994b). As Baird points out (Garrard *et al.* 1994b), the high

Type	Phase									
	1	2	3	4	5	6	7	8	9	10
Concave truncation	6	8	2	1	21	18	5	11	11	19
Transverse truncation	1	1	2	1	0	1	0	0	2	0
Oblique truncation	0	0	1	0	0	0	0	1	1	0
Dihedral	33	49	17	29	66	36	10	29	12	29
Offset dihedral	3	1	0	0	0	0	0	0	0	1
Multiple mixed	4	7	4	3	11	7	0	11	3	5
On break	16	26	11	6	23	26	11	14	31	26
Transverse	0	1	1	0	3	3	0	1	0	1
Nucleiform	0	0	0	0	0	3	1	0	2	1
Broken	10	25	16	6	27	17	5	32	15	17

Table 4.34 Burins: absolute tool counts by phase.

	Stage 1		Stage 2		Stage 3		Total	
Type	No.	%	No.	%	No.	%	No.	%
Concave trunc.	38	8.66	45	14.15	19	19.19	102	11.9
Transv. trunc.	5	1.14	2	0.63	0	0	7	0.82
Oblique trunc.	1	0.22	2	0.63	0	0	3	0.35
Dihedral	194	44.19	87	27.36	29	29.29	310	36.17
Offset dihedr.	4	0.91	0	0	1	1.01	5	0.58
Multiple mixed	29	6.6	21	6.6	5	5.05	55	6.42
On break	82	18.68	82	25.79	26	26.26	190	22.17
Transverse	2	0.45	4	1.26	1	1.01	7	0.82
Nucleiform	0	0	6	1.89	1	1.01	7	0.82
Broken	84	19.13	69	21.7	17	17.17	170	19.95
Total	439	99.98	318	100.01	99	99.99	856	100.00

Table 4.35 Burins: absolute and relative counts by stage.

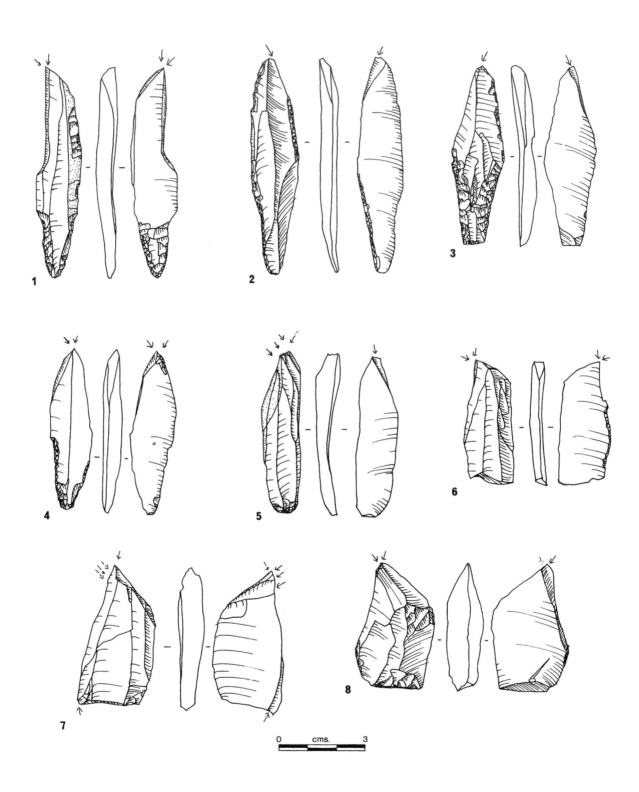

Figure 4.19   Chipped stone: Dihedral burins, 1, 6 Stage 1; 5 Stage 3; 4, 8 + ; Burin on break, 2 Stage 1; 3 +; Multiple mixed burin, 7 Stage 1.

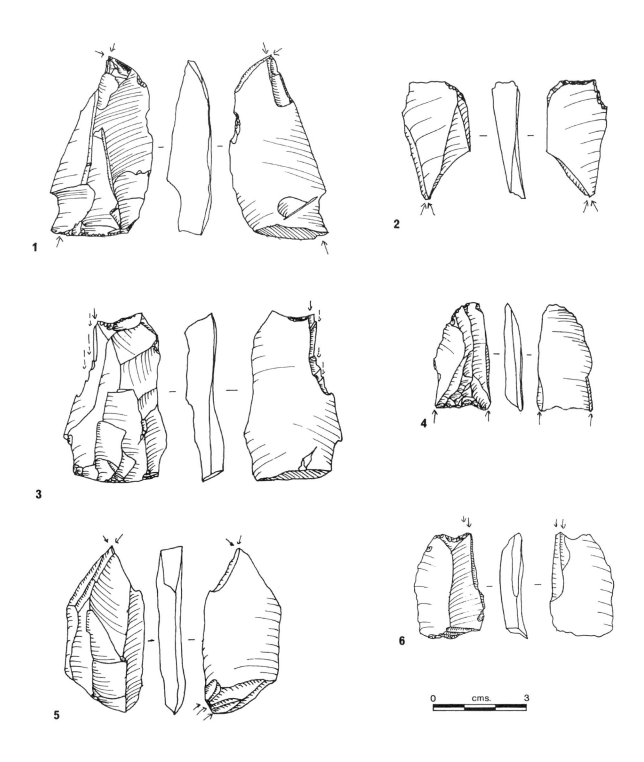

Figure 4.20   Chipped stone: Multiple mixed burins, 1 +; 5 Stage 2; Truncation burins, 3, 6 Stage 1; 4 Stage 2; Dihedral burin, 2
Stage 2.

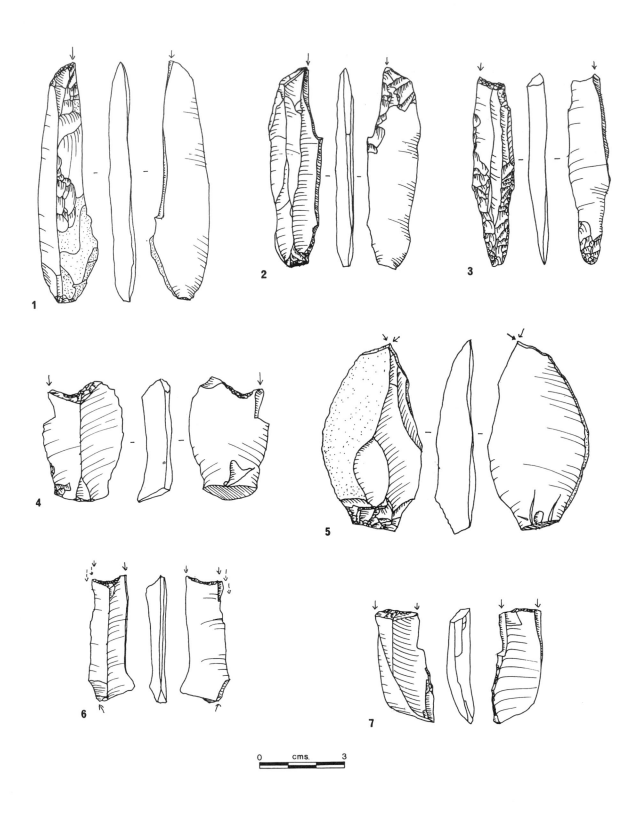

Figure 4.21   Chipped stone: Truncation burins 1, 3 Stage 1; ; 4, 6, 8 Stage 2; 7 +; Burin on break, 2 +; Dihedral burin, 5 Stage 2.

concentrations of truncation burins at certain steppic sites (cf. Betts 1987c: 227; 1987d) probably represent loci where limited activities were pursued. Dhuweila saw regular use over a protracted period of time. The low proportions of truncation burins may be a reflection of the types of activities carried out at the site, while the variety of tools may also be an indication of a wider range of activities. This variability is clear in the range of Neolithic sites within the *badia* (Betts 1993b; Garrard *et al.* 1994b: 90–1).

Burin function is a question which requires further research. The term 'burin' derives from the carpenter's or mason's graving tool of the same name and it is commonly assumed that all burins were used for engraving or incising, as in the making of bone or antler points, for example. Micro-wear studies of truncation burins (Finlayson and Betts 1990; Baird 1993: Sect 8.10) have indicated that this may not always be the case. A limited study on burins from Jebel Naja showed that truncation burins were not consistently used as cutting or engraving tools having the burin facet as the working edge. Some were used on the side of the piece; others may simply have been cores for the production of spalls. Rollefson (*et al.* 1992: 459, tab. 5) has figures for burin groups from 'Ain Ghazal comparing 'complex' burins (dihedrals, double burin edges and opposed burins) with truncation burins. Despite the difficulty of direct comparison with the Dhuweila tool counts, it seems that the proportions vary significantly, despite a general trend towards increasing numbers of concave truncation burins in the Late Neolithic.

Until the function of burins is better understood, it can only be suggested that the activities at Dhuweila involved a different range of priorities from those on other steppic sites.

Scrapers

The scraper typology is based on broad standard groupings (Tables 4.36–4.37). No finer subdivisions were clear within the groups (cf. Rollefson 1994: 446–7). The 'flake scraper' class comprises flakes with irregular or discontinuous working which do not fit into one of the other, more specific categories. Tabular scrapers are an anomalous group in that they are classified by the presence of extensive cortex rather than by the nature and location of retouch. The most marked change is the increase in tabular scrapers in Stage 2, consistent with the introduction of tabular scraper forms in the Late Neolithic. There is also a greater variety of scrapers in Stage 2.

Dhuweila is unusual in that tabular scrapers are an important feature of the assemblage in Stage 2. Rollefson *et al.* (1994: 454) note a reduction in the use of cortical flakes for scrapers in post-PPNB levels at 'Ain Ghazal, while at the Azraq/Jilat sites, scrapers "occur in diverse frequencies without broad temporal

Type	Phase									
	1	*2*	*3*	*4*	*5*	*6*	*7*	*8*	*9*	*10*
Flake	2	1	0	2	5	3	7	3	8	9
Tabular	1	1	0	0	1	7	5	8	17	5
End	3	3	0	3	8	7	2	7	10	7
Side	0	1	1	0	0	1	0	6	8	3
Steep	0	0	2	0	0	0	0	0	3	1
Round	0	0	0	0	0	0	0	0	3	1
Thumb	0	0	0	0	0	1	0	0	0	1
Denticulated	0	0	0	0	0	0	0	0	2	2
Fan	0	0	0	0	0	0	0	1	1	0
Other	0	0	0	0	0	0	1	2	2	0

Table 4.36 Scrapers: absolute counts by phase.

Type	Stage 1	Stage 2	Stage 3	Stage 4
Flake	10	21	9	40
Tabular	3	37	5	45
End	17	26	7	50
Side	2	15	3	20
Steep	2	3	1	6
Round	0	3	1	4
Thumb	0	1	1	2
Denticulated	0	2	2	4
Fan	0	2	0	2
Other	0	5	0	5
Total	34	115	29	178

Table 4.37 Scrapers: absolute counts by stage.

significance" (Baird 1993: Sect 8.10). At Dhuweila, scrapers increase in frequency throughout the sequence from 2.3% in Stage 1 to 5.7% in Stage 2 and 6.3% in Stage 3, while on the Azraq/Jilat sites scrapers comprise 1% or less of most Neolithic samples (Baird 1993: Sect. 8.10). The reason for this difference is not clear. It is possible that it relates to the specific activities at the site, perhaps those concerned with preparation of hunting equipment and carcase processing.

Bifaces

Foliate bifacial pieces are made almost exclusively on thin plaques of tabular flint. They are relatively large tools, characterised by an oval or pointed shape worked by invasive subscalar bifacial retouch, usually only leaving small traces of cortex on one or both faces. In some cases the edges have been trimmed by irregular pressure flaking. Most pieces look like large projectile points, but some are rounded at one or both ends and may perhaps have functioned as knives. Because of the ambiguity of function, such pieces have been classified simply as bifacial tools (Tables 4.38–4.39). While acknowledging this issue, Forstadt (in Rollefson *et al.* 1994: 454) classifies such pieces in the 'knife' category together with true 'tile knives' which, at Dhuweila, are quite distinct from the bifacial foliate pieces (see 'tile knives' below). Baird, in his analysis of the chipped stone from Wadi Jilat (Garrard *et al.* 1994b: 89), distinguished between 'ovate-lanceolate bifacials' and 'tile knives'. The Dhuweila bifacial foliate pieces correspond to the Azraq/Jilat 'ovate-lanceolate' group and to types K1a, K1b and K2a from 'Ain Ghazal

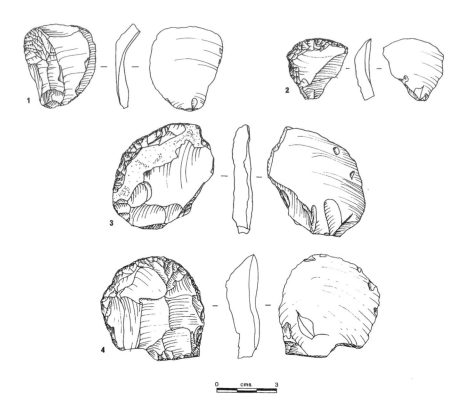

Figure 4.22   Chipped stone: Flake scraper, 1 Stage 3; End scraper, 2 Stage 2; Side scraper, 3 Stage 2; Round scraper, 4 Stage 2.

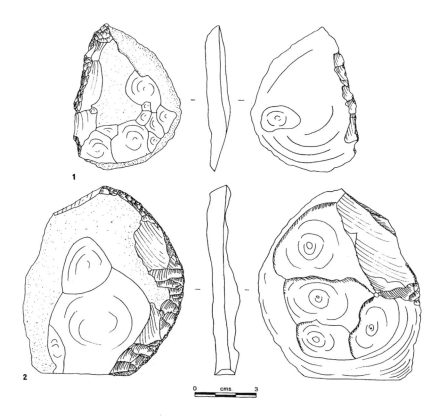

Figure 4.23   Chipped stone: Tabular scrapers, 1, 2 Stage 2.

106

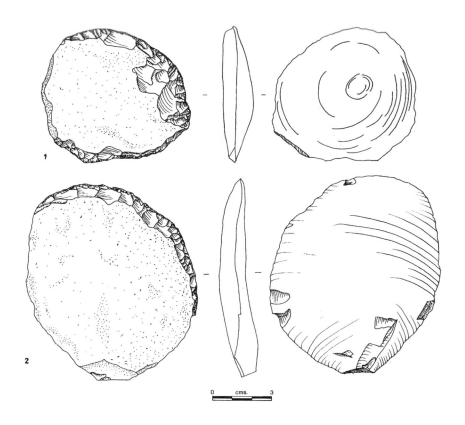

Figure 4.24   Chipped stone: Tabular scrapers, 1, 2 Stage 2.

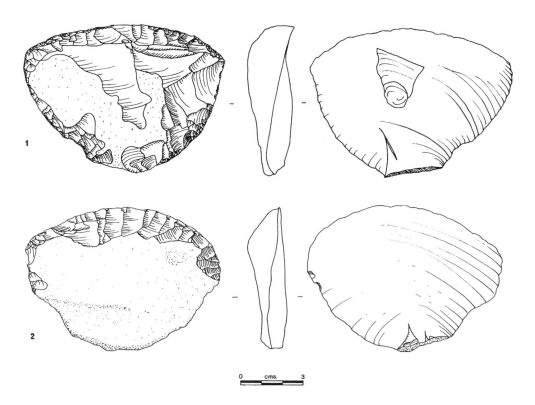

Figure 4.25   Chipped stone: Tabular scrapers, 1, 2 Stage 2.

(Rollefson *et al.* 1994: fig. 4). Since there is no clear division between the forms, especially if they are broken, they have been classified according to general shape and nature of retouch. Although a small number occur in levels of Stage 1, they appear predominantly to be a Late Neolithic form. In the Jilat/Azraq sequence they first appear in the mid-PPNB, but are more common in the Late Neolithic (Garrard *et al.* 1994b).There is a small concentration of bifacial foliates in Area B at Basta (Nissen *et al.* 1987) which Baird (in Garrard *et al.* 1994b: 89) suggests may indicate that they appear as part of developments marking the early Late Neolithic at Basta.

Foliate bifacial pieces of this type have been found in a number of steppic sites in the *harra*. A cache of four were found in the hide of a 'kite' near to Qa' Mejalla (Betts 1982: figs. 10, 12: 1–4). One had a distinct tang form at one end and all four could have functioned effectively as spearheads. Two other bifacial foliate pieces, almost identical to each other, were found hidden below a boulder on a knapping site near Qa' Mejalla. Unlike those from the 'kite', these were longer, perhaps too long for spearheads, and were more rounded at the ends. Their finely retouched edges made them seem more as if intended for use as knives. Roughly retouched bifacial foliates also occur in small numbers on many of the larger 'burin' Neolithic sites (Betts 1982: fig. 15: 34; 1993b: fig. 5: 6). Many of the 'burin' Neolithic sites in the *harra* are Late Neolithic in date.

Similar pieces are reported from Neolithic sites further afield. One piece from PPNB Kfar Horesh, near Nazareth, is classified under bifacial pieces and described as "a finely flaked complete dagger/knife" (Goring-Morris 1994: 423; fig. 12; see also Goring-Morris *et al.* 1995: fig. 12, 4-b), while the Late Neolithic Tuwailan of the Negev has a wide variety of similar bifacial forms (Goring-Morris 1993: fig. 7), here classified as knives as in Forstadt's typology (Rollefson *et al.* 1994). The Negev surveys identified production sites where both foliate forms and 'tile knives' were knapped from local tabular flint sources.

Tile Knives

Problems in identifying knives as a distinct class have been mentioned above (see 'bifaces' above). Forstadt (Rollefson *et al.* 1994: 454) has also discussed the problems associated with classifying 'bifacial foliate' pieces, as well as distinguishing knives from scrapers. Here, following the separation of bifacial foliate pieces, tile knives have been classified according to the nature of the blank (Tables 4.40–4.41). Tile knives are made almost exclusively on thin slabs of tabular flint. A small proportion, here classified in the 'other' category, are made on flakes or chunks without traces of cortex. Most are unilaterally retouched with natural backing. Some have bilateral retouch, usually much more extensive on

| | Phase | | | | | | | | | |
Type	1	2	3	4	5	6	7	8	9	10
Foliate	0	3	0	1	1	2	3	4	2	3
Other	0	0	0	0	0	0	0	1	0	0
Broken	0	0	0	0	0	1	0	0	0	0

Table 4.38 Bifaces: absolute counts by phase.

Type	Stage 1	Stage 2	Stage 3	Stage 4
Foliate	5	11	3	19
Other	0	1	0	1
Broken	0	1	0	1
Total	5	13	3	21

Table 4.39 Bifaces: absolute counts by stage.

| | Phase | | | | | | | | | |
Type	1	2	3	4	5	6	7	8	9	10
Tabular	3	1	4	4	6	17	8	12	16	19
Other	0	0	0	0	0	6	0	0	0	0

Table 4.40 Tile Knives: absolute counts by phase.

Type	Stage 1	Stage 2	Stage 3	Total
Tabular	18	53	19	90
Other	0	6	0	6
Total	18	59	19	96

Table 4.41 Tile Knives: absolute counts by stage.

one side. The working on the less retouched side may have been done to facilitate handling or hafting, if such pieces were hafted. The retouch on the working edge is bifacial, and often pressure flaked. Occasionally tile knives have scratches on the surface of the cortex, usually roughly parallel with and close to the retouched edge, which suggests that they were used with an up and down cutting motion, at least in some cases.

Borers

Borers are varied in shape, generally simply worked on blades and more rarely flakes. As Beck (Rollefson *et al.* 1994: 455) has pointed out, internal variability within the borer tool class has not been examined in detail by most analysts of Levantine Neolithic assemblages. This may be due to low frequencies and high variability, which makes for difficulties in identifying clear groupings. Here a simple classification has been used which is based primarily on blank and number of points. Here too, drills and borers have been classified as distinct tool classes (see 'drills' below) (Tables 4.42–4.43). Borers occur in low frequencies in all stages, but are slightly more common in Stage 2. Almost all the borers in Stage 1 are on blades while a greater proportion in Stage 2 are on flakes. The two in the 'other' class in Stage 1 are of a distinctive type with particularly long, extensively worked points. A small number of similar pieces occur in PPNB and early Late Neolithic contexts on sites in Azraq and Wadi Jilat (Garrard *et al.* 1994b: 89). They occur more commonly at sites around the Wadi Arabah, for example at Late PPNB Nahal Issaron (Gopher *et al.* 1994: fig. 8). Borer

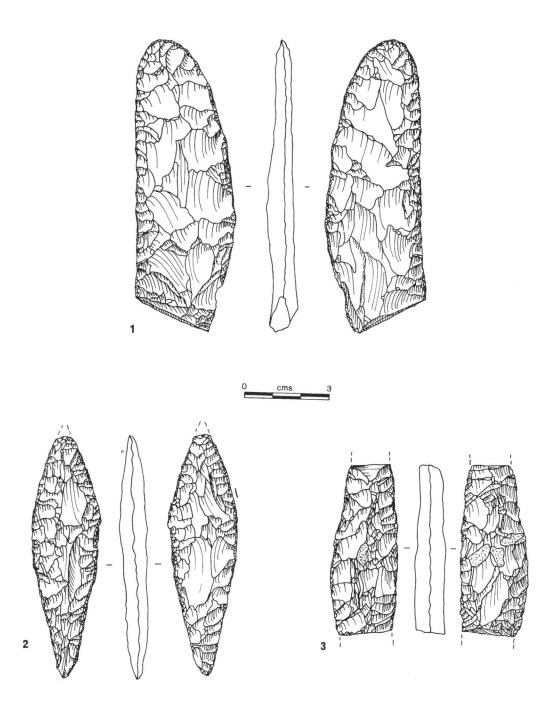

Figure 4.26   Chipped stone: Biface, 'other', 1 Stage 2; Foliate biface, 2 Stage 2; Foliate biface, 3 +.

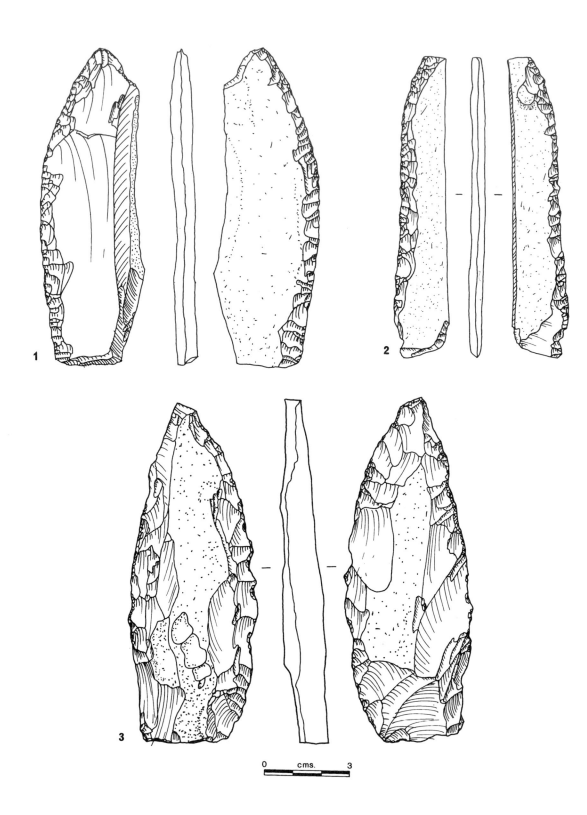

Figure 4.27   Chipped stone: Tile knives, tabular, 1, 3 Stage 2; 2 +.

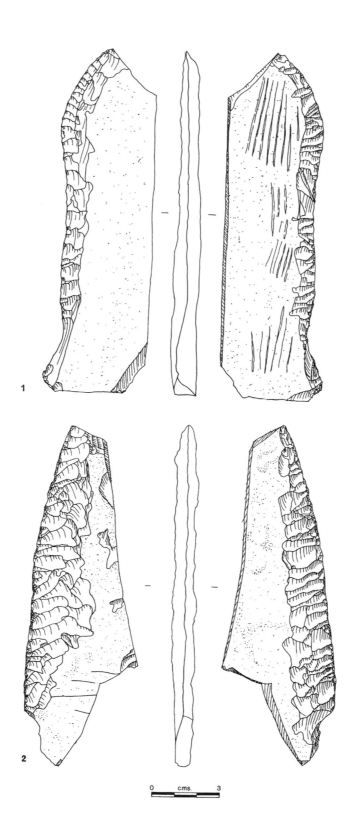

Figure 4.28   Chipped stone: Tiles knives, tabular, 1, 2 Stage 2.

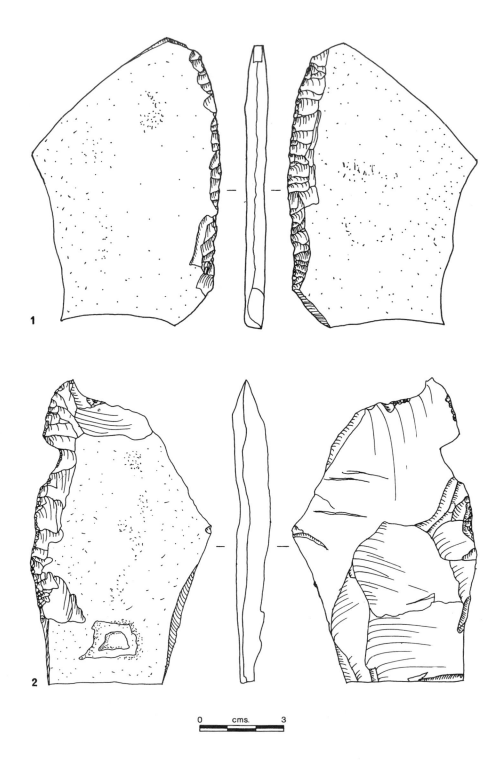

Figure 4.29   Chipped stone: Tile knife, tabular, 1 Stage 2; Tile knife, 'other', 2 Stage 2.

Type	Phase									
	1	*2*	*3*	*4*	*5*	*6*	*7*	*8*	*9*	*10*
Single on blade	2	10	2	1	8	9	5	13	5	6
Double on blade	0	0	0	0	0	0	0	1	0	0
Single on flake	0	2	0	0	2	3	4	2	5	0
Double on flake	0	0	0	0	0	0	0	0	1	0
Other	0	0	0	0	2	0	0	0	0	0

Table 4.42 Borers: absolute counts by phase.

Type	Stage 1	Stage 2	Stage 3	Total
Single on blade	23	32	6	83
Double on blade	0	1	0	0
Single on flake	4	14	0	0
Double on flake	0	1	0	0
Other	2	0	0	0
Total	29	48	6	83

Table 4.43 Borers: absolute counts by stage.

	Phase									
	1	*2*	*3*	*4*	*5*	*6*	*7*	*8*	*9*	*10*
Drill	0	2	1	0	2	3	0	0	4	2

Table 4.44 Drills: absolute counts by phase.

Type	Stage 1	Stage 2	Stage 3	Total
Drill	5	7	2	14

Table 4.45 Drills: absolute counts by stage.

	Phase									
	1	*2*	*3*	*4*	*5*	*6*	*7*	*8*	*9*	*10*
Sickle	1	4	0	2	2	0	1	1	2	2

Table 4.46 Sickles: absolute counts by phase.

Type	Stage 1	Stage 2	Stage 3	Total
Sickle	9	4	2	15

Table 4.47 Sickles: absolute counts by stage.

numbers relative to the whole tool assemblage are similar to those from Wadi Jilat throughout the PPNB and the Late Neolithic (Garrard *et al.* 1994b: 89).

Drills

Drill bits are small pointed pieces worked by use and/or retouch around the tip and for roughly a centimetre below the tip. They are usually made on burin spalls, but occasionally small pointed chips or bladelets are used. They are characteristic of the Transjordanian Neolithic and are associated with the occurrence of truncation burins. It is likely that some burins were used as cores for the production of drill bits, but this may not have been the sole function of the burins (see 'burins' above). Drill bits are also associated with bead production (Finlayson and Betts 1990). On the Azraq/Jilat sites drills on spalls occur from later PPNB occupations onwards, coinciding with an increase in truncation burins (Baird 1993: Sect 8.10; Garrard *et al.* 1994b: 90–1). At Dhuweila small numbers of drills, relatively low numbers of truncation burins and limited evidence for

on-site bead manufacture once again underlines the specialised nature of the site where non-hunting activities were carried out on a restricted basis.

Sickles

Sickles (Tables 4.46–4.47) are defined according to the presence of gloss and not according to the type of tool. Gloss is not necessarily an indication of harvesting (either wild or domesticated plants). It can be created by a variety of other activities including the working of soft and humid mineral materials or materials with minerals included. While such glosses appear similar to the naked eye, they can be distinguished under the microscope (Anderson 1994: 62). The Dhuweila glossed pieces have not been subject to microscopic analysis and so the precise use or uses cannot be determined. However, the low numbers suggest that the activity which created the gloss was not one carried out frequently at the site. Typically, the gloss on the Dhuweila pieces is slight, suggesting limited use. Cutting of plant material can create a gloss visible to the naked eye after one or two hours of use (Anderson 1994: 62), and presumably visible gloss can be created by cutting other materials for a relatively short time. The Dhuweila sickles are mostly blades with a light irregular gloss on an irregularly retouched blank. Only one, from phase 5, has unilateral inverse pressure flaking, and the piece from phase 8 has fine denticulations on one side.

The low number of sickles at Dhuweila is consistent with the evidence from the Azraq/Jilat sites where they occurred only very infrequently (Baird in Garrard *et al.* 1994b: 89).

Denticulates

Denticulated pieces are irregular and are made most frequently on flakes. They occur in relatively low proportions throughout all stages, with a significantly higher number in Stage 2 (Tables 4.48–4.49). The one anomaly is the 'Yarmoukian' piece from phase 5. This is a flake with the deep regular notches typical of Yarmoukian sickle blades. The piece had no obvious signs of gloss and so has been placed in the denticulate category rather than that of the sickles. Its occurrence in Stage 1 can be explained in that phase 5 contains an admixture of Late Neolithic material. Proportions of denticulates within the total assemblage are similar to those in the Jilat assemblages where they average from 1–3% throughout the sequence (Baird 1993: Sect 8.10).

Notches

Notched pieces are irregular and form no obvious subtypes. Most are on flakes but a small number are on blades or blade fragments. They occur in low numbers throughout the sequence (Tables 4.50–4.51).

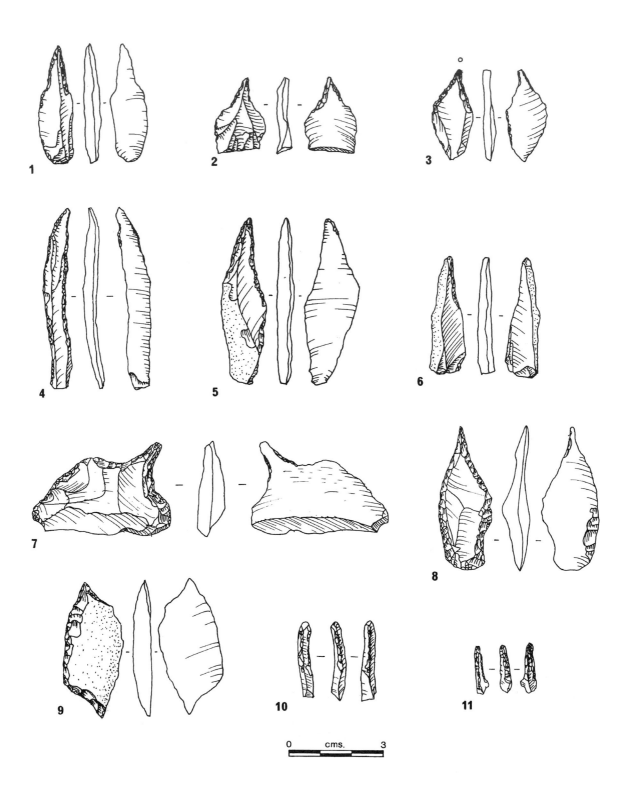

Figure 4.30   Chipped stone: Single borers on blade, 1 Stage 1; 3, 4 Stage 2; 6 +; single borers on flake, 2, 7, 8 Stage 2; double borer on flake, 9 Stage 2; drills, 10, 11 Stage 2.

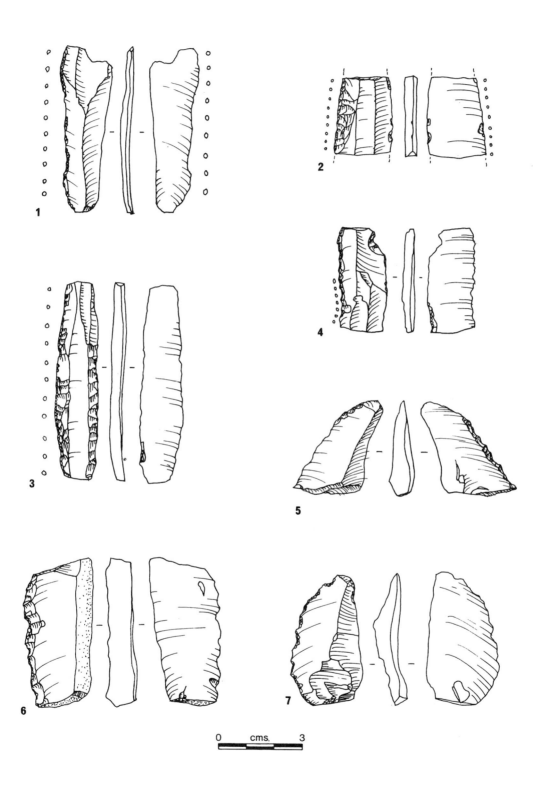

Figure 4.31   Chipped stone:Sickles 2, 3 Stage 1; 1, 4 Stage 2; Denticulates, 5-7 Stage 2.

Type	Phase 1	2	3	4	5	6	7	8	9	10
Flake	1	0	0	0	3	7	5	1	14	7
Blade	2	1	0	0	3	4	4	5	5	3
Yarmoukian	0	0	0	0	1	0	0	0	0	0

Table 4.48 Denticulates: absolute counts by phase.

Type	Stage 1	Stage 2	Stage 3	Total
Flake	4	27	7	38
Blade	6	18	3	27
Yarmoukian	1	0	0	1
Total	11	45	10	66

Table 4.49 Denticulates: absolue counts by stage.

Type	Phase 1	2	3	4	5	6	7	8	9	10
Single	0	1	2	1	4	3	2	2	3	2
Multiple	0	0	0	0	1	1	0	0	0	1

Table 4.50 Notches: absolute counts by phase.

Type	Stage 1	Stage 2	Stage 3	Total
Single	8	10	2	20
Multiple	1	1	1	3
Total	9	11	3	23

Table 4.51 Notches: absolute counts by stage.

Truncations

Truncations on flakes are a feature of the Late Neolithic on the Burqu' sites (Betts in McCartney 1992: 45). There they occur in two forms, one on a small flake or blade segment, and the other on cortical flakes struck from small pebble cores which came into use in the Burqu' sequence in the later part of the Late Neolithic (Betts 1993b: fig. 6, nos. 7,8). Similar truncated pieces also occur at al-Hibr with a steppic Chalcolithic toolkit including transverse arrowheads (Betts 1992). The Dhuweila truncations vary. None are of the pebble core variety but some are similar to the small truncated flakes from Burqu'. They are more common in Stage 2 than in Stage 1 (Tables 4.52–4.53).

Mixed Pieces

Many of the retouched pieces in the assemblage are, by broad definition, mixed pieces, but have been classified according to their most obvious attributes. Burins will often have traces of retouch on some part of the blank in addition to the burin blows, and miscellaneous retouched pieces in some cases clearly were put to a variety of uses. Pieces in the mixed category are only included if they show a range of attributes which put them clearly into two or more of the major tool groups, and where it would be inappropriate to place them in one, while ignoring the other (Tables 4.54–4.57).

Retouched Blades

Retouched blades form a large proportion of the tool kit in all stages (Tables 4.56–4.57). Despite their number, it is difficult to break them down into clear and meaningful subgroups. Most blades have irregular and usually discontinuous retouch, or small patches of retouch at various points around the blank. No clear patterns emerge from study of these and so the data is presented here in the form of broad retouch types. The analysis shows no obvious differences between stages. It is possible that other forms of analysis might prove more sensitive although the *ad hoc* use of blanks may simply be similar throughout the sequence.

Retouched Flakes

Retouched flakes form a smaller proportion of the toolkit than blades (Tables 4.58–4.59), but are similarly difficult to subdivide into meaningful groups. However, some patterns emerged. With flakes, the 'other' category has been separated into two groups which could be clearly isolated and which, in addition, showed apparent chronological variability. One includes cortical pieces, which occur in greater numbers in phase 5 of stage 1 and in the Late Neolithic, probably broadly coinciding with the appearance of cortical scrapers. Some of the cortical flakes from Stage 2 had faceted platforms. The second group consists of flakes with fairly extensive pressure flaking (Figure 4.33, 2–6). These form a consistent group and in other assemblages may have been classified in either the 'knife' or 'scraper' class (e.g. Rollefson *et al.* 1994: fig. 1). Because of their indeterminate function, here they have simply been counted as a sub-group of retouched flakes.

Type	Phase 1	2	3	4	5	6	7	8	9	10
Unipolar	0	0	2	2	3	2	1	2	6	4
Bipolar	0	1	0	0	1	1	0	2	2	3

Table 4.52 Truncations: absolute counts by phase

Type	Stage 1	Stage 2	Stage 3	Total
Unipolar	7	11	4	22
Bipolar	2	5	3	10
Total	9	16	7	32

Table 4.53 Truncations: absolute counts by stage

Type	Phase 1	2	3	4	5	6	7	8	9	10
Mixed pieces	0	0	0	0	1	2	0	0	0	0

Table 4.54 Mixed Pieces: absolute counts by phase.

Type	Stage 1	Stage 2	Stage 3	Total
Mixed pieces	1	2	0	3

Table 4.55 Mixed Pieces: absolute counts by stage.

116

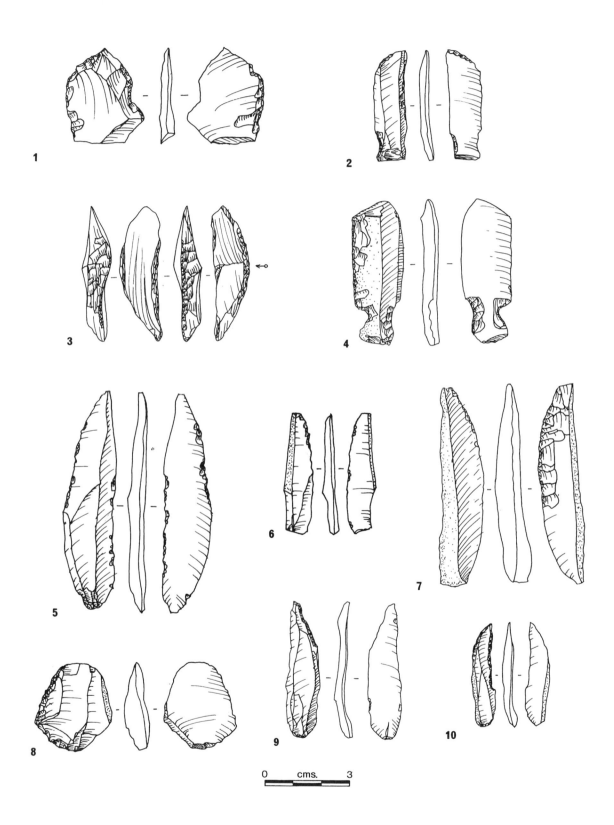

Figure 4.32   Chipped stone: Notched flake, 1 Stage 2; Notched blades, 2, 4 Stage 2; Truncation, 3 Stage 2; Retouched blades, 5-7, 9, 10 Stage 2; Retouched flake, 8 Stage 2.

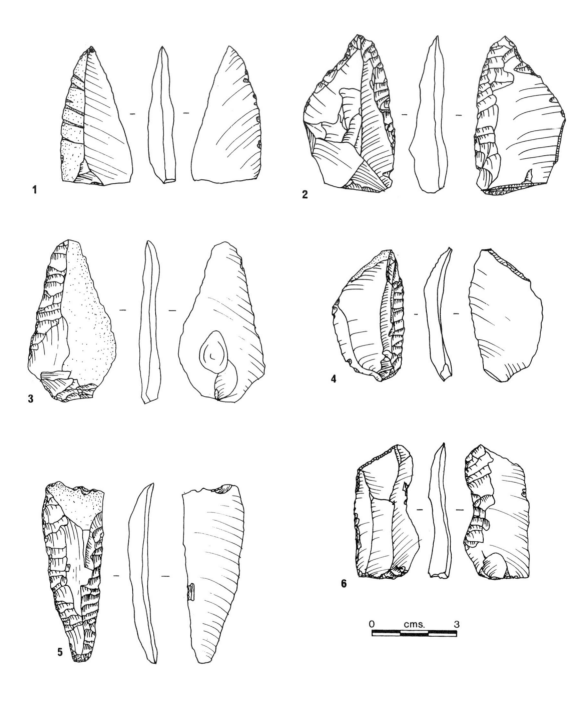

Figure 4.33   Chipped stone: Retouched flake, 1 Stage 2; Pressure flaked flakes, 2, 5, 6 Stage 2; 3, 4 Stage 1.

Retouch	Phase 1	2	3	4	5	6	7	8	9	10
Unilateral normal	33	38	17	17	46	50	22	67	37	31
Unilateral inverse	12	5	1	2	12	14	5	9	14	11
Bilateral normal	10	23	15	5	22	15	11	37	6	14
Bilateral inverse	1	2	0	0	0	0	0	0	9	2
Bifacial	0	2	0	0	1	1	1	1	1	2
Alternate	1	5	10	4	10	7	1	12	3	4
Irregular	21	16	18	12	51	80	30	48	56	57
Other	1	3	0	2	3	4	3	0	4	1

Table 4.56 Retouched Blades: absolute counts by phase.

Retouch	Stage 1 No.	%	Stage 2 No.	%	Stage 3 No.	%	Stage 4 No.	%
Unilateral normal	151	35.87	176	32	31	25.4	358	32.75
Unilateral inverse	32	7.6	42	7.64	11	9.02	85	7.78
Bilateral normal	75	17.81	69	12.55	14	11.47	158	14.46
Bilateral inverse	3	0.71	11	2	2	1.64	16	1.46
Bifacial	3	0.71	4	0.73	2	1.64	9	0.82
Alternate	30	7.13	23	4.18	4	3.28	57	5.21
Irregular	118	28.03	214	38.9	57	46.72	389	35.59
Other	9	2.14	11	2	1	0.82	21	1.92
Total	421	100.00	550	100.00	122	99.99	1093	99.99

Table 4.57 Retouched Blades: absolute and relative counts by stage.

	Phase 1	2	3	4	5	6	7	8	9	10
Unilateral normal	0	1	1	0	2	5	5	3	12	4
Bilateral normal	0	0	0	0	0	1	1	2	3	0
Inverse	0	0	0	0	5	2	6	7	3	4
Bifacial	0	0	0	0	0	0	0	2	0	0
Alternate	0	0	2	0	0	1	0	2	1	1
Irregular	8	18	11	6	25	37	18	45	57	25
Cortical	0	0	0	0	4	1	0	0	4	4
Pressure flaked	0	1	0	1	4	2	4	19	9	6

Table 4.58 Retouched Flakes: absolute counts by phase.

	Stage 1	Stage 2	Stage 3	Total
Unilateral normal	4	25	4	33
Bilateral normal	0	7	0	7
Inverse	5	18	4	27
Bifacial	0	2	0	2
Alternate	2	4	1	7
Irregular	68	157	25	250
Cortical	4	5	4	13
Pressure flaked	6	34	6	46
Total	89	252	44	385

Table 4.59 Flakes: absolute counts by stage.

Summary

While the PPNB of the Levant is well documented from a large number of sites over a wide range of environmentally diverse locations, the technology and tool forms are broadly similar. Dhuweila Stage 1 represents a late stage in the PPNB of the Levant. In chronological terms the chipped stone assemblage fits well with evidence for this period elsewhere. However, while the technology is generally typical of PPNB assemblages in a variety of environmental regions, the range of retouched pieces and their relative proportions demonstrate the distinctive and specialised nature of the Dhuweila economy. Both the association between the site and the 'kite' systems and the faunal evidence (see 'Animal Bones' below) strongly indicate that Dhuweila functioned predominantly as a hunting station. This would account for the unusually high proportions of arrowheads, many of them with impact fracture. Stage 2 represents a slightly different case as there is much less data available on Late Neolithic chipped stone assemblages and of the known sites (e.g. Kafafi 1993; Garfinkel 1993), most are in the fertile well watered areas and are associated with mixed farming economies (but see Goring-Morris 1993). As with the assemblage of Stage 1, the broad range of tools is generally typical of Late Neolithic industries in the Levant, but the specific proportions reflect the peculiar characteristics of the site. Again, arrowheads form an unusually large component of the assemblage, together with burins. Tile knives and tabular scrapers are particularly associated with sites in the more arid regions. Evidence from the Negev and Sinai (Goring-Morris 1993) suggests that tile knives are gradually replaced by tabular scrapers, a change which may also be reflected in the Dhuweila assemblage in the phase by phase breakdown of tool numbers in Stage 2 where the scraper numbers are markedly higher in phases 8 and 9, as well as in Stage 3. Goring-Morris (1993: 85) suggests that the two tool types might be functionally associated with pastoralism, but the Dhuweila evidence indicates that they may be common to steppic industries, but not necessarily exclusively associated with herding.

One particular aspect of the assemblage is significant, and that is the relative proportions of burin types. Unlike the Azraq/Jilat sites where there is a trend throughout the later PPNB into the Late Neolithic towards higher proportions of truncation burins, this is much less marked in the Dhuweila assemblage. This must be a result of economic variability and requires a better understanding of burin function to explain the diversity within the Neolithic of the *badia* (see also Stordeur 1993).

While Dhuweila is within the modern political boundaries of Jordan, the chipped stone assemblage reflects its location within the steppic zone of the greater Badiyat al-Sham, while the similarity of the Badia points to those from Um Dabaghiya indicate connections even as far as the Jezirah.

5.   Dhuweila: Ground Stone

Katherine Wright

Introduction

Ground stone technology can be understood as a form of lithic reduction in which abrasion of rock plays a prominent role. This technology is known from as early as the Upper Paleolithic in the Levant. In the Natufian time range, ground stone tools became much more elaborate and diverse, and this trend continued in the Neolithic. However, Near Eastern ground stone assemblages have been inconsistently documented and classified according to widely varying criteria. This has inhibited inter-assemblage comparisons so that the significance of variations in such assemblages has remained unclear.

Ground stone tools have the potential to inform on questions about subsistence, sedentism, site functions, and, possibly, the size and composition of social groups (e.g. Flannery 1972: 39; Flannery and Winter 1976: 43; Kraybill 1977: 514; Bar-Yosef 1970: 142, 1981c: 154ff., 1984: 157ff.; Hayden and Cannon 1984: 72ff.; Goring Morris 1987: 439; Wright 1990, 1991, 1992, n.d.; Wright *et al.* in press). While detailed discussion of these issues is beyond the scope of this report, the Dhuweila material contributes to an emerging picture of highly variable and locally differentiated Neolithic ground stone assemblages in the Levant (Wright 1990, 1992; Bar-Yosef 1981c: 151ff.). These variations are of particular relevance for questions about regional differences and changes in subsistence strategies as the Neolithic ran its course.

Certain problems confront any analysis of a ground stone assemblage. Ground stone tools may sometimes have very long use-lives in comparison with other kinds of artefacts. Re-use of very ancient tools is widely documented in the ethnographic record and the rate of entry of such tools into the archaeological record may be very slow (Lange and Rydberg 1972: 430; Binford 1977: 34, 1979: 262ff.; Hayden and Cannon 1983: 124; Kramer 1982: 33). These considerations make it difficult to interpret tool frequencies and care must be exercised in making the assumption that grinding artefacts recovered from a given context were actually used as such in that context.

Raw material availability and use

Ground stone assemblages are sharply conditioned by the nature and availability of raw materials for such tools. Fine-grained rocks lacking surface roughness (e.g. flint, fine limestone) have limited effectiveness as grinding tools and would have required frequent rejuvenation of a grinding surface. Rougher materials (e.g. travertine, basalt) should have demanded less retooling and in principle should have longer use-lives as grinding tools. Similarly, variables such as brittleness and compressive strength of raw materials will affect the use-lives of tools designed for either pounding or grinding (Speth 1972: tab. 1; Hayden 1987).

At Dhuweila all of the raw materials used for ground stone tools were immediately available on the site or very close to it (Betts 1985, 1988b). Dhuweila lies amid a vast field of basalt and this was by far the most common raw material in the assemblage (Table 5.2). All of the basalt used for such tools was either non-vesicular or a fine vesicular variety with very small vesicles. Other materials available nearby include flint, fine limestones and coarse limestones. At Dhuweila, the basalt nodules used for most tools were small- and medium-sized wind-abraded cobbles. Grinding slabs and querns were made on larger boulders.

Ground stone lithic technology

Studies of ground stone lithic technology are in their infancy by comparison to analysis of chipped stone artefacts (Hayden 1987; Wright 1992). The use of methodologies developed for the study of chipped stone is justifiable for the study of ground stone, but the term 'ground stone' itself obscures the complexity of the reduction techniques. Such tools may be made on large flakes detached from cores, some exhibit retouch, others are analogous to 'core tools' and some categories of debitage are recoverable. The chief technological difference is the prominent role of reduction by abrasion. In this report the class of 'ground stone' artefacts includes any artefacts in which abrasion has played a prominent role in manufacture or use. However, stone beads and figurines are excluded, although technologically they may fall within the ground stone category.

At Dhuweila, the ground stone technology is characterised by expedient use of immediately available stones and much of the lithic reduction seems to have been the result of use. The tools are often 'outils à posteriori' (Bar-Yosef 1981a: fig. 2) and there are relatively few instances of the modification of blanks by

No.	Context	Phase	Artefact Class	Type
1	****	*	handstone	Bifacial Irregular/Lens Handstone
2	****	*	pounder	Subspherical Pounder
3	****	*	worked cobble	Weight or Knobbed Handstone
4	****	*	axes, celts	Bifacial Miscellaneous Chopper
5	++++	+	perforated tool	Counterpoise Weight
6	****	*	multiple tool	Bifacial Handstone/Unipolar Pestle
7	****	*	multiple tool	Unifacial Handstone/Pestle
8	****	*	multiple tool	Handstone/Knife
Stage 1				
9	2126	2	fragment	Probable grinding slab
10	2210	3	handstone	Bifacial Loaf/Flat Handstone
11	4120	3	multiple tool	Handstone/Chopper
12	2112	5	mortar	Fragment
Stage 2				
13		6	grinding slab/quern	Basin Quern?
14		6	grinding slab/quern	Miscellaneous Grinding Slab
15		6	grinding slab/quern	Miscellaneous Grinding Slab
16		6	grinding slab/quern	Miscellaneous Grinding Slab
17		6	grinding slab/quern	Miscellaneous Grinding Slab
18	4228	6	mortar	Fragment
19	4229	6	handstone	Bifacial Ovate/Wedged Handstone
20	4114	6	handstone	Bifacial Loaf/Triangular Handstone
21	4114	6	pounder	Irregular Core Pounder
22	4228	6	worked cobble	Flaked Cobble
23	4228	6	grooved stone	Cutmarked Slab
24	4229	6	multiple tool	Basin Quern/Mortar
25		6	multiple tool	Bifacial Handstone/Bipolar Pestle
26	4229	6	multiple tool	Bifacial Handstone/Unipolar Pestle
27	4229	6	multiple tool	Handstone/Pestle/Chopper
28	4113	7	handstone	Bifacial Ovate/Planoconvex Handstone
29	4113	7	handstone	Bifacial Ovate/Planoconvex Handstone
30	4115	7	handstone	Unifacial Ovate/Planoconvex Handstone
31	4113	7	multiple tool	Bifacial Handstone/Pestle/Chopper
32	4111	8	handstone	Bifacial Ovate/Flat Handstone
33	4212	9	handstone	Bifacial Irregular/Lens Handstone
34	4212	9	worked cobble	Weight or Knobbed Handstone

Table 5.1   Ground Stone - context and class (**** = 1983 excavations; ++++ = surface)

deliberate manufacture. The form of the original nodule is in most cases retained and not obscured by intensive reduction. The impression is that in many cases the nodules were picked up and used in an *ad hoc* way with minimal preparation. Exceptions to this pattern include a basin quern/mortar (Figure 3.16, BA), a mortar fragment (Figure 5.2: 5), a perforated stone (Figure 5.1: 4) one handstone (Figure 5.3: 2) and possibly two 'weights' (?) (Figures 5.1: 2, 5.6: 2).

Coeval assemblages elsewhere in the Levant contain ground stone tools which were extensively reduced and even 'exhausted', and such assemblages contain high frequencies of flint pounders (Wright 1992). These pounders occur as slightly battered irregular cores which grade into those battered to an almost perfectly spherical shape. The latter are extremely consistent in size and suggest that they had lost utility as percussion tools and were abandoned. Experimental studies suggest that such pounders may have played a prominent role in ground stone manufacturing, especially in the process of 'pecking' (Abbes 1991). At Dhuweila such tools are missing and instances of 'exhausted' ground stone tools are absent.

Stylistic variation does not seem to be prominent in the Dhuweila assemblage, which seems to have been conditioned more by functional variables and progressive lithic reduction through the adaptation of old forms to new functions (cf. Dibble 1987). This kind of assemblage has parallels at some Neolithic sites in the Levant but contrasts with other coeval assemblages, where deliberate manufacture and stylistic variation are evident (Wright 1992). These observations suggest that comparison of specific tool *forms* between Dhuweila and other sites may not be particularly meaningful. On the other hand, comparison of whole assemblages and their underlying technologies may reveal significant patterns.

Definitions of types

A standard classification is a prerequisite for addressing questions about assemblage variations. Most published ground stone typologies are site-specific inventories, which often do not distinguish between the type definition and the sample description. Prehistorians working with chipped stone artefacts have developed

No.	Fig	Mat.	C/F	Wgt.	L.	W.	Th.	Use Traces
1	1.1	BA	C	538	105.2	104.2	36.0	Pigment
2		BA	C	650	93.8	92.1	55.0	Flake scars
3	1.2	BA	C	938	148.5	79.8	60.5	
4	1.3	BA	F	625	117.3	60.7	47.3	Pigment, flake scars
5	1.4	BA	C	1675	186.0	96.4	56.0	Polish
6	2.1	BA	C	780	122.0	75.6	47.1	Polish, flake scars
7		BA	F	625	123.7	79.6	37.4	Pigment
8	2.2	BA	C	275	118.0	52.6	28.2	

Stage 1

No.	Fig	Mat.	C/F	Wgt.	L.	W.	Th.	Use Traces
9		LS	F	1012	137.2	91.0	58.6	
10	2.3	BA	F	312	83.1	63.0	33.1	Pigment
11	2.4	BA	C	375	102.6	64.3	34.2	Polish, pigment
12	2.5	LS	F	450	120.8	65.9	43.0	Striae

Stage 2

No.	Fig	Mat.	C/F	Wgt.	L.	W.	Th.	Use Traces
13		BA	C					
14		BA	C					
15		BA	F					
16		BA	F					
17		BA	F					
18		LS	F	510	97.9	45.0	60.2	
19	3.1	BA	C	1575	149.0	120.2	65.8	Polish, pigment
20	3.2	BA	C	850	210.0	82.4	35.0	Pigment
21	3.3	BA	C	675	121.5	85.5	59.2	Flake scars
22		LS	C	368	95.0	83.9	45.0	Fractures, cracks
23	3.4	FL	C	525	143.3	116.3	22.0	Pigment
24		BA	C					
25	4.1	BA	C	650	117.5	81.7	36.2	Striae, pigment
26	4.2	BA	C	930	164.0	58.4	47.0	Pigment
27	4.3	BA	C	780	186.0	72.0	35.0	Pigment, flake scars
28	4.4	BA	C	780	95.2	77.9	65.4	Polish, striae
29	5.1	BA	C	1100	129.4	94.3	54.0	Polish
30	5.2	SS	C	875	126.0	75.5	65.3	Polish
31	5.3	BA	C					
32	5.4	BA	C	1960	147.2	116.0	68.7	
33	6.1	BA	F	1175	115.5	101.7	54.5	Polish
34	6.2	BA	C	2038	162.0	117.3	100.0	Pigment

Key: BA: basalt; LS: limestone; FL: flint; SS: sandstone;
Mat. = material; C/F = Complete/Fragment; L=Length;
W= Width; T=Thickness.

Table 5.2   Ground Stone - raw material, dimensions and use traces.

relatively standard classifications which have been useful for comparisons (e.g. Bordes 1961; Bar-Yosef 1970). The classification used here is defined in full elsewhere (Wright 1992) and is based on variations in raw material, blank type, primary reduction (flaking, pecking), secondary reduction (abrasion), and morphology of (and macroscopic wear traces on) use surfaces. The typology is regional in scope and hierarchical (Bar-Yosef 1970: 17). The following definitions are confined to the types relevant to the Dhuweila assemblage. The assemblage itself is described in subsequent sections.

Grinding slab/quern

The lower, stationary stone in a pair of (mainly) grinding tools. Most grinding is in a plane roughly parallel to the side on which the artefact rests. Blank type: core, flake, pecked blank or unmodified cobble/boulder. Use surfaces: oval or subrectangular in plan; concave or flat in section. 'Grinding slabs' refer to tools with surfaces indicating lateral grinding in a linear path. 'Quern' is reserved for tools with oval surfaces or *striae* indicating rotary grinding in an elliptical path.

Basin quern

Oval/concave use surface indicates rotary grinding.

Miscellaneous grinding slab/quern

Any grinding slab or quern not meeting the definitions of other types as given in Wright (1992).

Mortar

A lower stationary stone in a pair of (mainly) pounding tools. Most pounding occurs in a plane perpendicular to the resting surface of the artefact. Blank type: variable. Use surfaces: subcircular in plan and concave in section. The deepest part is often pitted with pounding marks. Wear from 'vertical' rotary grinding is often seen on the upper interior side walls. Mortars are formally distinguished from vessels (s.v.).

Handstone

Upper, mobile stone in a pair of grinding tools. Blank type: flake, core, pecked blank, or unmodified cobble. Use surfaces: elongated or constricted in plan; always either convex or flat in section. Marked evidence of pounding is absent (see Multiple Tools). Handstones were classified according to the number of use surfaces, the shape of the artefact in plan, and the shape of the artefact in section.

Bifacial ovate/planoconvex handstone

Blank type: variable. Ovate in plan. Two opposed use surfaces, one flat and one convex.

Bifacial ovate/flat handstone

Same as above but both surfaces are flat and parallel, and sides are approximately straight.

Bifacial ovate/wedged handstone

Same as above but opposed flat faces are not in parallel planes.

Bifacial loaf/flat handstone

Loaf-shaped in plan. Two opposed use surfaces which are flat and parallel.

Bifacial loaf/triangular handstone

Same as above but opposed faces are respectively flat and bevelled.

Bifacial irregular/lens handstone

Irregular in plan, gently convex in section and with straight sides, producing lens-shaped section.

123

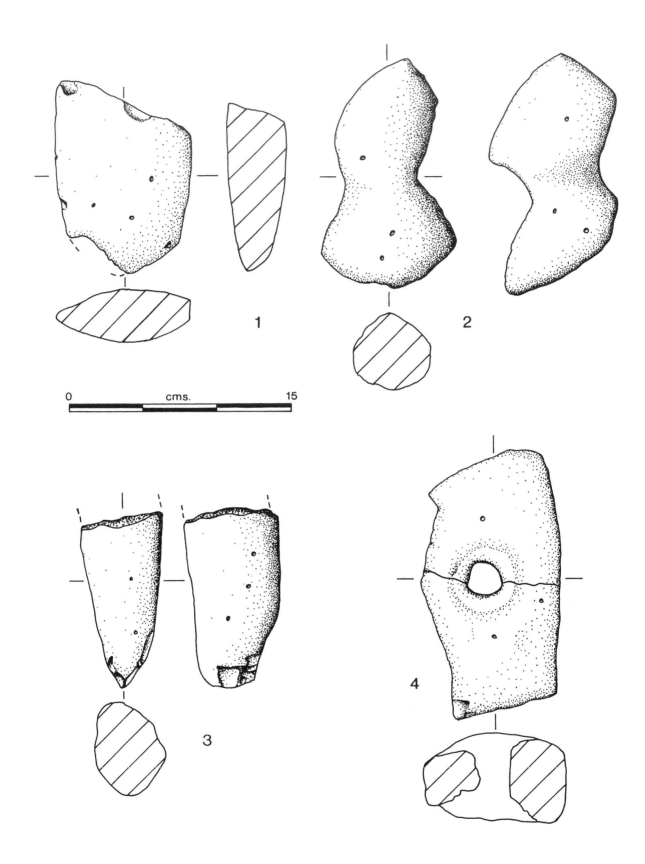

Figure 5.1 · Ground stone: 1 handstone; 2 worked cobble; 3 axe/celt; 4 perforated tool.

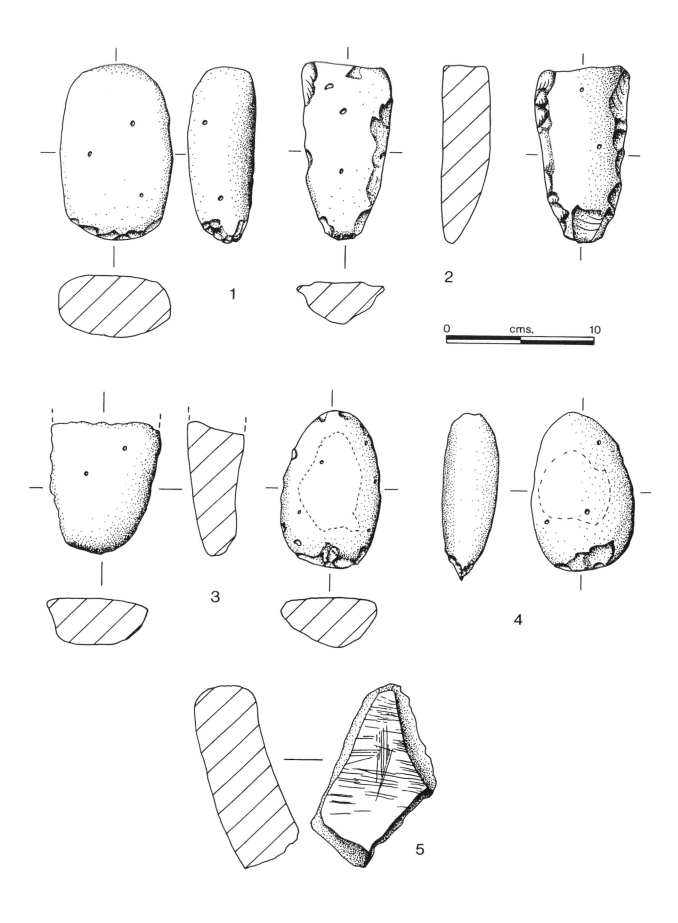

Figure 5.2   Ground stone: 1 multiple tool; 2 multiple tool; 3 handstone; 4 multiple tool; 5 mortar.

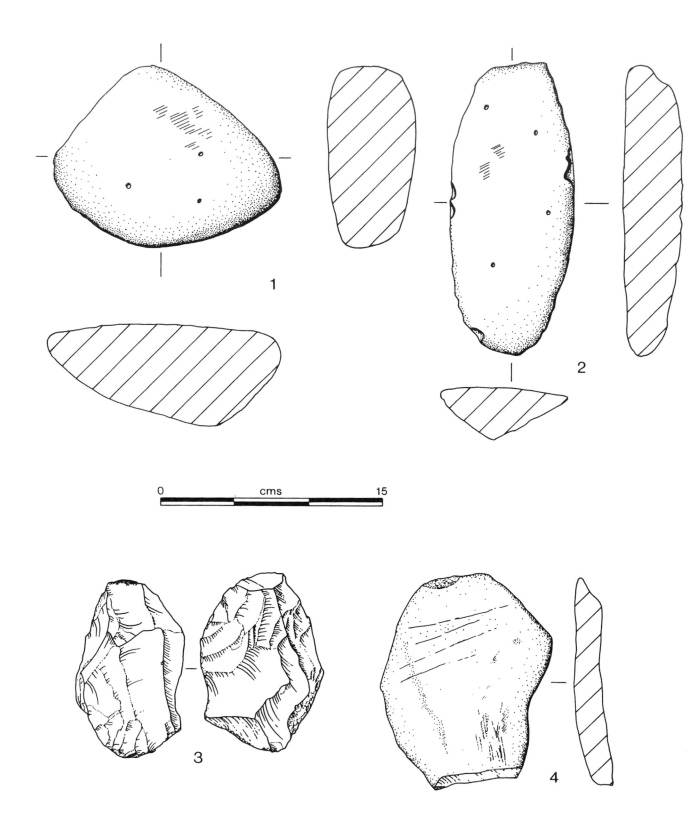

Figure 5.3   Ground stone: 1 handstone; 2 handstone; 3 worked cobble; 4 grooved stone.

Unifacial ovate/plano-convex handstone

Ovate in plan and plano-convex in section. Use surfaces: only one.

Pestle

Upper, mobile stone in a pair of pounding tools. Blank type: variable, often elongated. Use surfaces: subcircular or oval in plan and confined to one or more of the ends of the blank. In section they are convex or flat. There are often flake scars on the sides, with the negative bulb of percussion near the use surface, showing the direction of use. Pestles are classified by the number of use surfaces (bipolar, unipolar) and shape in plan.

Pounder

Blank type: core or unmodified angular nodule. Core tools with heavy battering marks on any or all sides. Battering marks are small, wedge-shaped internal fractures from pounding directed into the stone at a variety of angles. Forms range from irregular to spheroid.

Irregular core pounder

Blank type: cobble or core. Irregular, angular polyhedron shape. Battering marks restricted to a small area (<25%) of the blank.

Subspherical pounder

Blank type: as above. Battering marks cover between about 25% and 90% of the blank, but the tool is not completely spherical and there are angular edges remaining.

Worked pebbles and cobbles

Blank type: unmodified cobble. Artefacts with diffuse use surfaces lacking clear patterning.

Ground cobble/pebble

Blank type: unmodified cobble or pebble. Use surface: one or more ground faces, of irregular shape and distribution.

Flake cobble

Blank type: as above. One or more flake scars.

Axes, celts and choppers

Tools with cutting edges. Blank type: flake, blade or core. Manufactured by combinations of flaking, pecking and abrasion.

Flake/ground 'knife'

Blank type: flake, blade or a tabular core. Any elongated tool ground along the face but flaked along the lateral edges.

Miscellaneous flaked chopper

Any robust chopping tool with an irregular flaked bit.

Grooved stone

Any tool with a groove, defined as a concave use surface much longer than it is wide, lenticular in plan and V-shaped or U-shaped in transverse section.

Cut-marked slab

Blank type: variable. Use surface: always a long and very narrow cut mark, lenticular in plan, and always a sharply angled V shape in transverse section (cf. 'slicing slabs', Hole *et al.* 1969: 192).

Perforated stone

A tool with either a perforation (which connects two sides of an artefact), or one or more drill marks (which do not fully penetrate opposing sides). Perforations are always subcircular or circular in plan, and biconical or cylindrical in section.

Counterpoise weight

Blank type: large pebble or cobble, generally pecked and ground to symmetrical shape. Use surface: a single large off-centre perforation set into one end of the blank, usually the narrower end. The end opposite to the perforated end is usually the broader end.

Stone vessel

An artefact with (1) a well-defined, uniform rim; (2) a well-defined base; (3) one smooth continuous exterior wall surface; (4) consistent or gradually increasing or decreasing thickness of walls from rim to base; (5) grinding and/or finishing on exterior walls. Nothing is implied about whether such vessels in fact functioned as mortars (s.v.).

Multiple tool

Any artefact which fits into more than one category.

Basin/quern/mortar

Same as basin quern but with a mortar surface set into (superimposed onto) the grinding surface (cf. Hole *et al.* 1969: 176, Fig. 75).

Pestle/handstone

Any combination of the other categories of pestle and handstone as listed above.

Unidentifiable ground stone fragments

Possible handstone/grinding slab

A fragment with a single flat ground surface which could be either a handstone or grinding slab fragment.

Unknown

Unidentifiable ground stone fragment.

Artefacts from the 1983 excavation

Eight artefacts were recovered from the 1983 excavation. As these can be only broadly related to the stratigraphic sequence established in the 1986 excavations, they are listed separately from the later finds.

Handstones

1. Bifacial irregular/lens handstone

Handstone with two ground surfaces made on an irregular cobble (Figure 5.1: 1). The artefact has not been reduced by any percussion such as flaking or pecking. Instead, the reduction derives solely from use (grinding). The two faces are heavily worn and form a lens-shaped cross-section. Traces of pigment were found on one use surface.

Pounders

2. Subspherical pounder

A subspherical basalt pounder with battering marks on all sides.

Worked cobbles

3. Weight or knobbed handstone (?)

An enigmatic artefact which seems to have been ground on all sides of a 'waisted' basalt nodule (Figure 5.1: 2). One of the surfaces is broad, flat and somewhat more heavily ground than the others and the artefact may have served as a handstone with a 'knob' for grasping. Alternatively, the 'waisted' shape may suggest that the artefact was used as an anchor to which ropes were tied (compare Figure 5.6: 2b).

Axes, celts and choppers

4. Bifacial miscellaneous chopper

Fragment of an elongated basalt tool which has irregular flake scars on the distal end forming a robust bifacial cutting edge with an acute edge angle (Figure 5.1: 3). There is red pigment on one side of the shaft, but there was little evidence that the shaft had been abraded to any appreciable degree. It is unlikely that the flake scars were solely the result of use; they seem to have been intended to form the cutting edge. Possibly this was a multiple tool for grinding, pounding and chopping.

Perforated stones

5. Counterpoise weight

Counterpoise weight made on an irregular cobble which was only minimally ground across its surface but heavily ground in a depression surrounding the perforation (Figure 5.1: 4). The general shape of the original nodule is retained. The perforation is biconical in section and was formed by drilling from opposite ends. This artefact almost certainly functioned as a weight, perhaps for the support of a light organic roof.

Multiple tools

6. Bifacial handstone/uni-polar pestle

Handstone made on a small cobble and heavily ground on two surfaces (Figure 5.2: 1). The symmetrical shape does not seem to have been formed by pecking in manufacture. Rather, the shape seems to be the combined result of the form of the original nodule and heavy grinding. Pounding on the sides of hammerstones used in blade-making can also form symmetrical 'edge-ground cobbles' (Crabtree and Swanson 1968). The flake scars on one end of the artefact do not form a sharp edge but seem to be either (1) use-wear from pounding on that end; or (2) flaked intentionally to form a rougher surface, perhaps for coarse chopping or pounding.

7. Unifacial handstone/pestle

A miscellaneous handstone with one grinding surface and battering marks suggesting pounding at one end.

8. Handstone/knife

This artefact was bifacially flaked on all edges. The result is a knife-like tool with an acute edge angle (Figure 5.2: 2). The two faces retain the original cortex of the blank but were ground heavily, forming a bifacial handstone with a plano-convex cross section. Traces of pigment were seen on the flattest use surface.

Artefacts from Stage 1

Four artefacts were recovered from contexts in Stage 1 (Tables 5.1, 5.2).

Unidentifiable ground stone fragments (Phase 2)

9. Probable grinding slab

An unidentifiable fragment of limestone, probably part of a grinding slab.

Handstones (Phase 3)

10. Bifacial loaf/flat handstone

A fragment of a loaf-shaped handstone with two relatively flat grinding surfaces (Figure 5.2: 3). Evidence for deliberate shaping of the blank prior to use is confined to the edges which appear to have been slightly pecked.

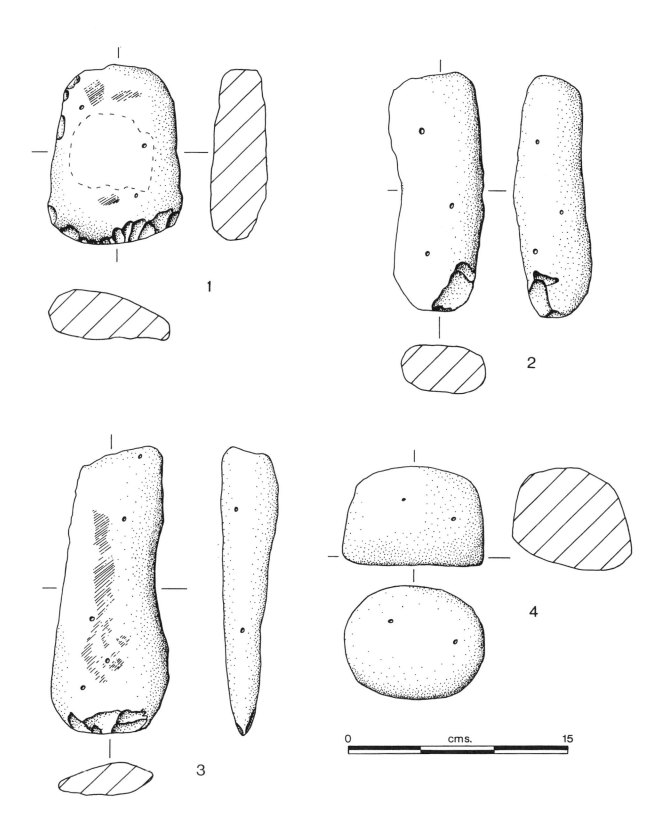

Figure 5.4   Ground stone: 1 multiple tool; 2 multiple tool; 3 multiple tool; 4 handstone.

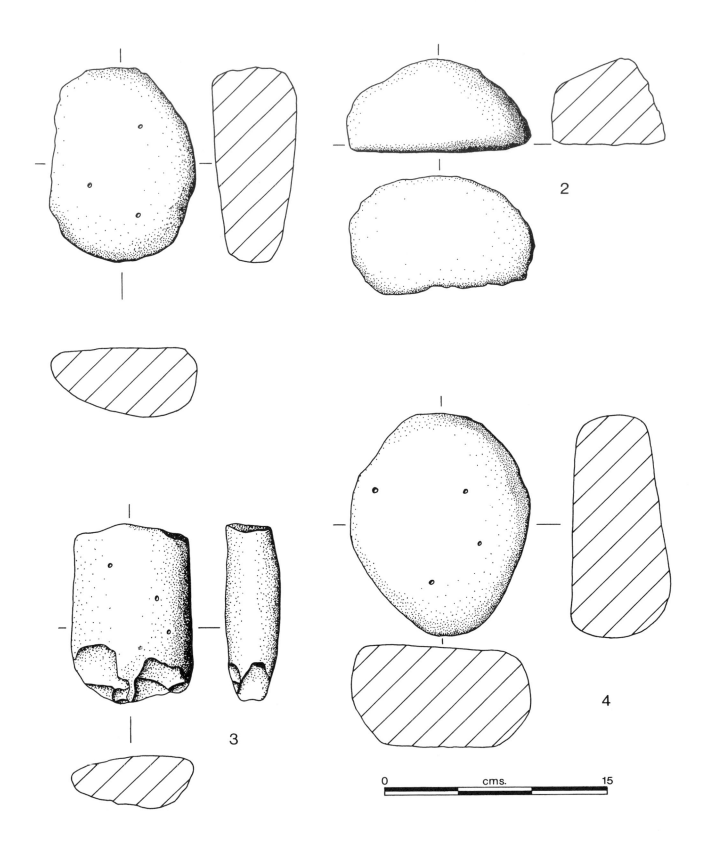

Figure 5.5   Ground stone: 1 handstone; 2 handstone; 3 multiple tool; 4 handstone.

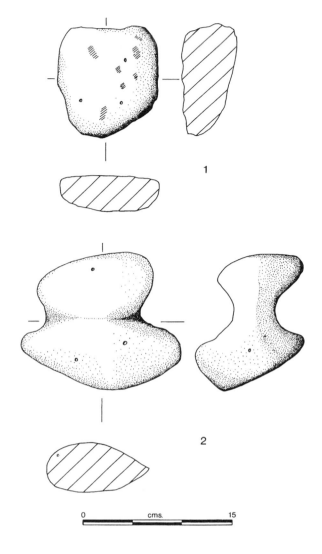

Figure 5.6   Ground stone: 1 handstone; 2 worked cobble.

Multiple tools (Phase 3)

11. Handstone/chopper

An ovate handstone with two grinding surfaces which form a plano-convex cross-section (Figure 5.2: 4). There is a bifacially flaked cutting edge (with an acute edge angle) at one end. There are a few flake scars distributed across the flat use surface and there is some evidence that the tool was slightly pecked and polished (from use?). There is a possibility that this artefact was actually a preform for an ovate celt, such as those seen in other PPNB sites (e.g. Kirkbride 1966: fig. 10, 5). A more conservative interpretation was adopted here.

Mortars (Phase 5)

12. Mortar fragment

A fragment of a limestone mortar (or vessel/mortar) which shows striations on the interior (Figure 5.2: 5).

These striations may have resulted from either manufacture or use and are visible mainly as a result of the soft raw material.

Artefacts from Stage 2

Twenty-two ground stone artefacts were recovered from Late Neolithic contexts. Most of these came from within or just above the phase 6 pavement (Table 5.1).

Grinding slabs/ querns (Phase 6)

Five grinding slabs or querns were built into the phase 6 pavement (Figure 3.16, stippled stones). This raises the question as to whether these tools represent *in situ* activity areas where they were used in place, or whether the slabs were used as grinding tools earlier and only re-used in making the pavement. However, it is likely that the complete basin quern, the complete grinding slab, and the combination basin quern/mortar (see below and Figure 3.16 BA) were used *in situ* by the occupants of the Late Neolithic structure. The three other grinding slabs are fragmentary.

13. Basin quern

A complete quern (Figure 3.16, stippled stones) with an oval use surface was found just to the south of the combination quern/mortar in the pavement (Figure 3.16, BA).

14. Miscellaneous grinding slab

A complete example (Figure 3.16, stippled stones) was found immediately adjacent to the quern/mortar on its northern side (Figure 3.16). The other three miscellaneous grinding slabs (15–17) appear to be fragmentary.

Mortar (Phase 6)

18. Mortar fragment

One limestone mortar fragment was found in the phase 6 contexts.

Handstones (Phase 6)

19. Bifacial ovate/wedge handstone

This artefact appears to have been only minimally reduced by pecking and retains the original shape of the nodule (Figure 5.3: 1). Extensive use of the two broad surfaces has resulted in a bright polish and there are traces of pigment on one use surface.

20. Bifacial loaf/triangular handstone

This tool was extensively used as a grinding tool and there are traces of pigment on the flat face (Figure 5.3: 2).

Pounders (Phase 6)

21. Irregular core pounder

A basalt flake core with a few traces of battering on one side (Figure 5.3: 3).

Worked cobbles (Phase 6)

22. Flaked cobble

A basalt cobble with a few flake scars.

Grooved stones (Phase 6)

23. Cut-marked slab

A tabular flint nodule with cut-marks and pigment on the cortex (Figure 5.3: 4).

Multiple tools (Phase 6)

24. Basin quern/mortar

This artefact (Figure 3.16, BA) is a sub-circular quern with a simple rim and a central depression suggesting rotary grinding on the upper surface and pounding of small quantities on the lower surface.

25. Bifacial handstone/bipolar pestle

This handstone was heavily ground on two sides of a rectilinear nodule (Figure 5.4: 1). Flake scars are distributed along two lateral edges possibly as a means of straightening the edges. On one edge there are numerous flake scars but the flaking is unifacial and does not form a cutting edge. These scars may have resulted from use in pounding, but it is more likely that they are the result of trimming the sides of the artefact to obtain a certain symmetry.

26. Bifacial handstone/unipolar pestle

This pestle bears flake scars from use at one end and exhibits light abrasion around the shaft (Figure 5.4: 2). The irregular form of the original cobble is still evident.

27. Handstone/pestle/chopper

The irregular form of the original nodule is retained in this multiple tool (Figure 5.4: 3). Traces of grinding and pigment can be seen on one surface. The distal end bears scars from bifacial flaking. These scars do not quite meet to form a cutting edge and thus they may have resulted from use in pounding as a pestle.

Handstones (Phase 7)

28 - 30. Bifacial ovate/planoconvex handstone

Three of these artefacts were recovered, of which two are basalt and one (Figure 5.5: 2) is sandstone. One (Figure 5.4: 4) resembles the distal end of a pestle or a 'bell muller' such as occur in PPNB sites (Kirkbride 1966: Figure 5.7: 2). All three were extensively used and were pecked to shape. None have traces of pigment.

Multiple tools (Phase 6)

31. Bifacial handstone/pestle/chopper

This fragment of a flat handstone/pestle has irregular flake scars at one end (Figure 5.5: 3). These are bifacially distributed but do not form a sharp cutting edge. They may have resulted from use as a pestle but also form a blunt edge suitable for coarse chopping activities.

Handstones (Phase 8)

32. Bifacial ovate/flat handstone

A thick and heavy basalt handstone, pecked to an ovate shape and heavily ground on two flat surfaces (Figure 5.5: 4).

Handstones (Phase 9)

33. Bifacial irregular/lens handstone

A handstone made on an irregular cobble which was not shaped by pecking or any other process except grinding from use (Figure 5.6: 1). The two use surfaces are ground heavily, forming a lens-shaped cross-section.

Worked cobbles (Phase 9)

34. Weight or knobbed handstone

This artefact (Figure 5.6: 2) is similar to Figure 5.1: 2 but is larger and heavier. There is no direct evidence of pecking to obtain this shape, although such reduction is likely to have been obscured by the intensive grinding. Since another example exists of this enigmatic tool type, it is likely that this shape was intended. The artefact may have served as a weight or as a 'knobbed' handstone, or both.

Discussion and comparisons

Stage 1

The sample from Stage 1 is too small to permit detailed comparisons with other contemporary assemblages. It is quite possible that a number of the artefacts in Late Neolithic contexts were originally manufactured in Stage 1 and re-used later. This is the more likely since the main structure was rebuilt and the mixing of artefacts in Stage 2 has been alluded to elsewhere (see 'stratigraphy' above). Even accounting for this probability, the data suggest that a limited range of grinding and pounding activities were being conducted at Dhuweila. This would be consistent with an interpretation of Dhuweila as a campsite occupied intermittently for relatively specialised activities (cf. Betts 1989c: 13ff.).

Botanical remains from PPNB contexts at Dhuweila include wild-type einkorn (see 'Botanical Remains' below). This plant requires some form of pounding for dehusking if it is to be consumed on any significant scale (Hillman 1984a, b; Stahl 1989). However, specific grinding and pounding stone tool types cannot be linked convincingly with specific plant resources in the absence of residue studies (Wright 1991, 1992). The scarce material from PPNB contexts at Dhuweila does not inform on the question of einkorn exploitation.

Variations in PPNB ground stone assemblages in the southern Levant are marked. These variations may reflect regional and chronological differences in subsistence and settlement. They may be briefly summarised as follows.

Early/Middle PPNB

Woodland and moist steppes: In the Early and Middle PPNB, assemblages in the woodlands are often immense in size, even accounting for differences in the exposure of excavated deposits (Stekelis and Yizraeli 1963; Kirkbride 1966; Noy *et al.* 1973; Dorrell 1983; Wright 1990, 1992; cf. Nierlé 1983). These large assemblages are closely linked with large sites containing elaborate architecture, burials and other evidence of permanent facilities and year-round occupation (e.g. Beidha, Jericho, Nahal Oren I-II). There is good evidence for cultivation at these sites.

Semiarid and arid zones: In the Azraq Basin, the earliest substantial assemblage comes from Jilat 7, which dates to the mid-eighth to mid-seventh millennium BC. At Jilat 7, large numbers of grinding stones and pounding stones appear in conjunction with the earliest evidence for cereals in that region; the cereals already include domesticated forms (Garrard *et al.* 1988a, b). However, shaft straighteners are one of the most abundant tool types at Jilat 7 and testify to the emphasis on hunting activities at that site (Wright 1990, 1992). Nearby sites contemporary with late phases of Jilat 7 have thus far produced much smaller assemblages (Jilat 32, Jilat 26). Of these sites, Jilat 32 has produced one or two grinding/pounding tools that are similar in form to those recovered from Jilat 7; Jilat 26 has a paucity of such tools (Wright 1992). A coeval site in the Negev Desert (Nahal Divshon) produced no ground stone tools apart from a pair of shaft-straighteners (Servello 1976). These assemblages are quite distinct from Dhuweila's small Late PPNB assemblage.

Late PPNB

Woodland and moist steppes: In the Late PPNB, woodland-zone assemblages are sometimes immense (e.g. Basta: N. Qadi pers. comm.; Nissen *et al.* 1987; Gebel *et al.* 1988); elsewhere they are somewhat more modest but still large (e.g. 'Ain Ghazal: Rollefson and Simmons 1988a: 103, 1988b; Rollefson *et al.* 1989). They are also associated with large sites containing elaborate architecture, burials and other evidence of

permanent facilities and year-round occupation, and there is solid evidence for cultivation at these sites.

Semiarid and arid zones: In the Azraq Basin, few sites can be securely dated to this time range (A. Garrard pers. comm.). Only the PPNB deposits at Dhuweila and Azraq 31 fill this gap and have produced similar C14 dates indicating occupation in the middle to late seventh millennium BC ('radiocarbon chronology' above; Baird *et al.* 1992). Excavated deposits in the Azraq Basin suggest that 'burin sites', which are common in the sixth millennium BC (Betts 1988b: 15) also occur much earlier, as phases in stratified sites of the Early/Middle PPNB (e.g. Jilat 7 and Jilat 26: Baird 1989). None of the secure Late PPNB deposits at Azraq 31 produced ground stone tools (Baird *et al.* 1992).

In the southern Negev, Nahal Issaron C has a large assemblage associated with substantial domestic structures and is dated to the end of the seventh millennium bc (Goring Morris and Gopher 1983: 156 ff.). In the southern Sinai, Ujrat el-Mehed has a very large assemblage (some 201 handstones and 192 broken bowls; Bar-Yosef 1984: 153) which occurs in tandem with circular structures and a burial ground. Ujrat el-Mehed, Abu Madi I, Abu Madi III and Gebel Rubsha have been interpreted as highland, summer camps with high proportions of ground stone tools. Sites at low elevations with small assemblages include Wadi Jibba and Wadi Tbeik (some 30 handstones and 34 broken grinding bowls) and have been interpreted as lowland winter camps of mobile groups (Bar-Yosef 1981b: 565, 1984: 157 ff.). According to this model, Dhuweila and its ground stone assemblage would fit the 'lowland winter camp' category, although Dhuweila's four PPNB artefacts hardly compare with the substantial assemblage from Wadi Tbeik.

Stage 2

A noticable feature of Dhuweila's Late Neolithic assemblage is the high proportion of tools which suggest grinding (handstones, slabs) and cutting or chopping (butchery?) functions. This combination may mirror (in 'impoverished' form) the activities reflected in the Early/Middle PPNB Jilat 7 assemblage, which has high proportions of grinding tools and shaft straighteners. Both assemblages suggest 'base-camp' activities related to hunting and plant-food processing (cf. Betts 1988b: 16). The Dhuweila assemblage also contains weights (for the support of lightweight organic roofs?). The distribution of the tools is consistent with the caching of tools as 'site furniture' (Binford 1978a: 338ff.) in or near a seasonally occupied structure. Most of the grinding equipment was closely associated with the pavement or floor of the structure.

Elsewhere in the region, Late Neolithic levels at Azraq 31 produced a small set (N= 13) of miscellaneous ground stone artefacts of which only a very few were grinding or pounding tools. At Azraq 31, the emphasis on cutting and grinding tools (seen at Dhuweila) is absent. However, Azraq 31 did produce three perforated basalt weights. These were of finer manufacture than the one recovered from Dhuweila, but may have served similar functions (Baird *et al.* 1992). The Azraq 31 assemblage also contained a shaft straightener, a type missing from Dhuweila.

The small size of, and lack of tool diversity in, the Dhuweila assemblage may be part of a larger pattern which seems to characterise the PPNB- late Neolithic transition in the southern Levant. In the well-watered regions, at large village sites such as Jericho and 'Ain Ghazal, ground stone artefacts appear to diminish in frequency and variety from the PPNB to the Late Neolithic (Dorrell 1983; Rollefson *et al.* 1989; Wright 1990, 1992; cf. Hole *et al.* 1969: 351-352, 356, 359). Within the Azraq Basin, there appears to be a marked decline in the frequency and diversity of grinding and pounding tools in sites post-dating Early/Middle PPNB

Jilat 7 (e.g. Azraq 31, Jilat 25, Jilat 13). Ground stone assemblages are often (but not always) absent from 'burin Neolithic sites' of the mid-seventh to sixth millennia bc. (Wright 1992; Betts 1988b; Baird 1989; Baird *et al.* 1992).

If this pattern is confirmed, it may be consistent with the hypothesis that more mobile subsistence systems, including hunting and gathering, and especially early pastoralism, coexisted with or developed from sedentary farming in this time range (Bar-Yosef 1981c: 156, 1984: 157; Smith *et al.* 1984: 106; Betts 1988a,b; Gebel 1988: 94; Köhler-Rollefson 1989; Garrard *et al.* 1988a: 334; Baird *et al.* 1992). Ethnoarchaeological research indicates that present-day mobile pastoralist groups in the Near East use a limited number and range of domestic grinding tools which are not often abandoned at temporary occupations (e.g. Digard 1975: 177ff.; Hole 1978: 153ff.; Cribb 1982: Appendix C, 1991; but see Solecki 1979).

6. Dhuweila: Pottery, Miscellaneous Objects and Imported Items

A.V.G. Betts

with contributions by D.S. Reese, L. Cooke and C. McClintock

Introduction

The excavations at Dhuweila produced only a small number of miscellaneous objects and imported items. Those recovered from Stage 1 were all beads in a variety of materials; bone, shell and different stones, including Dabba 'marble'. There were also stone bead blanks, suggesting that bead making was carried out at the site. Stage 2 had a more varied collection including more beads, an animal figurine, a fragment of stone ring, two bone points and a few potsherds. Beads, sherds and incised chert flakes came from Stage 3 and surface levels. Some may be of Late Neolithic date. The most unusual finds of this stage were small chunks of white plaster, some with fabric impressions on one face. Traces of fibre remaining embedded in the plaster made it possible to identify the fabric as cotton.

Pottery

Stage 1 is aceramic, while only a few sherds were found stratified in levels of Stage 2. A number of sherds was also recovered from surface contexts of Stage 3 (Figure 6.1). Some may be of Late Neolithic date. The sherds are from simple bag-shaped or open vessels. The common ware is a coarse red fabric with basalt inclusions, fired at low temperature. Surfaces of the vessels are either smoothed or burnished. Several of the sherds come from a pot or pots where the clay has been applied in layers (Figure 6.1:3–5). This may be the result of slab construction, a technique which is known from prehistoric Anatolia. A second possibility is that the vessels were form made, with the clay applied in layers over a simple mould. This technique is not reported from other sites, but a similar method was used for the construction of white-ware vessels at el-Kowm (Dornemann 1986: pls. 11, 13).

One sherd is buff ware, made of better levigated clay with chaff temper and limestone inclusions, fired at a higher temperature. It is from a hand-built vessel with a slurred surface (Figure 6.1:2).

Forms are crude and simple, but might be loosely compared with vessels from contemporary Pottery Neolithic/Yarmoukian assemblages in Syria/Palestine (see among others Kenyon and Holland 1982: fig. 8, 6–8; Kafafi 1988: figs. 2–3). It is also possible that No 7 (Table 6.1; Figure 6.1:2) could belong to Stage 3, with a date in the late fourth millennium to early third millennium BC. Bag-shaped vessels are a typical form of the late Chalcolithic/EB IA period (e.g. Betts ed. 1991: see generally genre E, particularly fig. 136.5; Betts ed. 1992: see generally genre 16, particularly fig. 177.2 [with 'finger streaking']; 177.6 [with 'finger streaking' and punctate decoration]; Hanbury Tenison 1986: fig. 25.3–5 [with painted band]; Commenge-Pelerin 1987: fig. 51.3). It stands out from the other sherds as the only piece without basalt inclusions, and must be imported from beyond the *harra*. Although it was found in levels of Stage 2, these were loose ashy deposits quite close to the surface and the sherd might have moved down through the soil.

No.	Context	Phase	Description
1.	4229	6	bodysherd, coarse dark red ware, basalt inclusions, dark burnished interior and exterior (Figure 6.1:1)
2.	2103	6	bodysherd, coarse red ware, smoothed exterior and interior surfaces, basalt inclusions
3.	4210	8	bodysherd, coarse red ware, smoothed exterior and interior surfaces, basalt inclusions
4.	4213	8	two bodysherds, coarse red ware, smoothed exterior and interior surfaces, basalt inclusions (Figure 6.1:5); one rimsherd from form-made vessel, coarse red ware, smoothed exterior and interior surfaces, basalt inclusions (Figure 6.1;4)
5.	4216	8	two bodysherds, coarse red ware, smoothed exterior and interior surfaces, basalt inclusions; one rimsherd from form-made vessel, coarse red ware, smoothed exterior and interior surfaces, basalt inclusions (Figure 6.1:3)
6.	4107	9	bodysherd, coarse red ware, smoothed exterior surface, basalt inclusions
7.	4204	9	rimsherd from bag-shaped vessel, buff ware, chaff temper, limestone inclusions (Figure 6.1:2)
8.	4206	9	bodysherd, coarse red ware, basalt inclusions
9.	0000	+	four bodysherds, coarse red ware, smoothed exterior surface, basalt inclusions

Table 6.1   Pottery Catalogue

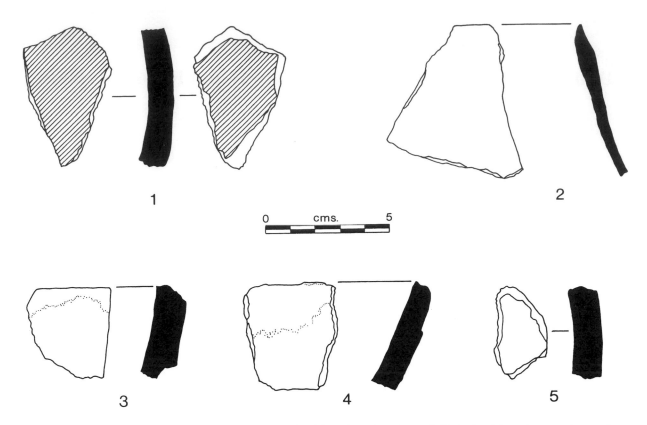

Figure 6.1   Pottery: 1. burnished red bodysherd; 2. rimsherd from bag-shaped vessel; 3. rimsherd from form-made vessel, coarse red ware; 4. rimsherd from form-made vessel, coarse red ware; 5. bodysherd, coarse red ware.

Miscellaneous objects and imported items

Figurine

One figurine was found during excavation. It is a small limestone sculpture of a resting quadruped (Figure 6.2). Bodily outlines are only lightly defined. The legs are folded under the body and the head is held up. There is no indication of a tail, and no details on the head such as eyes, ears or horns. Of the animals familiar to the occupants of the site, the figurine most closely resembles a gazelle. It was found in a Late Neolithic context (Stage 2, Phase 9). The closest parallel for this type of figure is a small animal figurine in limestone from the Pre-Pottery Neolithic site of Jilat 7 (Garrard *et al.* 1986: fig. 9d). Recent excavations at Basta have also produced a similar figurine from a Late Neolithic context (Gebel, pers. comm.)

Stone Ring

A fragment of a limestone ring was found in a Late Neolithic context (Stage 2, Phase 8; Figure 6.3). The inner face has traces of fine horizontal striations and the sides are polished smooth. The outer surface is slightly rougher. Similar rings are known from Neolithic sites over much of the Near East including, in Jordan, Baga, Basta and 'Ain Ghazal (Starck 1988) and also Burqu' (Sites 03 [Betts *et al.* 1990, fig. 10]; 11; 27). At 'Ain

Ghazal stone rings were found in levels of all periods at the site; the PPNB, the intermediate stage of the PPNC, and the PNA. At Baga and Basta they occur in the final PPNB. At Burqu' they were found in Late Neolithic contexts.

Starck (1988) has made a comprehensive study of stone rings from Near Eastern sites. He concludes that there is little variety over a wide area, and that the rings must have served similar functions wherever they were found. The Dhuweila stone ring fragment conforms to Starck's basic type. He notes that most pieces have the same pattern of surface incisions, presumably resulting from the manufacture of the blank. These include horizontal scratches on the inner face, as in the Dhuweila piece. The traditional assumption is that these rings were used as bracelets, but Starck suggests that the wide range of variation in diameters makes this improbable, and offers an alternative explanation that they functioned as pendants or clasp-like ornaments.

Incised chert

Chert flakes with incisions on the cortex have not been widely reported from Near Eastern sites, and there is no particular indication as to what purpose they might have served. There are three examples from Dhuweila, all from unstratified surface contexts (Figure 6.4). The scratches form patterns which appear to be deliberate, rather than the result of use wear, but the designs have no obvious significance. They may be abstract, and are

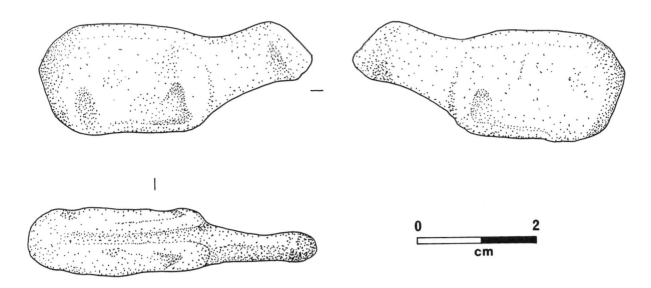

Figure 6.2   Limestone figurine.

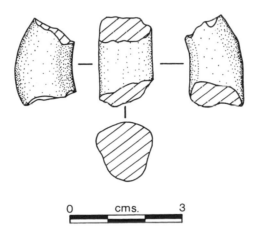

Figure 6.3   Fragment of limestone ring.

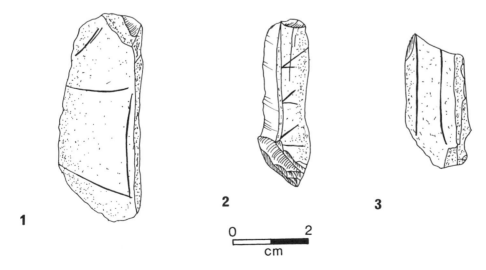

Figure 6.4   Incised chert flakes.

certainly incomplete as all three have lines interrupted at the edge of the flake. There is a published parallel from Pre-Pottery Neolithic levels at Jilat 7 (Garrard *et al.* 1986: fig. 9c), which suggests that these pieces might belong with Stage 1 at Dhuweila, but the evidence is inconclusive at present.

Worked bone

Two worked bone points were recovered from levels in Stage 2, phases 6 and 7. Both are approximately 5 cm in length, and made on longbones of unidentified species. The bone points were not included in Martin's faunal study. Simple bone points of this type occur in both PPNB and Late Neolithic contexts elsewhere in Jordan (e.g. Rollefson *et al.* 1991: 101–2)

Beads

Marine shells (*D.S. Reese*)

Dhuweila today, as the crow flies, is about 200 km from the Mediterranean Sea and 275 km from the Red Sea at Aqaba. Marine shells from both seas are present in the small collection (Table 6.2). Most are Mediterranean forms, but *Engina* and *Nerita* must come from the Red Sea. None of the shells from Stage 1 need come from the Red Sea; all could originate in the Mediterranean. The Dhuweila collection is comparable with other Neolithic shell collections from the Near East (see Reese 1991a for a recent summary).

Cockles and/or *Glycimeris*, generally holed, are known from early to mid-PPNB Jilat 7 and late PPN/PN Azraq 31 (eastern Jordan), from PPNB Beidha and late PPNB Basta (south Jordan), PPNA Gilgal and PPNA

No.	Context	Phase	Description
Stage 1			
1.	****	*	gastropod apical bead, marine origin
2.	4117	1	*Glycimeris* – waterworn, holed at umbo
3.	2126	2	*Cerastoderma* – waterworn, ground-down hole at umbo
4.	2126	2	*Cerastoderma* – waterworn, drilled hole on upper body
5.	2127	2	*Cypraea* (Cowrie) – fragment
6.	2216	2	gastropod apical bead
7.	2108	5	worked nacre (mother of pearl)
Stage 2			
8.	4115	7	*Engina* – ground-down at apex, irregular hole on body
9.	4113	7	Nerita (Nerite) – ground-down hole at apex
10.	4104	9	*Cerithium* (Horn shell) – hole opposite mouth
Stage 3			
11.	3202	10	*Engina* – open apex, two holes on body, one ground-down
12.	3201	10	*Conus* (Cone shell) – waterworn, open apex
13.	4101	10	*Conus/Columbella* (Cone shell/Dove shell) – small, open apex (possibly ground-down)

Table 6.2   Shells (**** = 1983 excavations).

Netev Hagdud, PPN/PN Jericho, PPNB Abou Gosh and Beisamun, and PPNB-C 'Ain Ghazal (Jordan Valley area), early PPNB Sefunim rockshelter, PPN Rakefet, and Neolithic Mugharet Abu Usba (Mount Carmel), PPNB Yiftah'el (Lower Galilee), PPNB Nahal Hemar cave (Judean Desert).

Conus or *Columbella*, usually holed on the apex, body, or made into apical beads, are known from Jilat 7, mid to late PPNB Jilat 26, Azraq 31, PPN Sabra 1 and PPNB 'Ain Abu Nekheileh (south Jordan), Jericho, Sefunim, Rakefet, Abu Usba, Yiftah'el, PPNB/PN Nahal Issaron (southern Negev), and PPNB Wadi Tbeik (south Sinai).

Cyprea are known from Beidha, Basta, Sabra 1, Jilat 26, Yiftah'el, Nahal Hemar, Nahal Issaron and Wadi Tbeik.

Nerita and *Engina* have been widely traded from their Red Sea/Indo-Pacific sources for a long period of time (Reese 1991b). Holed *Nerita* are known from Azraq 31, Beidha, Basta, 'Ain Abu Nekheileh, late PPNB Baga 1 (southern Jordan), Jericho, 'Ain Ghazal, Yiftah'el, Nahal Hemar, Wadi Tbeik and PPNB Ujrat el-Mehed (south Sinai) (Reese 1991a: 617-20, 622). *Engina* are also present at Beidha and Nahal Hemar. The Dhuweila PPNB worked nacre is probably made of *Pinctada margaritifera*, the (Black-lip) Pearl oyster. Ornaments made from this shell are known from various PPN sites: Beidha (43 worked pieces), Basta, Abou Gosh, Beisamun, 'Ain Ghazal (13 worked pieces), Nahal Issaron and Bouqras in Syria.

Stone and Bone Beads (*L. Cooke*)

4119 (Phase 1): bead, possibly a pendant, material unidentified (tooth fragment?), thickness 5.6 mm; length (max.) 23 mm; diameter of hole 3 mm (Figure 6.5:10).

The artefact has had a hole deliberately drilled through from both sides. It is nearly white in colour, and has a greyish line clearly visible running longitudinally. It has a surface which may be incisal, although a dental radiograph shows that it is opaque to X-ray, and does not have a usual tooth (or bone) internal structure.

4233 (Phase 1): green stone (probably apatite) fragment (45%) of long faceted ellipsoidal bead, length 9.8 mm; diameter across middle 5.9 mm; diameter at end 4.3 mm; diameter of hole 1.2 mm (Figure 6.5:7).

The ridge, striations and relative angles of the hole show that it was drilled from both ends. The outer surface has been faceted, and horizontal scratches can be seen. One relatively unscratched area shows a 'spoon-shaped' facet which may have been made by pressure flaking.

2216 (Phase 2): pink stone disc bead (probably limestone), length 1.2 mm; diameter 7.1 mm; diameter of hole 1.7 mm (Figure 6.5:11).

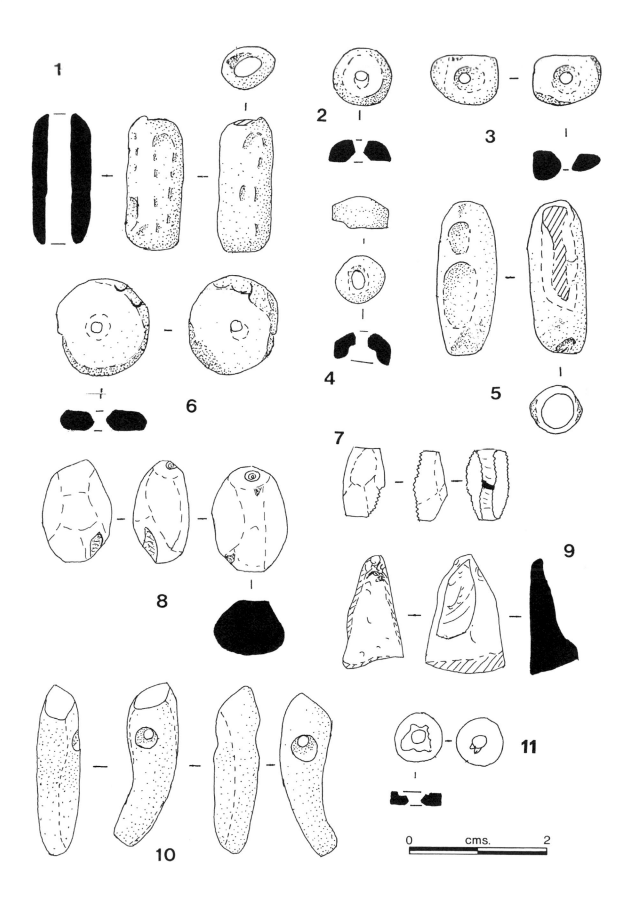

Figure 6.5   Beads (scale 1 cm): 1. bone bead; 2. bone bead; 3. green stone bead; 4. shell bead; 5. bone bead; 6. pink stone bead; 7. broken green stone bead; 8. green stone bead blank; 9. flaked green stone; 10. pendant bead (on tooth?); 11. pink stone bead.

A slight ridge is visible approximately midway down the hole, under a thin layer of accretion, suggesting that the bead was drilled from both ends. The circumference has been rounded and clearly shows longitudinal scratches, indicating directional polishing with a substance harder than that of stone. At one end there is a declivity of irregular circumference surrounding the hole, a feature which was not seen on any other beads. At the other end, there are two small declivities close together and near the hole. The position of these features, and the lack of damage to the rest of the bead, may indicate that they were caused during manufacture rather than through post-depositional damage.

2210 (Phase 3): bone long tube bead, length 18 mm; diameter 7.5 mm; diameter of hole 3.7 mm (Figure 6.5: 1).

This bone is brownish and considerably less clean and fresh than the other bone beads from the site. Dirt is adhering to much of the surface. Some ridging can be observed macroscopically on the shaft. These may be natural features, although there is a possibility that they are the result of deliberate shaping. It is not clear if the hole is natural, enlarged, or man-made.

2209 (Phase 4): green stone fragment (probably apatite), length 16.5 mm; diameter 11.5 mm; diameter of hole 7.4 mm (Figure 6.5: 9).

This bead is five sided, roughly flat at one end, and tapering to a point at the other. One surface appears less weathered than the others, and shows a 'spoon-shaped' declivity, probably due to deliberate working.

2108 (Phase 5): green stone (probably apatite) partly made long bead, length 13.5 mm; diameter 10.3 mm; depth of hole 0.2 mm; diameter of hole 1.2 mm (Figure 6.5: 8).

The piece is both faceted and rounded; scratches indicating deliberate polishing are not apparent. The round declivity at one end has signs of drilling, and is apparently the start of a perforation. The overall shape is not regular, but is roughly the shape of a long ellipsoidal bead.

2108 (Phase 5): short bone bead with curved profile, length 6.0 mm; diameter 8.6 mm; diameter of hole 0.7 mm (Figure 6.5: 2).

The bead shows the typical hour-glass effect of drilling from both sides. The bead resembles a half barrel bead (divided laterally), with a distinct curved, sloping profile and flat ends. The diameter of one end is noticeably greater than that of the other. The bone is cream coloured and appears dense, glossy and undamaged.

2110 (Phase 5): pink stone disc bead, length 3.1 mm; diameter 13.5 mm.; diameter of hole 1.6 mm (Figure 6.5:6).

This bead shows the hour-glass effect of drilling from either end. The outer face is polygonal and has not been rounded by abrasion. It appears to show tool marks, probably the result of pressure flaking. It does not appear to have been completed.

2110 (Phase 5): green stone short bead of irregular form, length 5.1 mm; max. diameter 10. 4 mm; diameter of hole 1.1 mm (Figure 6.5:3).

The hole shows the typical hour-glass effect of drilling from either side. The surface is mostly angular, but curved in places. In cross-section the bead tapers down from thick at one side to thin at the other. The colour of the stone is particularly bright.

4108 (Phase 8): green stone bead fragments, approx. dimensions, length 3 mm; diameter 4.5 mm; diameter of hole 1 mm.

The largest fragment (30%) shows recognisable features from which approximate dimensions were estimated. The piece was probably a short annular or barrel bead drilled from both ends.

2101 (Phase 10): long bone bead, incomplete, length 21.6 mm; diameter 7.6 mm; diameter of hole 2.5 mm (Figure 6.5:5).

A fragment of approximately 40% of the length and 20% of the circumference is missing from this piece. The bone is cream-coloured and appears dense and glossy. Two ovoid spoon-shaped tool marks are clearly visible on the circumference. A triangular nick is apparent at one end. Where the circumference is complete, the hole is filled with dirt, but where it is broken there is no clear evidence of drilling or hole enlargement. The comparatively robust quality of the bone, together with the tool marks, suggest that the removal of the fragment is unlikely to have been the result of a natural process. It is possible that the bead was broken in manufacture.

Impressed plaster

The plaster fragments

Nine fragments were recovered from the excavations. Most of these were flat on one side and rough on the other, with a variety of linear impressions on the flat surfaces. Some of the impressions appeared to have been caused by woven fabric being pressed onto the plaster while it was still soft. The pieces range in size from 1–3 mm in width and 3–5 mm in thickness. On all but one piece (No. 9), one face is rough and irregular while the other is flat. Two pieces (Nos. 5 and 7) show definite fabric imprints, although no evidence of twist or ply of the fibres is evident. Traces of fibres are also present on some of the fragments (Plate 7).

1. 12–2114 (1.9 x 1.5 cm). This fragment has three broad (3 mm) parallel markings across it which are unlikely to be of textile origin.

Context	Phase	Description	
Stage 1			
****	*	shell/bead	
4117	1	shell/bead	
4119	1	bone bead	6.5:10
4233	1	bead, Dabba 'marble'	6.5:7
2126	2	shell/bead	
2126	2	shell/bead	
2127	2	shell	
2216	2	stone bead	6.5:11
2216	2	shell/bead	
2210	3	bone bead	6.5:1
2209	4	bead blank, Dabba 'marble'	6.5:9
2108	5	bone bead	6.5:2
2108	5	shell fragment	
2108	5	bead blank, Dabba 'marble'	6.5:8
2110	5	stone bead	6.5:6
2110	5	bead, Dabba 'marble'	6.5:3
Stage 2			
2103	6	potsherd	
4229	6	potsherd	6.1:1
4229	6	bone point	
4113	7	shell/bead	
4113	7	bone point	
4115	7	shell/bead	
4108	8	stone bead	
4210	8	stone ring, fragment	6.3
4210	8	potsherd	
4213	8	three potsherds	6.1:4,5
4216	8	three potsherds	6.1:3
4104	9	shell/bead	
4107	9	zoomorphic figurine, stone	
4107	9	potsherd	
4204	9	potsherd	6.1:2
4206	9	potsherd	
Stage 3			
2101	10	bone bead	6.5:5
3201	10	shell/bead	
3202	10	shell/bead	
4101	10	shell/bead	
Surface			
++		chip, Dabba 'marble'	
++		incised chert	6.4
++		incised chert	6.4
++		incised chert	6.4
++		four potsherds	

Table 6.3   Pottery, miscellaneous objects and imported items. (**** = 1983 excavations)

2. 14–2208 (1.9 x 1.4 cm). The impression may be a fabric imprint. It has strong linear markings in one direction with no evidence of twist or ply.

3. 22–2214 (1.5 x 1.5 cm). The impression may be a fabric imprint. It has strong linear markings in one direction with no evidence of twist or ply. Some fibres still adhere to the plaster.

4. 25–4102 (2.0 x 2.1 cm). This has linear markings in two directions at right angles to each other. The markings in one direction are more pronounced in one direction than the other. There is no visible evidence of twist or ply of threads but there are traces of charred thread ends preserved (Plate 13).

5. 26–4202 (2.1 x 1.5 cm). This piece has two definite zones. One, as with the previous fragment, shows linear markings at right angles, one more pronounced than the other. The second zone shows four definite bands of a Z-twisted and Z-plyed yarn.

6. 29–4202 (0.8 x 1.3 cm). This fragment has strong linear markings in one direction only, but no evidence of twist or weave. There are several traces of charred fibre ends embedded in the plaster.

7. 30–4104 (3.3 x 2.8 cm). This fragment has three definite zones, two with linear markings in both directions on either side of a zone with nine bands of a Z-twisted and Z-plyed yarn. There are also fibres embedded in the plaster.

8. 35–4208 (1.8 x 2.0 cm). This has linear markings in both directions, with the markings in one direction more pronounced than in the other.

9. 43–4210 (1.8 x 1.6 cm). This has faint markings in both directions, with those in one direction more pronounced than the other. Both sides of this piece are flattened. The reverse of the fabric-impressed side has irregular ridges which appear to indicate that the plaster was pressed up against a hard surface and then pulled away before it had completely set.

Fabric and fibres (*C. McClintock*)

Fabric technology

Since the results of the first analysis were published (Betts *et al.* 1994), further work has been carried out on the fabric technology with results which revise the findings of the preliminary study. The linear markings at right angles could be a tabby (plain) woven structure (Figure 6.6:1), but there is no evidence of twist or ply in the imprints. The bands of Z-twisted yarns (Figure 6.6:2) could have been formed by weft twining where two or more weft threads have been manipulated by hand, introducing a twist between the warp threads (Figure 6.6:3). This is a simple procedure requiring no complicated equipment and can be done in the hand. However, the juxtaposition of the twisted band with the tabby woven structure (assuming for the moment that it is a woven structure) would suggest the use of some sort of loom. Another possible and simple explanation is that the imprints are from lengths of a Z-plyed yarn laid parallel for some unknown purpose.

It is not possible to draw any conclusions as to exactly what textile structure might have caused the imprints. The parallel bands imprinted on two of the fragments are certainly of spun threads, but what they were or why they should be left as imprints remains a mystery.

Identification of fibres

Linen and wool are the two types of fibres used in the ancient world which might be expected in such a context. Linen has a great antiquity in the Near East. Woven linen was found in Nahal Hemar cave in the Judean desert, in contexts dating to the 7th millennium BC, and at the slightly later site of Çatal Hüyük in

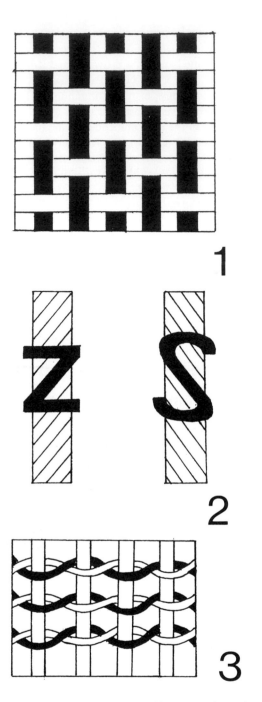

Figure 6.6   Fabric technology: 1. tabby weave; 2. z twist and s twist; 3. weft twining.

Anatolia (Bar-Yosef and Alon 1988; Burnham 1965). Traces of textile were found on a bone object from Çayönü in south-eastern Turkey. The fabric has not yet been identified, but it is likely that it may be a bast fibre, possibly linen (Vogelsang-Eastwood 1993). In Egypt, linen fabric was found at a site of the 5th millennium BC in the Fayum Depression. There is some dispute as to the exact date of the earliest use of wool, but it was clearly in relatively common use by the 4th millennium BC (Barber 1991).

Various methods of analysis are available for identifying fibres. Visual analysis is the first step. Fragments of the mortar containing the fibres were subject to analysis using a scanning electron microscope (SEM). Wool, even very degraded wool, has scales or traces of scales on the surface and can have a dark line: the medulla running along the centre. It also has a fairly straight profile. None of this was present. Bast or stem fibres such as hemp or flax have a long linear profile with transverse dislocation marks at frequent intervals along the fibre appearing as black lines across the fibre. Degradation would add to this appearance.

Cotton is a seed fibre and has a very typical convoluted profile. This is caused when the cotton boll ripens and bursts open, and the individual fibres have dried out and collapsed in on themselves, giving this convoluted, ribbon-like form. Degradation may cause splits in the fibre as it breaks down, but it does not have the straight linear profile of a bast fibre.

Several microphotographs were taken of the embedded fibre at various magnifications. These showed a convoluted profile rather than a linear one, and there was no trace of scales. The fibres, whilst obviously showing signs of degradation did not have the transverse markings of a bast fibre (Plate 7). It was therefore concluded that the fibre was cotton.

Summary

The dates for the samples fall within the Levantine Chalcolithic to Early Bronze Age period, later than the last clearly identifiable Late Neolithic occupation levels at the site (see 'Radiocarbon Chronology' above). This suggests that the fabric fragments found their way to the site through casual visits by nomadic hunters or shepherds. The site does not lie on any important routes and would only have attracted visitors because of the shelter offered by the ruins of the prehistoric structures. It is impossible to determine what the plaster was used for. There are no archaeological or ethnographic parallels which could provide clues, although it might at least be assumed that the plaster was impressed onto scraps of waste fabric rather than on good cloth. Modern beduin frequently make use of fabric scraps for a variety of purposes such as bandages, hobbles for animals, storing small valuables, or as bottle stoppers. The scraps may have been picked up in a town or village beyond the steppe and accidentally discarded at Dhuweila when the plaster ceased to be of functional importance.

7. Dhuweila: Rock Carvings

A.V.G. Betts

Over eighty prehistoric carvings were recorded at Dhuweila and sites in the vicinity. Carvings were found on loose rocks and bedrock outcrops around the sites, and carved stones were recovered from stratified contexts at Dhuweila (see 'stratigraphy' above). All but one of the stratified stones were associated with Stage 1, the late Pre-Pottery Neolithic period. Carvings recorded from surface contexts at two nearby sites, Abu Masiade al-Sharqi and Abu Masiade al-Gharbi, are of the same style, and are also associated with late Pre-Pottery Neolithic occupation sites (see 'area survey' below). Carvings found at other sites in the area were noted but not copied (but see Figure 7.11: 1–3). Most of the carvings showed animals, but anthropomorphic and abstract subjects were also found.

Technique

The most common technique is an outline produced by fine semi-continuous scratched lines. In some cases detail has been added by light, even pecking, particularly on the bodies of the animals. C9 (Figure 7.1), the representation of anthropomorphic figures, was created by heavily pecked outlines, with detail and contrast provided by lighter pecking around the bodies and heads of the figures. It is possible that the final result was based on an incised outline or preparatory cartoon.

All the carvings are on basalt. The weathered surface of the basalt boulders is covered by a thin, black patina. Scratching or pecking this surface exposes the unweathered rock in its natural state. This is whitish grey in colour and stands out in considerable contrast to the darker background. As the exposed surface weathers, it gradually darkens through yellow into reddish-orange until it returns to the colour of the surrounding rock. Most of the carvings have reverted almost totally to weathered black and are only visible in oblique light.

Recording methodology

Each carved rock was given a number. Its dimensions were recorded, together with a description of the carvings. Photographs (B/W and colour) were taken where details would show up on film. Each carving was then outlined in white water-soluble paint and photographed (B/W and colour). Transportable rocks were brought back to the laboratory at the British School in Amman where transcripts were made by tracing off the designs onto sheets of polythene. Carvings left in the field were transcribed from photographs. (Conservation and in-field recording of the carvings was carried out by C. McLaughlin.)

Design and content

Zoomorphic

A large proportion of the carvings are of animals, usually quadrupeds, shown in profile. Some have short, upright or curving horns and a short tail. A few lack horns but have a series of short, oblique lines along the crest of the neck, perhaps a mane. The animals are shown singly or in groups, sometimes overcut one on another. The majority face to the right. Most are standing or running, some are looking back over their shoulder, and one or two appear to be grazing. Two carvings may show females suckling their young. All the zoomorphic carvings are similar in style. The animals are well observed and surprisingly lifelike, given the difficulty of controlling the form of a line on such intractable material. Bearing in mind the faunal evidence from Dhuweila which shows its first occupants above all to have been gazelle hunters, it might be assumed that most of the carvings are of gazelle, drawn by people who were familiar with gazelle behaviour (Figures 7.3–7.10; Plates 8–12).

Anthropomorphic

Two carvings of human figures have been found, one in a stratified context at Dhuweila and the other on a large stone beside the 'kite' wall at Abu Masiade al-Gharbi. Both show groups of figures, face on. They appear to be wearing costumes and headdresses, and carrying sticks or perhaps weapons (Figures 7.1–7.2).

The Dhuweila carving is broken, damaged before it was incorporated into the Early Neolithic pavement. There are three complete figures, and part of a fourth. The Abu Masiade al-Gharbi carving shows two figures, incised in outline with pecking on the bodies. The heads and upper torsos have been damaged, perhaps at a later date. Their costumes are quite clearly represented — they seem to be wearing trousers. These are gathered at the waist, voluminous around the hips, narrow down the thighs, and gathered or cut off just at the knee.

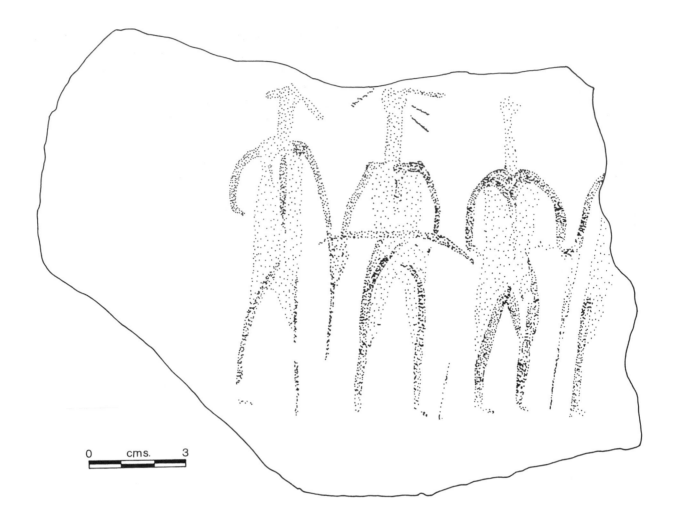

Figure 7.1   Rock carving: Dhuweila (C9) series of human figures.

Abstract

Abstract or ambiguous motifs occur in isolation and in conjunction with zoomorphic designs. In two scenes horned quadrupeds are shown above or beside a pair of parallel wavy lines. Two carvings consist of crossed lines in some form of 'net' pattern. Both of these are small and not apparently associated with depictions of animals.

The third type of abstract motif is the most distinctive. There are three examples, only one of which includes animals. In each case, specially shaped rocks were selected. These are large, flat slabs, roughly triangular in plan, and averaging 60 x 40 cms across. Around some or all of the edges have been cut a series of short, straight incisions. These cuts are fairly regularly spaced, with larger gaps at intervals. No specific pattern can be detected in their length or distribution.

Stratified carvings

Nine carved stones came from stratified contexts. All were loose rocks. Several of the carvings were on the undersides of the rocks or on surfaces covered by other stones. Some were upside down. One carved rock (C6) formed part of a ring of stones around a firepit (P14) sealed by occupation deposits of Stage 1. The stone was badly fractured and had four animals carved on it, two upside down on the face exposed to the fire and two on the side, covered by other rocks forming the rest of the hearth. The anthropomorphic carving (C9) formed part of a stone pavement and was laid at an angle with part of the design covered by another slab. Other carved stones also formed part of pavements and walls. All the stratified carvings appear to have been included in structures without regard for the design. The carvings seem to have held no special significance after they had been created.

0   2

Figure 7.2   Surface carving: Abu Masiade al-Gharbi, two human figures, incised on boulder, detail filled out by pecking.

Discussion

The significance of the carvings

Research into hunter/gatherer art in other areas of the world has shown that motives behind artistic expression are usually complex and often metaphorical. In some cases interpretation is possible through study of the

No.	Context	Phase	Description
C1	2126	2	Incomplete outline of horned animal facing right
C2	2126	2	Incomplete outline of animal(s)
C5	2126	3	Hindquarters of animal facing right
C6	2118	3	Four horned animals, incised on two sides of a stone
C8	****	3	Incomplete outline of single animal (?)
C9	2126	3	series of human figures, full face, pecked
C7	****	5	Two horned animals facing right, incised on two sides of a stone
C4	6002	*	Horned animal facing right
C3	4218	8	Incomplete outline of animal(s)

Table 7.1   Dhuweila: Stratified Rock Carvings

beliefs and practices of modern hunter/gatherer groups (see for example Lewis Williams 1987), but in the absence of similar data for north Arabia, interpretation of the Dhuweila carvings must be limited to basic observation and some tentative hypotheses. Compared to other examples of rock art, the content of the Dhuweila carvings is simple. There are no complex scenes depicting interaction between men and animals, and the designs are strictly limited to three basic images; animals, humans and abstract motifs. This simplicity may be in part a result of the medium. Other, more complex scenes occur elsewhere in Arabia where the local stone is more easily worked (Betts n.d.). However, later Safaitic carvings in the *harra* frequently show complex battle and hunting scenes, carved on the same intractable basalt. This suggests that the Neolithic thematic simplicity was deliberate rather than a function of the carving medium. It can be assumed that the Pre-Pottery Neolithic population was largely pre-occupied with hunting, especially the hunting of gazelle, and that the zoomorphic carvings, at least, reflect this. It cannot, however, be assumed that the images of animals were intended as literal representations of living beasts; the images may well have had a symbolic significance which cannot be determined. Similarly, the anthropomorphic carvings could have a number of meanings. Even apparent representations of weapons, clothing and head-dresses may not be as they seem. Hunter-gatherer art often shows potency, spiritual possession and other abstract notions through additions to the human figure; for example a line extending from the body or an enlarged head. Certainly the abstract designs have meanings which cannot be interpreted.

Evidence for artistic and/or ritual expression has been found at other seventh millennium BC sites in the Near East (Cauvin 1994). The anthropomorphic 'statues' from Jericho (Garstang 1935) and 'Ain Ghazal (Rollefson 1986; Rollefson *et al.* 1992: 464 ff.), animal figurines from a number of sites (e.g. Rollefson *et al.* 1992), and painted plaster floors at Abu Hureyra (Moore 1975: 60) are but a few examples. Ritual disposal of objects was also common in the period, as evidenced by burial practices at 'Ain Ghazal and Jericho involving removal, decoration and separate interment of skulls, and by apparent 'ritual' disposal of the 'Ain Ghazal' 'statues'.

There is no indication that the Dhuweila carvings had any significance beyond their immediate creation. They are not grouped in any obvious way, and when they are 'disposed of', as in their re-use in structures at the site, there is no evidence that the images on the rocks had any bearing on the placing of the rock within the structure. However, it must be assumed that while the Dhuweila carvings may be simple representations of hunters and their prey, it is equally possible that they have complex symbolic meaning.

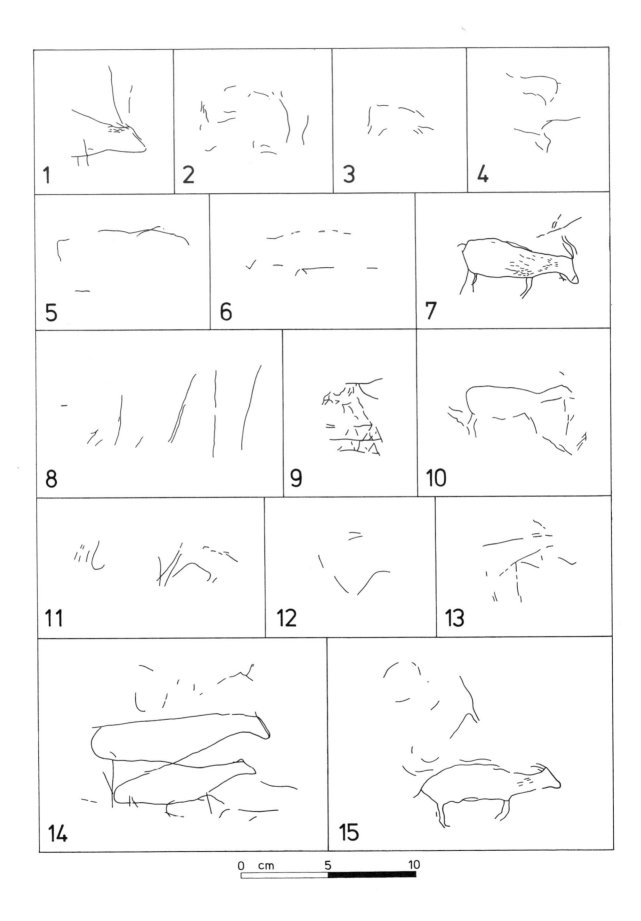

Figure 7.3   Carvings from surface contexts at Dhuweila.

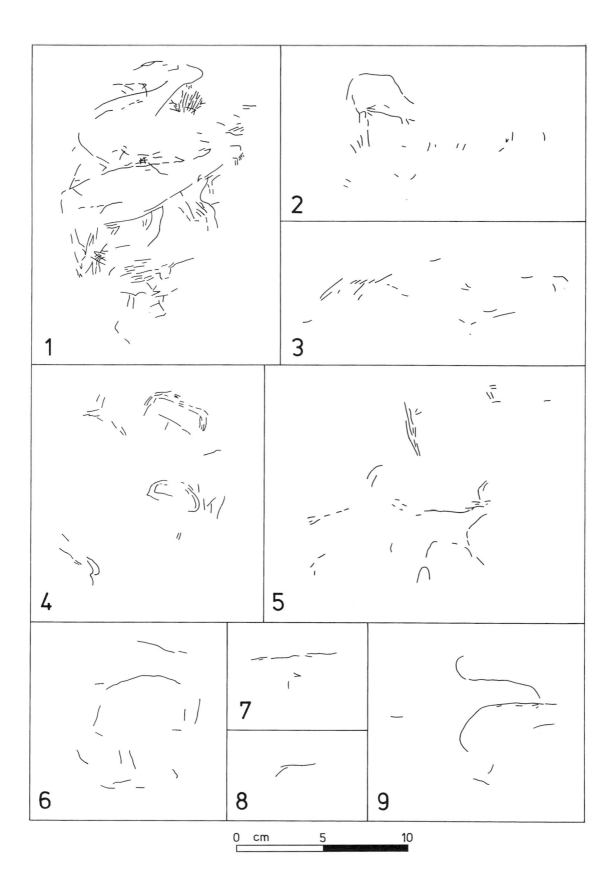

Figure 7.4   Carvings from surface contexts at Dhuweila.

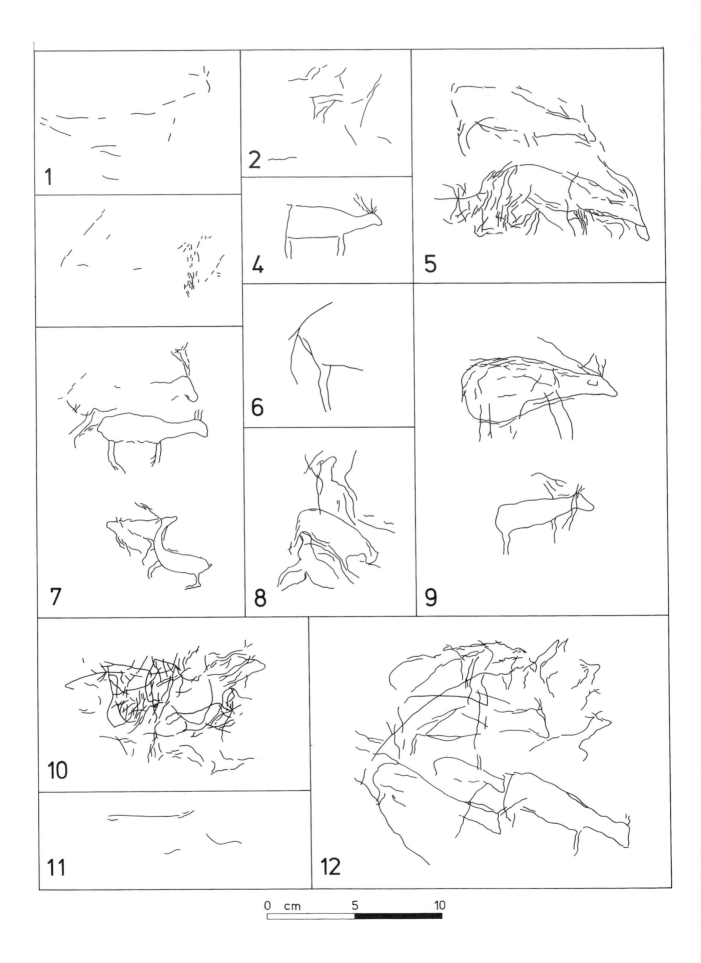

Figure 7.5   Carvings from stratified and surface contexts at Dhuweila.

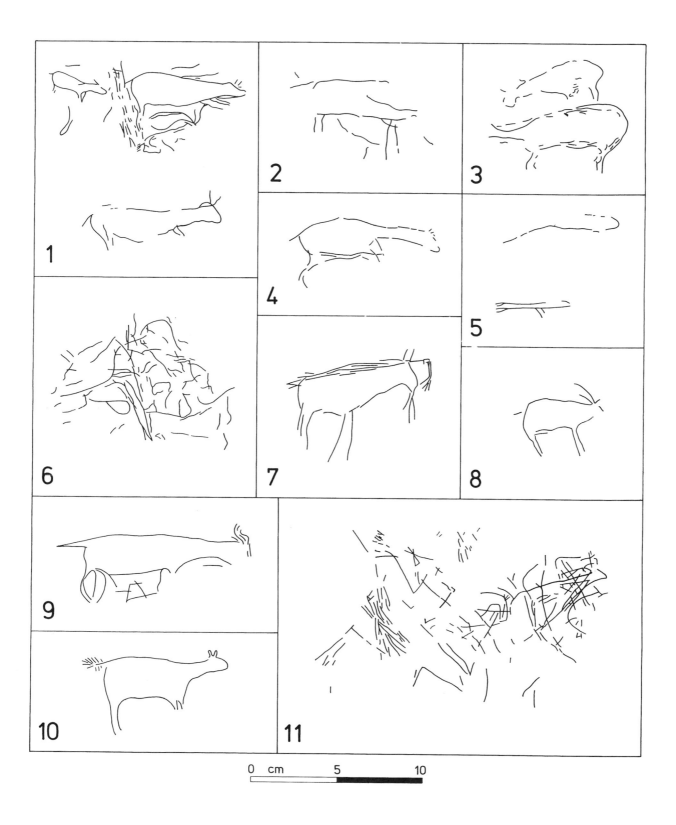

Figure 7.6   Carvings from suface contexts at Abu Masiade al-Sharqi.

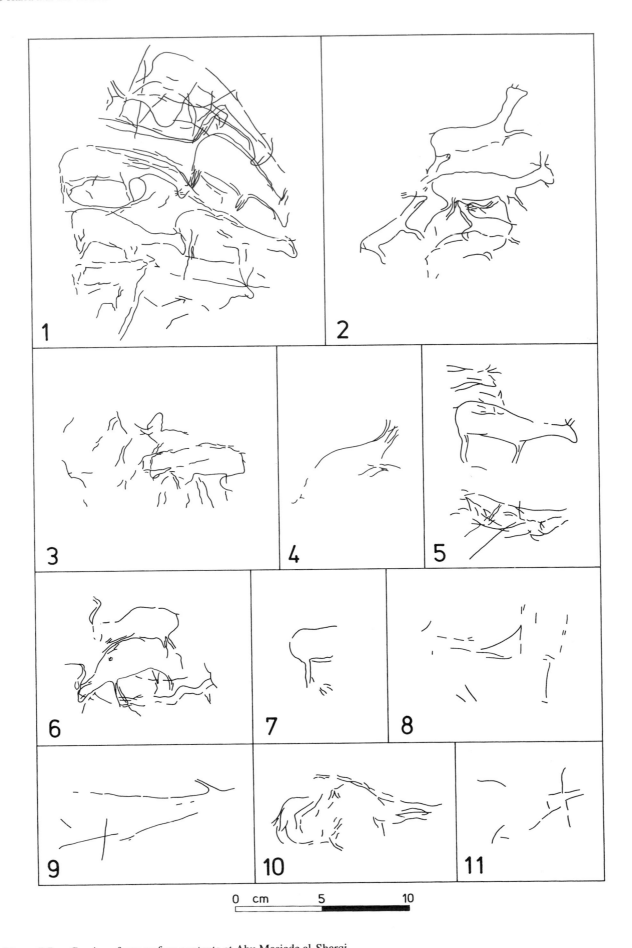

Figure 7.7   Carvings from surface contexts at Abu Masiade al-Sharqi.

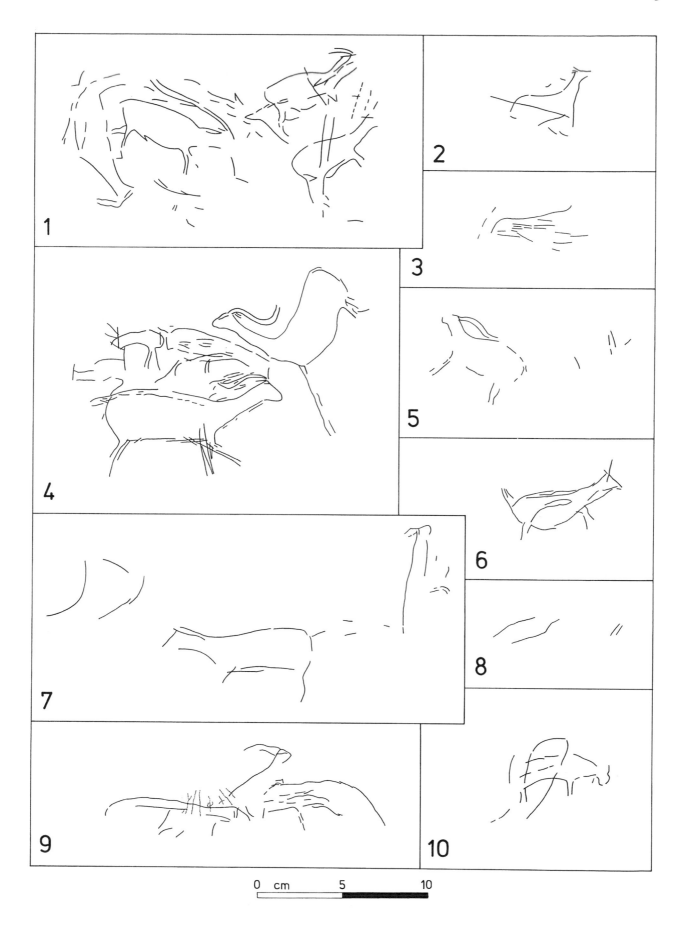

Figure 7.8   Carvings from surface contexts at Abu Masiade al-Sharqi.

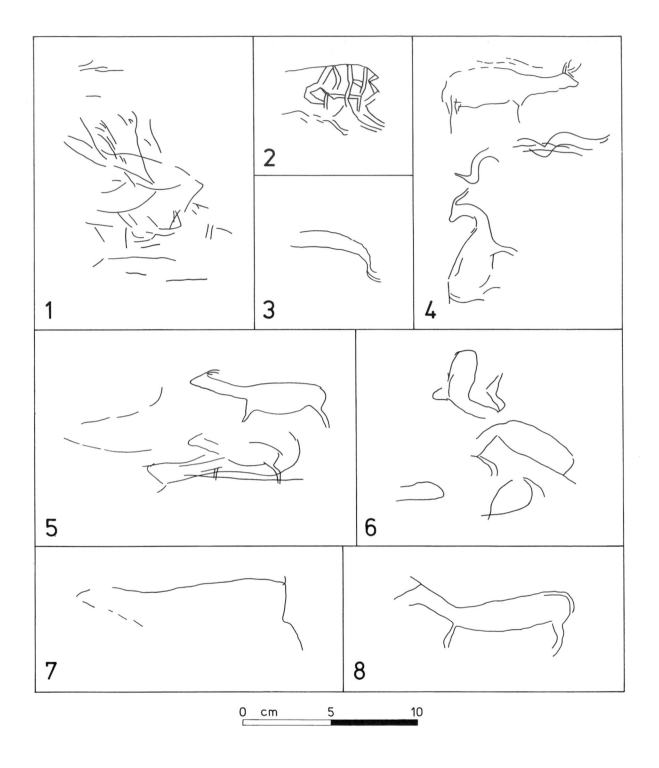

Figure 7.9   Carvings from surface contexts at Abu Masiade al-Sharqi.

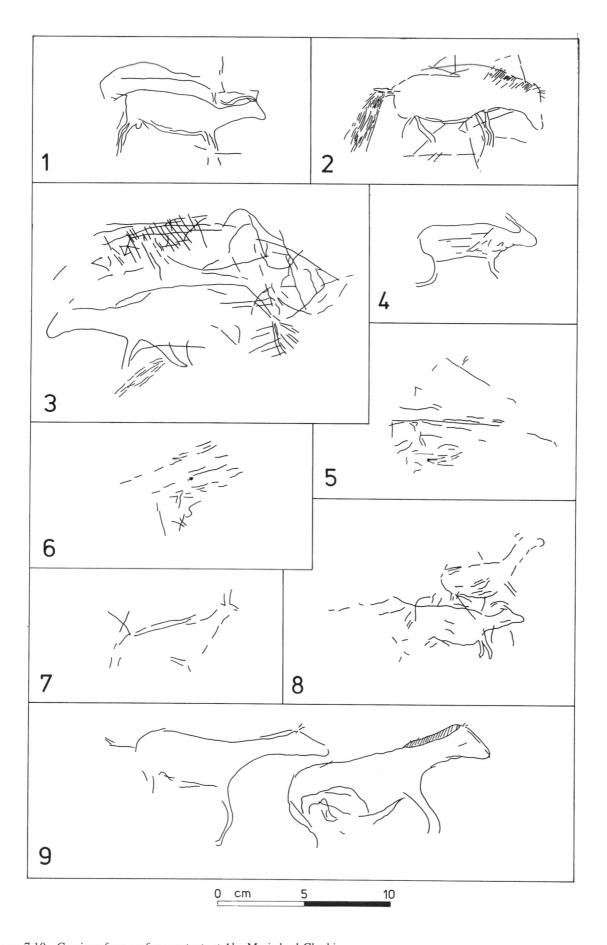

Figure 7.10   Carvings from surface contexts at Abu Masiade al-Gharbi.

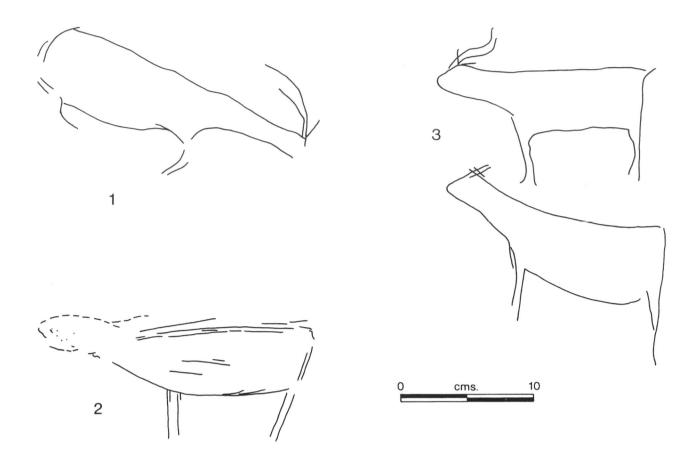

Figure 7.11   Animal carvings: 1. Zumlat 'Arus; 2. Jawa area; 3. region of Bir al-Ghusain.

Parallels and dating

On the basis of stratigraphic evidence the Dhuweila carvings cannot be dated later than the end of the seventh millennium BC. In theory, it is possible that the carvings predate the Early Neolithic occupation of the site, and were either on the hilltop when the site was first occupied, or were brought in from a nearby, and earlier, site. There is no trace of earlier occupation at Dhuweila or in the immediate vicinity. Similarly, there is no evidence that carvings in the 'Dhuweila' style are associated with earlier sites elsewhere in the *harra*. Where they do occur elsewhere (see 'other carvings' below), they are usually close to, or in the rubble of, sites with Early Neolithic flint scatters.

Unfortunately, the Dhuweila carvings have no close parallels beyond the *harra*. A wide variety of rock art styles exists within the Arabian peninsula. Of these various styles, the Dhuweila carvings most closely resemble the 'Early Hunters' group defined by Anati (1968:5, 1972:29). Anati's group encompasses at least three different styles, in two of which human figures are absent or rare. Of the three styles, the closest to the 'Dhuweila' style is his 'Outlined Animals' Style I (*cf.* Anati 1968: 26, fig. 10). These are horned animals carved in thin outline with patinas identical to that of the

surrounding rock face. The style is relatively rare in central Arabia. Anati compares it to carvings from Kilwa (Rhotert 1938; Horsefield and Glueck 1933) in northwestern Saudi Arabia, and from the central Negev (Anati 1979). The 'Dhuweila' style most closely resembles the Central Arabian examples.

Zarins (1990:46) has suggested that the carvings of human figures from Dhuweila have been wrongly attributed to the Early Neolithic, and that the style closely resembles scenes found near Hail and at Jubba (Parr *et al.* 1978: pls. 28–31) which he considers to be Late Neolithic in date. While there is no doubt of the stratigraphic context of the Dhuweila carvings, other Arabian rock art is dated principally on the basis of nearby artefact scatters, and a Late Neolithic date for the Jubba and Hail carvings is not firmly established. However, there are broad stylistic parallels between the 'Dhuweila' style and both Zarins' 'Late Neolithic' and Anati's 'Hunter-Herder' group. The latter includes rows of human figures in pecked outline which might provide a general thematic parallel for the Dhuweila human figures. Zarins *et al.* (1980) mention carvings of *E. hemionus*, caprids and other now unrecognisable subjects at al-Hafna in the region of Mahd adh-Dhahab. The equids, although pecked rather than outlined (1980:

154

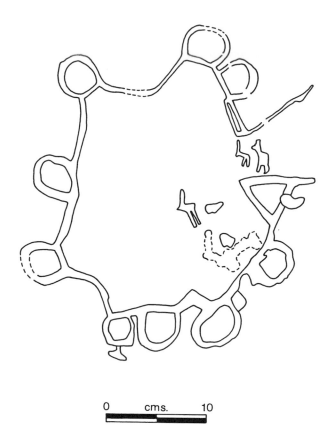

0   cms.   10

Figure 7.12   'Kite' carving from the lower Wadi Rajil.

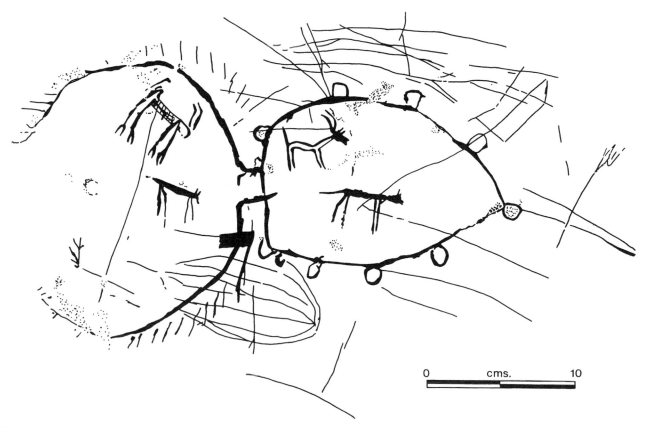

0   cms.   10

Figure 7.13   'Kite' carving from the Burqu' region.

pl. 13a) might provide a general parallel for the Dhuweila wild ass. The same scene also includes rows of pecked human figures, possibly forming part of a hunting scene (1980: pl. 13b). Rock art of apparently early date (Zarins' 'Late Neolithic') has been found in the Northern Province of Saudi Arabia, particularly at Jubba (Parr *et al.* 1978). The so-called 'Jubba' style includes bovids, often with body markings, 'stick' style anthropomorphic figures and also more realistic human portrayals including details of dress and ornament.

Other carvings

Carvings in the 'Dhuweila' style have been found elsewhere in the *harra*. Many were found around the sites of Abu Masiade al-Sharqi and Abu Masiade al-Gharbi (Figures 7.6–7.10; Plates 10–12). A horned animal (Figure 7.11.1) was found carved on a rock near the Neolithic site of Zumlat 'Arus, north of Dhuweila (see 'area survey' below). A carving of two horned quadrupeds (Figure 7.11.3) was found on a stone built into a 'kite' wall beside Wadi Ghusain, just east of the Jebel Ashaqif watershed, and another was found by an Early Neolithic flint scatter on the slopes of 'Maitland's Fort', on Wadi Qattafi. A number of animal carvings in the 'Dhuweila' style have been found around Jawa. Helms recorded one (Figure 7.11.2) near the waterfall above the site (Helms 1981; Betts [ed.] 1992), Macdonald's epigraphic survey team recorded two or three examples about a kilometre upstream from Jawa (Macdonald pers. comm.), and recent survey work located several more on flat slabs used in the construction of pool P1 of the Jawa water system (Helms 1981; Betts [ed.] 1992). Parallels for the human figures may have been found in Wadi Salma, on the eastern side of the Shubeiqa mudflats (King and Montague pers. comm.).

The Jawa carvings are close to 'kite' systems, but are not obviously associated with Early Neolithic sites. However, the largest collection of carvings, those on stones around P1, have all been moved from their primary location. There is no sign of any site nearby, but the area around P1 was cleared for fields and animal pens in antiquity, probably originally in the fourth millennium BC. Consistent use of the area may have destroyed evidence of earlier occupation. The carvings in Wadi Salma were found near a large site with an extensive flint scatter (Montague pers comm.), but the date of the site has not yet been established.

The Dhuweila carvings are associated with gazelle hunters and use of the 'kite' systems (see '"kite' systems' below). While none of the Dhuweila carvings show 'kites', 'kite' carvings , mostly undated, have been found in the *harra*. These fall into two basic groups. The first is a very simple style in which the surface of a boulder is treated as a landscape in miniature (Betts and Helms 1986; see also Tresguerres 1991: fig. 2 for a possible example of this type). The outline of a 'kite' enclosure is pecked around the edge of a boulder, with the 'hides' and guiding arms curving around the stone as if hidden over a hillslope. Most examples have no further decoration, but one, (Figure 7.12) appears to show animals (or possibly ostrich) entering the enclosure. The second group consists of carvings which date in, or are likely to date in, the period of Safaitic inscriptions, broadly from the 4th century BC to the 4th century AD. One such carving is dated in the Safaitic period on the basis of an accompanying inscription and a second one, without inscription but in a similar style, is from a cairn with many Safaitic inscriptions and carvings. Two others are from an area with many Safaitic carvings and appear to be in a similar style. The dated example is the famous 'Cairn of Hani' carving (Harding 1953) which shows (horned?) quadrupeds being driven into a 'kite' enclosure (see '"kite' systems' below). The second example is from the Burqu' area (Figure 7.13). It shows a 'kite' with four animals, two inside and two in the entrance to the enclosure. The upper two animals may be gazelle or goat, while the lower two might possibly be dogs. This carving is interesting in relation to Musil's account of hunting by means of a 'kite'. He describes a trap somewhat different from the 'star-shaped' 'kites' common in the *harra*, but similar to that shown in Figure 7.13. Musil's 'kite' was:

> '... a wall about one and a half metres high, shaped like a figure of eight... The lower loop is only half finished. Where the two loops meet, a narrow opening... is left' (Musil 1928: 26).

The gazelle were driven into the open loop which was said to be about 1000 paces apart at the entrance, narrowing towards the second loop. Once through the narrow gap between the loops, dogs were set on the animals, forcing them to leap over the lower parts of the enclosing walls into pits dug beyond.

Lancaster, in surveys of the eastern *harra* located other, somewhat similar, carvings in the Ghadir al-Wisad (Lancaster, pers comm.). One shows a carving of an oval enclosure with circles attached to its circumference. The entrance and guiding walls are represented by long lines radiating from the right side of the circle. A second carving shows what is probably a 'kite', with an animal, possibly an oryx, inside it. Around the circumference at irregular intervals there are semi-circular projections (Macdonald, pers. comm.). While no direct association can be made between most of these various carvings and the 'kites' themselves, they appear to confirm evidence from archaeology and ethnography that 'kites' were used for hunting in the *harra*, sporadically, if not continuously, from the prehistoric periods up to the recent past.

Catalogue of figures

Figure 7.1   Rock carving: Dhuweila (C9) series of human figures.

Figure 7.2   Surface carving: Abu Masiade al-Gharbi, two human figures, incised on boulder, detail filled out by pecking.

Figure 7.3   Carvings from surface contexts at Dhuweila.

1. head and fore-quarters of horned animal facing right, incised on cobble, some fine scratches on head and shoulders.
2. outline of (?) two animals, incised on cobble.
3. incomplete outline of animal facing right, incised on cobble.
4. incomplete outline of (?) two animals, incised on cobble.
5. (?) incomplete outline of animal incised on cobble.
6. (?) incomplete outline of animal incised on cobble.
7. horned animal facing right, incised on cobble, fine scratches on fore-quarters.
8. series of fine, roughly parallel line incised on edge of large flat boulder.
9. series of criss-cross lines forming crude net pattern incised on cobble.
10. animal facing right, incised on cobble.
11. (?) incomplete outline of two animals, incised on cobble.
12. hindquarters of animal facing right, incised on cobble.
13. incomplete outline of horned animal facing right, incised on cobble.
14. two (?) horned animals facing right, faint outlines of other (?) animals, incised on cobble.
15. horned animal facing right, fine scratches on forequarters, incomplete outline of (?) two other animals, incised on cobble.

Figure 7.4   Carvings from surface contexts at Dhuweila.

1. incomplete outline of two animals facing right, pecking on bodies, other (?) random lines, incised on cobble.
2. hindquarters of animal facing right, other (?) random lines, incised on cobble.
3. series of lines incised on cobble.
4. series of lines forming enigmatic design, incised on cobble.
5. incomplete outline of horned animal facing right, other lines, incised on cobble.
6. (?) incomplete outline of animal(s), incised on cobble.
7. series of lines, incised on cobble.
8. two lines, incised on cobble.
9. (?) incomplete outline of animal facing right, incised on cobble.

Figure 7.5   Carvings from stratified and surface contexts at Dhuweila

1. incomplete outline of horned animal facing right, incised on cobble (C1).
2. (?) incomplete outline of animal(s), incised on cobble (C2).
3. (?) incomplete outline of animal(s), incised on cobble (C3).

4. horned animal facing right, incised on cobble (C4).
5. two horned animals facing right, incised on cobble.
6. hindquarters of animal facing right, incised on cobble (C5).
7. four horned animals, incised on two sides of cobble (C6).
8. incomplete outlines of three animals, one (?) suckling, incised on cobble.
9. two horned animals facing right, incised on two sides of cobble (C7).
10. series of animals incised on cobble (C8).
11. (?) outline of single animal incised on cobble.
12. series of horned animals facing right, incised on cobble.

Figure 7.6   Carvings from suface contexts at Abu Masiade al-Sharqi.

1. three horned animals facing right, other lines, incised on cobble.
2. (?) incomplete outline of animal, incised on cobble.
3. two animals, facing left, pecking on body of upper one, incised on cobble.
4. horned animal facing right, incised on cobble.
5. series of lines, incised on cobble.
6. (?) animals incised on cobble.
7. horned animal facing right, pecking on body, incised on cobble.
8. horned animal facing right, incised on cobble.
9. horned animal facing right, pecking on body, incised on bedrock.
10. (?) horned animal facing right, tufted tail, pecking on body, incised on bedrock.
11. (?) series of animals, incised on bedrock

Figure 7.7   Carvings from surface contexts at Abu Masiade al-Sharqi.

1. series of horned animals facing right, pecking on bodies, incised on cobble.
2. three horned animals facing right, one (?) suckling, pecking on body of central animal, other lines, incised on cobble.
3. (?) series of animals, incised on cobble.
4. incomplete outline of animal, incised on cobble.
5. series of horned animals facing right, other lines, incised on cobble.
6. two horned animals facing left, pecking on bodies, wavy parallel lines below, incised on cobble.
7. hind-quarters of animmal facing right, incised on cobble.
8. (?) outline of animal, incised on cobble.
9. (?) outline of animal, incised on cobble.
10. (?) outline of animal incised on cobble.
11. series of lines, incised on cobble.

Figure 7.8   Carvings from surface contexts at Abu Masiade al-Sharqi.

1. series of horned animals, three facing right, one upside down, pecking on body of central animal, other lines, incised on cobble.
2. incomplete outline of horned animal facing right, incised on cobble.

3. (?) outline of animal, incised on cobble.
4. series of horned animals, incised on cobble.
5. horned animal facing left, other lines, incised on bedrock.
6. animal facing right, incised on cobble.
7. incomplete outlines of animals, incised on bedrock.
8. series of lines, incised on cobble.
9. incomplete outlines of series of animals, overcut by Safaitic inscription, incised on bedrock.
10. incomplete outline of animal.

Figure 7.9   Carvings from surface contexts at Abu Masiade al-Sharqi and Abu Masiade al-Gharbi.

Abu Masiade esh-Sharqi.
1. series of lines, incised on bedrock.
2. series of sets of parallel lines forming geometric design, incised on bedrock.
3. pair of parallel wavy lines, incised on bedrock.
4. two horned animals, set of parallel wavy lines, incised on cobble.
Abu Masiade al-Gharbi.
5. series of incomplete outlines of animals, incised on cobble.
Abu Masiade esh-Sharqi.
6. incomplete outlines of (?) several animals, incised on bedrock.
Abu Masiade al-Gharbi.
7. incomplete outline of animal facing left, incised on cobble.
8. horned animal facing left, incised on bedrock.

Figure 7.10   Carvings from surface contexts at Abu Masiade al-Gharbi.

1. horned animal facing right, pecking on body, other lines, incised on cobble.
2. (?) equid, facing right, pecking on body, other lines, incised on cobble.
3. incomplete outline of animal facing left, bushy tail, other lines, incised on cobble.
4. horned animal facing right, scratches on body, incised on cobble.
5. series of lines, incised on cobble.
6. series of lines, incised on cobble.
7. incomplete outline of animal facing right, incised on cobble.
8. incomplete utlines of two animals facing right, incised on cobble.
9. two (?) equids facing right, incised on cobble.

Figure 7.11   Animal carvings: 1. Zumlat 'Arus; 2. Jawa area; 3. region of Bir al-Ghusain.

Figure 7.12   'Kite' carving from the lower Wadi Rajil.

Figure 7.13   'Kite' carving from the Burqu' region.

8. The Animal Bones

Louise Martin

Introduction

The 1986 excavations at Dhuweila produced over 11,000 identifiable fragments of animal bone which derive from both major stages of occupation. The majority are from the Late Neolithic (LN) levels (Stage 2), although there is also a fairly large sample from the late Pre-Pottery Neolithic B (PPNB) deposits (Stage 1), and a smaller sample from the post Late Neolithic deposits (Stage 3). It should be stressed, though, that remains from Stage 3 could well be residual Late Neolithic material, and may not represent a distinct occupation.

By the late PPNB, many sites in the Levant show high proportions of sheep and goats in their faunal assemblages (Davis 1987), although agreement has not been reached as to whether these remains belonged to animals of morphologically 'domestic' status (Horwitz 1989). It is generally accepted, though, that by the Late Neolithic, herding, and therefore domestication, of sheep and goats was widespread in the region. A glance at the proportions of animal taxa represented at Dhuweila (Table 8.2a and 8.2b) shows that one animal, the gazelle, dominates the assemblage in all levels, indicating that this was not a herding site, but rather that some form of hunting was the mainstay throughout the occupation of the site.

Gazelle hunting has been widely discussed, particularly in relation to the Epipalaeolithic and early Neolithic periods in South West Asia. Suggestions have been advanced as to the nature of gazelle hunting strategies and the degree of human control over this animal. The fauna from the seemingly very specialized hunting and processing site of Dhuweila allows examination of some aspects of gazelle hunting in a steppic environment.

Overview of the sample

All deposits from Dhuweila were dry-sieved through a 5 mm mesh, minimizing retrieval biases against small bones. The animal bones are generally highly fragmented; for medium and large sized animals (gazelles, caprines, equids), the only complete elements found were small compact bones such as carpals, tarsals and phalanges. Long bones are typically only represented by ends and shaft splinters, and teeth are rarely found intact. Possible reasons for this degree of fragmentation will be discussed below (see 'fragmentation'). Here it is necessary only to point out that fragmentation of bone and teeth, plus a high incidence of burning (e.g. 45% of identifiable gazelle bones show signs of burning), has hindered both the determination of gazelle cull patterns, and metrical analyses for all taxa, despite the large sample of bones.

As can be seen in Table 8.1, approximately 17% of the total bone fragment count was identified, and 31% by weight. These figures are low when compared for example with the PPNB site of Basta in southern Jordan where 55% (by count) and 83% (by weight) were identified (Becker 1991: 61). The low identification rate at Dhuweila is likely to result from the high fragmentation of the bone. The higher figure for weights suggests, not surprisingly, that the heavier, larger bones were more identifiable.

What is counted?

What is considered 'identifiable' is always subjective. From the Dhuweila assemblage, all body parts were recorded with the exception of the vertebral column (of which only atlas and axis were counted) and ribs. In the case of long bones, the proximal and distal halves of the bone were treated as separate anatomical units for pur-

	Unidentified Count	Unidentified Weight g	Identified Count	Identified Weight g	Total Count	Total Weight
STAGE 3	3339 (82%)	1943 (73%)	731 (18%)	735 (28%)	4070	2678
STAGE 2 (LN)	39535 (82%)	23144 (69%)	8418 (18%)	10202 (31%)	47935	33346
STAGE 1 (PPNB)	16191 (85%)	10159 (67%)	2786 (15%)	4925 (33%)	18977	15084
TOTAL	59065 (83%)	35246 (69%)	11935 (17%)	15862 (31%)	71000	51108

Table 8.1   The unidentified versus identified bone fragments from the three stages of occupation at Dhuweila, expressed by bone count and bone weight (g) (percentages are shown in brackets).

159

	1	2	3	4	5	PPNB total (Stage 1)	6	7	8	9	LN total (Stage 2)	10	Total Taxa
Mammals													
Half-ass/Donkey	-	-	-	-	1	1	3	-	-	-	3	-	4
Equid	2	5	5	2	14	28	15	8	17	15	55	1	88
Large Herbivore	-	-	-	-	-	-	-	-	3	1	4	1	5
Goitred Gazelle	-	-	-	-	-	-	-	1	-	1	2	-	2
Gazelle	911	264	479	203	744	2601	2222	2220	2295	1180	7917	558	11076
Sheep	1	-	-	-	-	1	1	1	1	6	9	2	12
Goat	-	-	-	-	-	-	2	-	1	-	3	-	3
Sheep/Goat	1	2	-	-	1	4	7	-	11	9	27	3	34
Medium Herbivore	21	6	49	10	3	89	39	67	33	63	202	5	296
Brown Hare	9	5	7	4	12	37	26	19	23	70	138	137	312
Wolf/Dog/Jackal	1	-	1	-	1	3	11	-	1	3	15	-	18
Fox	2	3	3	-	6	14	1	2	1	-	4	2	20
Badger	-	-	-	-	-	-	-	-	-	3	3	-	3
Hedgehog	2	-	1	-	1	4	2	2	4	1	9	-	13
Jird	-	-	-	-	-	-	-	-	1	6	7	7	14
Jird/Gerbil	-	-	-	-	-	-	-	1	1	1	3	-	3
Birds													
Black-bellied Sandgrouse	1	-	-	-	-	1	-	-	-	-	-	1	2
Pin-tailed Sandgrouse	-	-	-	-	-	-	-	-	1	5	6	-	6
Pallas's Sandgrouse	-	-	-	-	-	-	-	-	-	1	1	-	1
Sandgrouse	-	-	-	-	-	-	2	-	-	-	2	-	2
Houbara Bustard	-	2	-	-	-	2	-	-	-	-	-	-	2
c.f. Partridge	-	-	-	-	1	1	-	-	-	-	-	-	1
Quail	-	-	-	-	-	-	-	3	-	1	4	3	7
c.f. Little Owl	-	-	-	-	-	-	-	1	-	1	2	1	3
Little Bittern	-	-	-	-	-	-	-	1	-	-	1	-	1
Cream-coloured Courser	-	-	-	-	-	-	-	-	-	-	-	1	1
Reptiles													
Tortoise	-	-	-	-	-	-	-	-	-	1	1	-	1
Unid. mandibles	-	-	-	-	-	-	-	-	-	-	-	9	9
TOTAL	951	289	545	219	784	2786	2331	2326	2393	1368	8418	731	11935

Table 8.2a The relative proportions of taxa for each phase and stage of occupation at Dhuweila, expressed as the Number of Identifiable Specimens (NISP).

poses of recording and counting (see Smith and Halstead 1989). For the scapula and the pelvis, only the articular areas of each were counted. This method allows for the calculation of both the total number of identified fragments (NISP) and the minimum number of bone ends (MNE) for each taxon. Due to generally poor representation of cranial parts, the following areas were selected for recording: horncore, occipital condyles, petrous temporal, maxillary dentition, mandibular dentition (including root sockets with missing teeth), and mandibular condyles.

All bone fragments that could be identified to anatomical element, either to genus, species, or to a general size category (e.g. large herbivore, medium-sized herbivore) were counted.

Level of analysis

For most taxa, results are discussed for each period (i.e. Stage 1 – PPNB; Stage 2 – LN; Stage 3). Gazelle bones, however, were numerous enough to allow analysis for each substage, which are here termed 'phases' (1-10). Although there is likely to be a degree of mixing between phases, caused by reworking of deposits, reoccupation and deflation of surfaces (see 'stratigraphy' above), these units have been used as the most detailed level of analysis for the large sample of gazelle bones, in an attempt to reduce the 'blurring' of patterns inevitably created by the lumping of material into long periods of occupation (Edwards 1991: 111).

The degree of horizontal patterning within the structure will not be dealt with, since repeated clearing and dumping is likely to have made this meaningless. Phase 5 alone represents material from deposits external to the structure; all others are from internal contexts.

Bone measurements used follow von den Driesch (1976) and Davis (1985) and are expressed in mm.

The relative proportions of taxa

The Dhuweila assemblage includes at least 10 species of mammal, a reptile and a minimum of 9 bird species. The relative frequencies of these remains are expressed as the Number of Identified Specimens (NISP) (Table 2a) and their percentages (Table 8.2b). Table 8.3 shows the Minimum Number of Individuals (MNI) for each taxon per stage/period, calculated using body-side and ageing data. In the discussion of individual taxa which follows, however, the tables present either the Minimum Number of Ends (MNE) or the Minimum Number of Bones.

	1	2	3	4	5	**Phases** PPNB total *(Stage 1)*	6	7	8	9	LN total *(Stage 2)*	10	Total Taxa
Mammals													
Half-ass/Donkey	-	-	-	-	0.1	**0.3**	0.1	-	-	-	**<0.1**	-	**<0.1**
Equid	0.2	1.7	0.9	0.9	1.8	**1.0**	0.6	0.3	0.7	1.0	**0.7**	0.1	**0.7**
Large Herbivore	-	-	-	-	-	**·**	-	-	0.1	0.1	**<0.1**	0.1	**<0.1**
Goitred Gazelle	-	-	-	-	-	**·**	-	-	-	0.1	**<0.1**	-	**<0.1**
Gazelle	96	92	88	93	95	**93**	95	95	96	86	**94**	76	**93**
Sheep	0.1	-	-	-	-	**<0.1**	<0.1	<0.1	<0.1	0.4	**0.1**	0.1	**0.1**
Goat	-	-	-	-	-	**·**	0.1	-	<0.1	-	**<0.1**	-	**<0.1**
Sheep/Goat	0.1	0.7	-	-	0.1	**0.1**	0.3	-	0.5	0.7	**0.3**	0.4	**0.3**
Medium Herbivore	2.2	2.0	9.0	4.5	0.4	**3.2**	1.7	2.8	1.4	4.6	**2.4**	0.7	**2.5**
Brown Hare	0.9	1.7	1.0	1.8	1.5	**1.3**	1.0	0.8	1.0	5.0	**1.6**	19.0	**2.6**
Wolf/Dog/Jackal	0.1	-	0.2	-	0.1	**0.1**	0.5	-	<0.1	0.2	**0.2**	-	**0.2**
Fox	0.2	1.0	0.6	-	0.8	**0.5**	<0.1	0.1	<0.1	-	**<0.1**	0.3	**0.2**
Badger	-	-	-	-	-	**·**	-	-	-	0.2	**<0.1**	-	**<0.1**
Hedgehog	0.2	-	0.2	-	0.1	**0.1**	0.1	0.1	0.2	0.1	**0.1**	-	**0.1**
Jird	-	-	-	-	-	**·**	-	-	<0.1	0.4	**0.1**	1.0	**0.1**
Jird/Gerbil	-	-	-	-	-	**·**	-	<0.1	<0.1	0.1	**<0.1**	-	**<0.1**
Birds													
Black-bellied Sandgrouse	0.1	-	-	-	-	**<0.1**	-	-	-	-	**·**	0.1	**<0.1**
Pin-tailed Sandgrouse	-	-	-	-	-	**·**	-	-	<0.1	0.3	**0.1**	-	**0.1**
Pallas's Sandgrouse	-	-	-	-	-	**·**	-	-	-	0.1	**<0.1**	-	**<0.1**
Sandgrouse	-	-	-	-	-	**·**	0.1	-	-	-	**<0.1**	-	**<0.1**
Houbara Bustard	-	0.7	-	-	-	**0.7**	-	-	-	-	**·**	-	**<0.1**
c.f. Partridge	-	-	-	-	0.1	**<0.1**	-	-	-	-	**·**	-	**<0.1**
Quail	-	-	-	-	-	**·**	-	0.1	-	0.1	**<0.1**	0.3	**0.1**
c.f. Little Owl	-	-	-	-	-	**·**	-	<0.1	-	0.1	**<0.1**	0.1	**<0.1**
Little Bittern	-	-	-	-	-	**·**	-	<0.1	-	-	**<0.1**	-	**<0.1**
Cream-coloured Courser	-	-	-	-	-	**·**	-	-	-	-	**·**	0.1	**<0.1**
Reptiles													
Tortoise	-	-	-	-	-	**·**	-	-	-	<0.1	**<0.1**	-	**<0.1**
Unid. mandibles	-	-	-	-	-	**·**	-	-	-	-	**·**	0.1	**0.1**

Table 8.2b The relative proportions of taxa for each phase and stage of occupation at Dhuweila, expressed as percentages (NISP).

Species list

MAMMALS

Equus hemionus/asinus	Asiatic half ass/donkey
Equus spp.	ass/donkey/horse
Gazella subgutturosa	Goitred gazelle
Gazella spp.	gazelle
Ovis spp.	wild sheep/sheep
Capra spp.	wild goat/ibex/goat
Lepus sp.	hare
Canis spp.	wolf/dog/jackal
Vulpes spp.	fox
Meles meles	badger
Hemiechinus/Paraechinus spp.	hedgehog
Meriones sp.	jird
Meriones/Gerbillus spp.	jird/gerbil

BIRDS

Pterocles orientalis	black-bellied sandgrouse
Pterocles alchata	pin-tailed sandgrouse
Syrrhaptes alchata	Pallas's sandgrouse
Pterocles/Syrrhaptes	sandgrouse
Chlamydotis undulata	Houbara bustard
cf. *Perdix perdix*	partridge
Coturnix coturnix	quail
cf. *Athene noctua*	little owl
Ixobrychus minutus	little bittern
Cursorius cursor	cream-coloured courser

REPTILES

Testudo graeca	tortoise

Individual taxa

Equids

A total of 88 equid bones was recovered, constituting less than 1% of the total fragment count (1.3% in the PPNB and 0.7% in the LN). Table 8.4 shows anatomical elements - expressed in MNE - for each period.

Equid finds from both early and late Neolithic contexts in the Near East are generally believed to belong to wild animals (Uerpmann 1982; Meadow and Uerpmann 1986) although the timing of the introduction of the first domesticates into the area remains an open question (Clutton-Brock 1992: 56). The wild horse (*Equus caballus*) (and possibly also *Equus tabetti* described by Eisenmann 1992) is assumed to have disappeared from the Levant before the end of the Pleistocene, with domestic horses being introduced to the area by the Bronze Age (Davis 1976), although Grigson has recently identified the earliest known domestic horses in the Levant, from the 4th millennium BC (Chalcolithic) of the Negev (Grigson 1993).

Concerning the smaller equids, the wild Asiatic half-ass (*Equus hemionus*) is known from Middle Palaeolithic sites in the area and survived until the present century, but was never domesticated. Another small equid, (*Equus hydruntinus*), sometimes referred to as the European wild ass, inhabited the area in the late Pleistocene but had disappeared by the Neolithic (Garrard 1991: 240; Uerpmann 1987). Remains of domestic donkey (*Equus asinus*) are frequently found in western Asia from the early 3rd millennium BC onwards, with earlier examples known from Egypt (Clutton-Brock 1992). The distribution of the wild ass

Taxa	Stage 1	Stage 2	Stage 3
Equus spp.	2	3	1
Ovis spp.	1	1	1
Capra spp.	-	2	-
Gazella sp.	67	152	17
Lepus sp.	3	8	6
Canis spp.	1	1	-
Vulpes spp.	1	2	1
Meles meles	-	-	1
Erinaceidae	-	1	2
birds	3	5	4
rodents	3	5	-
Testudo graeca	1	-	-

Table 8.3   The Minimum Number of Individuals (MNI) of each taxon for the three stages of occupation at Dhuweila.

(*Equus africanus*), the progenitor of the domestic donkey, is not well known although it has been identified from PPNB Basta in southern Jordan (Becker 1991), and tentatively recorded from other prehistoric sites in Jordan, Palestine and Syria (Uerpmann 1987:28).

Most equid remains from Dhuweila are too fragmented to allow morphometric analysis to suggest which species are present. Four mandibular teeth, however, have been assigned to *Equus hemionus/asinus* using the criteria in the dental enamel patterning described by Davis (1980b). One of these teeth is from phase 5; the other three are from phase 6 and are likely to derive from the same individual (Figure 8.1). Davis states that unless a large sample of complete metapodia are available, which they are not from Dhuweila, then further separation of *Equus asinus* (donkey) from *Equus hemionus* (half-ass) is difficult (Davis 1980a: 297). From Dhuweila the only equid measurements obtainable are the following (in mm):

	Phase	GL	BP	Dp	SD	BD	Dd
Phalanx I							
(anterior)	9	75.4	38.4	-	26.2	33.5	18.7
(ant/post)	9	-	34.8	-	26.5	-	-
Phalanx II							
GH	9	38.8	37.7	25.8	33.5	35.7	20.9
Astragalus	1		43.9				

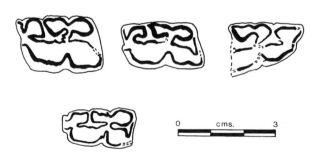

Figure 8.1   Equid teeth (the three above are from Stage 1, and one below is from Stage 3) assigned to *Equus hemionus/asinus* on the basis of enamel patterning.

The size of the complete phalanx I, when compared with both the modern comparative material plotted by Compagnoni (1978: fig. 4), and the material from Halafian Shams ed-Din and early Neolithic Mureybet (Uerpmann 1982: 50, fig. 2) falls within the overlapping ranges of *Equus hemionus* and *Equus asinus*, and supposedly also for *Equus africanus*.

Since no other large herbivores have been identified from the site, the five bone fragments which come into this category could probably be assigned to *Equus* spp..

Although equid representation is relatively low at Dhuweila, these large animals could have been important contributions to the diet. The wild ass, for example, has a body weight ranging from 200–400 kg. (Garrard 1980: Table 8.3B), approximately half of which would be meat weight.

Age

The majority of equid bones are from adult individuals, but the following elements are unfused: proximal tibia (phase 5), distal tibia (phase 1), 2 distal metapodia (phases 5 and 6), and a proximal phalanx II (phase 8). Of the two unfused distal metapodia, one was fairly large and the other appeared almost neonate, indicating that at least two immature animals were killed.

Body part

The number of equid remains is too few for analysis of body part representation to be meaningful. The skull, upper limbs and lower limbs, however, are all

Element	Stage 1	Stage 2	Stage 3	Total
mandibular tooth	2	2	-	4
maxillary tooth	3	-	-	3
scapula	2	1	-	3
radius p	-	1	-	1
pelvis	-	1	-	1
femur p	-	1	-	1
tibia p	1	-	-	1
tibia d	1	1	-	2
metatarsal p	-	2	-	2
metapodial p	-	4	-	4
metapodial d	4	-	-	4
phalanx I	2	3	-	5
phalanx II	-	2	-	2
phalanx III	-	2	-	2
sesamoid	1	4	-	5
scaphoid	1	-	-	1
semi-lunaire	2	-	-	2
pyramidal	1	-	-	1
capetum-trapezoid	-	-	1	1
astragalus	1	6	-	7
navicular-cuboid	-	2	-	2

Table 8.4   The minimum number of equid elements for each stage (p=proximal; d=distal). Long-bones are shown as Minimum Numbers of Ends (MNE).

represented (Table 8.4). The lower leg extremities are slightly more frequent than other categories, but this may be a preservational bias, rather than a cultural one.

Processing

Three fragments of phalanx I (phase 5) (Figure 8.2) and one proximal metapodial (phase 8) show longitudinal breakage, uncharacteristic of such strong bone elements. It is suggested that this may reflect splitting, possibly for marrow extraction.

Gazelles

Gazelles are by far the most frequently represented animal at Dhuweila, with at least 11,078 bones being identifiable to this genus (constituting over 90% of each of the two main periods). At least three different species of gazelle are likely to have been present in the Levant in the early Holocene: *G. gazelle*, *G. dorcas* and *G. subgutturosa* (although Tchernov *et al.* 1986/87 argue for the expansion of *G. dorcas* into the area only after the PPNB). The distributions of the three species today tend to adhere to different environmental zones, with *G. gazella* preferring woodlands and lush grassland, *G. dorcas* inhabiting deserts and *G. subgutturosa* being steppic. Broad overlap has been noted in places, however, although it is believed that different species generally do not mix within herds (Mendelssohn 1974: 725). Their separation in archaeological bone assemblages is only secure when using horncore morphology; the postcranial bones are not distinctly different, although they do cover a range of overlapping sizes, with those of *G. subgutturosa* being the most robust, *G. dorcas* the most gracile, and *G. gazella* falling between them (Harrison 1968). Both the size of bones and a knowledge of modern distributions has often been used to suggest the presence of one or other species in the archaeological record (Uerpmann 1987).

On the basis of male horncore morphology, two specimens from Dhuweila have been identified as *G. subgutturosa* (from phases 7 and 9 — both LN). The first criterion used for these identifications is the lyrate twisting of the horncore (Uerpmann 1982: 27;

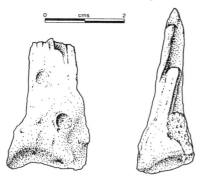

Figure 8.2 Two equid proximal phalanx fragments, showing longitudinal breakage (all from Stage 1 deposits).

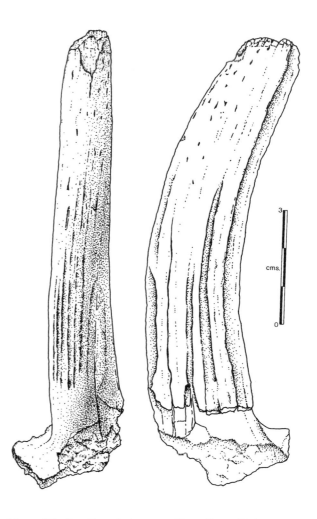

Figure 8.3 Gazelle male horncore (from Stage 2) showing lyrate twisting, assigned to *Gazella subgutturosa*; a) anterior view; b) lateral view.

Compagnoni 1978:119) (see Figure 8.3). Secondly, the deep lachrymal pit seen at the base of the horncore in Figure 8.4 separates *G. subgutturosa* from other gazelles (Harrison 1968: 361), as does the closeness of the horncores on the skull, which is inferred from the proximity of the horncore base to the medial suture on the same specimen.

For female horncores, of which there are several from Dhuweila, separation of *G. subgutturosa* and *G. gazella* is problematic. The Dhuweila examples (e.g. Figure 8.5) do not appear to belong to *G. dorcas*, whose females tend to have long, straight horncores, but they compare equally well with those of both *G. subgutturosa* (*marica* subspecies) and *G. gazella*, and therefore cannot be assigned to either with any certainty.

Turning to body size, it must be stressed that the number of bones upon which metrical analysis is based is fairly small, mainly due to the extensive fragmentation and/or burning of the bone (see Appendix B for full list of measurements). In addition, the possibilities for size variation in gazelles are not well understood, particularly in *G. subgutturosa* and especially in earlier

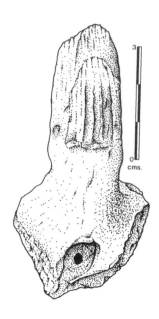

Figure 8.4 Gazelle male horncore (from Stage 2) showing deep lachrymal pit on frontal, assigned to *Gazella subgutturosa*.

Element	Measurements (von den Driesch)	Range (mm.)	S.D. Size	Sample Size
Humerus	BT (breadth of trochlea)	19.6-24.6	1.12	34
Radius	BP (breadth of prox. end)	22.8-26.9	1.19	12
Tibia	Bd (breadth of dist. end)	18.2-24.1	1.46	20
Astragalus	GLl (greatest length of lateral half)	21.1-27.8	1.52	72
Calcaneum	GL (greatest length)	51.0-57.6	3.65	3
Metacarpal	Bd (breadth of dist. end)	17.8-20.8	0.93	14
Metatarsal	Bd (breadth of dist. end)	19.0-21.2	0.98	14

Table 8.5 The ranges of measurements for selected gazelle elements from both PPNB and LN levels from Dhuweila. (measurements follow von den Driesch 1976).

times. Any conclusions, therefore, can only be tentative.

Table 8.5 shows the ranges of measurements for selected elements. In a review of some of the published gazelle bone measurements, Helmer gives the ranges for certain modern identified specimens of *G. gazella*, *G. dorcas* and *G. subgutturosa*, and also for selected archaeological material (Helmer 1991: 362–363, figs. 4, 5). Comparing the Dhuweila ranges presented in Table 8.5 with Helmer's figures, it was found that they consistently fell within the overlapping size ranges of modern *G. gazella* and *G. dorcas*, but that for each element some Dhuweila bones fell within the sole range of the smaller animal, *G. dorcas*. Amongst distal metapodia, calcanea and distal tibiae, the larger Dhuweila examples overlap in size with the smallest recorded examples of *G. subgutturosa* (which in turn overlap with *G. gazella*), although it should be noted that the sample of modern comparative material used for this species is very small (see Compagnoni 1978 for original publication).

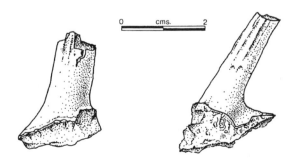

Figure 8.5 Gazelle female horncores (Stages 1 and 2).

Tchernov *et al.* (1986/87) give the ranges of variability and their means for distal metacarpi of both recent *G. gazella* and *G. dorcas*. These are compared in Table 8.6 with the Dhuweila data, showing that the Dhuweila bones again fall into the overlap between the two modern samples of *G. gazella* and *G. dorcas*.

Uerpmann on the other hand, who identified *G. subgutturosa* from the Late Neolithic site of Shams ed-Din in Syria, finds their bones fairly small, especially when compared to the gazelles of neighbouring Mureybet, which are likely to be of the same species (Uerpmann 1987: 100–101). He offers a possible explanation for the smaller size of *G. subgutturosa* in the early Holocene: following Bergmann's rule, rising temperatures caused a decrease in average size of the animals. The known modern examples of *G. subgutturosa*, however, are larger, and have been subject to continuously higher temperatures than those in the late Pleistocene/early Holocene.

The metrical results, then, are inconclusive. Using Helmer's figures (Helmer 1991) and the ranges shown by Tchernov *et al.* (1986/87), the size ranges of the Dhuweila gazelles is more consistent with that of *G. gazella* or *G. dorcas*. It must be noted, however, that our knowledge of the possible variations is limited. There may be more than one species of gazelle represented at the site, although this is unlikely for ecological reasons. Also, the size ranges presented in Table 8.6, and the measurements shown in Figure 8.6 for the breadth of the distal end of the astragalus (the most frequently measurable bone), do not appear too widely spread for a single species. The two identified *G. subgutturosa* horncores, which represent the most morphologically sound criteria for species identification, would then be at odds with the much larger sample of measurements.

Species	Range (mm)	Mean (mm)	SD	Sample Size
Gazella gazella Recent	18.64–22.37	20.41	0.90	24
Gazella dorcas Recent	17.62–17.70	17.66	0.06	2
Gazella sp. Dhuweila	17.80–20.80	19.15	0.93	14

Table 8.6 Ranges of distal breadth of metacarpal for recent *Gazella gazella* and *Gazella dorcas* from Israel (from Tchernov et al. 1986/87), and Dhuweila gazelle material, from both PPNB and LN levels.

Dental age

An absence of teeth in jaws, and the extremely poor survival of teeth in general, led to difficulty in determining dental age. The creation of cull patterns based on tooth wear or cusp heights (e.g. Davis 1977; Legge and Rowley-Conwy 1987) proved impossible due to the very small numbers of intact teeth. One method that was applied, however, was to use a count of teeth root-sockets in the mandibular bone (with the teeth themselves missing), which could be identified as having held either a deciduous or permanent dentition. In Israeli zoo-bred gazelles (*G. gazella*), the permanent dentition fully replaces the deciduous by 16–20 months (Davis 1980a). The exact figures here are not important; they only serve to show that decidous dentition would belong to an animal below 2 years of age. A total of 35 fragments from Dhuweila showed such root patterns, and results are given in Table 8.7. Wear stages of the few complete mandibular 3rd molars (following an adaptation of Payne 1973) are also given.

Although the sample is very small and any results should be treated with caution, the totals show more adults than juveniles in the PPNB, and the opposite in the LN (juvenile:adult ratio for PPNB=5:8; for LN=4:3), and the lack of heavily worn M3s suggests a scarcity of old aged animals.

Fusion

A large number of gazelle bones yielded fusion information; the data for each phase are presented in Appendix A.

						Phases							
Mandibles (MNI)	1	2	3	4	5	PPNB Total	6	7	8	9	LN Total	10	Total
Deciduous	0	0	4	0	1	5	1	0	6	5	12	0	17
Permanent	1	2	2	0	3	8	3	1	4	1	9	1	18
M3 wear stage					F				D	GH			
			GH						GH				
									GH				
									H				
									I				

Table 8.7 The top part of the table shows the number of gazelle mandibles in each phase/stage with root-socket evidence for either deciduous or permanent dentition. The lower part shows the wear stages for eight mandibular M3s, following Payne's (1973) codes.

In his study of a sample of zoo-bred Israeli gazelles (*G. gazella*), Davis has shown that all the bones in the skeleton have fused by the time the animal is roughly 18 months old (Davis 1980a: 133; 1987: 40). Again, the exact ages are unimportant since they may be subject to variation, but the relative sequence of fusion times for different bones in the body can be used to build up a picture of kill patterns up until the time of complete fusion. The main problems with this technique are firstly that unfused bones are generally much less durable than fused ones (Klein and Cruz-Uribe 1984:43), and secondly that since all bones have fused by a relatively young age, fusion can necessarily only give information about a short early stage of the animal's life.

Fusion information for the Dhuweila gazelles is shown in Tables 8.8 and 8.9 for the PPNB and Late Neolithic layers respectively (as can be seen from the tables in Appendix A, the fusion data for each phase tends to adhere to the general patterns seen in Tables 8.8 and 8.9, but there is also a wide range of variation, e.g. phases 2 and 4 show a very high proportion of juveniles compared to the other PPNB phases). The percentage of fused bones reflects the animals surviving beyond a certain age, while the percentage of unfused bones represent those that died before, or during, the known ranges of fusion times.

From Table 8.8 it can be seen that 55% of the PPNB bones are unfused, and therefore belong to juveniles (meaning approximately less than 18 months old). Table 8.9 shows the Late Neolithic material to include 45% juveniles. Further, the percentages of unfused distal humeri and proximal radii (the earliest fusing bones), suggest that for the PPNB, 17% of gazelles were culled by approximately 2 months of age, whilst for the Late

Element	Fusion Age* (months)	Number Unfused	Number Fused	% Fused
d humerus	c.2	21	68	76.4
p radius	c.2	2	45	95.7
TOT >c.2 months	**-**	**23**	**113**	**83.1**
scapula-coracoid	3-6	9	56	86.2
p phalanx I	5-8	33	71	68.3
TOT >3-8 months	**-**	**42**	**127**	**75.1**
d tibia	8-10	32	42	56.8
TOT >8-10 months	**-**	**32**	**42**	**56.8**
p femur	10-16	14	25	64.1
calcaneum	10-16	58	23	28.4
d metacarpal	10-16	21	32	60.4
d metatarsal	10-16	26	22	45.8
d femur	10-18	17	14	45.2
p humerus	12-18	6	3	33.3
p ulna	12-18	8	10	55.6
p tibia	12-18	26	19	42.2
d radius	12-18	24	18	42.9
TOT>10-18 months	**-**	**200**	**166**	**45.4**

Total number of bones with fusion data=745

Table 8.8 Gazelle fusion data for PPNB deposits (phases 1-5), using the approximate ages (*) of fusion given by Davis (1980a:133, 1987:40), based on zoo-bred Israeli *Gazella gazella*. The total number of bones with fusion data=745.

Element	Fusion Age* (months)	Number Unfused	Number Fused	% Fused
d humerus	c.2	38	145	79.2
p radius	c.2	2	150	98.7
TOT >c.2 months	-	**40**	**295**	**88.1**
scapula-coracoid	3-6	5	40	88.9
p phalanx 1	5-8	74	247	76.9
TOT >3-8 months	-	**79**	**287**	**78.4**
d tibia	8-10	70	113	61.7
TOT >8-10 months	-	**70**	**113**	**61.7**
p femur	10-16	51	86	62.8
calcaneum	10-16	52	97	65.1
d metacarpal	10-16	50	47	48.5
d metatarsal	10-16	59	74	55.6
d femur	10-18	34	35	50.7
p humerus	12-18	10	10	50.0
p ulna	12-18	8	32	80.0
p tibia	12-18	44	36	45.0
d radius	12-18	68	52	43.3
TOT>10-18 months	-	**376**	**469**	**55.5**

Total number of bones with fusion data=1729

Table 8.9   Gazelle fusion data for Late Neolithic deposits (phases 6-9), using the approximate ages (*) of fusion given by Davis (1980a:133, 1987:40), based on zoo-bred Israeli *Gazella gazella*. The total number of bones with fusion data=1729.

Neolithic the same figure is 12%. These patterns will be discussed below.

Sex determination

Two methods exist for determining the presence of males and females in archaeological gazelle bone assemblages. One uses horncores, which are distinct for each sex, and the other measurements.

Unfortunately, horncore representation is low at Dhuweila, and the preservational biases against the small thin female horncores would anyway make this an unreliable means of quantification. Table 8.10, however, shows at least that both males and females are present at the site.

The principal bone measurements which various authors have used to exhibit sexual dimorphism in the gazelle are those for the atlas, axis, scapula, astragalus, distal metacarpal and metatarsal (Cope 1991; Davis 1987: 44; Garrard 1980; Haaker 1986; Horwitz *et al.* 1990). From Dhuweila, the only one of these bones which was frequently measurable was the astragalus. Measurements for this element (following Horwitz *et al.* 1990: 6) are shown in Figure 8.6.

The interpretation of these histograms is problematic for the following reasons. Firstly, it is not known which species of gazelle are present at the site, and so this scatter might represent more than one species of different size. Secondly, there is a lack of comparative measurements taken from gazelles of known sex; Horwitz *et al.* (1990) show astragalus measurements for recent sexed *G. gazella*, but the Dhuweila astragali are much smaller than these. The third problem is that the astragali do not fall into two distinct size clusters. A tentative suggestion may be (if it is assumed that the

assemblage consisted of one gazelle species only) that the larger astragali to the right-hand of the graphs represent males, and the smaller ones to the left are females. An area of overlap will almost certainly exist between the sexes (Cope 1991: 344). Following this interpretation, both adult males and females appear to be present, in roughly similar proportions, in both periods. An alternative view might be that the larger bones are from females of *G. gazella* size, and the smaller ones are from a smaller species (ie. *G. dorcas*), but as argued above, the presence of two species is unlikely. With so little firm comparative data, any interpretation must remain tentative.

Discussion of gazelle behaviour and hunting

Two questions are of prime interest concerning possible hunting practices at Dhuweila:

1) Are there indications that hunting occurred at particular times of the year?
2) Is there evidence for particular hunting strategies, e.g. selection of age or sex groups, random predation or whole herd killing?

Seasonality of gazelle hunting has been inferred in a number of ways. Legge and Rowley-Conwy found high proportions of newborn and one year old animals in the Late Natufian levels at Abu Hureyra in Syria, and therefore suggest spring killing (Legge and Rowley-Conwy 1987: 90). For a number of prehistoric sites in the Levant, Davis argues that if the overall proportions of juveniles in an assemblage are seen as a mirror of their proportions in nature, then a low juvenile count may indicate winter hunting, whilst a higher count could imply year-round hunting (Davis 1983), although he does not take into account hunting strategies or selection. Others have also proposed that hunting occurred at specific times of the year through a comparison of any age/sex groups evident in their assemblages with the compositions of modern gazelle herds (Butler *et al.* 1977; Hovers *et al.* 1988; Tchernov and Bar-Yosef 1982). Most assume spring birth peaks for gazelles, although Hovers *et al.* advise caution when applying modern animal behaviour patterns to past populations (Hovers *et al.* 1988: 44).

Phase	Total Horncores	Female Horncores	Male Horncores
1	3	2	0
2	0	0	0
3	1	0	1
4	1	0	1
5	6	1	1
6	9	2	5
7	1	0	1
8	1	0	0
9	5	2	3
10	2	1	1

Table 8.10   The total number of gazelle horncores for each phase with numbers identifiable to either female or male.

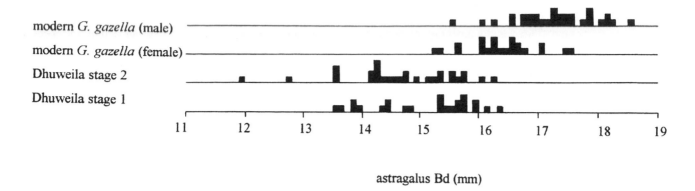

modern *G. gazella* (male)

modern *G. gazella* (female)

Dhuweila stage 2

Dhuweila stage 1

11　12　13　14　15　16　17　18　19

astragalus Bd (mm)

Figure 8.6 The size of gazelle astragali (breadth of distal end - Bd) from Dhuweila Stages 1 and 2, compared to modern *Gazella gazella* males and females (data from Davis, pers. comm.).

There has been less discussion of hunting strategies. Legge and Rowley-Conwy use the overall age patterns of gazelles — individuals from every age group including very old and very young — combined with historic accounts for the use of gazelle drives, to conclude that whole herds were killed using mass kill structures (Legge and Rowley-Conwy 1987: 91). Campana and Crabtree also argue for a 'catastrophic' kill profile for gazelles from Salibiya I (Campana and Crabtree 1990). On the subject of catastrophic age profiles, Davis believes that the same pattern could just as well indicate different age groups culled at random (Davis 1983: 55).

Clearly, a prerequisite to answering any questions about prehistoric gazelle hunting is an understanding of the animal's birthing times, group structures, group sizes and densities, and seasonal movements, and the likely variations of these in different environments (Simmons and Ilany 1977). The interpretation of gazelle bones from Levantine sites has placed heavy reliance on observations of modern gazelles, drawing particularly on studies of the populations of *G. gazella* in the Galilee and *G. dorcas* in the Negev (Baharav 1974a; 1974b; 1981; 1982; 1983a; 1983b). These, however, cannot be applied directly to eastern Jordan, an area with a very different environment. Here, the gazelle survives only in very small numbers today due to extreme overhunting during this century, and these animals cannot serve as a model for earlier behaviour. A single study of the behaviour of *Gazella subgutturosa* has been found (Habibi *et al.* 1993); this is based mainly on gazelles enclosed in a wildlife reasearch centre in Saudi Arabia, and for this reason the authors point out that the behaviour observed may not resemble that shown under more normal conditions, i.e. in the wild (Habibi *et al.* 1993: 42).

Instead of using gazelle behaviour studies directly, an ecological approach has been used to predict the past behaviour of the species for this area. The underlying assumption of behavioural ecology is that it is possible to understand an animal's reproductive cycle, seasonal movements, group composition, group size and density, through a detailed knowledge of the food and water resources available to it, the existing predators and commensals, and the design of the animal itself (such as body size, nutritional requirements and feeding constraints) (Clutton-Brock and Harvey 1978; Krebs 1978; 1984; Rubenstein 1989). A full review of the factors shaping the adaptive behaviour of five species of Arabian and African gazelles is presented elsewhere (Martin 1994). It is argued that the actual species present would be unimportant: Baharav finds two populations of different species (*G. gazella* and *G. dorcas*), living far apart, using the same reproductive strategy, whilst two populations of the same species (*G. gazella*) in close proximity exhibit different birthing patterns (Baharav 1983b: 449–51). The underlying determinant is the timing of peak vegetational conditions. In brief, the predictions for the behaviour of early Holocene gazelles in eastern Jordan are as follows:

1) In an Irano-Turanian zone, gazelles could be expected to concentrate births in the spring, when the increase in temperatures and seasonal rains would cause a flush of new vegetation growth. Prior to March-May, the steppe would probably be too cold for fawn survival; summers are too hot and dry, and birthing in autumn would be hazardous for fawns due to the arrested plant growth in winter.

2) Concerning seasonal and annual movements, the two well studied Arabian gazelles have small home-ranges (up to 25 km²), and do not migrate. Populations in areas of lush Mediterranean vegetation make small seasonal movements up and down valley sides, whilst others in areas of sparse vegetation (with less than 50mm of rainfall a year) will roam along wadi bottoms. These arid-adapted populations use a strategy of minimizing movement in the summers in order to reduce energy and water loss (Baharav 1982). African gazelles migrate seasonally from the bush in the dry seasons, to the open plains during the rains (Brooks 1961; Estes

1967; Walther 1972). They appear to do so to feed on lusher vegetation, to move with their commensals, and to avoid wet ground. There is documentary evidence to suggest that *Gazella subgutturosa* was a migratory or nomadic species in the recent past (Mendelssohn 1974: 726). Habibi *et al.* (1993: 42) also observe this species as being 'mobile' at non-reproductive times, since they tend to form larger groups (as an anti-predator response to its adherence to open terrain?), and thus create high group nutritional needs, necessitating movement.

In light of these examples, gazelles in eastern Jordan would probably have moved on a seasonal basis, but it is unlikely that the relatively small body sizes inferred by the bone measurements (with a maximum average body weight of 24 kg, following Garrard 1980: tab. 3B) would have allowed them to migrate long distances, as has been suggested by Legge and Rowley-Conwy (1987: 91), particularly at times of the year when vegetation is sparse. The African Grant's gazelle, which moves over distances of 290km^2 a year, is a larger animal with an average weight of 75 kg. (Estes 1967). It consequently has absolutely higher nutritional needs, and relatively lower locomotion costs. Arabian gazelles are more comparable in size with Thomson's gazelle, which utilizes a much smaller area of 140 km^2 per year. A comparison, therefore, between the home ranges of Grant's and Thompson's gazelles shows how, even in their lush habitats, the animal's body size influences the distances they will move.

3) Variations in the social structure of herds would be similar to those for most gazelles because they are integral to mating and birthing strategies. If a spring birth is assumed for gazelles in eastern Jordan, then the autumn mating season would see active adult males defending territories. Sub-adult and non-mating males could be expected to form bachelor herds for much of the year. Reproductive females would wander through male territories during the mating season. When birthing, females often become solitary, and after being born fawns tend to 'lie out' in protected or hidden areas until weaning. During this period, nursery herds, composed of mothers, other females and fawns, may form. At other times of the year, males, females and juveniles would form mixed herds.

4) The size and density of groups would be determined by the size and distribution of vegetation patches in the area, and to a lesser degree by the need for anti-predator clustering (Rubenstein 1978). Some gazelles are virtually independent of standing water and it is possible that, in summers, their distribution may be influenced by available shade and the need for low movement feeding, rather than by water. By rough comparison with known situations, it may be safe to predict very low density groups roaming widely, but mainly through wadi bottoms in the summers, and higher densities (probably approximately 40 animals per km^2) aggregating in areas where water collection stimulates denser vegetation growth, from autumn to spring. The mud-flats and wadi systems present throughout the *harra* would be attractive locations at such times.

If the data from the Dhuweila gazelles are viewed in the light of the above behavioural reconstruction, several points can tentatively be made. Fusion data show that 17% of animals in the PPNB and 12% in the Late Neolithic died within the first two months of life. Since birthing is assumed to be in spring, this shows some hunting at least to have taken place at that time, or in early summer at the latest. Both periods of occupation see a significant number of animals being culled at, or before, 8–10 months of age. Although the nature of fusion data is that they can only specify whether a bone is fused or unfused, and therefore from an animal below or above a certain age (range), it may be worth noting here that 15 out of 16 measurable unfused distal tibiae (1 from the PPNB and 14 from the LN) overlap in size with the fused distal tibiae, as opposed to a single example (from the LN) which is much smaller. This might be taken to suggest that these 15 distal tibiae were approaching full size, and fusion time, which occurs at 8–10 months. This may be used to conjecture winter/spring killing.

Regarding hunting strategies, the lack of sufficient dental ageing data and the questionable interpretation of the sex ratio, makes consideration of this issue problematic. If, however, it is believed that some hunting was taking place during winter and spring, it may be useful to consider which types of herds could be expected to form at these times. Winter would probably see large mixed herds, including juveniles, and possibly also separate bachelor herds. Spring would find mothers becoming solitary to fawn. If the astragalus measurements (see Figure 8.6) are interpreted as representing both males and females, then the targetting of male bachelor herds in the winter/spring might have been an option, as would the taking of females and very young animals (evidenced in fusion data), which may reflect some opportunistic hunting of newly-born fawns or nursery groups in spring/early summer. Equally, the larger mixed winter groups could have been the object of the hunt. The assemblage shows relatively high proportions of juveniles when compared to other sites (Davis 1983) (55% in the PPNB, 45% in the Late Neolithic) and these patterns will be discussed elsewhere (Martin 1994).

The suggestion by Betts (1988b: 13; 'stratigraphy' above) that a 'kite' wall may be in direct association with the Late Neolithic structure at Dhuweila, raises the issue of drive techniques of hunting. When one animal is so clearly the object of hunting, such as gazelles were at Dhuweila, it would be perhaps likely that groups participated in planned, communal hunts (*cf.* Driver 1990). Animals which are predictable in their behaviour, and hence location, at certain times of the year are

	Humerus		Radius		Femur		Tibia		Metacarpal		Metatarsal		Phalanx I		Phalanx II	
	n	%	n	%	n	%	n	%	n	%	n	%	n	%	n	%
End only	98	18	50	10	7	1	59	10	18	3	21	3	413	57	219	81
End splinter and end+shaft splinter	321	60	402	81	586	93	494	81	482	93	768	95	265	37	34	13
Shaft splinter	94	18	31	6	32	5	43	7	11	2	14	2	26	4	10	4
Shaft cylinder	18	3	16	3	3	1	11	2	8	2	5	1	17	2	9	3
Total	531	-	499	-	628	-	607	-	519	-	808	-	721	-	272	-

Table 8.11 The fragmentation classes for gazelle longbones and phalanges, for both PPNB and LN. Both counts (n) and percentages (%) are shown.

frequently seen to be the focus of organized hunting tactics (*cf.* Davis and Reeves 1990; Ingold 1980; Frison 1978; Spiess 1979). Gazelles in the steppic landscape of eastern Jordan would have been likely to represent such predictable prey. The bones themselves, however, do not allow the resolution of age and sex ratios needed to consider whether 'whole herd' killing or serial predation was being undertaken, particularly since the complexities of gazelle social organization mean that the 'whole herd' is a variable entity. Alone, the bones do not permit the extrapolation of hunting techniques, but can only point to the selection (whether intended or not) of certain animal groups.

Gazelle bone modification and body part representation

Fragmentation

As has been stated above, the assemblage is highly fragmented, with only small compact bones being found complete, whilst the majority of pieces were longitudinal splinters of longbone ends, shafts or both. The most interesting question concerning these fragmentation patterns is whether the high incidence of splintering occurred before or after deposition, or rather, whether the bone shattering is a result of deliberate human activity (for marrow or grease extraction) or natural or general depositional action (such as weathering, trampling or disturbance of deposits). An attempt was made to characterize and quantify fragmentation by recording each identifiable fragment to one of the following categories: end only, end and/or end and shaft splinter, shaft splinter alone, or shaft cylinder. The results of the fragmentation analysis for gazelle longbones and phalanges are shown in Table 8.11.

It is well known that weathering can cause splitting in bone (Behrensmeyer 1978; Tappen 1969; Tappen and Peske 1970), and this could be expected particularly in areas of extreme seasonal and diurnal temperature ranges, such as the Jordanian steppe, and especially if bone has already been weakened by soil action or burning. The implication, however, is that longitudinal fractures resulting from weathering occur mainly on the compact bone of the shaft, rather than on the ends (Miller 1975: 219). From the fragmentation patterns

seen for the Dhuweila gazelle longbones — namely that there is a high proportion of end splinters or end and shaft splinters relative to whole ends — it is argued that intentional cracking is partly responsible for the patterns observed. Table 8.11 shows that 60–95% of the longbone pieces have splintering on the ends or end-and-shaft fragments, whilst only 1–18% have complete ends present (the low percentage of shaft splinters is probably a result of these fragments being less identifiable than those with ends. Also note that phalanges have different breakage patterns with a higher proportion of whole ends).

The suggestion of intentional breakage is supported by evidence that certain elements appear unambiguously split in ways that would not arise through weathering. Figure 8.7 shows an assortment of gazelle longbone and phalanx fragments which have been longitudinally split.

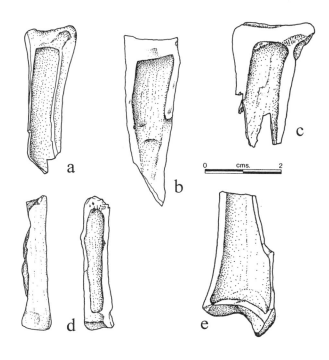

Figure 8.7 Gazelle bones showing longitudinal breakage suggestive of splitting: a) proximal radius (Stage 2); b) proximal radius (Stage 2); c) proximal metatarsal (Stage 1); d) proximal phalanx (Stage 2); e) distal tibia (Stage 1).

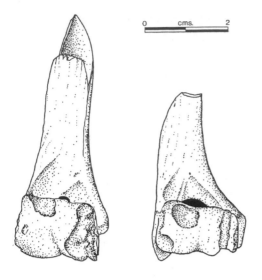

Figure 8.8 Gazelle distal humeri (Stages 1 and 2) showing pitting characteristic of carnivore gnawing.

It is, therefore, suggested here that human processing, probably for extraction of bone marrow or bone grease, is partly responsible for the observed bone fragmentation patterns, although weathering is likely to have been an additional factor.

Carnivore activity

The Dhuweila bone assemblage has produced very little evidence of carnivore activity; only 0.1% of bones show the characteristic gnawing marks produced by either wild or domestic carnivores (see, for example, Figure 8.8). This might be taken as an indication that domestic dogs, although evidenced in the Near East during and since the Natufian, were not present on the site (Marean and Spencer 1991). The absence of 'digested bone' (Payne and Munson 1985; Davis 1987:148) supports this, although the possibilities of both gnawed and digested bones being removed from the site by carnivores and deposited elsewhere, should not be ignored.

Body part representation

This section aims to explore which parts of gazelle carcasses may have been brought to the site, and the kind of activities, such as butchering, processing or consumption, which may have been undertaken.

Figures 8.9 and 8.10 show the relative representation of different skeletal elements for the PPNB and Late Neolithic deposits respectively. (Data for individual phases has not been given since they follow broadly similar trends).

Before these patterns can be taken to reveal any kind of human activity, the factors which can potentially influence the original deposited assemblage must be taken into account. Bone density has a major effect on the survival of bones (Brain 1981; Lyman 1984),

meaning, for example, that the proximal ends of humerus and tibia are much more prone to destruction than their denser distal ends (see Figures 8.9 and 8.10). Skeletal age, condition and state of articulation when deposited are all likely to influence bone survival (Brain 1981), and if carnivores have ravaged an assemblage they will differentially alter the pattern of body parts (Binford and Bertram 1977; Marean and Spencer 1991).

As discussed above, carnivore activity is believed to have been slight at Dhuweila, and the high number of ends, many unfused, attests to this. The histograms show that most parts of the body are represented to some degree, including heads, which may suggest that the animals were carried whole to the site. Any suggestion of Dhuweila being a primary kill/butchery site can probably be ruled out if Binford's study of Nunamiut (Eskimo) hunting sites is taken into account. Binford shows that primary kill-butchery sites have a high representation of skulls and foot bones, which tend to be removed first in the butchery process, and low representation of most other elements (Binford 1978b). The pattern seen at Dhuweila is almost opposite to this.

The relatively low frequency of phalanges, which would survive well, may suggest a trend of lower leg removal off-site, maybe during skinning, although the slightly higher representation of metapodia (especially distal ends) may suggest that these parts, which can be also lost during skinning (e.g. Binford and Bertram 1977: 91) may be arriving on site for other processing reasons (such as marrow or grease extraction). An alternative explanation for the low frequency of phalanges is that they are leaving the site attached to skins.

Most of the denser longbone parts which would be expected to survive well show a fairly high representation (e.g. distal humerus, radius, distal tibia and distal metapodials). It has already been suggested above that the high degree of splintering reflects bone marrow removal, or maybe even bone grease extraction (Binford 1978b). What is actually happening to the meat before this stage, however, is more difficult to infer. The two main possibilities are that meat is being primarily consumed on site, or that it is being preserved for storage (e.g. through removal from the bone and drying/salting), although the observed body part representation appears fairly consistent with both alternatives. In addition, the potential 'over-patterning' which could result from the accumulated consumption and/or processing activities is considerable and makes the patterning difficult to interpret.

Mandibles show low representation, maybe as a result of the observed tooth shattering from weathering. Horncores are not frequent, especially compared to the other cranial part count (taken on the admittedly very durable petrous temporal). One suggestion for this difference is that complete skulls are arriving on the site, but the horncores are later removed, maybe for working or trophies.

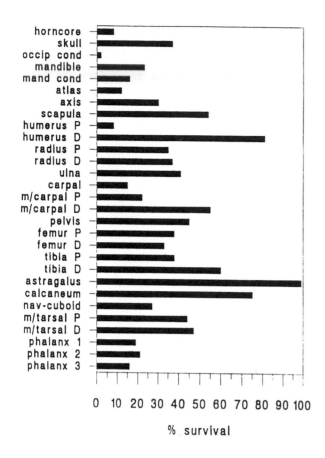

Figure 8.9 Gazelle body part representation for Stage 1.

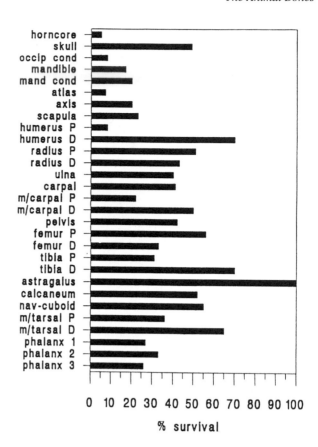

Figure 8.10 Gazelle body part representation for Stage 2.

That the astragalus is consistently the best represented element is a result of its density and survival potential.

There are many possible interpretations for the gazelle body part frequencies shown; the discussion here mentions just some of the means by which these bone patterns may have been formed. The different ways of using animal body parts is obviously culturally variable, but animals such as gazelles provide potential sources of hides, meat, fat, marrow, grease, tendons, bone and horncores and sheaths.

Butchery and pathology

Only one bone — a metapodial condyle — showed a cut mark (Figure 8.11). This paucity of marks might indicate either that carcasses were generally not butchered with sharp tools (which is unlikely given the chipped stone assemblage at the site), or that the butchers were highly experienced and skilled, and their stone tools rarely came into contact with bone. Several other bones showed likely evidence for chopping or splitting. These included 2 proximal tibia ends (phase 5) transversally cut (Figure 8.12); a distal tibia (phase 5) longitudinally split; a metatarsal shaft (phase 5) longitudinally split; a proximal metatarsal (phase 8) longitudinally split; a phalanx 1 (phase 8) longitudinally split, and 2 proximal radii (phase 9) evidencing longitudinal splitting (Figure 8.7).

Three pathological bones were found (Figure 8.13). A phalanx I (phase 5), and a phalanx II (phase 1) both had bony outgrowths on their proximal ends, similar to those described by Davis (1985) from Hatoula. A scaphoid from phase 8 had a similar extra bone growth.

Sheep/Goat

Dhuweila produced a total of 49 caprine bones (5 PPNB, 39 LN, 5 Post-LN), constituting less than 1% of the assemblage in each period. Of these, 12 were identified as sheep (1 PPNB, 9 LN, 2 Post-LN)) and 3 as goats (all LN), using criteria described by Boessneck (1969) and Prummel and Frisch (1986). Table 8.12 shows the elements present in each phase for sheep, goat and sheep/goat, and gives any fusion evidence; Table 8.13 presents measurements.

The species to which these bones belonged, and whether they were wild or domestic, are issues which cannot be satisfactorily answered from this small sample of fragmentary remains. The criteria for recognizing domestic sheep and goats have been much discussed (see Meadow 1989; Horwitz 1989), and include morphological evidence (encompassing size change), demographic changes within the species, zoogeographic evidence, species spectrum change and inferences from pathology. The Dhuweila caprine remains show no morphological traits which would

	Phase	Element	Fusion
SHEEP	1	metapodial distal	Fused
	6	humerus distal	Fused
	7	calcaneum	
	8	phalanx I	Fused
	9	humerus distal	Fused
	9	radius distal	Unfused
	9	ulna	
	9	metacarpal distal	Fused
	9	tibia distal	Fused
	9	phalanx III	Fused
	10	astragalus	
	10	metatarsal distal	Fused
GOAT	6	femur proximal	Fused
	6	phalanx II	Fused
	8	phalanx II	Fused
SHEEP/GOAT	1	tooth fragment	
	2	scapula	Fused
	2	metatarsal distal	Fused
	5	phalanx I proximal	Fused
	6	humerus distal	Fused
	6	femur distal	Unfused
	6	tibia distal	Unfused
	6	metacarpal proximal	
	6	metapodial distal	
	6	phalanx II	Fused
	6	phalanx II proximal	Unfused
	8	scapula proximal	Fused
	8	femur proximal	
	8	semi-lunaire	
	8	semi-lunaire	
	8	phalanx I proximal	Fused
	8	phalanx I proximal	Fused
	8	phalanx I proximal	Fused
	8	phalanx I distal	
	8	phalanx II	Fused
	8	phalanx III	Fused
	9	M	
	9	mandibular condyle	
	9	capetum-trapezoid	
	9	capetum-trapezoid	
	9	metapodial distal	
	9	phalanx I proximal	Fused
	9	phalanx III proximal	Fused
	9	phalanx III proximal	Fused
	10	capetum-trapezoid	
	10	phalanx I	Fused
	10	phalanx I proximal	Fused

Table 8.12 Sheep, goat and sheep/goat representation by phase (expressed as MNE), also showing states of fusion.

assign them to either wild or domestic species. The measurements permitted are too scanty for comparison with size indices (e.g. Uerpmann 1979, quoted in Davis 1987:138) and the sample is too small and fragmentary for an analysis of age/sex to be conclusive. In addition, the relative proportions of the caprines to other species are similar in both the PPNB and the Late Neolithic deposits. For any elightenment, therefore, the zoogeographic evidence must be considered.

Eastern Jordan could possibly have been within the distributions of all three wild caprines. The wild goat (*Capra aegagrus*) generally had a more northerly range than ibex, but is known to have extended as far south as Beidha (Uerpmann 1987). The Nubian ibex (*Capra nubiana*) is more arid-adapted and found further south, although it is also known from Syria (Harrison 1968: 333). Both prefer rocky habitats but their presence in the

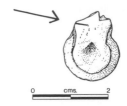

Figure 8.11 Gazelle distal metapodial condyle, showing cut mark.

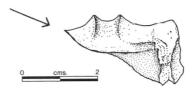

Figure 8.12 Gazelle proximal tibia (Stage 1) showing likely evidence for chopping.

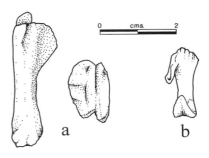

Figure 8.13 Pathological gazelle phalanges (Stage 1): a) anterior and proximal views of a proximal phalanx showing pathological bony outgrowth; b) anterior view of an intermediate phalanx showing pathological bony outgrowth.

Sheep	**Phase**	**Bd**	**BT**	**HT**
				(Davis 85)
humerus	9	35.6	35.0	16.4
		BPC		
ulna	9	19.3		
		Bd	**Dd**	
tibia	9	26.5	21.6	
		DLS	**Ld**	
phalanx III	9	34.3	27.7	
Goat		**DC**		
femur	6	21.2		
		GL	**Bp**	
phalanx II	6	25.7	11.7	
phalanx II	8	20.9	13.2	
Sheep/Goat				
phalanx I	8	-	14.4	
phalanx II	6	24.0	11.0	

Table 8.13 Measurements of sheep, goat and sheep/goat bones in mms (following von den Driesch 1976 and Davis 1985).

flat boulder field areas of the *harra* cannot be ruled out. With different tolerances, the wild sheep or Mouflon (*Ovis orientalis*) would be better suited to flat, open territory, and they have been reported from sites in a variety of habitats (Uerpmann 1987: 127; Davis *et al.* 1982; Henry and Turnbull 1985; Payne 1983).

In the more fertile areas of the Levant the question of whether domestic sheep and goats are present in the late PPNB remains debated. In her review of the evidence, Horwitz concludes that there is no evidence for domestic caprines in this period based on morphological or metrical changes (1989: 169). Köhler-Rollefson, however, has argued that on the basis of cull patterns and pathologies in the PPNB goats from 'Ain Ghazal, domestication is well under way (Köhler-Rollefson 1989). Whatever the actual status of caprines, it is clear that some sites see an increase in the relative frequency of sheep and goats in the PPNB (e.g. Jericho, Abu Hureyra). The possibility, therefore, that caprines under some form of human control may have been present during both periods of occupation at Dhuweila must be considered.

Baird *et al.* have recently reviewed the evidence for late Pleistocene and early Holocene caprine remains from eastern Jordan (Baird *et al.* 1992: 28–29). In short, they report that the Epipalaeolithic sites in both Wadi Jilat (limestone region) and the Azraq oasis, have produced only 3 caprine bones out of a total of more than 12,000 identifiable fragments. Early/middle PPNB sites in Wadi Jilat contain no caprines, whilst the late PPNB site of Azraq 31 includes 2 from a small sample of 56 identifiable bones. It is not until the Early Late Neolithic in the area that caprines constitute over 10% of faunal assemblages (Baird *et al.* 1992; Mylona 1992; Powell 1992). Further northeast, in the basalt area, the Natufian site of Khallat 'Anaza produced a small faunal assemblage of 29 bones, of which 18 were caprines, and 2 of these identified to *Capra* sp. (Garrard 1985; see 'Natufian sites' above). The late PPNB in the basalt area

is represented by the site of Ibn el-Ghazzi, where 2 of a total of 20 bones were found to be from caprines. These finds indicate that wild caprines, specifically goats, were present in the *harra* of eastern Jordan, but the very low frequencies in which they appear at sites with adequate samples prior to the Late Neolithic imply either that they were sparse, only irrupted into the area on occasions, or that they were avoided as large-scale game.

Since there is evidence for wild goats in the area, and wild sheep would not be unexpected in this habitat, it is tempting to interpret the extremely low proportions of caprines as evidence for their being wild animals, occasionally hunted amongst the array of other game. The presence of over 50% caprines in the unambiguously Late Neolithic phase of Burqu' 27 (McCartney 1992) — a site 50 kms northeast of Dhuweila — suggests however, that herding had reached the *harra* by the 6th millennium BC, and the possibility that the Late Neolithic or even PPNB Dhuweila caprines represented herded animals cannot be entirely dismissed.[1]

Hare

The bones of hare (*Lepus* sp.) are the second most numerous after those of gazelle, being represented by 312 fragments (2.6% of total), although their small size would make them a much less important resource in terms of meat weight. Table 8.14 shows the minimum number of bones for each stage, and measurements are given in Appendix B. It must be pointed out that some of the hare bones from Stage 3 appeared quite fresh, and stood out from the rest of the assemblage in terms of surface patination.

Most of the bones are from adult individuals, although a total of 11 longbones had unfused ends, therefore belonging to immature animals. Meat yields from an average sized hare would be approximately 2.25kg (Garrard 1980: tab. 3B), and they could also have provided skins.

Wolf/Dog/Jackal

Eighteen fragments belong to *Canis* spp. and could be from either wolf, dog or jackal (Table 8.15 gives the minimum number of bones). None of the bones allow meaningful measurements, and there are no M^1 teeth, which have been used metrically to suggest whether specimens from prehistoric Levantine sites belonged to wolves or domestic dogs (Davis 1981; 1987: 138).

Fox

A total of 19 fox bones was recovered, and the minimum number of elements these represent is shown in Table 8.16. The fox species likely to have been present around the site are *Vulpes vulpes* and maybe also the smaller desert fox, *Vulpes ruppelli* (Harrison 1968). The main distinguishing criterion is size, and in this respect two measurements from Dhuweila (radius

Element	PPNB	LN	EB	Total
mandible	1	10	3	14
maxilla	1	5	2	8
atlas	0	1	0	1
scapula	2	1	2	5
humerus	5	16	9	30
radius	1	6	5	12
ulna	3	4	4	11
pelvis	5	13	12	30
femur	2	1	5	8
tibia	1	8	8	17
metapodials	6	24	39	69
phalanx I	0	8	4	12
phalanx II	0	0	1	1
phalanx III	0	0	0	0
astragalus	0	3	6	9
calcaneum	4	17	15	36
naviculo-cuboid	0	0	2	2

Table 8.14 The minimum number of hare bones for each period.

Phase	Element
1	humerus proximal
3	humerus proximal
5	metapodial proximal
6	femur proximal
6	patella
6	metapodial proximal
6	metapodial distal
6	metapodial distal
6	phalanx I distal
6	phalanx II
6	phalanx II
6	mandibular tooth fragment
8	phalanx I proximal
9	phalanx I
9	phalanx II distal

Table 8.15 Representation of *Canis* spp. (wolf/fox/jackal) by phase, shown as the minimum number of bones.

Phase	Element
1	phalanx II
2	mandible
3	scapula
3	humerus distal
3	pelvis
5	scapula
5	pelvis
5	metapodial distal
5	mandible
6	M_1 (deciduous)
7	radius distal
7	femur proximal
8	maxillary tooth
10	pelvis
10	phalanx I

Table 8.16 The minimum of fox bones by phase.

	Phase	SLC	GLP	BG	Bd
scapula	5	13.6	14.6	08.3	-
humerus	3	-	-	-	15.5
		Bp			**Bd**
radius	7	10.1	-	-	12.5
		LAR	**SH**	**SB**	**SC**
pelvis	3	12.4	03.6	10.2	27.7
	5	12.1	04.9	09.0	25.7

Table 8.17 Measurements of fox bones, by phase (mms).

Bp and pelvis LAR, seen in Table 8.16) show a similarity with the Palaeolithic fox bones from Douara Cave which Payne implies are mostly *Vulpes vulpes* (Payne 1983: 51–52). One measurement, however, (humerus Bd in Table 8.16) is significantly smaller than those from Douara Cave. The most frequently used element for comparing archaeological fox material is the carnassial tooth, or mandibular M1 (Davis 1977; 1981); the single adult example from Dhuweila is broken and unmeasurable, thus not permitting wider comparisons.

Badger

A total of 3 bones was identified to badger (*Meles meles*). These were a scapula, an astragalus and a calcaneum, all from phase 9. One measurement was taken (mm):

	Phase	GL	GB
Calcaneum	9	29.3	14.8

Hedgehog

Six hedgehog mandibles were found (phases 1, 3, 8, 9); 1 maxilla (phase 5); 4 distal humeri (phases 1, 7, 8), and 2 proximal femurs (phase 6). Of the distal humeri, the one from phase 1 and two from phase 7 have supracondylar foramena, suggesting either *Hemiechinus* or *Paraechinus*, the more arid-dwelling species, as opposed to the larger *Erinaceus* which inhabits moister areas (Payne 1983: 12–13). One measurement was taken (mm):

	Phase	Bd
Humerus	3	09.3

Rodents

Seventeen mandibles were identified as either jird (*Meriones* sp.) or jird/gerbil (*Meriones/Gerbillus* spp.). The presence of these bones only in the upper levels of the site suggests that they may have been incorporated into the assemblage after the main periods of occupation. Both jirds and gerbils are burrowing animals.

Birds (identified by Barbara West)

Table 8.18 shows the list of bird bones recovered in each phase.

Most of these birds are likely to have been found year-round in the area of the site. The little bittern, however, is today a spring/autumn visitor to the area, due to its need for standing water, and both the pin-tailed sandgrouse and Pallas's sandgrouse are currently present only in winter.

Tortoise

A single fragment of tortoise carapace (*Testudo graeca*) was found in phase 8.

Reptile mandibles

Nine small reptile mandibles (probably lizards) were found in phase 10. They are unlikely to be related to the occupation of the site.

Summary

Gazelle bones make up over 90% of the assemblage from the PPNB and Late Neolithic deposits. *G. subgutturosa* is identified from two horncore fragments. The small size of most of the gazelle remains may reflect the presence of another species, or could equally suggest that the early Holocene *Gazella subgutturosa* in the area were much smaller than known modern comparative material.

If one assumes spring birth peaks for gazelle, there is evidence for killing in spring/early summer, and maybe also in autumn/winter. A behavioural reconstruction for gazelles in the east Jordanian steppe is presented. Juveniles constitute 55% of the gazelle remains in the PPNB layers, and 45% in the Late Neolithic.

Phase	Species	Element
1	Black-bellied Sandgrouse	dist. humerus Bd:10.8
2	Houbara Bustard	dist. tibiotarsus
2	cf. Houbara Bustard	dist. carpometacarpus
5	cf. Partridge	dist. humerus
6	Sandgrouse	coracoid (juvenile) coracoid
6-8	Quail	complete humerus GL:33.2 Bp:7.8 SC:2.6 Bd:5.3
6-8	cf. Little Owl	dist. tarsometatarsus
7	Quail	prox. humerus prox. humerus dist. humerus Bd:5.6
7	Little Bittern	dist. tarsometatarsus
7	cf. Little Owl	prox. tarsometatarsus
8	Pin-tailed Sandgrouse	coracoid GL:30.5
9	Pin-tailed Sandgrouse	tarsometatarsus SC:3.5 dist. humerus Bd:9.8 tarsometatarsus Bd:6.2 SC:2.8 carpometacarpus GL:31.2 Bp:8.8
9	cf. Pin-tailed Sandgrouse	carpometacarpus
9	Pallas's Sandgrouse	prox. humerus
9	Quail	prox. humerus Bp:7.5
9	cf. Little Owl	dist. femur
10	cf. Black-bellied Sandgrouse	dist. humerus
10	Cream-coloured Courser	dist. humerus Bd:7.0
10	Quail	prox. humerus prox. humerus tarsometatarsus
10	cf. Little Owl	dist. tarsometatarsus

Table 8.18 Bird bones identified from each phase, with any measurements (codes follow von den Driesch 1976) given below the element (in mms).

Fragmentation patterns suggest that gazelle bones were intensively cracked for marrow or grease extraction. Carnivore ravaging of the assemblage was probably low.

All gazelle body parts are present at the site, although a low representation of phalanges may point to skinning taking place elsewhere, or skins being exported with phalanges attached. Body-part frequencies resemble patterns for consumption or processing sites, rather than kill-butchery sites.

Besides gazelle, the rest of the assemblage is made up of equids (*Equus hemionus/asinus* being positively identified), caprines (both sheep and goat), hare, fox, canids (wolf/dog/jackal), badger, hedgehog, birds and a single fragment of tortoise.

Morphologically it cannot be determined whether the caprines and canids are of wild or domestic status, or include both. From their low proportions in the assemblage, and comparison with similar period sites, it is tentatively suggested that the caprine remains belonged to wild species.

Three of the identified bird species would today only visit the area in wetter seasons, inferring that they were hunted in autumn-spring.

Conclusions

The interpretation of Dhuweila as a hunting camp is attested by the over-riding dominance of gazelle bones at the site. Seasonal use of the site has been suggested (Betts 1988 and this volume), and the gazelle cull patterns lend support to this, with indications of hunting in spring/early summer and maybe also autumn/winter. The presence of a little bittern, pin-tailed sandgrouse and Pallas's sandgrouse also imply hunting during the wetter months of the year (i.e. autumn to spring), at least. Occupation at other times of the year, however, cannot be ruled out.

There is no positive evidence for the presence of any domestic species at Dhuweila. The diagnostic equid remains can only be identified to a general category of wild ass/donkey, but in view of what is known of equid domestication, the Dhuweila specimens are likely to belong to the wild ass, a common inhabitant of steppic areas. The caprine remains also provide no firm evidence as to their wild/domestic status, although through comparison with other PPNB and Late Neolithic faunas in the area and consideration of their consistently low proportions, it is suggested that they are from wild animals. Whether the canid remains may include representation of domestic dog is uncertain. Ecologically, the species found are all representative of dry steppe, although lack of positive identification in many instances hinders more detailed habitat inferences.

Sites which show high proportions of a single wild species, particularly gazelle, are common in the Levantine Epipalaeolithic. Kebaran and Natufian sites such as Nahal Oren, Kharaneh IV, Urkan e-Rub, El Wad B, Hayonim Terrace and Salibiya I, all have assemblages in which gazelles make up over 75% (Noy *et al.* 1973; Hovers *et al.* 1988; Bate 1937; Henry *et al.* 1981; Crabtree *et al.* 1991; Martin 1994). By the Late PPNB many sites in the more fertile areas show significant frequencies of sheep and goat in their assemblages, such as 'Ain Ghazal (Köhler-Rollefson *et al.* 1988) and Basta (Becker 1991). There are, however, PPNB sites which compare with Dhuweila in that they are interpreted as hunting camps. Ujrat el-Mehed is a late PPNB site in the southern Sinai, which has a totally wild fauna consisting mainly of ibex/goat with much less gazelle (Dayan *et al.* 1986). Also in the southern Sinai, Wadi Tbeik (which is dated slightly earlier) shows a similar faunal spectrum (Tchernov and Bar-Yosef 1982).

Suggestions have been forwarded that a focus on hunting of gazelles in areas of the Levant may have led to over-predation (Legge and Rowley-Conwy 1987; Davis 1983), or some form of cultural control (Legge

1972) or loose-herding (Saxon 1974) of the animal. Most of these ideas find supporting evidence in the recognition of high proportions of juveniles at sites. The percentages of juveniles at Dhuweila is higher than at many other sites (see Davis 1983), particularly Epipalaeolithic ones, and although Baharav (1974) finds an equally 'high' juvenile/yearling component in modern gazelle herds in the Galilee, this can be explained by their double annual births, which steppic gazelles are unlikely to have. It is necessary, therefore, to look at arguments for over-predation or animal selection to explain the high proportions of juveniles at Dhuweila, and in this respect, it is of interest to compare the Dhuweila data with the proportions of juveniles from earlier sites in the eastern Jordanian steppe (Martin 1994).

It is noteworthy that the two main periods of use at Dhuweila show very similar relative proportions of species and animal exploitation patterns. It could be argued that the site saw similar hunting activities over repeated occupations.

Acknowledgements

I would like to thank Alison Betts for allowing me to study the Dhuweila faunal remains.[2] I am also grateful to Douglas Baird, Simon Davis, Andrew Garrard and Paul Halstead for reading an earlier draft of this report and for each providing very helpful comments. Additional thanks are due to Simon Davis for help with identifications, and for allowing me to use the unpublished recent *Gazella gazella* measurements used in Figure 8.6. I would also like to thank Adrienne Powell for valuable assistance in the preparation of this report. The study of the Dhuweila faunal remains was made possible by grants from the Wainwright Fund and the SERC. The Department of Archaeology and Prehistory, University of Sheffield, and the British Institute at Amman for Archaeology and History provided support of many kinds. The bird bones were identified by Barbara West.

Notes

1 Context 4210 (phase 8) produced 36 sheep bones which have not been included in the above counts since they are probably intrusive. These remains all derived from one area and differ in surface patination from the majority of the Dhuweila assemblage. In addition, the observations that all the diagnostic elements can be identified to sheep, that the minimum number of individuals represented is one, and that states of fusion consistently give ages of approximately 3 years old, all strongly suggest that these bones belong to one animal which may have arrived on the site under different circumstances from the rest of the bones.

2. This chapter was originally submitted for publication in 1992, and the text remains largely unchanged since that date.

Appendix A

Gazelle Fusion Data

Gazelle fusion data for phases 1–9 are presented below. The approximate ages of fusion (*) are taken from Davis (1980a:133, 1987:40), based on zoo-bred Israeli *Gazella gazella*.

Dhuweila Phase 1

Element	Fusion Age *(months)	Number Unfused	Number Fused	% Fused
d humerus	c.2	9	18	66.7
p radius	c.2	1	15	93.8
TOT >c.2 months	-	**10**	**33**	**76.7**
scapula-coracoid	3-6	3	7	70.0
p first phalanx	5-8	8	24	75.0
TOT >3-8 months	-	**11**	**31**	**73.8**
d tibia	8-10	8	10	55.6
TOT >8-10 months	-	**8**	**10**	**55.6**
p femur	10-16	6	12	66.7
calcaneum	10-16	16	9	36.0
d metacarpal	10-16	3	7	70.0
d metatarsal	10-16	6	3	33.3
d femur	10-18	4	6	60.0
p humerus	12-18	2	0	00.0
p ulna	12-18	2	1	33.3
p tibia	12-18	8	5	38.5
d radius	12-18	12	7	36.8
TOT>10-18 months	-	**59**	**50**	**45.9**

Total number of bones with fusion data=212

Dhuweila Phase 3

Element	Fusion Age (months)*	Number Unfused	Number Fused	% Fused
d humerus	c.2	6	7	53.8
p radius	c.2	1	12	92.3
TOT >c.2 months	-	**7**	**19**	**73.1**
scapula-coracoid	3-6	2	17	89.5
p first phalanx	5-8	4	7	63.6
TOT >3-8 months	-	**6**	**24**	**80.0**
d tibia	8-10	7	12	63.2
TOT >8-10 months	-	**7**	**12**	**63.2**
p femur	10-16	5	3	37.5
calcaneum	10-16	15	4	21.1
d metacarpal	10-16	4	9	69.2
d metatarsal	10-16	4	8	67.7
d femur	10-18	2	1	33.3
p humerus	12-18	1	0	00.0
p ulna	12-18	2	3	60.0
p tibia	12-18	4	2	33.3
d radius	12-18	5	5	50.0
TOT>10-18 months	-	**42**	**35**	**45.5**

Total number of bones with fusion data=152

Dhuweila Phase 2

Element	Fusion Age (months)*	Number Unfused	Number Fused	% Fused
d humerus	c.2	0	7	100.0
p radius	c.2	0	6	100.0
TOT >c.2 months	-	**0**	**13**	**100.0**
scapula-coracoid	3-6	1	8	88.9
p first phalanx	5-8	8	7	46.7
TOT >3-8 months	-	**9**	**15**	**62.5**
d tibia	8-10	4	3	42.9
TOT >8-10 months	-	**4**	**3**	**42.9**
p femur	10-16	0	3	100.0
calcaneum	10-16	7	3	30.0
d metacarpal	10-16	2	3	60.0
d metatarsal	10-16	4	2	33.3
d femur	10-18	5	0	00.0
p humerus	12-18	1	0	00.0
p ulna	12-18	1	0	00.0
p tibia	12-18	6	1	14.3
d radius	12-18	1	1	50.0
TOT>10-18 months	-	**27**	**13**	**32.5**

Total number of bones with fusion data=84

Dhuweila Phase 4

Element	Fusion Age (months)*	Number Unfused	Number Fused	% Fused
d humerus	c.2	2	7	77.8
p radius	c.2	0	3	100.0
TOT >c.2 months	-	**2**	**10**	**83.3**
scapula-coracoid	3-6	1	7	87.5
p first phalanx	5-8	4	4	50.0
TOT >3-8 months	-	**5**	**11**	**68.8**
d tibia	8-10	2	4	66.7
TOT >8-10 months	-	**2**	**4**	**66.7**
p femur	10-16	2	1	33.3
calcaneum	10-16	6	0	00.0
d metacarpal	10-16	3	1	25.0
d metatarsal	10-16	2	3	60.0
d femur	10-18	2	1	33.3
p humerus	12-18	2	0	00.0
p ulna	12-18	1	1	50.0
p tibia	12-18	3	2	40.0
d radius	12-18	2	2	50.0
TOT>10-18 months	-	**23**	**11**	**32.4**

Total number of bones with fusion data=68

Dhuweila Phase 5

Element	Fusion Age (months)*	Number Unfused	Number Fused	% Fused
d humerus	c.2	4	29	87.9
p radius	c.2	0	9	100.0
TOT >c.2 months	**-**	**4**	**38**	**90.5**
scapula-coracoid	3-6	2	17	89.5
p first phalanx	5-8	9	29	76.3
TOT >3-8 months	**-**	**11**	**46**	**80.7**
d tibia	8-10	11	13	54.2
TOT >8-10 months	**-**	**11**	**13**	**54.2**
p femur	10-16	1	6	85.7
calcaneum	10-16	14	7	33.3
d metacarpal	10-16	9	12	57.1
d metatarsal	10-16	10	6	37.5
d femur	10-18	4	6	60.0
p humerus	12-18	0	3	100.0
p ulna	12-18	2	5	71.4
p tibia	12-18	5	9	64.3
d radius	12-18	4	3	42.9
TOT>10-18 months	**-**	**49**	**57**	**53.8**

Total number of bones with fusion data=229

Dhuweila Phase 7

Element	Fusion Age (months)*	Number Unfused	Number Fused	% Fused
d humerus	c.2	4	33	89.2
p radius	c.2	0	30	100.0
TOT >c.2 months	**-**	**4**	**63**	**94.0**
scapula-coracoid	3-6	1	13	92.9
p first phalanx	5-8	17	69	80.2
TOT >3-8 months	**-**	**18**	**82**	**82.0**
d tibia	8-10	12	30	71.4
TOT >8-10 months	**-**	**12**	**30**	**71.4**
p femur	10-16	16	21	56.8
calcaneum	10-16	12	28	70.0
d metacarpal	10-16	10	13	56.5
d metatarsal	10-16	13	15	53.6
d femur	10-18	7	7	50.0
p humerus	12-18	3	3	50.0
p ulna	12-18	0	7	100.0
p tibia	12-18	8	9	52.9
d radius	12-18	11	19	63.3
TOT>10-18 months	**-**	**80**	**122**	**60.4**

Total number of bones with fusion data=411

Dhuweila Phase 6

Element	Fusion Age (months)*	Number Unfused	Number Fused	% Fused
d humerus	c.2	15	27	64.3
p radius	c.2	2	42	95.5
TOT >c.2 months	**-**	**17**	**69**	**80.2**
scapula-coracoid	3-6	0	8	100.0
p first phalanx	5-8	21	59	73.8
TOT >3-8 months	**-**	**21**	**67**	**76.1**
d tibia	8-10	19	25	56.8
TOT >8-10 months	**-**	**19**	**25**	**56.8**
p femur	10-16	18	22	55.0
calcaneum	10-16	12	19	61.3
d metacarpal	10-16	12	9	42.9
d metatarsal	10-16	16	21	56.8
d femur	10-18	10	8	44.4
p humerus	12-18	4	3	42.9
p ulna	12-18	3	8	72.7
p tibia	12-18	13	9	40.9
d radius	12-18	25	10	28.6
TOT>10-18 months	**-**	**113**	**109**	**49.1**

Total number of bones with fusion data=440

Dhuweila Phase 8

Element	Fusion Age (months)*	Number Unfused	Number Fused	% Fused
d humerus	c.2	12	45	78.9
p radius	c.2	0	44	100.0
TOT >c.2 months	**-**	**12**	**89**	**88.1**
scapula-coracoid	3-6	3	14	82.4
p first phalanx	5-8	25	77	75.5
TOT >3-8 months	**-**	**28**	**91**	**76.5**
d tibia	8-10	21	30	58.8
TOT >8-10 months	**-**	**21**	**30**	**58.8**
p femur	10-16	10	27	73.0
calcaneum	10-16	17	32	65.3
d metacarpal	10-16	19	18	48.6
d metatarsal	10-16	19	24	55.8
d femur	10-18	13	12	48.0
p humerus	12-18	2	2	50.0
p ulna	12-18	4	8	66.7
p tibia	12-18	16	11	40.7
d radius	12-18	22	12	35.3
TOT>10-18 months	**-**	**122**	**146**	**54.5**

Total number of bones with fusion data=539

178

Dhuweila Phase 9

Element	Fusion Age (months)*	Number Unfused	Number Fused	% Fused
d humerus	c.2	7	40	85.1
p radius	c.2	0	34	100.0
TOT >c.2 months	-	**7**	**74**	**91.4**
scapula-coracoid	3-6	1	5	83.3
p first phalanx	5-8	11	42	79.2
TOT >3-8 months	-	**12**	**47**	**79.7**
d tibia	8-10	18	28	60.9
TOT >8-10 months	-	**18**	**28**	**60.9**
p femur	10-16	7	16	69.6
calcaneum	10-16	11	18	62.1
d metacarpal	10-16	9	7	43.8
d metatarsal	10-16	11	14	56.0
d femur	10-18	4	8	66.7
p humerus	12-18	1	2	66.7
p ulna	12-18	1	9	90.0
p tibia	12-18	7	7	50.0
d radius	12-18	10	11	52.4
TOT>10-18 months	-	**61**	**92**	**60.1**

Total number of bones with fusion data=339

Appendix B

Gazelle and Hare bone measurements

Measurements follow von den Dreisch (1976) and Davis (1985). All measurements in mm.(uf) = unfused

Gazelle

Gazelle mandible

phase	L decid row	L Premolar row	L Molar row	L Premolar and Molar row
5	-	21.5	40.7	62.3
5	-	17.9	41.4	59.4
5	-	20.1	-	-
8	-	19.5	-	-
8	25.5	-	-	-
8	25.4	-	-	-

Gazelle horn core

phase	basal circumference	greatest diameter at base	least diameter at base
4	80.5	28.1	19.8
7	85.8	29.2	20.3
9	82.1	29.0	20.3

Gazelle scapula

phase	SLC	GLP	BG
2	15.5	28.4	19.0
2	15.2	27.3	-
3	16.1	31.6	23.6
3	-	30.3	21.6
3	15.6	28.7	21.6
3	15.6	22.5	-
3	-	30.3	21.3
3	14.1	30.7	21.6
3	-	27.6	20.6
4	-	29.4	20.4
5	-	30.9	23.8
5	14.8	-	-
5	14.8	-	-
6	16.0	-	-
6	15.7	-	-
9	15.5	27.1	18.9

Gazelle humerus

phase	Bd	BT	HT
1	-	23.7	-
1	-	22.9	12.9
1	-	22.6	12.5
1	-	23.5	14.3
4	25.6	24.2	-
4	25.4	23.3	-
4	26.8	-	-
4	-	24.6	-
4	-	24.1	-
5	26.5	24.2	-
5	25.0	23.5	-
5	-	20.4	-
5	-	21.7	-
6	-	24.4	-
6	-	23.8	13.9
6	-	24.2	14.0
6	-	23.3	13.5
6	27.2	23.8	13.9
6	24.3	21.6	12.6
7	22.8	19.6	12.2
7	-	22.1	-
7	-	23.9	13.4
8	26.3	23.7	-
8	25.7	-	-
8	-	24.5	13.9
8	-	22.5	13.6
8	-	23.6	13.4
8	-	22.9	13.5
8	25.9	23.8	13.1
8	-	24.1	13.6
8	24.8	23.0	13.3
8	-	23.5	13.5
8	-	22.9	13.3
9	23.2	-	-
9	23.1	22.3	14.5
9	-	22.9	13.2

Gazelle radius

phase	Bp	Dd	Bd
1	-	-	21.2
1(uf)	-	-	18.5
1(uf)	-	-	20.1
1(uf)	-	-	23.8
3	26.1	15.1	-
3	24.6	14.4	-
3	24.3	13.8	-
3	23.6	13.7	-
6	23.0	12.8	20.9
6(uf)	-	-	22.3
6	24.3	13.8	-
6(uf)	-	-	21.7
6(uf)	-	-	20.4
7(uf)	-	-	20.4
7(uf)	-	-	22.9

179

phase			
7(uf)	-	-	20.0
7(uf)	-	-	21.3
7(uf)	-	-	21.1
7(uf)	-	-	21.5
8	24.7	14.8	-
8	23.9	13.6	-
8	23.4	12.8	-
8	22.8	-	-
8(uf)	-	-	16.7
8(uf)	-	-	22.2
8(uf)	-	-	22.9
8(uf)	-	-	22.1
8	-	-	22.3
8(uf)	-	-	18.9
8(uf)	-	-	21.0
8(uf)	-	-	20.0
8(uf)	-	-	21.2
8(uf)	-	-	21.9
9	-	-	21.8
9	-	-	23.9
9	26.9	14.5	-
9	23.1	13.1	-
9(uf)	-	-	21.2
10	23.9	13.4	-

Gazelle ulna

phase	DPA	SDO	BPC
1	-	16.1	-
3	22.3	-	13.7
3	20.0	-	12.3
4(uf)	20.4	15.6	11.9
5(uf)	-	17.5	-
5(uf)	19.5	15.4	-
5	-	15.9	-
5	21.8	17.1	13.1
6	19.6	15.9	13.1
6	18.2	15.5	12.6
6(uf)	19.1	16.0	12.9
6	20.5	15.3	-
6	-	16.3	-
6	20.9	17.0	14.4
6(uf)	18.2	15.3	-
7	20.4	16.1	12.7
8	-	16.2	-
8	20.0	16.5	13.4
8(uf)	22.8	18.1	-
8	19.5	16.4	-
9	22.0	17.7	12.7
9	-	18.2	-
9	19.2	15.6	-
9	21.4	16.8	-
9	19.1	15.6	-
9(uf)	20.0	17.1	-

Gazelle calcaneum

phase	GL	GB
1	57.0	18.0
3	57.6	19.0
9	51.0	15.0

Gazelle pelvis

phase	MinH LAR	MinW Pubis	Pubis
2	25.1	-	-
2	-	06.5	10.9
3	-	05.0	08.3
3	-	04.1	05.5
3	-	06.2	09.4
3	-	05.6	09.1
3	-	06.2	09.5
3	-	04.9	06.5
5	25.3	-	-
6	-	06.6	08.9
7	23.2	-	-
7	-	07.6	09.5
7	-	03.9	07.9
8	-	05.0	07.1
8	-	04.8	07.6
8	-	05.4	07.0
8	-	05.9	08.7
8	-	05.0	06.4
8	-	05.6	09.8
8	-	05.3	09.8
9	-	07.3	10.6
9	25.2	-	-
9	-	05.1	07.6
9	-	06.3	09.3

Gazelle femur

phase	Bp	DC	Bd
4	-	-	31.6
5	44.3	17.9	-
5	-	-	32.6
6	-	17.3	-
7	-	15.9	-
7	-	17.3	-
8	-	17.9	-
8	-	17.6	-
8	-	17.9	-
8	-	17.8	-
9	-	17.4	-
9	-	16.8	-

Gazelle naviculo-cuboid

phase	GB	GD
1	20.0	18.5
1	20.5	19.0
1	19.5	20.0
1	18.5	17.0
3	20.0	18.5
3	20.0	18.5
4	20.0	18.5
5	19.5	18.0
5	20.5	18.5
6	17.0	16.0
6	17.5	17.0
6	17.0	17.0
7	19.0	18.5
7	18.0	17.5
7	20.5	18.0
7	19.0	17.5
8	19.5	17.0
8	18.0	16.0
8	18.0	16.0
8	18.0	17.0
8	18.0	18.0
8	16.5	15.5
8	19.0	18.0
8	18.5	17.5
8	19.0	17.0
8	17.0	16.5
9	21.5	19.5
9	18.5	17.5
10	18.5	18.0
10	16.7	16.0
10	18.5	19.0
10	21.0	21.0

Gazelle tibia

phase	Bp	Bd	Dd
2(uf)	-	21.8	17.8
5	-	24.1	16.7
5	-	23.8	18.8
5	-	20.9	16.1
5	30.4	-	-
6	-	20.9	17.4
6(uf)	-	20.8	18.7
7	-	20.5	17.8
7	-	21.4	18.3
7	-	19.6	16.6
7	-	21.7	18.8

phase			
7	-	21.5	19.1
7	-	22.2	18.7
7(uf)	-	17.7	14.5
7	30.2	-	-
8	-	18.2	15.4
8	-	21.0	18.8
8	-	22.0	17.8
8	-	18.9	16.1
8(uf)	-	20.0	17.2
8(uf)	-	22.7	-
8(uf)	-	20.4	-
8(uf)	-	22.1	18.1
8(uf)	-	21.5	18.0
8	-	21.1	18.9
8(uf)	-	22.4	17.5
9(uf)	-	20.5	18.0
9	-	21.6	-
9	-	19.3	16.5
9(uf)	-	20.1	17.1
9(uf)	-	21.1	17.3
9(uf)	-	19.0	15.2
9(uf)	-	21.9	17.2
9	-	20.8	16.9
9(uf)	-	21.3	16.2
9	-	22.4	17.1
10	-	20.6	17.3

Gazelle metacarpal

phase	Bp	Dd
1	18.5	13.4
1	-	13.5
5	19.8	14.6
6	17.5	12.3
7	16.6	12.7
7	17.8	13.2

phase	Bd	Height Condyle	Width Condyle	Width Trochlea	
1	19.7	-	09.0	11.7	(med)
	-	-	08.7	11.0	(lat)
1	18.9	14.0	08.3	11.0	(med)
	-	13.8	08.4	10.4	(lat)
2	20.5	14.8	09.7	11.1	(med)
	-	14.7	09.2	11.4	(lat)
3	18.9	15.5	08.6	12.2	(med)
	-	15.4	08.3	11.5	(lat)
3	20.3	-	09.6	11.4	(med)
			09.4	11.0	(lat)
5	20.8	-	08.5	10.5	(med)
		08.6	09.7		(lat)
5	18.2	13.6	08.5	10.6	(med)
	-	13.8	08.7	10.5	(lat)
8	17.8	-	08.2	11.2	(med)
	-	14.1	08.1	10.6	(lat)
8	19.3	-	-	-	
9	18.7	-	-	-	
9	18.0	-	-	-	
9	19.6	15.0	09.0	11.6	(med)
	-	14.8	09.1	11.2	(lat)
10	18.4	-	-	-	
10	19.0	-	-	-	

Gazelle metatarsal

phase	Bp	Dp	Bd	Dd
1	-	-	20.3	14.3

phase				
1	18.0	18.0	-	-
3	-	-	-	14.3
4	-	-	21.2	17.5
4	19.5	21.8	-	-
4	-	-	19.9	14.7
5	-	-	19.8	15.4
6	-	-	19.5	14.0
6	-	-	21.2	15.6
6	-	-	19.0	14.5
8	-	-	19.4	15.0
8	-	-	19.4	14.3
8	-	-	20.2	15.7
9	-	-	19.6	14.2
9	-	-	18.7	14.4
9	-	-	19.1	14.8

Gazelle astragalus

phase	GLl	GLm	Dl	Dm	Bd
1	24.9	22.9	-		
-	-				
1	27.5	25.6	15.0	15.0	16.0
1	27.1	25.0	15.1	14.8	16.0
1	26.1	24.8	-	-	-
1	25.5	24.2	14.1	13.2	-
1	26.1	24.5	14.5	-	-
1	-	25.1	15.1	-	15.8
1	24.2	22.1	12.8	11.9	13.9
1	26.4	24.8	14.2	14.5	15.8
3	26.4	24.5	14.5	15.1	14.8
3	27.8	26.0	14.9	-	15.6
3	27.7	25.9	15.3	15.2	16.2
3	25.6	23.8	13.9	14.1	15.4
3	27.0	25.2	15.1	-	15.8
3	25.6	24.0	14.5	14.1	15.7
3	26.5	24.5	14.8	-	16.5
3	27.5	25.3	14.7	15.1	15.4
4	25.2	24.0	13.2	14.4	13.9
4	26.0	24.2	13.8	13.1	-
4	25.7	24.2	13.8	14.0	13.7

Gazelle astragalus (continued)

phase	GLl	GLm	Dl	Dm	Bd
4	24.3	22.4	14.0	-	14.5
5	24.9	23.7	13.8	14.2	15.7
5	26.1	24.4	14.8	14.2	16.4
5	25.3	22.9	14.2	14.0	14.0
5	26.9	24.5	14.9	-	14.9
5	26.8	23.9	15.9	-	15.4
5	24.7	23.5	13.6	13.9	14.4
5	23.4	-	13.5	13.9	14.5
5	26.0	-	14.4	14.5	15.5
6	25.0	24.0	13.6	13.8	15.4
6	26.2	24.0	14.7	14.6	15.7
6	24.8	23.6	13.6	13.2	15.8
6	25.1	23.5	13.9	-	14.3
6	23.3	22.5	13.1	-	13.6
6	25.2	23.8	14.2	14.0	14.4
6	24.3	23.1	13.0	13.2	14.2
6	24.8	23.5	13.6	13.6	-
6	27.0	25.1	14.6	14.9	15.6
6	25.7	23.6	-	14.0	14.8
6	26.6	24.3	14.3	14.3	14.3
6	25.4	23.8	14.0	14.0	14.5
6	25.7	23.1	14.2	14.3	15.3
6	25.2	23.9	13.9	13.9	14.3
7	26.1	24.0	13.9	14.6	-
7	23.2	22.2	12.8	12.4	13.6
7	23.5	21.2	-	-	-
7	23.2	21.3	-	-	-
7	-	-	14.5	-	14.2
8	-	23.5	-	13.7	15.0
8	26.5	-	14.3	-	-
8	22.5	-	12.1	-	12.8
8	26.7	24.0	14.3	14.0	14.8
8	-	25.7	15.0	15.0	16.1

8	24.9	23.1	14.4	15.4	15.4
9	22.7	20.9	-	-	-
9	21.1	18.7	11.3	11.5	12.0
9	25.1	23.2	13.6	13.2	13.6
9	24.5	23.2	-	-	-
9	26.1	24.4	15.0	14.4	15.6
9	24.1	22.6	13.1	13.2	-
9	-	-	-	-	14.6
9	25.6	23.9	14.5	14.4	15.8
9	25.3	23.2	13.7	13.6	14.3
9	27.1	25.3	14.8	14.4	15.2
9	-	21.7	-	-	-
9	24.0	-	-	-	-
9	26.0	24.0	14.3	14.4	16.3
10	25.1	23.6	-	-	-
10	25.5	24.3	-	-	-
10	24.9	24.1	-	-	-
10	25.9	24.7	-	-	-
10	23.8	21.6	12.6	12.3	13.3
10	22.4	21.0	11.9	11.9	-
10	21.5	20.3	11.8	11.7	12.6
10	23.2	22.2	12.1	11.5	12.6
10	23.9	22.2	13.1	12.5	13.0
10	21.3	20.1	11.8	-	12.1

Gazelle 1st phalanx

phase	GL	Bp
1	39.0	10.9
1	32.0	09.2
1	41.0	09.2
1	34.0	09.5
2	40.5	09.4
2	34.0	09.2
3	36.0	08.9
3	33.5	10.4
3	36.0	09.6
4	41.5	08.8
5	37.5	11.4
5	34.0	10.5
5	39.0	10.9
5	40.5	09.2
6	40.0	08.7
6	34.5	09.7
6	33.5	10.4
6	34.5	09.2
6	32.0	09.1
6	32.0	08.7
7	36.0	09.5
7	35.5	07.6
7	35.0	08.5
7	36.5	10.5
7	31.0	07.8
7	34.5	08.4
8	33.5	09.0
8	38.5	08.6
8	30.0	07.5
8	31.0	07.8
8	34.5	09.5
8	40.5	09.4
8	40.0	09.4
8	34.0	09.7
8	33.5	09.0
8	35.5	08.4
8	35.0	07.7
9	33.0	08.6
9	34.5	09.2
9	37.5	10.6
9	36.0	09.7
9	32.5	08.4
9	39.0	07.6
9	36.0	08.6
9	34.5	08.4
10	32.5	08.0

Gazelle 2nd phalanx

phase	GL	Bp
1	21.0	08.5
1	21.0	08.8
1	20.5	08.5
1	17.0	07.1
1	17.0	07.0
1	16.5	07.8
1	17.5	08.5
2	20.0	08.1
3	17.0	08.3
3	17.0	08.5
3	22.0	09.7
4	20.0	08.8
5	22.5	09.0
5	21.0	09.2
5	20.5	08.5
5	21.0	09.3
5	21.0	08.4
5	19.0	07.6
5	20.0	08.4
5	20.5	08.6
5	19.5	09.2
5	20.0	08.4
5	19.0	08.2
5	20.0	08.4
5	18.5	07.6
6	20.0	07.6
6	20.5	08.5
6	20.0	08.4
6	20.0	08.4
6	20.0	08.5
6	18.0	07.2
6	19.5	08.9
6	21.5	09.0
6	18.5	06.8
6	20.0	08.6
6	17.0	07.4
6	19.5	08.5
6	20.0	09.1
6	17.0	08.3
6	18.0	09.0
7	17.0	0.65
7	18.5	08.4
7	19.5	08.3
7	16.0	06.2
7	19.0	07.9
7	15.5	06.9
7	19.0	07.6
7	20.0	08.0
7	20.0	08.2
7	18.5	07.4
7	18.0	07.1
7	17.0	06.2
7	20.5	08.5
7	15.0	07.1
8	18.0	07.6
8	21.0	08.5
8	19.0	07.5
8	17.5	07.5
8	18.0	07.1
8	18.5	07.1
8	18.0	06.7
8	18.0	07.5
8	19.0	07.4
8	17.5	07.0
8	17.5	07.3
8	18.0	07.0
8	21.0	08.6
8	17.5	06.8
8	18.5	06.6
8	20.0	08.5
8	19.0	07.3
8	17.0	06.7
8	18.0	06.6

8	18.0	07.2
8	19.0	07.5
8	20.0	08.5
8	20.0	08.4
8	18.0	06.8
8	20.5	08.2
8	18.0	07.3
8	17.5	07.3
8	19.0	08.3
8	16.0	08.0
8	19.0	08.4
8	18.0	07.9
8	18.0	08.4
8	17.0	08.3
8	18.0	07.9
8	18.0	08.0
8	17.0	09.1
9	18.0	07.6
9	18.0	06.9
9	18.0	07.6
9	18.5	07.3
9	19.0	06.7
9	17.5	06.9
9	20.0	08.5
9	18.5	06.8
9	16.0	06.9
9	16.0	07.0
9	18.0	07.3
9	18.5	07.1
9	17.5	07.1
9	19.5	08.9
9	19.0	09.0
10	19.0	07.7
10	18.0	0.73
10	19.5	08.1
10	16.5	06.6
10	21.0	10.5
10	18.5	07.9
10	10.5	08.9
10	18.0	06.6
10	18.0	07.1
10	17.5	07.0
10	18.0	06.7
10	18.0	07.2
10	18.0	06.1
10	19.8	07.1
10	20.1	06.8

Gazelle 3rd phalanx

phase	DLS	Ld
1	23.8	19.2
1	25.7	21.5
1	26.4	21.4
1	24.6	19.7
1	24.6	20.0
1	25.1	20.7
1	26.8	21.5
3	23.6	19.5
3	23.9	20.3
3	26.1	20.7
4	25.5	20.6
5	24.7	20.9
5	21.3	17.3
5	25.4	20.0
6	24.0	19.4
6	23.5	18.9
6	24.5	19.8
6	23.3	18.8
7	24.5	20.0
7	21.7	18.1
7	22.9	18.0
7	26.1	21.5
7	23.5	20.7
8	22.5	18.0
8	24.2	19.7

8	20.8	16.2
8	23.3	18.5
8	23.7	18.7
8	18.9	14.8
8	21.9	17.3
8	22.6	17.8
8	24.9	20.3
8	26.2	22.2
8	23.8	19.7
8	24.4	19.5
8	24.1	19.2
8	22.0	17.5
8	25.5	20.9
8	22.9	19.8
8	23.4	18.5
8	23.4	18.5
8	24.1	20.2
8	24.0	20.1
9	24.7	19.9
9	22.8	18.3
9	25.3	20.8
9	22.9	18.3
9	21.3	17.1
9	23.9	19.7
9	24.0	19.3
9	22.7	18.5
9	24.8	21.3
9	23.4	18.3

Hare

Hare humerus

phase	GL	Dp	Bd	Dd
1	-	-	08.4	06.5
1	-	-	08.6	06.8
2	-	-	09.3	07.0
3	-	-	09.2	07.1
6	-	-	08.7	06.5
7	-	-	07.9	-
8	-	-	08.6	06.4
8	-	-	08.1	06.5
8	-	-	08.4	06.3
9	-	-	08.7	06.7
9	-	-	08.1	06.1
9	-	-	08.4	06.4
9	-	-	08.4	06.2
9	-	-	08.1	06.4
9	-	-	08.2	06.6
10	71.6	11.0	08.4	06.7
10	-	-	08.2	06.3
10	-	-	08.4	06.3
10	-	-	07.7	05.9
10	-	-	07.9	06.3
10	-	-	08.4	06.1

Hare radius

phase	Bp	SD	Bd
6	06.7	-	-
8	06.8	-	-
9	07.1	-	-
9	06.0	-	-
10	-	-	07.2
10	-	04.1	07.0
10	06.6	-	-
10	-	03.8	07.6
10	05.7	-	-

Hare pelvis

phase	LAR	SH	SB	SC
3	09.5	05.0	07.5	24.9
4	08.5	-	-	-
4	09.2	-	-	-
8	09.6	-	-	-
9	08.2	-	-	-

9	09.6	-	-	-
10	09.1	04.8	07.4	24.9
10	-	05.8	09.0	25.6
10	09.0	05.3	07.9	25.0
10	09.4	05.1	07.8	20.1
10	07.9	-	-	-
10	09.5	05.1	08.0	25.1
10	-	04.6	08.1	25.3
10	08.2	-	-	-

Hare scapula

phase	GLP	LG	BG
5	09.2	05.5	07.9
10	10.0	06.1	08.3

Hare mandible

phase	L premol row	LP and M row
5	-	14.6
10	10.8	-
10	06.7	14.5

Hare femur

phase	GL	Bd
5	-	13.1
10	85.7	13.7

Hare tibia

phase	Bp	Bd	Dd
5	-	10.4	07.1
5	12.8	-	-
9	-	10.0	06.6
9	-	10.8	07.1
10	13.5	-	-
10	13.9	-	-
10	-	10.8	06.8
10	-	11.5	06.5
10	-	11.4	07.1
10	-	10.4	06.1
10	-	10.5	06.0
10	-	10.7	06.7

Hare astragalus

phase	GL
6	11.8
7	11.1
9	11.9
10	11.7
10	11.1
10	11.7
10	11.1
10	10.8

Hare calcaneum

phase	GL	GB
3	21.2	07.4
5	22.4	07.7
5	24.1	07.7
7	23.7	07.3
8	23.7	07.2
9	22.2	07.3
9	22.4	06.9
10	23.3	07.8
10	22.1	07.3
10	23.0	07.9
10	24.0	07.7
10	22.3	07.1
10	23.2	08.0
10	23.8	07.5

9. Dhuweila: Botanical Remains

S. Colledge

with a contribution by J. Hather

Introduction

Ten small samples were collected for archaeobotanical analyses from ashy deposits in PPNB and Late Neolithic contexts. Water flotation was undertaken to separate charred plant remains from the mineral matrix of the samples. Identifiable whole/fragmentary plant items were extracted from the flots. Preservation of the remains was poor. Three of the ten samples did not contain any identifiable plant material.

Dhuweila is situated in the dry steppe of eastern Jordan. The flora of the area is composed of elements of Irano-Turanian and Sudanian vegetation.

Taxa represented by charred seeds in the samples

Wild cereals

Identification of wild cereals

Identifications which require a distinction to be made between ancient wild and domestic cereal species are always problematic. For most species of wheat and barley identifications based on the diagnostic characteristics of spikelet and rachis morphology are far more reliable than those which are based on grain morphology alone. At Dhuweila no cereal chaff was found accompanying the cereal grains in the samples.

It has been possible only to state that the few grains from the Dhuweila samples resemble certain present-day cereal species. The suffix 'type' has been added to the species names to indicate the limitations of identifications based only on the knowledge of modern populations.

The two wild cereals represented by the grains found in the Dhuweila samples are both closely related to the domestic species. Zohary and Hopf state that the wild barley is cross-compatible and fully inter-fertile with the cultivated species (1988: 28). In fields where the wild species infested the domestic crop, there would have been the possibility for inter-breeding and also for producing hybrids which could have shown morphological characteristics of both forms.

Triticum boeoticum type

Context 2124 produced two embryo end fragments of a grain resembling *Triticum boeoticum*, wild einkorn. The small grain size and the prominent dorsal ridges of the two specimens were indicative of the wild species. The illustration of the better preserved specimen from 2124 shows how, in all views, the fragment tapers to the embryo tip and this, together with the lateral compression of the grain, are distinguishing features of einkorn.

Today wild einkorn is widely distributed over western Asia and the southern Balkan peninsula (Zohary 1989:360). The primary habitats for the species are in the herbaceous cover of oak-park-forest and in steppe-like formations. In areas further away from the distribution centre it is found in secondary habitats, and as Zohary and Hopf state, 'at sites which were very probably not available before the opening up of these areas to agricultural activity' (1988: 32). Wild einkorn has a wide ecological amplitude with respect to both soils and climates. It is extremely common in basalt areas (Zohary 1971; Zohary and Hopf 1988).

Grains identified as *Triticum boeoticum* have been found on several other PPNB sites. In Syria it has been identified at the sites of Mureybet and Ramad. At Mureybet (van Zeist and Bakker Heeres 1984) wild einkorn was present in samples with wild barley and here, as at Dhuweila, there was no evidence of domestic cereals. On early Neolithic sites it has been found more commonly in contexts which also contain domestic wheat and/or barley. At Ramad (van Zeist and Bakker Heeres 1982) it was identified in many of the PPNB contexts and in all cases it occurred with domestic einkorn and/or emmer. Wild einkorn and domestic einkorn and emmer were in Aceramic Neolithic samples from Abu Hureyra (Hillman 1975). At Wadi Jilat 7 wild einkorn was found in three contexts, together with the two species of domestic hulled wheats. The sites recorded here are situated well outside the present distribution centre for the wild species. Pollen evidence from the Hula and Ghab valleys (Baruch and Bottema 1991; van Zeist and Woldring 1980) indicated that in the northern and southern Levantine regions at the beginning of the Holocene there was an increase in the relative humidity caused by an increase in precipitation. For the earlier site of Abu Hureyra, Hillman suggested that with the increase in moisture at the Pleistocene/Holocene boundary wild einkorn could well have spread into areas of steppe, beyond the limits of the

Other wild plants

Wild grasses

Stipa sp.

Remains of grains of species of steppe grasses, *Stipa* spp., were found in two contexts on the site. The grains of this genus are more or less cylindrical, the embryo ends of the grains tend to be 'chisel-shaped', and the ventral furrows are indistinct. Both of the Dhuweila specimens showed these features. The poor preservation of the grains precluded identification to the species level. *Flora Palaestina* records six species of *Stipa*. Four of the species favour steppic habitats (Feinbrun-Dothan 1986: 262–5).

Hordeum sp. (weed species)

In context 4118 there was one grain of a weed barley. The specimen is illustrated alongside the wild barley grains and the differences and similarities of the two species of the genus are apparent. No attempt was made to identify to species on the basis of only one grain. In the *Flora Palaestina* six wild/weed species of *Hordeum* are recorded. The ecological range of the species includes saline marsh habitats (Feinbrun-Dothan 1986: 179–83).

Other taxa

Arnebia decumbens/linearifolia

The embryos of the two seeds found in the Dhuweila samples were charred, proving that they were not modern intrusions. The four species of *Arnebia* recorded in the *Flora Palaestina* all grow in deserts (Feinbrun-Dothan 1978: 68–70). The roots of plants of this genus are collected for their purple dyes (Musil 1928). The presence of the seeds of the two species in the Dhuweila contexts does not prove conclusively, however, that the plants were being collected for this purpose.

Atriplex sp. – bracts

A pair of bracts (which enclosed a seed) of a species of *Atriplex* were found in the sample from context 2133. Ten species of *Atriplex* are recorded in the *Flora Palaestina*. The habitats favoured by the species include wadi beds or depressions in desertic sandy soils, and several members of the genus grow in saline environments (Zohary 1966: 143–150).

Erodium sp.

Three PPNB contexts produced seeds of the genus *Erodium*. Two specimens have been illustrated. Identification to the species level was not possible. Several species of *Erodium* favour desertic/steppic habitats. *Flora Palaestina* records that two of these, *E. Hirtum* and *E. glaucophyllum,* are known to be collected for their edible tubers/roots (Zohary 1972: 231–243).

Again, however, the presence of seeds of a certain taxa is no proof that other plant parts were being used.

Leguminosae indet.

No attempt was made to identify specimens to genus in the categories 'small' and 'large legumes'. The 'small legume' category included the genera *Astragalus*, *Trigonella*, *Trifolium*, *Melilotus* and *Medicago*. Of these, the first two genera comprise large groups of species favouring steppic/desertic habitats (Zohary 1972). The 'large legume' category included the genera *Vicia* and *Lathyrus*.

Liliaceae, types i and ii

Specimens of types i and ii have been illustrated. On the broken fragment of the type ii specimen, it is possible to see the pattern of cells radiating from the central cavity in the seed. It was easy to identify fragments of Liliaceae seeds on this basis. Poor preservation of the seeds in the PPNB and LN contexts prevented the possibility of further identification.

Plantago sp.

The ecological range of species of *Plantago* includes sandy desertic habitats (Feinbrun-Dothan 1978: 220–232).

	2124	2128	2133	2125	2111	4118	4214
Triticum boeoticum type embryo end fragments	2	-	-	-	-	-	-
Hordeum spontaneum type							
whole grains	1	-	-	-	-	-	-
embryo end fragments	1	-	-	-	-	-	-
cf. Stipa sp.							
whole grains	-	-	-	-	-	1	-
grain fragments	-	-	-	1	-	-	-
Hordeum sp. (weed type)							
whole grains	-	-	-	-	6	-	-
Gramineae indet.							
grain fragments	-	-	-	1	-	1	-
Arnebia decumbens	1	-	-	-	-	-	-
Arnebia linearifolia	-	-	-	-	-	-	1
Atriplex sp. - bracts	-	-	1	-	-	-	-
Chenopodiaceae/ Caryophyllaceae	-	-	-	-	-	3	
Erodium sp.	2	1	1				
Small legume indet.	7	5	4	3	1	-	2
Large legume indet. cotyledons	1	-	-	-	-	-	-
Liliaceae							
type i	-	2	-	2	1	6	5
type ii	-	1	1	-	-	1	-
indet.	-	-	-	-	1	3	1
Plantago sp.	1	-	-	-	-	1	-
Scirpus sp.	-	-	-	-	-	1	-
Type X fragments	1	3	4	7	-	5	2
Root/tuber remains (cf. *Orobancheaceae*)	x	-	-	-	-	x	-
Unidentifiable	1	-	-	3	3	1	1

Table 9.2   List of taxa represented in the samples.

Scirpus sp.

One Scirpus seed was found in the LN context 4118. The six species recorded in the *Flora Palaestina* favour marsh habitats, and of these *Scirpus maritimus* grows on saline soils (Feinbrun-Dothan 1986:348–51).

Type X fragments

Type X fragments were found in six of the seven contexts. Type X has also been found in samples from Wadi Jilat 7 and Azraq 31. The fragments are from the leafy parts of a plant, but so far it has been impossible to identify them further.

Root/tuber remains

In two samples there were charred remains of parenchymatous material.

The parenchymatous charcoals (*J. Hather*)

Identifiable parenchymatous fragments were found in contexts 2124 and 4118 (Plates 13, 14). While the preservation of these tissues is not excellent, due mostly to the post-charring effects of abrasion, certain characters are easily visible and are of diagnostic value. the fragments are small, no more than 3 mm across and composed largely of uniform parenchymatous tissue and vascular bundles. In places the parenchyma had deteriorated to solid carbon, but generally the cells were easily visible. These are thin-walled, ovoid in shape and randomly oriented, or spherical, measuring between 30–55 microns across. Occasional cells appear to have thicker cell walls, though this was uncommon.

Vascular tissue is collected into distinct concentric bundles with an amphicribal organisation. The xylem tissue is preserved more or less intact though the phloem has been reduced to a narrow band of solid carbon. This is not unusual in tissues of this type. No epidermal, endodermal or analagous structure was found.

The occurrence of such vascular bundles within a large body of parenchymatous storage tissue indicates that these remains are of swollen stem rather than of any other stem or root structure. Considering the environment and presuming that the present flora is more limited than that of any previous time, the number of possible plants that these fragments could be the remains of is restricted. The particular combination of characters presented by these charcoal fragments leads to a tentative identification as *Cistance tubulosa* (Orobancheaceae) and compare favourably with modern reference material.

Ethnographic data suggesting a use as food for *Cistance tubulosa* is given by Bailey and Danin (1981). They state that the roasted swollen stem may be used as food.

Comments on the plant remains from Dhuweila

There are many problems associated with the interpretation of ancient assemblages which consist entirely of the remains of wild plants. There is bound to be ambiguity regarding the use of the species represented, and particularly as there are no obvious 'crop' components in the sample. At Dhuweila the low numbers of seeds further limited any interpretation of the significance of the presence of certain taxa and it has not been possible, therefore, to suggest that there was deliberate collection of any of the plants.

Using the notes based on the ecological preferences of modern populations of the taxa represented, it could be argued that most of the plants would have been growing in areas nearby to the site, on the playa, or out in the steppe. The weeds may have been collected with dry brushwood and brought onto the site for fuel. There are perhaps more explanations for the accidental presence of seeds on sites (and in the fires on those sites). The deliberate use of the wild cereals as a source of food, however, cannot be discounted. The PPNB occupation at Dhuweila has been interpreted as a seasonal hunting station which was visited in the late winter/early spring to catch migrating gazelle. The area would not have supported cultivation and so the inhabitants may have supplemented their diet of wild game with locally grown wild cereals which could have been collected and processed with relatively little effort. Hather's comment on the possible use of *Cistanche tubulosa* as a food source supports the idea of local foraging.

In the Dhuweila samples there was an absence of seeds of perennial Chenopodiaceae, common in the steppe, which flower and fruit in late summer/autumn. In contrast, several species were identified in PPNB contexts at Wadi Jilat 7. Absence of these taxa is hardly proof that the site was abandoned late in the year, but the comparison of the composition of the Dhuweila samples with those from Wadi Jilat 7 may be significant.

10. Dhuweila: Area Survey

A.V.G. Betts

Area survey

Regional survey has produced evidence for relatively extensive use of the *harra* in the Neolithic period, particularly as an area for hunting. Sites include hilltop knapping/lookout stations, small camps like Dhuweila with a few irregular structures, 'kite' enclosures with impact-fractured arrowheads and isolated flint scatters (Plates 15, 16). Sites in the Dhuweila area have been surveyed in some detail, and a sounding was made at one small occupation site, Abu Masiad al-Sharqi.

Dhuweila lies on a chain of 'kites', running north–south down the eastern edge of a series of mudflats (Figure 10.1). Three similar hunting stations have been found in the area, together with knapping sites, rock carvings (see 'rock art' above) and broken arrowheads in 'kite' enclosures. The two sites Abu Masiad al-Gharbi and Abu Masiad al-Sharqi are single occupation sites of the Early Neolithic period, with one or more small structures built into 'kite' walls. Around each were found rock carvings in the 'Dhuweila' style. Further north is the larger site of Zumlat 'Arus. This lies just below the crest of a high hill, has deep occupation deposits, and, like Dhuweila, was occupied in both the Early Neolithic and Late Neolithic periods. 'Kite' walls run off the hill and a carving in the 'Dhuweila' style was found nearby.

Survey in the Dhuweila area has shown a specific pattern of site location in these periods. Hunting stations with structures are sited on high or rising ground, usually just below the crest of a hill, but high enough to provide a good view of the surrounding country. Sites are also located with regard to water supply. In the Dhuweila area, they are concentrated along the two main wadi systems of Wadi Dhuweila and Wadi al-'Asaji al-Janubi (Figure 10.2). Both wadis are deeply incised and hold water in *ghudran* into the dry season. Sites are also placed in relation to the 'kite' systems, often built into 'kite' walls.

Abu Masiad al-Sharqi

A sounding of one metre by one metre was put into the site of Abu Masiad al-Sharqi (Figures 10.3; 10.4). The aim of the sounding was to test the nature of occupation at the site and to establish whether the structures were bonded into the 'kite' wall. The sounding revealed loose sandy occupation layers with Early Neolithic (PPNB) artefacts from topsoil to bedrock (Figure 10.5: 5). The

range of lithics from the site were similar to that from Stage 1 at Dhuweila. Fragments of bone were also recovered. The occupation layers ran up against two massive boulders which also formed part of the 'kite' wall. A stone with a carving in the 'Dhuweila' style was resting partly on topsoil and partly on one of the boulders. The evidence strongly suggests that 'kite' wall and site were contemporary.

Abu Masiad al-Gharbi

Abu Masiad al-Gharbi is similar to Abu Masiad al-Sharqi. It presently consists of a low mound of rubble with a scatter of flint and fragments of bone in and around the boulders. Traces of small structures can be seen among the tumble and the mound lies alongside and abutting a 'kite' wall. While no soundings were carried out to determine the precise relationship of the 'kite' wall to the structures, the two seem to be linked in the same way as Abu Masiad al-Sharqi. A number of carvings of animals and one of human figures (see 'Rock art' above) were found on and around the site. The flint scatter indicates that it was occupied in the Early Neolithic (PPNB) period.

Zumlat 'Arus

Zumlat 'Arus is similar to Dhuweila, in that it is relatively large and was apparently established in the PPNB and re-occupied in the Late Neolithic period. It is not built on a 'kite' wall, but lies on the line of 'kites' passing through the other sites and the location of the site affords a good view over open country to the south and west (Figure 10.1). Recent disturbance revealed ashy occupation layers rich in bone and chipped stone. Flints from the site are similar to those from Dhuweila and include exhausted bipolar cores, Byblos points and broken Nizzanim points. An animal carving in the 'Dhuweila' style was found on a rock at the mouth of the wadi to the southwest of the site (see 'Rock art' above).

The 'Kite' Systems

The system of 'kite' walls and enclosures in the Dhuweila area is complex and impossible accurately to plan on the ground. It is clear that the system was in use over a long period of time. There is evidence of overbuilding and reconstruction; some walls have eroded away or have been robbed out both for the

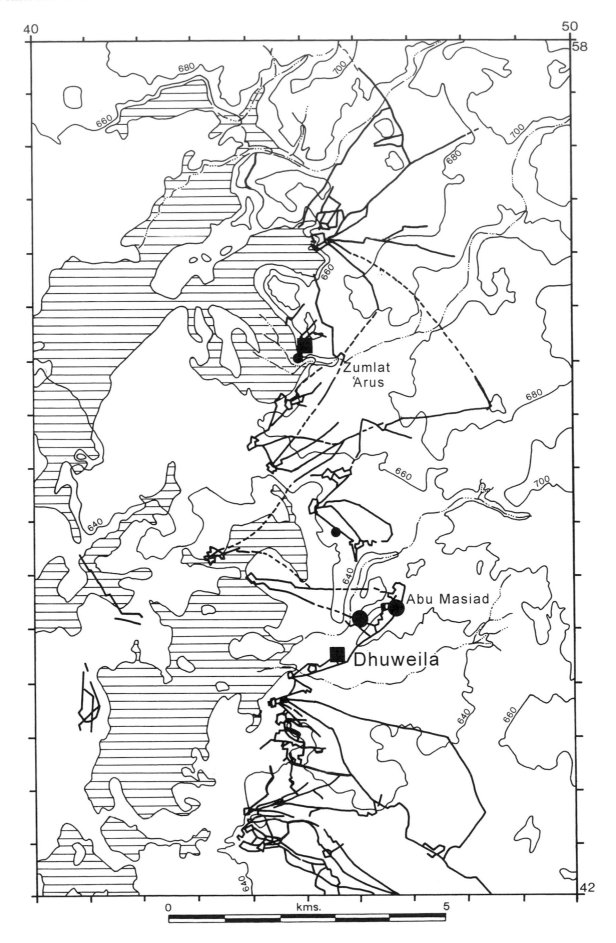

Figure 10.1   Sites and 'kites' in the Dhuweila area. (based on 1: 50,000 Map series).

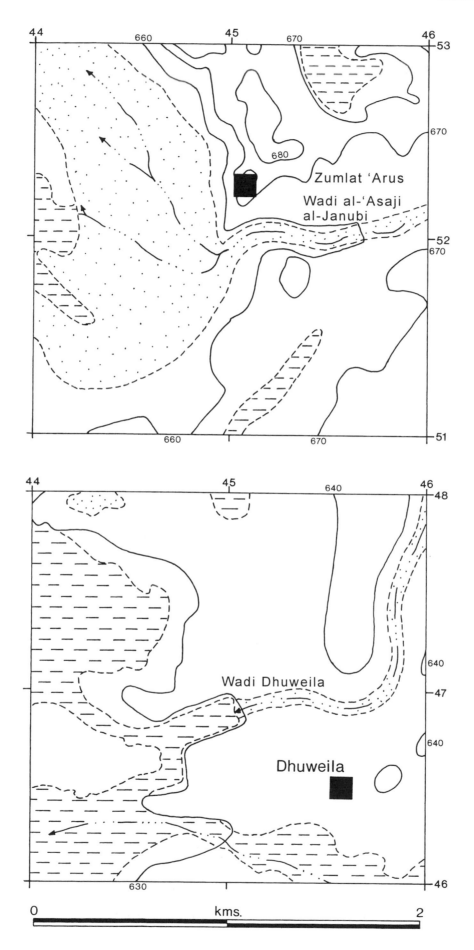

Figure 10.2   Zumlat 'Arus and Dhuweila: site location in relation to local topography and drainage.

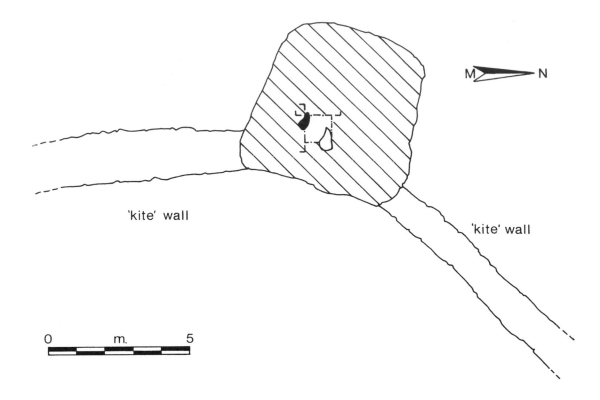

Figure 10.3   Abu Masiad al-Sharqi: plan of site, 'kite wall' and sounding.

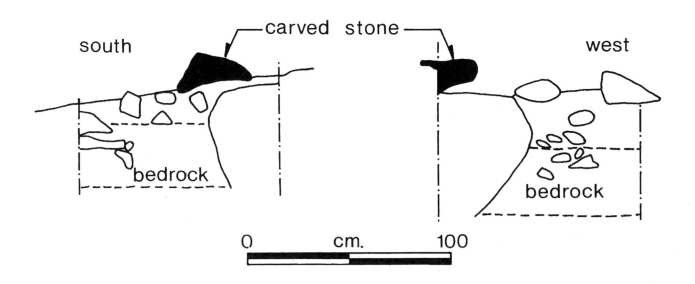

Figure 10.4   Abu Masiad al-Sharqi: sections.

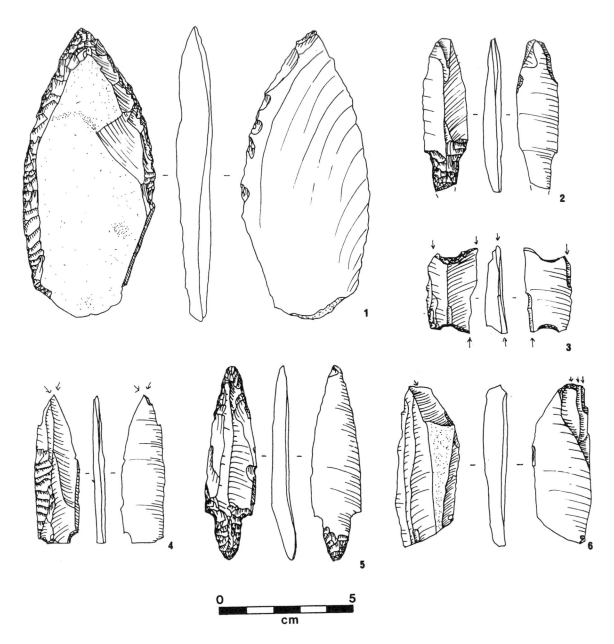

Figure 10.5 Chipped stone: 1. tabular scraper, Zumlat 'Arus; 2 Byblos point, Zumlat 'Arus; 3. concave truncation burin, Zumlat 'Arus; 4. dihedral burin on pressure flaked blade, Zumlat 'Arus; 5. Byblos point, Abu Masiad al-Sharqi; burin nucléiform, Zumlat 'Arus.

building of new walls or for more recent beduin corrals. Most of the enclosures, where preserved, are of the 'star-shaped' variety (Figure 10.6; Helms and Betts 1987: fig. 14 D). The wall running to the west of Abu Masiad al-Sharqi zigzags along the crest of the hill and may have formed a simple trapping system of its own. The main line of 'kites' lies along a ridge overlooking an extensive series of mudflats, with the guiding walls leading up the slope to the west and the enclosures located over the crest on the downslope, out of sight of animals being driven up towards them. All the walls are low with a spread of tumble around them, and appear to be ancient. Broken points which can be dated typologically in both stages of the Neolithic have been

found in some of the enclosures (Figure 10.7: 4, 5, 8, 10, 12; see also 'Survey sites in the *harra*' below).

Dating of 'kite' systems is problematical. The main difficulty is the lack of stratified deposits directly associated with the 'kite' enclosures. This is a issue which is common to many non-residential structures such as field walls, water harvesting systems and roads. In the case of the 'kites', the issues both of date and function are somewhat controversial (e.g. Echallier and Braemer 1995; Garrard *et al.* 1996: 217–8). With regard to dating of the Dhuweila systems, there are various strands of evidence which, combined, make a strong case to link the hunting camps with some of the 'kites' in the area. The stratified evidence from Abu Masiad al-

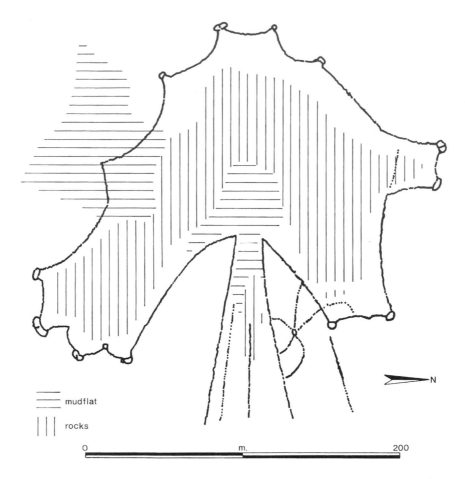

Figure 10.6   K 2.1: Plan of a 'kite' enclosure showing walls, rocks and mudflat.

Sharqi clearly links the occupation deposits to boulders set into the 'kite' wall. Dhuweila itself lies along the guiding wall of a 'kite'. Part of this was incorporated into the Late Neolithic structure and is therefore securely stratified in the excavations. At the northwestern end of the site is a guiding wall which was interrupted at some time, probably as a result of reconstruction during the Late Neolithic period. Its original line may be reconstructed as running up to the occupation site, jogging eastwards and then south again. By analogy with Abu Masiad al-Sharqi and Abu Masiad al-Gharbi, the Early Neolithic structure and the original 'kite' guiding walls were probably bonded together. Critics might argue that the walls could have been built later, incorporating the sites as convenient features in the landscape. However, it is difficult to accept that in a region covered in loose stones and rocky knolls, later 'kite' builders deliberately chose to align their walls with not just one, but three insignificant rubble mounds in the construction of at least two, if not three, separate traps. Similarly, it seems unlikely that to the east, near Wadi Ghusain, on a slope covered in many thousands of basalt boulders, post-Neolithic 'kite' builders managed to select one stone with a lightly scratched 'Dhuweila' style carving and place it in the wall in such a way that it was visible and correctly aligned. The evidence of broken points in and around the enclosures is more

tenuous, in that Neolithic hunters were active in the region, and could have left their broken arrows anywhere. However, the weight of evidence from the Dhuweila area and elsewhere in the *harra* (see 'survey sites in the *harra*' below) suggests some connection between broken arrowheads and the use of a number of the 'kites'. Some problems in accepting the evidence from the *harra* have arisen through misunderstanding. On the basis of earlier and more limited publication of the Dhuweila evidence (Helms and Betts 1987), Echallier and Braemer (1995: 54) believed that the structures at Dhuweila were attached not to a guiding wall, but to the outer face of a 'kite' enclosure wall like the small circular structures found around the perimeter of most 'kite' enclosures. Correctly, they argued that the site was too complex to represent such a structure; this led them to believe that the evidence linking the site to the walls was tenuous. It is hoped that the full evidence presented here will resolve further doubts as to the Neolithic date of at least some of the 'kites'.

The archaeological evidence connecting Dhuweila, Abu Masiad al-Sharqi and Abu Masiad al-Gharbi to the 'kite' walls indicates that at least part of the system was in use as early as the 7th millennium b.c. Although there is no evidence for earlier sites in the area, pre-Neolithic use of the 'kites' cannot be ruled out. Given that the available evidence implies sporadic use of the Dhuweila

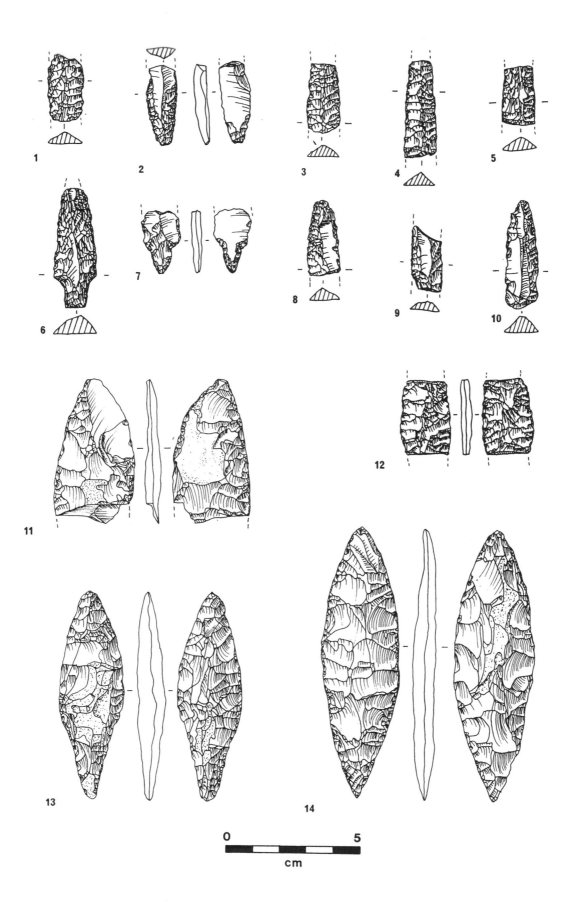

Figure 10.7   Chipped stone artefacts from 'kites': arrowheads - 1, 2 (1505); 3, 7 (1524); 4, 8 (2241); 5, 10 (2240); 6 (1523); 9 (2108); foliate bifacial pieces - 11, 13, 14 (1635); 12 (2242).

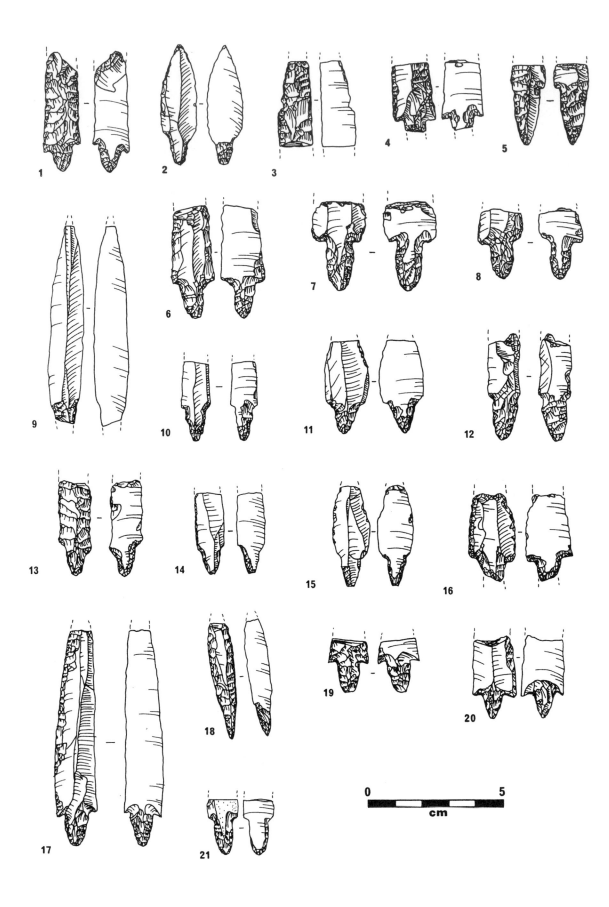

Figure 10.8   Chipped stone artefacts from knapping sites: 1, 2 (1605); 3, 9 (1612); 6, 7 (1656); 8, 11 (1670); 10, 12 (1671); 13 (1682); 14, 15, 16 (1684); 17 (2306); 18, 19, 20, 21 (3120).

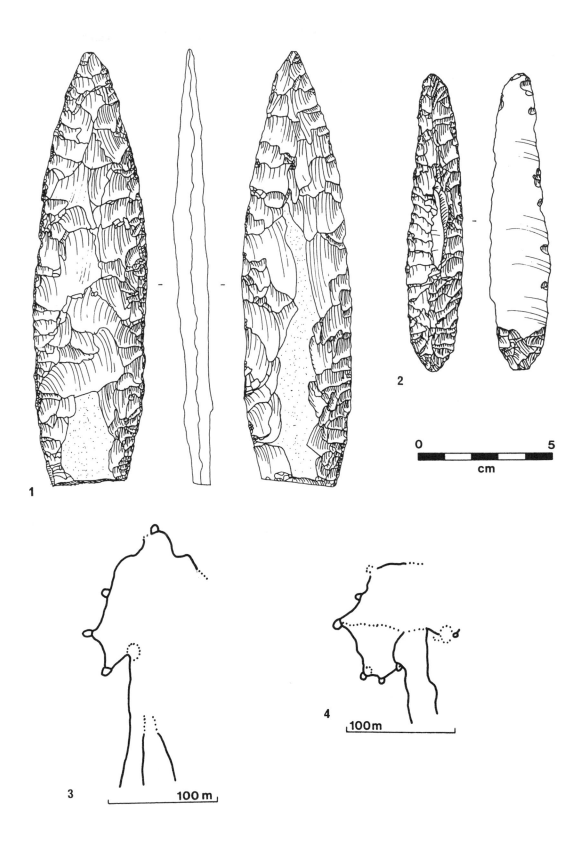

Figure 10.9 Chipped stone artefacts from knapping sites, and 'kites' with associated Neolithic projectile points: 1. foliate biface (1605); 2. pressure flaked point (2228); 3. BDS 1635; 4. BDS 1657.

'kite' systems over perhaps one and a half thousand years at least, it is possible that most of the rebuilding and changes to the system took place within this time period. However, with the ethnographic evidence showing that similar traps were in use until recent times, it is also possible that some parts of the system are more recent.

Survey sites in the *harra*

'Kites'

Several 'kites' throughout the *harra* were planned and surveyed for artefacts. Broken arrowheads were found in and around a number of the enclosures (Figure 10.7). Most of the arrowheads found in 'kite' enclosures were Byblos or Amuq points, and almost all showed evidence of impact fracturing. The apparent dominance of large, extensively retouched arrowheads may be because these are easier to find in surface survey. Less extensively retouched points may not have been identified if the diagnostic tangs or tips had been lost. Similarly, the smaller forms of Late Neolithic arrowhead would be less likely to snap off and drop to the ground. If broken, the tip would probably remain embedded in the carcase, while the tang would be left in the shaft and carried away for replacement. Only those 'kites' which yielded arrowheads are listed here.

BDS 1505 Map Ref. 3454 III 514185

'Star-shaped' 'kite', part of a chain running across the T.A.P.-line west of qa' Awiyah. Two broken points were found around the enclosure (Figure 10.7: 1, 2).

BDS 1523 Map Ref. 3454 III 512185

'Star shaped' 'kite', part of a chain running across T.A.P.-line. A tanged, pressure flaked point was found in the enclosure (Figure 10.7: 6).

BDS 1524 Map Ref. 3454 III 492182

'Star-shaped' 'kite', part of the same chain as 1523. A Byblos point and a broken pressure flaked point were found near the enclosure (Figure 10.7: 3, 7).

BDS 1635 Map Ref. 3453 IV 203310

'Star-shaped' 'kite' running down to Wadi Rajil near qa' Mejalla. Three foliate bifaces were found in one of the hides (Figure 10.7: 11, 13, 14).

BDS 2108 Map Ref. 3454 I 768365

'Kite'. One impact fractured point was found nearby (Figure 10.7: 9).

BDS 2240 Map Ref. 3454 II 457443

'Star-shaped' 'kite' forming part of the chain running south from Dhuweila. Two broken pressure flaked points were found in the enclosure (Figure 10.7: 5, 10).

BDS 2241 Map Ref. 3454 II 437438

'Star-shaped' 'kite', also part of the Dhuweila chain. Two broken pressure flaked points were found around the enclosure (Figure 10.7: 4, 8).

BDS 2242 Map Ref. 3454 II 436439

'Star-shaped' 'kite' on the same hillslope as 2241. The mid-section of a bifacially pressure-flaked foliate piece was found in the enclosure (Figure 10.7: 12).

Knapping sites

Knapping sites are located on hilltops and high slopes offering clear views along wadi systems and over open ground. The sites consist of a spread of knapping debris including cores, blanks and waste. Most of the worked pieces found on these sites are arrowheads. These are normally broken, with only the base preserved, suggesting that shafts with broken points were brought up to the site and replaced with new arrowheads, leaving the broken ones as discards (Figure 10.8).

BDS 1605 Map Ref. 3453 IV 205259

A large, multi-period knapping site on a high basalt covered peak overlooking Wadi Rajil near Jebel Qorma. Finds included several Byblos points and a pair of large foliate bifaces (Figure 10.8: 1, 2; Figure 10.9: 1).

BDS 1612 Map Ref. 3453 IV 181238

A small knapping site on the main peak of Jebel Qorma. Finds included a broken pressure-flaked point (Figure 10.8: 3, 9).

BDS 1617 Map Ref. 3453 IV 181234

A small knapping site on the bank of Wadi Rajil below Jebel Qorma. There were no cores but a scatter of fine punch-struck blades.

BDS 1633 Map Ref. 3453 IV 320311

A knapping site near qa'a Mejalla with many bipolar cores, debitage and a broken foliate biface.

BDS 1656 Map Ref. 3453 I 318345

A large knapping site on high, isolated basalt capped hilltop east of qa' Mejalla. Finds included a scatter of truncation burins, possibly associated with the knapping floor. The blanks consisted of two types of blades, one group very fine and thin with punctiform platforms and the other group more robust, struck from bipolar cores. There were two bipolar cores, two flake cores and one roughout for a bipolar core. Other debitage included waste, crested blades and plunging flakes from bipolar cores, and three broken Byblos points (Figure 10.8: 6, 7).

BDS 1670 Map Ref. 3453 I 355380

A small knapping site on slope of low promontory near qa' Mejalla. There were no cores but the debitage included a crested blade and a core tablet, together with broken Byblos points (Figure 10.8: 8, 11).

BDS 1671 Map Ref. 3453 I 354381

Small knapping site on ridge of low promontory near qa' Mejalla. Finds comprised several bipolar cores, one discoidal core, a tabular scraper, a side-scraper on tabular flint reworked into a bipolar core, three truncation burins, one of them on a crested blade, and some broken points (Figure 10.8: 10, 12).

BDS 1682 Map Ref. 3453 I 349386

Small knapping site just below the top of a ridge near qa' Mejalla. Most of the debitage was from Epipaleolithic knapping debris, but there was also one bipolar core, a few larger blades and a broken Amuq point (Figure 10.8: 13).

BDS 1684 Map Ref. 3453 I 353398

An extensive knapping site on a hilltop, probably mixed in period. Finds include four bipolar cores, several crested blades, dihedral and truncation burins, two bifacially-worked pieces and six broken Byblos points (Figure 10.8: 14, 15, 16).

BDS 2228 Map Ref. 3454 II 497386

A small knapping site around a later cairn. Debitage included bipolar blade cores, flake cores, blanks and a pressure-flaked point (Figure 10.9: 2).

BDS 2302 Map Ref. 3453 I 240551

A small knapping site east of Biyar Qattafi with bipolar cores and miscellaneous debitage.

BDS 2306 Map Ref. 3453 I 328429

Small knapping site on 'Tell A' near Biyar Qattafi with a scatter of debitage and one broken arrowhead (Figure 10.8: 17).

BDS 3120 Map Ref. 3553 IV 302798

A knapping site on slope above Wadi Subhi with a scatter of debitage and several broken arrowheads (Figure 10.8: 18, 19, 20, 21).

Date and function of 'kites'

The technique of using traps or enclosures to hunt game in the Badiayat al-Sham is a well-known one, with a long history. The remains of 'kites' have also been recorded by a number of researchers (Maitland 1927; Rees 1929; Poidebard 1928, 1934; Kirkbride 1946; Meshel 1974; Helms and Betts 1987; Legge and Rowley-Conwy 1987; Echallier and Braemer 1995). A number of ethnographic accounts have appeared in print; only a few will be mentioned here to show the nature of available evidence. Several 19th century travellers recorded use of such systems. Burckhardt (1831: 220) described a hunt in the steppe east of Damascus. An area of one and a half miles square was

enclosed on three sides by walls of loose stone, with gaps and ditches beyond. The enclosure was sited near a water source which attracted gazelle in summer. Herds were monitored visually and then driven into the trap. The panicked animals leapt through the gaps in the enclosing walls into the pits beyond, where they were slaughtered in their hundreds. Wright (1845: 42) reported on hunting in the same region. About 125 kilometres northeast of Damascus on the route to Palmyra:

> '...we passed several gazelle-traps, near Karyetein. Little walls converge to a field from a great distance, increasing in height as they approach the field. The field is walled round, leaving gaps at intervals, outside of which there are deep pits. The gazelles, led on by curiosity, and guided by the little walls, march boldly into the field, and when they are startled, they rush out wildly in a panic, at the breaches, and tumble into the pits. Sometimes forty or fifty are taken out of a pit alive at one time'.

Burckhardt, Wright, and also Musil (1928: 26–37), record that such hunts were conducted both by beduin and villagers (*fellahin*). They were also used by another group, the Solubba, a non-pastoral nomadic people who lived among the beduin and made their livelihood by a variety of activities including hunting, donkey breeding, acting as guides for the beduin and itinerant crafts such as metalworking and entertainment (Betts 1989b; Simpson 1994). While a number of accounts describe Solubba hunting individual animals, there are also references to their use of 'kites' (Simpson 1994). Mitford (1884: 157–8) was told that a tribe called the 'Sleibe', living between Palmyra and Aleppo subsisted entirely on gazelle:

> 'Their method of taking the gazelle is peculiar: when they have found a place frequented by them, an extensive tunnel wall is constructed, gradually narrowing down to an angle, at which point it is partially broken down, and a deep fosse dug on the other side; the herd is then surrounded, and naturally presses to the widest opening to escape, when the Arabs close in and pursue them down the tunnel, where, finding no other outlet, they leap the broken wall and fall into the pit prepared on the other side.'

Earlier parallels for this type of hunt are also known. Murals at 8th century Qasr Amra northeast of Amman show a hunting cycle involving at least two separate forms of hunting: one using a net with guiding arms, flagged and manned by torchbearers, with game driven by horsemen; the other a stampede of onagers driven by dogs over open ground. Two end-walls depict the

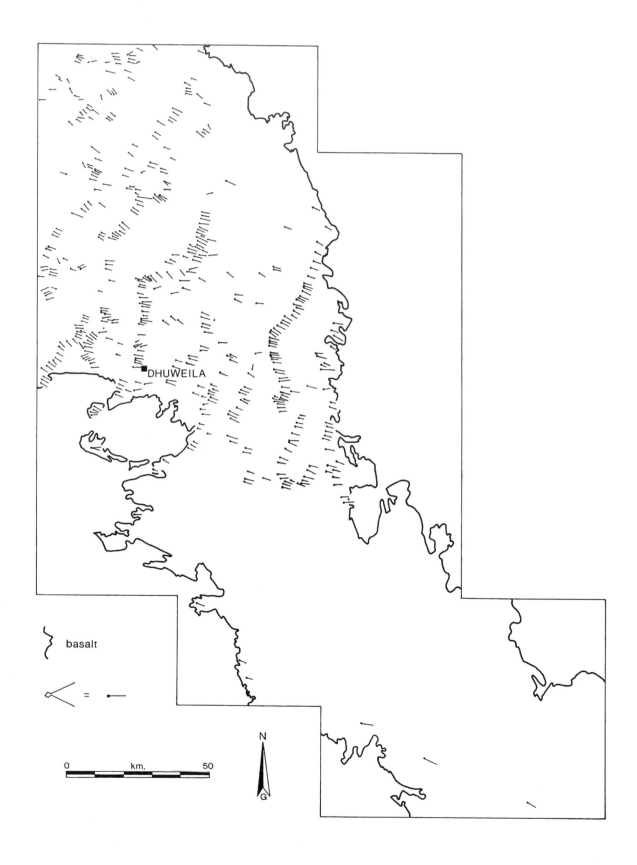

DHUWEILA

basalt

0   km.   50

N
G

Figure 10.10 General distribution of 'kites' in the *harra* (based on 1: 100,000 Map Series).

Figure 10.11 Examples of 'kites' in the *harra*: 1. (1508); 2. (1422); 3. (0701); 4. (0703); 5. (2108); 6. (1506)

slaughter of onagers inside a net and men butchering onagers beneath some trees. The net in this case is a mobile form of the stone-built 'kite'. An eastern version of the net hunt is given in *The Thousand Nights and One Night* (Mardrus and Mathers 1951: 652):

> '...the prince gave the signal for a hunt, and a great net was spread around an area covered with small trees. The beaters worked inwards towards the centre, driving the frightened animals before them. Then panthers, dogs and hawks were set free to chase the swifter prey, and a multitude of gazelles and other light game were taken.'

Egyptian and Mesopotamian reliefs, wall paintings and texts also record the use of nets to hunt a variety of game, mainly large ungulates (cf. Helms and Betts 1987: 58–61). Rock engravings from the *harra* show 'kites' (see 'Rock Carvings' above). The most famous of these is the 'Cairn of Hani', a Safaitic rock carving which shows a 'kite' with animals being driven into it (Harding 1953; see also 'Other carvings' above).

Stone enclosures of 'kite' type are known from many areas of the Near East (Helms and Betts 1987), although the greatest concentration appears to be in the *harra*, especially in the northern and central sectors. Farther south into Saudi Arabia, the long interlocking chains appear to give way to isolated individual traps (Figure 10.10). The enclosures vary considerably in plan, possibly reflecting differing construction techniques through time (Figure 10.11). However, the greatest number are of one general type. These have a large enclosure up to 150 metres across with a series of small stone circles along the perimeter. The guiding walls lead up from the grazing areas to a break of slope, a watershed, on the other side of which is the enclosure. The enclosure walls often return along the guiding walls and form a *cul de sac* where animals would be forced back on themselves, following the walls past the stone circles (Figure 10.6). The construction of the 'kite' walls aids the efficiency of the trap by clearing rubble and stones from an area beside the wall, making a path which the animals would be likely to follow, in preference to running directly over the cobbles which strew the rest of the enclosure. The long chained systems running across the *harra* are made up mostly of this type of 'kite'. Dhuweila lies on one such chain, and appears to be associated with the use of 'kites' of this type.

The ethnographic accounts mostly document use of 'kites' in the Syrian steppe. No accounts exist of 'kite' use in the *harra*, quite possibly because the *harra* is remote and difficult terrain which was seldom penetrated by 19th century travellers. This has given rise to two important topics of debate. Firstly, were the stone structures preserved in such large numbers in the *harra* the same as those described in the Syrian plains? If not, then what was their function? The first people to document 'kites' in the *harra*, principally pilots whose affairs took them over the desert region, suggested that they were fortified enclosures, possibly for the protection of domestic flocks (Maitland 1927; Rees 1929; Poidebard 1928, 1934; Kirkbride 1946). With increasing study of ethnographic data from the Near East and elsewhere in Central Asia, Northern Europe and North America (e.g. Nissen 1974; Binford 1978b; Ingold 1980; Raymond 1982; Pendleton and Hurst Thomas 1983; Barth 1983; Arkush 1986; Yagodin 1991; Benedict 1992) which provided a wealth of examples of the use of similar structures for hunting herds of game, the 'hunting trap' explanation became quite widely accepted (e.g., Meshel 1974; Helms and Betts 1987; Legge and Rowley-Conwy 1987). Recently however, the debate has been re-opened after new archaeological studies in the areas of the *harra* around Jebel Druze in southern Syria (Echallier and Braemer 1995).

The second issue concerns the exact method of killing. Most of the ethnographic accounts describe traps where the animals were driven from the enclosure into pits or ditches, where they fell, injured, and were easily killed. The Syrian steppe is gravel strewn with only occasional rocky outcrops. The looser gravel permits excavation of pits in a way which is almost impossible in the basalt region where bedrock rises close to the surface. The 'kites' in the *harra* provide no clear evidence for use of pits or ditches into which the animals might be driven. Where 'kites' are preserved intact, the enclosure walls show no signs of breaks. These two issues have been used by Echallier and Braemer to suggest that the 'kites' in the *harra* were not used for hunting, but possibly as enclosures for holding domestic flocks. The discrepancies between the ethnographic accounts and the nature of the *harra* 'kites' has led them to the conclusion that: 'nous ne pouvons donc pas interpréter la fonction réelle des monuments anciens par analogie avec les récits modernes' (1995: 57). However true this may be for the limited number of ethnographic accounts of hunting in the Syrian steppe, a wider survey of the ethnographic literature suggests that many similar traps were constructed for use without pits. In the case of the data from North America, use of pits seems to have been the exception, rather than the rule. To cite but a few examples, Benedict (1992) describes game drive systems in the Colorado ranges, used to hunt bighorn sheep, elk, or possibly mule deer. He has recorded more than fifty game-drive systems involving a combination of stone walls and natural features used to funnel animals from grazing areas to a confined kill area where hunters were concealed in rock-walled blinds. Some drive walls are more than a kilometre in length, made of loosely piled rock. The largest and best preserved are up to a metre high, but most are subtle rock alignments only a few stones high, without evidence of ever having been much bigger. The drive blinds are circular or semi-circular in shape, ranging from 1.1 to 2.7 m in interior diameter, excavated into subsoil where possible, with a peripheral wall making a total depth of between 50 to 110 cms. Some blinds were attached to the drive walls, while others were free-standing. Of the blinds excavated, 10–20% produced charcoal and/or chipped stone artefacts, primarily hunting and butchering tools. Arkush (1986) describes the hunting of pronghorn (*Antilocapra americana*) in the Great Basin. The drives were either rock or sagebrush alignments with a gap in the centre. Drivers on foot would herd the pronghorn in the general direction of the fence, where archers would be hiding in blinds along the passageway (Arkush 1986: 243; Kelly 1964: 50; Kelly 1943: 32). Parr and Newman report on pronghorn traps from Nevada (1992) where they excavated a number of small circular rock-built structures interpreted as windbreaks or blinds on high ground adjacent to game drives. The features contained no debris of domestic occupation or hearths. The artefacts recovered from them comprised the debris of mid and late-stage lithic reduction, projectile points and tools associated with the production, repair and maintenance of hunting equipment such as stone drills and gravers. In addition to the evidence for archers concealed in blinds, there are records of hunters clubbing exhausted pronghorn to death in the enclosures (Raymond 1982: 31; Steward 1943: 293). There is also an account of the use of pits used in combination with nets to kill rabbits (Raymond 1982: 32; Steward 1943: 267).

Echallier and Braemer base part of their argument on the results of the excavation of a stone circle attached to a 'kite' enclosure (K9) in the south Syrian *harra*. At the base of the small structure they found an occupation layer containing faunal remains of a variety of animals including both gazelle and domesticated species, together with a considerable amount of lithic material comprising debitage and some scrapers and three fragments of pottery. Survey of a number of other such stone circles attached to 'kite' enclosures showed that the walls stood, or once had stood, up to 2.5 m high. On one 'kite' (K52), the walls had small openings or 'windows' roughly 60 centimetres large some 40 cms above the ground surface of the enclosure and from 90 to 120 cms above the ground surface of the small structure. Other structures had small entrances with steps leading up into the enclosure (Echallier and Braemer 1995: 40–41). It is argued, quite correctly, that these stone circles show no signs of having functioned as the pits described in the various ethnographic accounts. The authors thus propose that the *harra* 'kites' were not hunting traps but enclosures for domestic flocks (Echallier and Braemer 1995: 58–59). However, considering the wealth of data from North American game drives, it is possible that the small circles could be considered as blinds. While the height of the walls would prevent hunters from shooting directly from inside the circles, they may still have served as shelters and places of concealment until the animals were driven into the main enclosure, at which point the hunters could easily reveal themselves to shoot since the animals would by then be so frightened that the appearance of more humans would have little effect on their behaviour. One obvious reason why this method should have been chosen for the *harra* 'kites' is simply the difficulty of digging suitable pits in the shallow soil cover. The material recovered from the excavations on K9 fits well with accounts of similar material recovered from North American hunting blinds. The absence of projectile points from a single structure is not a great problem as the excavators suggest a date in the early Bronze Age where arrowheads are not clearly identifiable in chipped stone assemblages. Transverse arrowheads may have been used in this period, but these are small, and would not be subject to re-working after use damage. Likewise, as the records clearly show, hunting has always supplemented the food procurement strategies of herders and villagers in the *badia*, and so the presence of domesticated species in the faunal remains of an early Bronze Age site would not be unusual. Clearly, this explanation cannot absolutely refute the arguments of Echallier and Braemer that the 'kites' were not hunting traps, but it should leave open the debate as to function. All the evidence from the Dhuweila area points to their use as hunting traps. A further consideration is that the evidence from Dhuweila indicates the use of 'kites' in the Early Neolithic period, the PPNB. While domestic animals were kept by Neolithic villagers in this period, there is a weight of evidence to suggest that widespread herding of sheep/goat was not carried out in the *badia* until the beginning of the sixth millennium b.c. (Cauvin 1990; Betts 1993b: 51–2; Garrard *et al.* 1996: 218). Thus, even if some 'kites' were used for containing domestic flocks, their initial function must have been as hunting traps.

Other arguments put forward by Echallier and Braemer against the use of the *harra* 'kites' as hunting traps include the exact interpretation of the 'Cairn of Hani' carving, and the relatively low height of the guiding walls, or in some cases their absence. The translation of the text associated with the 'kite' carving from the 'Cairn of Hani' is ambiguous (Harding 1953: 30–31). Harding's translation reads: 'By Mani'at, and he built for Hani'. And he drew a picture of the pen (or, enclosure) and the animals pasturing by themselves'. Translation of the phrases for 'the pen', 'to drive animals' and 'animals pasturing by themselves' were problematical, and while the final translation as published by Harding is a careful scholarly rendering of the most likely interpretation, it gives no indication as to whether the animals were domestic flocks or wild game (see also Meshel 1974: 140). The associated picture is similarly ambiguous in that it could equally well show either herding of sheep and goat, or the pursuit of gazelle into a trap. As to the relative height of guiding walls, this too does not provide evidence for or against use of the 'kites' as hunting traps. High walls are not a requirement for guiding game into traps as a simple linear feature will encourage fleeing game to follow along the line of the structure rather than leap over it. Natural paths created by the removal of surface stones for the construction of 'kite' walls would also encourage the animals to follow the line of the wall rather than cross over the barrier, however slight, into the rough rocky ground on either side.

In summary then, it is suggested here that the evidence from the Dhuweila area indicates the use of 'kites' as hunting traps in the Neolithic period. Bedouin in the Dhuweila area recognised the 'kite' walls as associated with hunting. This, combined with the weight of ethnographic evidence from Syria and elsewhere, suggests that some 'kites' were used in later periods for hunting. This does not rule out the use of 'kites' for the herding of domestic flocks, but such an interpretation requires further evidence before it can be accepted as valid.

11. 'Arrow-shaped' Structures in the Aralo-Caspian Steppe

Vadim N. Yagodin[1]

Introduction

Ustiurt is a plateau sharply defined by steep cliffs, lying between the Aral and the Caspian Seas. The average rainfall on the plateau is 100 mm per annum or less. With such low rainfall, dry farming is impossible except in the few oases where fields can be irrigated by groundwater. To the south and south-east, the plateau borders on more well watered areas, including the valley and delta of the Amu-Dar'ya (the ancient Oxus River and Khorezm).

As the main part of Ustiurt has almost no snowcover in winter, it provides favourable conditions for herds of wild animals which migrate here in the cold season. It is also used as winter pasture by cattle-herding nomads. Through archaeological fieldwork on the Ustiurt plateau, numbers of animal traps have been recorded. Because of their distinctive shape, these have been given the name 'arrow-shaped' structures (Yagodin 1991).[2] Some of these are apparently ancient, but the use of such structures is also recorded in recent ethnographic studies.

Information about the 'arrow-shaped' structures has been collected from a variety of sources. Their general distribution has been plotted using aerial photography and large-scale topographic maps. Specific details have been obtained through a combination of archaeological investigation and low-level aerial photography. Additional information has been gathered from ethnographic sources.

History of research

The first 'arrow-shaped' structures were discovered in 1952 during excavations at the site of Erburun-kala, a medieval town on the Khantersek promontory, at the edge of the Ustiurt plateau. The leader of the expedition, Tolstov, noted:

'... in many places on the edge of the Ustiurt plateau very strange structures have been discovered which consist of trenches radiating across the landscape, paved with rubble or stone slabs, long embankments and shallow circular pits. Some scanty pottery remains allow us to date these structures to the medieval period. These structures of unknown function are situated mostly on promontories at the edge of the Ustiurt plateau. The nature of the relief precludes their use as water storage reservoirs; they might have been used to trap animals driven inside them' (Tolstov 1958: 18, fig. 34).

In the early 1970s the Department of Archaeology of the Institute of History, Language and Literature of the Uzbek Academy of Science, Karakalpak Branch (Republic of Uzbekistan) began an extensive programme of archaeological research on the Ustiurt plateau. Aerial photography showed a group of 'arrow-shaped' structures running for dozens of kilometres from the Duan promontory to the sandy desert area of Mataikum. In 1975 research continued in the area of the Duan promontory. It was established that the North Ustiurt group of 'arrow-shaped' structures were combined in one system which was divided into subsystems. Two structures were studied on the ground. Data from this work provided evidence for a relative date and possible function of the structures (Yagodin 1978: 70–83).

In 1984 further 'arrow-shaped' structures on the Dekcha peninsula and on the western cliffs were investigated by the Povolzhsko-Uralskaya expedition of the Institute of Archaeology of the Russian Academy of Sciences. It was suggested that they were used as enclosures for driving in and trapping mouflon. No date could be established for their use (Galkin 1983: 433). A year earlier, similar structures had been discovered in the Aibuiir district. Four of them were excavated by the Ustiurt Archaeological Expedition. In 1984 further work was carried out on structures near the Duan peninsula. Soil scientists participated in this work, studying deposits under and around the structures (Gubin 1985).

In 1985 the North Ustiurt Archaeological Expedition found a new group in the remote region of the Zhar'inkuduk salt marshes. A topographical survey was carried out and some of the structures were excavated. In 1986 an 'arrow-shaped' structure was discovered near North Beineu. It was suggested that it could be dated not earlier than the 9th century AD (Galkin 1987: 566). In the same year, the extensive programme of archaeological and topographical research was completed with the use of a helicopter. Aerial reconnaissance made it possible to extend the study and to examine areas which were difficult of access. Several new 'arrow-shaped' structures were discovered as a result of this work. Further fieldwork continued in 1987 and 1988, so that by the end of 1988 fifty-four 'arrow-shaped' structures had been studied.

A review of the research conducted in Ustiurt shows that the 'arrow-shaped' structures are located in specific areas of the plateau. At present five groups can be identified (Figure 11.1).

1. North Ustiurt group: two sub-groups (Figure 11.2)
2. Aibuiir-Prisar'ikam'ish group: some sub-groups (Aibuiir, Berniyaz-3, Kazgan, Prisar'ikam'ish) are located separately within this group.
3. Zhar'inkuduk group
4. Kend'irlisor group
5. Beineu group

The North Ustiurt and Aibuiir groups are on the eastern cliffs of Ustiurt, the Kend'irlisor and Beineu groups are on the western cliffs, and the Zhar'inkuduk group is in the central plateau. However, it is likely that more are still to be found. According to unconfirmed information there are similar structures in the areas of the southern and northern cliffs, and even beyond the plateau, particularly in the region of Donguztau below the northern edge of Ustiurt.

The 'arrow-shaped' structures

North Ustiurt group

This group (Figures 11.1, 11.2) is situated on the flat plain near the cliffs, south of the North Ustiurt depression. The environment is typical of complex loamy desert with vegetation consisting of three main elements: *boyal'ich*, *biiurgun* and grey wormwood (Viktorov 1971: 53). In the hollows formed by the ditches of the 'arrow-shaped' structures and in natural depressions are plants unusual to loamy deserts, plants more typical of steppic conditions. These include feather-grass, *khurchavka*, and *kharagan* shrubs.

The location and linear structure of the 'arrow-shaped' structures of the North Ustiurt group are determined to some extent by the landscape, particularly by an extensive depression lying along an ancient tectonic fault which stretches for about 50 km across the plateau. As was noted above, the North Ustiurt group of 'arrow-shaped' structures is a single system sub-divided into two sub-systems. Within these, the form of the 'arrow-shaped' structures is quite uniform. Each consists of two triangular 'arrow-shaped' features linked by an enclosure wall, open at the lower end. The lower walls of each triangle are broken in the middle and point sharply inwards. On each corner are circular walls. Unconnected guiding walls lead up towards the centre of the main enclosure. The guiding walls of each structure run out at an angle until they almost meet up with those of the next structure, so that from the air it appears as if a series of structures is linked in a continuous chain. All the 'arrow-shaped' structures point in the same direction, with the apex of the arrows to the north.

Only one of the structures in this group (N3) has been subject to detailed archaeological investigation. The enclosure is defined by a ditch and accompanying earth bank. The triangular features are reinforced on the inside by limestone slabs and there is evidence of rebuilding on a slightly different line. The circular walls are hollowed out on the inside and are internally ringed with stone flagging. A trench excavated within the enclosure revealed some signs of short-term occupation, including ashy deposits with fragments of bone and pottery. Surface survey of other 'arrow-shaped' structures within the North Ustiurt group also produced occasional fragments of pottery, polished quartzite artifacts and a slate whetstone.

Aibuiir-Prisar'ikam'ish group

This group of 'arrow-shaped' structures (Figure 11.1) is located on the southeastern cliff of the Ustiurt plateau and forms a system running for more than 90 km. Unlike the straight cliffs of the eastern plateau this part of the plateau falls away in a broken and irregular line cut by numerous ravines. Below the cliffs there are many landslides forming large terraces and gentle slopes running down to the alluvial plain of the ancient delta of the Amu-Dar'ya. All the structures are either on the edge of the cliff or above the steep slopes of the larger ravines.

Aibuiir

From the air the structure takes the form of a triangle formed by low rubble walls. The base of the triangle lies on the cliff edge, with the apex to the north, pointing onto the plateau. The 'arrow-shaped' terminal enclosure lies on the apex of the triangle, with an opening at the southern end. The enclosure is formed by earth banks with shallow ditches running parallel on the inside.

On each corner of the enclosure are circular earth banks, reinforced on the inner face by limestone slabs. In the centre of each ring wall is a mound of earth, rising slightly higher than the surrounding bank (Figure 11.4).

Berniyaz 3

The structure is very degraded and barely visible on the ground, but can be seen from the air. Again it takes the form of a triangle. The base is about 770 m across and the sides about 250–300 m long. The sides end about 100 m from the cliff edge. The enclosed area of the triangle is roughly 30 hectares.

On each corner of the base are two smaller enclosures. The base of each of these turns inwards and is broken in the middle, leaving an opening about 20–25 m. wide. The sides are between 100 and 130 m. in length. On the three corners of each small triangle are ring-shaped banks with traces of limestone slabs in places around the

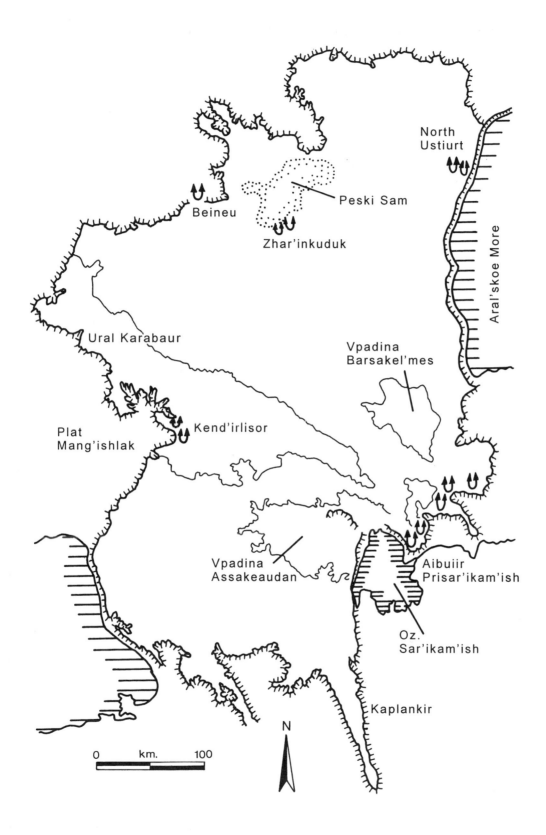

North
Ustiurt

Peski Sam

Beineu

Zhar'inkuduk

Aral'skoe More

Ural Karabaur

Vpadina
Barsakel'mes

Plat
Mang'ishlak

Kend'irlisor

Vpadina
Assakeaudan

Aibuiir
Prisar'ikam'ish

Oz.
Sar'ikam'ish

Kaplankir

N

0   km.   100

Figure 11.1   Distribution of 'arrow-shaped' structures on the Ustiurt plateau.

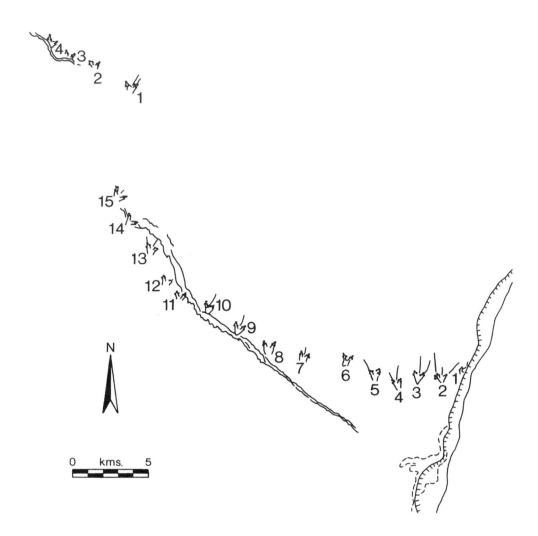

Figure 11.2   North Ustiurt group of 'arrow-shaped' structures.

internal faces. Mounds of earth are also visible in the centres of the rings. The main enclosure slopes down towards the cliff, and the smaller triangles are located on knolls at either side. Small gulleys lead up to the entrances.

The structure is unique in this group in that it has two small 'arrow-shaped' structures, suggesting that it is a system of two 'arrow-shaped' structures linked by a single triangular wall. Excavations were carried out across a rounded depression about 8–10 m. in diameter outside the western wall. In the centre of this depression was a shallow pit five m across and roughly 1 m. deep. Ash traces show that fires were lit several times in the pit. The ashes contained fragments of burnt animal bone.

The Kazgan sub-group

The Kazgan sub-group includes Aksaimak 2 and 4, Ibrakhimsha 2 and 3, Kazgan 1 and 3, Karamata 1, 3 and 7 and Khantersek. Aksaimak 2 and 4 are single

'arrow-shaped' structures, fairly heavily eroded and sited on steep ravines near the edge of the plateau. Ibrakhimsha 2 is another single structure, the outer walls of which have partly collapsed in a rock fall at the plateau cliff face. The remaining wall ends before the cliff edge, leaving a wide entry into the enclosure. Ibrakhimsha 3 lies on a peninsula with one of the enclosure walls cutting the promontory off from the rest of the plateau. The smaller triangular enclosure is sited on a low rise towards the end of the promontory. The structure has an unusual arrangement of double circles on the corners of the small enclosure.

Kazgan 1 is sited at a point where the plateau cliffs reach a height of 80–100 m. Kazgan 3 and Karamata 7, 3 and 1 lie above ravines. Khantersek lies on the Khantersek promontory adjacent to the ruined medieval town of the same name. The structure here consists of a single small triangular enclosure with ring walls at the corners which lies at the apex of a larger open-ended triangular walled area. The burial ground associated with the town stretches across the 'arrow-shaped'

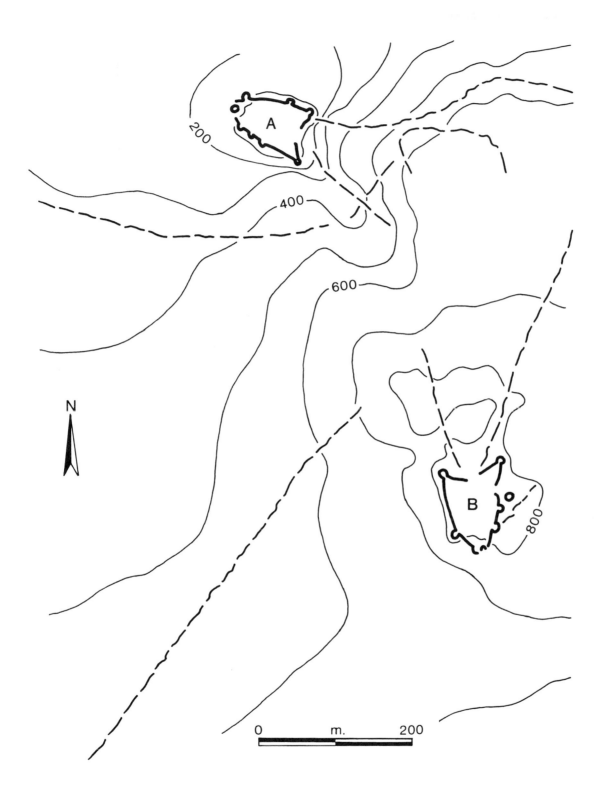

Figure 11.3   Zhar'inkuduk: 'arrow-shaped' structure.

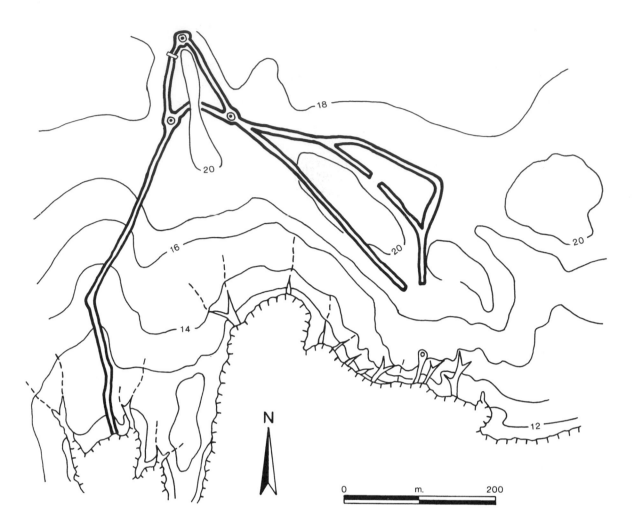

Figure 11.4   Aibuiir: 'arrow-shaped' structure.

structure, suggesting that the burial ground is later in date. All of the Kazgan structures are single traps. In each case, the ring walls on the corners of the smaller triangular enclosures have interior ring ditches surrounding an earth mound, and are reinforced at the outer face by stone slabs. Near Karamata 7 were traces of occupation in the form of a roughly rectangular limestone structure with fragments of pottery scattered around it.

The Prisar'ikam'ish sub-group

The Prisar'ikam'ish sub-group includes Dar'yal'ik 1 and 2, Dekcha 1, 2, 3 and 6, Erburun 1 and Chalburun 1. Dar'yal'ik 1 and 2 are both single 'arrow-shaped' structures on the cliff edge with traces of earlier structures visible. Dar'yarl'ik 1 has faint wall lines indicating one earlier enclosure, while Dar'yal'ik 2 is a complex system formed by five successive structures, each using elements of the previous one in the reconstruction. Dekcha 1 cuts across the neck of a promontory on which are the remains of a medieval

tower, built using limestone slabs robbed from the 'arrow-shaped' structure. Pottery from the tower dates it broadly within the 13th–14th centuries. Dekcha 2, 3 and 6 are badly eroded single enclosures. It is possible that Dekcha 2 was never completed. Chalburun 1 is a system consisting of two separate 'arrow-shaped' structures on a now inaccessible promontory.

Summary

In all, seventeen structures of the Aibuiir-Prisar'ikam'ish group have been located in this region. All have a number of common features distinct from structures elsewhere on the plateau, although each differs in detail. The structures are quite separate from one another, and clearly did not function as part of a unified system. They are particularly characterized by plans which include two major elements; a small 'arrow-shaped' enclosure and a larger triangular enclosure combined in one structure. The larger enclosure usually incorporates part of the cliff edge.

Zhar'inkuduk group

Zhar'inkuduk is an area of salt marsh in North Ustiurt, broken by banks of sand dunes. The marsh lies in a depression up to 60 kms across and in winter turns into a shallow lake. Geomorphological studies indicate that the area has been under water for a long period of time. Mesolithic and Neolithic sites are located around the marsh at about the same level, probably just above an ancient shoreline. Kurgans and 'arrow-shaped' structures are located closer to the base of the depression and may have been built when sinking water levels caused a reversion to marshland.

The Zhar'inkuduk group includes five 'arrow-shaped' structures and two other sites: Zhar'inkuduk 6b, an occupation site; and Zhar'inkuduk 10, a feature associated with the 'arrow-shaped' structures (Figure 11.3). Zhar'inkuduk 6b consists of a structure built of limestone slabs surrounded by a scatter of pottery, burnt bone and a few stone tools. It lies between two 'arrow-shaped' structures, Zhar'inkuduk 6a and Zhar'inkuduk 6c, both of which are badly damaged by erosion. Zhar'inkuduk 8 is also badly damaged; aerial photography shows an earlier structure underneath, following a different line. Zhar'inkuduk 12 appears to have only the smaller enclosure with peripheral ring walls at the corners. The structure lies on a slope and its configuration is governed partly by topography. Zhar'inkuduk 14 is a well preserved structure with all the elements typical of the North Ustiurt 'arrow-shaped' structures: an outer enclosure with an opening formed by inturned walls, two smaller 'arrow-shaped' enclosures with ring walls at the corners, a linking wall between the two, and a long guiding wall. Zhar'inkuduk 10 lies on a gentle slope on the southern edge of the salt marsh, just beyond the outer enclosure of Zhar'inkuduk 14. It consists of an outer, roughly rectangular, enclosure of limestone slabs containing a scatter of sherds and burnt bone and a series of circular structures also built of limestone slabs. On excavation the round structures proved to be cut into bedrock and filled with layers of ash, burnt bone and fragments of pottery.

Kend'irlisor group

This group is located on the western cliffs of Ustiurt. Most of the plateau here is relatively flat except near the edge of the cliff where the land falls away in a series of deeply cut gullies, screes and rocky promontories. There are numerous wells and springs in the area. Below the cliff lies a large salt marsh, the Kend'irlisor marsh, after which the group is named. Over an area of roughly 16 kms, eleven 'arrow-shaped' structures were located along the edge of the cliffs and two more a little further into the plateau. The structures in this group include Karamaya 1 to 13 and Kogusem 2.

Beineu group

The group is located on the western chink of Ustiurt, in the area of Old Beineu. The exact number of 'arrow-shaped' structures is not known. They were discovered by Galkin (1987: 561) who dated them in the medieval period.

Typology and chronology

Typology

'Arrow-shaped' structures can be arranged in four types. Type 1 (all of the North Ustiurt examples; some of the Zhar'inkuduk examples) consists of two or three guiding walls leading to a pair of 'arrow-shaped' enclosures linked by a wide curving enclosure wall (Figure 11.3). All of these structures point in the same direction and are linked to each other, forming a chain (Figure 11.2). Type 2 (Aibuiir-Prisar'ikam'ish) uses the cliff edge as one side of a large triangular enclosure. The apex of the triangle leads to one or two 'arrow-shaped' enclosures entered through a narrow gap between two in-turned walls (Figure 11.4). Type 3 (some examples from Zhar'inkuduk; some from Kend'irlisor) usually has one guiding wall (Karamaya 7 has two) which leads to an enclosure, one side of which is often made up of the chink or cliff (Figure 11.5). Type 4 (Kend'irlisor) consists of an odd combination of fences with circular structures (Figure 11.6).

Chronology

North Ustiurt group

Relative chronology

A number of the 'arrow-shaped' structures in this group show traces of earlier structures beneath the most recent walls. In the case of structure N15, the earlier western 'arrow-shaped' enclosure has only a single ring wall, while the later enclosure has a doubled ring wall. This suggests that doubled ring walls may be a later feature. The relatively small number of 'arrow-shaped' structures in sub-system II suggests that it was in use for a shorter period of time than sub-system I which seems to have functioned over a longer period with indications of more changes and additions to the structures.

Absolute chronology

The only tool for dating the 'arrow-shaped' structures is pottery, obtained both from the surface of sites and from excavation. Both crudely fired handmade pottery and well fired wheel-made pottery have been found. The pottery associated with sub-system I was poorly made, hand-turned blackish ware with slip applied to the outer surface. The only vessel shapes were flat-bottomed pots, some with incised or raised decoration. Similar vessels are characteristic of the Dzhet'iasar culture, from the

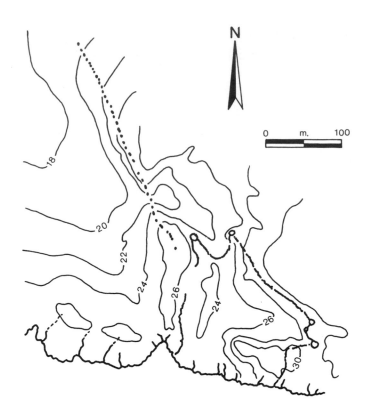

Figure 11.5   Karamaya: 'arrow-shaped' structure.

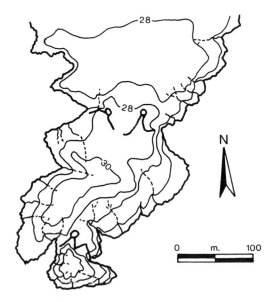

Figure 11.6   Karamaya: 'arrow-shaped' structure.

mouth of the S'ir-Dar'ya (the ancient Jaxartes). Dzhet'iasar 2 and 3 have been dated in the 4th to the late 8th/early 9th centuries AD (Levina 1971: 71, 74–5). Similar pottery is also characteristic of the 'swamp town culture' (Levina 1971: 78–80) as well as to the earlier stage of development of the Kerder culture in the *Priarali* delta of the Amu-Dar'ya river, dated in the late 7th to early 8th centuries AD (unpublished material from the Kurgancha settlement: Department of Archaeology of the Institute of History, Language and Literature of the Uzbek Academy of Science, Karakalpak Branch [Republic of Uzbekistan]). The presence of features such as vertical 'ribs' applied to the surface of the vessel makes it possible to limit the date of the system to the last quarter of the 7th century AD into the first half of the 8th century AD as in the Dzhet'iasar culture similar vessels appear only in Dzhet'iasar 3 (Levina 1971: 74–5). In the Kerder culture such applied decoration is typical of jars in the earlier stages (unpublished material from the Kurgancha settlement: Department of Archaeology of the Institute of History, Language and Literature of the Uzbek Academy of Science, Karakalpak Branch [Republic of Uzbekistan]).

Fewer pottery remains were recovered from sites in sub-system II. Most are jugs, two of which are of the so-called 'Afrigid' type. These jugs have a wide neck narrowing towards the body. The body of the vessel is egg-shaped, with a flat base and a single handle. The jugs were of fine clay, wheel-made with some limestone inclusions. Such vessels were first documented by Terenozhin (Terenozhin 1940; see also Tolstov 1948: 42, figs. 51–3). They have been found over a wide area on both banks of the Amu-Dar'ya in Khorezm and can be dated within the last quarter of the 7th century to the first half of the 8th century AD.

One jug neck fragment associated with sub-system II had an almost rectangular cross-section. It was wheel-made and evenly fired to a brownish-grey colour. Such vessels are typical of pottery group II of the Dzhet'iasar culture (Levina 1971: 68, 73, 75). Another sherd has ribbing applied horizontally as plastic decoration on the outside of the vessel. Such decoration is typical of all three stages of the Dzhet'iasar culture (Levina 1971: 68, 73, 75). Other sherds associated with this group also find parallels in vessels known from sites of the Dzhet'iasar culture in all stages, as well as the late Kerder pottery group dated in the second half of the 8th into the 10th century AD (Yagodin 1981: 87, 98, figs. 5, 6) and the early stages of the Kerder culture (Gudovka and Yagodin 1963: 261). There is also a separate pottery group which finds parallels almost exclusively in the 9th or 10th centuries AD. This latest group comes from the 'arrow-shaped' structure N10 in sub-system I. On the basis of the relative chronology of form and stratigraphy, N10 appears to be the latest in the North Ustiurt sequence.

Besides the 'arrow-shaped' structures there are a number of other archaeological remains in the area which might relate to use of the structures. The large Duan complex includes several cemeteries and cultic structures. The earliest burials date in the period from the 4th to the 2nd centuries BC and consist of single or collective interment in stone boxes. Burials of the 3rd to 4th centuries AD appear to be the most numerous. These consist of single graves in shallow earth pits, often reinforced by stone slabs, and oriented to the north. Two cultic structures are also included within the Duan complex. On the basis of typical Dzhet'iasar pottery from the structures, they can be dated in the 1st to 8th centuries AD. The evidence suggests that there are three stages in the development of the Duan complex: 2nd to 4th centuries BC, 3rd to 4th centuries AD and the 7th to 8th centuries AD. During the first two periods the complex was used as a burial ground and as a religious centre, while in the third period it was used only as a religious centre.

It seems likely then that during these periods this region of Ustiurt was used as winter camping grounds by nomadic groups who, in addition to herding, engaged in the hunting of migrating animals by means of the 'arrow-shaped' structures. The dates for the Duan complex may coincide with those of the structures, giving a date in the second half of the first millennium BC as the earliest time range for the establishment of the hunting systems.

Abuiir-Prisar'ikam'ish group

Relative chronology

Despite the fact that the 'arrow-shaped' structures in this group are generally similar, there are distinguishing features which suggest that some developments took place over time. In certain cases there is evidence that structures were modified and extended with the addition or replacement of enclosures and guiding walls.

Absolute chronology

Absolute dating for this group has been obtained from a number of sources which include pottery from several of the structures, the relationship of the Khantersek structure to the adjacent archaeological site and also radiocarbon dating. Pottery styles include forms with close parallels in Khorezmian vessels dated from the 9th to 14th centuries AD (Vakturskaya 1959), in late Kerder complexes from the *Priarali* delta of the Amu-Dar'ya river (Yagodin 1981:87), in forms associated with the Kerder culture (7th to 8th centuries AD) and in pottery from the ancient town of Kurgancha (late 7th to early 8th centuries AD).

The town of Khantersek on its exposed promontory is dated in the 12th to early 13th centuries AD (Tolstov 1958: 78; Yagodin *et al.* 1975; Manilov 1978: 214–220). The 'arrow-shaped' structure lying across the neck

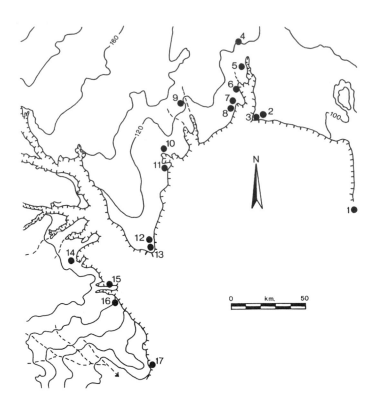

Figure 11.7 The Aibuiir-Prisar'ikam'ish group of 'arrow-shaped' structures: 1. Khantersek, ruined city, burial ground, 'arrow-shaped' structures; 2. Kazgan 1, 'arrow-shaped' structures; 3. Kazgan 2, kurgan group; 4. Kazgan 7, group of archaeological sites; 5. Kazgan 3, 'arrow-shaped' structures; 6. Kazgan 4, group of archaeological sites; 7. Kazgan 5, group of kurgans; 8. Kazgan 6, stone enclosure for livestock; 9. Aksaimak 2, 'arrow-shaped' structures; 10. Aksaimak 4, 'arrow-shaped' structures; 13. Ibrahimshah 2, 'arrow-shaped' structures; 14. Karamata 7, 'arrow-shaped' structures; 15. Karamata 2, signal tower; 16. Karamata 3, 'arrow-shaped' structures; 17. Karamata 1, signal tower.

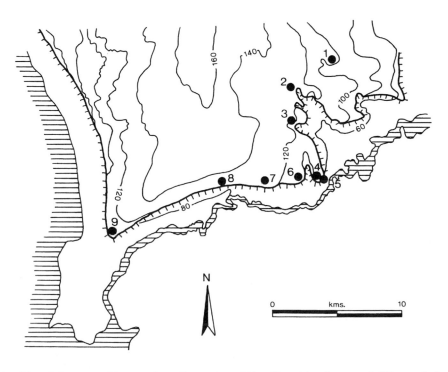

Figure 11.8 Aibuiir-Prisar'ikam'ish group of 'arrow-shaped' structures, Prisar'ikamish subgroup: 1. Erburun 1, 'arrow-shaped' structure; 2. Dekcha 2, 'arrow-shaped' structure; 3. Dekcha 3, 'arrow-shaped' structure; 4. Dekcha 1, 'arrow-shaped' structure; Dekcha 5, signal tower; 6. Dekcha 6, 'arrow-shaped' structure'; 7. Dar'yal'ik 1, 'arrow-shaped' structure; 8. Dar'yal'ik 2, 'arrow-shaped' structure; 9. Chalburun 1, 'arrow-shaped' structure.

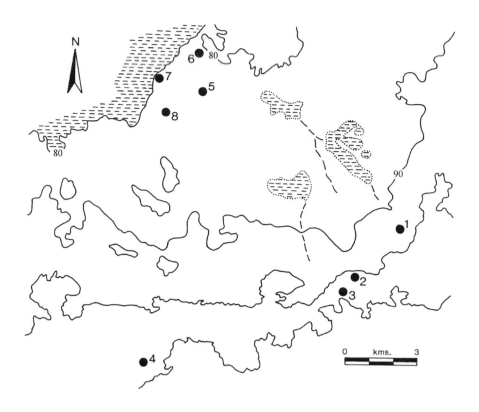

Figure 11.9 Schematic map of archaeological sites on the eastern edge of the Zhar'inkuduk salt-marsh: 1. Zhar'inkuduk 6a, 'arrow-shaped' structure; 2. Zhar'inkuduk 6b, 'stations'; 3. Zhar'inkuduk 6b, 'arrow-shaped' structure; 4. Zhar'inkuduk 7, 'stations'; 5. Zhar'inkuduk 8. 'arrow-shaped' structure; 6. Zhar'inkuduk 12, 'arrow-shaped' structure; 7. Zhar'inkuduk 4, groups of burials; 8. Zhar'inkuduk 14, 'stations', 'arrow-shaped' structure, solitary kurgan.

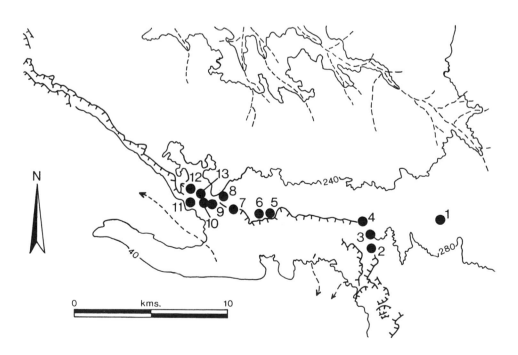

Figure 11.10 Schematic map of the disposition of the Kend'irlisor group of 'arrow-shaped' structures: 1. Kogusem 2; 2. Karamaya 1; 3. Karamaya 2; 4. Karamaya 3; 5. Karamaya 5; 6. Karamaya 6; 7. Karamaya 7; 8. Karamaya 8; 9. Karamaya 9; 10. Karamaya 10; 11. Karamaya 11; 12. Karamaya 12; 13. Karamaya 13.

of the promontory must be earlier than the town as it cannot have been in use while the town was occupied, and cannot be later as the cemetery associated with the town stretches across the enclosure: thus the Khantersek structure can be dated not later than the 11th century AD. Radiocarbon samples from excavations at Dekcha 1, Aibuiir and Berniyaz 3 have provided dates around the period from 550 to 750 AD (Yagodin 1991: 92).

It seems from the evidence cited above that this group of structures covers a relatively long period with several stages of growth and development. The earliest structures may have been built around the late 6th to early 7th centuries AD while the latest appear to date around the 13th to 14th centuries AD.

Zhar'inkuduk group

Chronology

Zhar'inkuduk 14 is provided with a *terminus post quem* by a number of graves located across the entrance to the enclosure, effectively blocking entry. Stone slabs were taken from the structure to build the grave mounds. Finds from the graves give a date in the 9th to 10th centuries AD. Pottery associated with this group was recovered from excavations at the 'settlement' of Zhar'inkuduk 10 and from the graves. Parallels for the forms can be found in vessels from the late second and the third stage of the Dzhet'iasar culture dated in the late 7th to early 9th centuries AD (Levina 1971), the 'swamp town' culture dated in the late 7th to early 9th centuries AD (Tolstov 1947; Levina 1971) and the pottery of the Kerder culture dated in the last quarter of the 7th to the first half of the 8th centuries AD.

With one exception, the Zhar'inkuduk structures relate to the period from the 7th to the early 9th centuries AD. The structures were repeatedly rebuilt during this time. The exception is the northern enclosure of Zar'inkuduk 8 which, on the basis of disruption by later burials, can be dated in the mid-1st millennium BC

Kend'irlisor group

There is little dating evidence for structures of this group. A *tamga* sign (a tribal mark) was found on a slab in one of the structures. The location of the sign suggests that it dates to the construction of the enclosure wall. These signs are also found on graves of the medieval periods and can provide a broad date for the structure from the 13th to the 14th centuries AD.

Beineu group

The structures in this group have been dated by Galkin to the medieval period (Galkin 1987: 561).

Summary

Dating evidence for the 'arrow-shaped' structures on the

Ustiurt plateau shows a sequence of five major stages in the history of their development: (i) second half of the 1st millennium BC; (ii) 3rd–4th centuries AD (Sarmato-Alan); (iii) 7th–early 9th centuries AD (Dzhet'iasar-Kerder); (iv) 9th–11th centuries AD (Oguz); and (v) 13th–14th centuries AD (Turkmen-Kipchak).

Functions of the 'arrow-shaped' structures

Ethnographic studies

The functions of the various 'arrow-shaped' structures can best be explained through both archaeological and ethnographic studies. Archaeological research provides two kinds of evidence: the structures themselves and any associated features; and the material remains derived from excavation. However, neither of these sources provide direct evidence of function, and this is where ethnographic data can provide some useful parallels to aid in the interpretation of the archaeological evidence. Ethnographic data from the Aralo-Caspian region dates to the 19th and early 20th century and relates to the Kazakh-Adaoi and Tab'inoi, nomadic cattle-breeders of Ustiurt, and to the Karakalpaks, semi-settled inhabitants of the delta regions of the S'ir-Dar'ya and Amu-Dar'ya. There are many descriptions of structures similar to the 'arrow-shaped' structures in these areas. Members of the 1925–6 expedition to Ustiurt noted:

> '... there are *kulans* [wild ass], *tarpans* [?] and *saiga* [antelopes] here. Hunters chase the *saiga*, directing them into stone enclosures with deep ditches in which they [the *saiga*] fall down.' (*Perv'ie russkie...*: document N15:98).

Dr Eversmann, a member of the same expedition, gave a similar description of the hunting techniques of people living on the Ustiurt plateau.

> 'In Ustiurt or on the upper edge of this cliff .... which is called *chink* by the Kirgiz people ... antelopes are caught using the following method: an appropriate place about 300 paces long and of varying width is fenced by a wall which is three or four feet high. The wall is made roughly and very quickly. It is built from stones laid one on the other. A small hole is left on one side of the wall. On the steep slope below there is a ravine surrounded by the wall which is so high that the animals cannot jump over it. For this purpose only the convenient places are chosen, to make it easier for the hunters to build the structure. One of the hunters rides a horse across the steppe for about 25 kilometres where he lures male antelopes with

sounds similar to the call of the female and drives the herd to the trap. When they are close to the trap, the hunter leaves his horse and comes into the enclosure through the hole along with the animals. After that another hunter who is waiting for the herd to step into the enclosure stands up and closes the hole, shouting very loudly. The frightened animals try to run away and jump over the wall to the lower enclosure and cannot escape. They are trapped.' (Eversmann 1850: 262).

When Eversmann's book was published, there was an expression of disbelief that the information he recorded was true (*Perv'ie russkie...*: 294, note 66). However, this method of hunting was widespread and there are repeated references to it in the ethnographic literature. For example, the Tuvintsoi-Todzhintsoi lure the animals using a wooden pipe which they called *murga*. Its sound imitated the scream of the male *maral* (stag). Another sound-imitating instrument was described. It belonged to the same people and was called *ediski*. This instrument could reproduce the sound of a kid and attracted the roe (Vainshtein 1961: 44, 46).

Eversmann also noted the presence of similar permanent structures which had been used for hunting not only in Ustiurt but in other regions of *Prikaspi* and *Priarali*:

'Kirgiz people kill *saiga* in a very strange manner: on the level ground of the steppe covered with wormwood, the favourite food of *saiga*, they make small hillocks from earth or turf about three feet high. The hillocks form direct radiating lines meeting at angles of 45 to 60 degrees. Towards the angles the hillocks are located very close to each other, a distance of about three to five paces, but the farther from the corner, the further apart they are located. The large entrance .... may be as much as three miles wide while the narrow end is about fifteen feet across, and is also left open. In front of the narrow end stalks of cane are placed with their points outwards one to two feet from each other. The cane is fairly firm and hard. Kirgiz hunters on horseback wait for a herd to appear. When the herd approaches the wide passage the hunters try to drive the animals inside the enclosure. Shy animals take the small earthen hillocks to be people and do not dare to approach them but continue to run towards the narrow end of the corner followed by the loud screams of the hunters. When they run up onto the sharp ends of the cane stalks they impale themselves.' (Eversmann 1850:261).

Despite the difference in materials and configuration, the general plan of these structures is similar to those of the 'arrow-shaped' structures in Ustiurt.

In 1832, during his voyage in the Caspian Sea, G.S. Karelin observed Kazakhs hunting for wild ass (*kulan*), *saiga*, and wild goats in the deserts of western Ustiurt (Karelin 1883: 484). The hunting techniques incorporated the special permanent structures which broadly coincide with the 'arrow-shaped' structures in the west *chink* of Ustiurt described above. Kazakhs of the older generation whose ancestors were nomads in Ustiurt still remember methods of hunting which are very similar to those of the 'arrow-shaped' structures. According to informants, these structures were called *aran*, and the pointed cane stalks placed in the round pits of a triangular fence were called *zhebe*. Several special pits, hiding places for hunters, were also dug. About 30 to 40 riders chased the animals into the *aran* where they were slaughtered. The hunt would normally take place in autumn. An *aran* was built by several nomad families. Sometimes the families were united in a tribe. After the hunt the kill was distributed among the tribe. In this connection it is interesting to note one of the meanings of the term *aran* as 'people' and 'tribe' (Radlov 1893: 251).

Modern explorers whose speciality is different hunting techniques describe the Kazakh hunting method using *aran*, including the special systems of structures in the form of a crater with sharp cane stalks placed at the entrance. *Saiga* were driven into these craters, impaled themselves on the canes and became the prey of hunters (Sludskii 1955: 50, 51). The same cruel method was also been used in Kazakhstan and in Kalm'ik land (Levshin 1832; Geptner *et al.* 1961: 483–85). The Karakalpak people also used *aran* as a hunting method. According to an informant, *aran* described as pits with sharp cane stalks placed vertically were in use as a hunting technique in the early 19th century in the region of the Zhan'i-Dar'ya in the southwestern *Priarali*. *Aran* as a hunting construction with a wide open entrance is known in Karakalpak folklore. For instance, in the epic poems *Er Ziiuar* and *K'irkk'iz* in a number of places such expressions as 'opened the mouth widely like an *aran*' was used (e.g., *arandai auz'in ashad'i*: see *Karakalpak fol'klor'i* 1980: 382; 1981: 57). The term *aran* is an ancient one in Turkic languages. It was mentioned in the dictionary by Makhmud Kashgar (1072–1074) with the meaning of 'stable' and 'farmyard' (*Drevnetiurkskii slovar'* [*Dictionary of the ancient Turkic language*], 1969:51). Another etymology is 'sharp tree which is placed in the way of wild animals' (Radlov 1893: 251).

Despite the fact that vast areas had been explored in the deserts of the Aralo-Caspian region, archaeologists and topographers did not manage to locate permanent hunting structures which could be directly connected with the means of livelihood of the Kazakh-Adaoi and Tab'inoi in the 18th and 19th centuries in Ustiurt. Historical documents describe them as both herders and hunters. There is also evidence that Kazakhs used *aran* for hunting animals in Ustiurt. The method was described in 19th century literary sources (Karelin 1883: 484, 495). Numerous hunting scenes with antelopes are illustrated on rock carvings in Ustiurt and Mang'ishlak (Medoev 1969: 146–52). It is quite possible that *aran* constructed by Kazakhs were not monumental and solid as they used to be in the Middle Ages, and so have not survived. However, it is also possible that medieval *aran* in good condition could have been used later by Kazakhs. The 'arrow-shaped' structures of the Kend'irlisor group, some of the 'arrow-shaped' structures of the Zhar'inkuduk group and the so-called 'system of stone fences' belonging to the topographical structures of the burial grounds of Duan in the eastern chink of Ustiurt were built from stone. They are all well-preserved and could easily have been re-used at a later date. The *aran* used in *Priarali* beyond the borders of Ustiurt were constructed of less durable materials and are thus far less well-preserved which might explain why archaeological expeditions in the deserts of the eastern and southeastern *Priarali* regions were unable to find evidence of 'arrow-shaped' structures or similar features.

At present there is no reliable information about the existence of similar structures in Central Asia and Kazakhstan. However, it seems unlikely that installations such as the 'arrow-shaped' structures could be associated only with the Ustiurt plateau. It is quite possible that similar hunting techniques were used in the desert regions of Central Asia and Kazakhstan. It is also possible that if such structures were used, they were built in materials which have decayed and eroded away. There are some reports which hint at this. Valikhanov decribed so-called *Dzhanibe* and *Tamerlan* knolls which were used to hunt for *kulan* (wild ass). According to Valikhanov one of these knolls was located between the Tarbagatai chain of mountains and the river Ili (Valikhanov 1904; Solomatin 1973: 127). Similar evidence is given by Masson who writes that:

> '... in the eastern part of Kazakhstan there are two large ancient ravines which were probably used to hunt for *kulan*; one is in the Khantau mountains and is called Kulan-K'ir'ilgan ['slaughter of the *kulan*'], the second ravine stretches from Lake Balkhash down to the northwestern spurs of Dzhungar Alatau and the river Ili.' (Masson 1984:116).

It is certainly possible that some of the ancient structures usually described simply as knolls are the remains of 'arrow-shaped' structures (see for example: *Trud'i Orenburgskoi*: 50–54, 57; *Arkheologicheskaya karta*:116).

Archaeological and ethnographic parallels for installations like the Ustiurt 'arrow-shaped' structures are found in forest and tundra zones throughout the continent of Asia, in the north of Scandinavia, in the Ural Mountains, and in western and eastern Siberia. In the Ural Mountains and in Siberia explorers have noted that among the numerous rock carvings found there hunting scenes are represented with forms resembling 'arrow-shaped' structures, with animals trapped inside them. Usually there are no human figures in such carvings. According to Okladnikov these are 'scenes of the hunt without a hunter' or, alternatively, 'the passive type of hunt with the use of permanent fencing devices' (Okladnikov 1966: 125). Similar scenes were noted in rock carvings from the Ural Mountains (Chernetsov 1971). It is believed that the hunting techniques shown in the rock art are fairly old in these regions. According to Chernetsov these types of scenes appear in the Urals 'earlier than the beginning of the second millennium BC' (Chernetsov 1971: 110).

In Siberia similar scenes can be traced back to Paleolithic times (Okladnikov 1966: 125). To explain their origin scholars have used ethnographic material with descriptions of permanent fencing structures for hunting in areas where wild game migrated each season. Such features are known in Ural-Siberian ethnography as *ogorod'i* or *zagorodi*: i.e., 'fencings' (Tret'yakov 1934: 236; Okladnikov 1966: 125; Chernetsov 1971: 73; Kosarev 1984: 83).

'Fencings' were large structures built by the inhabitants of the Urals from the 18th to the early 20th centuries along the rivers and in the woods. They were made of branches or logs and the walls ran for dozens of kilometres. A certain number of openings or entrances were left by the hunters. Traps in the form of deep pits were hidden behind the openings. The walls of the pits were revetted with branches or with wooden posts. On the bottom of the pits sharpened stakes were driven into the ground. Several reports mention that crossbows were deployed in the openings instead of stakes inside the pit. Some scholars believe that pits and stakes are early while the use of crossbows is a later innovation.

'Fencings' were constructed along the seasonal animal migration route from the western side of the mountains towards the eastern side. For this reason they were directed in the meridinal direction and are found on all mountain paths and the banks of rivers along which the herds usually migrated (Teploukhov 1880: 26–7; Glushkov 1900: 36).

According to Kosarev the use of fencing as a hunting technique had been widespread not only in the Urals but in all the mountain regions of Siberia where migrating game was forced to use narrow mountain paths (Kosarev 1984: 85). Tret'yakov believes that 'fencings' were used in vast areas from the Baltic Sea to the Amur River (south-east of Lake Baikal to the Sea of Okhotsk) to hunt elk, deer and other small ungulates (Tret'yakov 1934: 238). The permanent structures used for passive hunting have also been described by a number of ethnographers and biologists (e.g. Vainshtein 1961;

Vasilevich 1969; Simchenko 1976; Gurvich 1977; S'iroechkovskii 1986).

In the tundra regions of northern Europe and Asia another form of hunting was also used, an active form. The enclosures were oriented to catch the whole herd of animals rather than a single animal or part of a herd as were the 'fencings'. The techniques used were generally similar throughout different regions and among different peoples. The structures consisted of two converging lines built from stones, earth mounds, poles with flags and feathers, with traps where the lines joined. This type of hunt was recorded in Scandinavia and in the Kol'sk peninsula (Manker 1960: 406; Nesheim 1961: 210; Simchenko 1976: 87–88; Semenov Tyan-Shanskii 1977: 85–88). During the hunt elk and deer were driven into the traps. The pits serving as snare traps were found everywhere in the places where Laplanders live: northern Sweden, Norway, and some regions of Finland (Simchenko 1976: 88). It is believed that in front of the pits there were wooden fences. The fences crossed in front of the pit forming an acute angle. The fact that they had been built of wood may explain why they have disappeared (Semenov Tyan-Shanskii 1977: 85–86; S'iroechkovskii 1986: 209–210). Manker believes that hunting techniques similar to those under discussion appeared in Scandinavia in the Neolithic period (Manker 1960: 406). The same techniques used by Laplanders in the Kol'sk peninsula have been described by Tret'yakov (1934: 246–7) and S'iroechkovskii (1986: 209–10).

Animal behaviour and the use of 'arrow-shaped' structures

Data on animal populations in the Ustiurt region have been obtained from both archaeological and ethnographic sources. The region was once home to gazelle, *saiga* antelope, Ustiurt sheep and *kulan* (wild ass - *equus hemionus*).

Kulan (*equus hemionus*)

The *kulan* were once the most numerous animals in the deserts of Eurasia, from Manchuria in the east to Romania in the west. In Ustiurt *kulan* survived up until the end of the 19th century AD (Lomakin 1983). Herds in the north migrated seasonally over hundreds of kilometres. The size of individual herds may have been as much as a thousand animals. In late summer the herds moved south. In the 18th–19th centuries AD one of the migration routes ran along the eastern cliffs of the Ustiurt plateau. In some areas, such as the desert surrounding the Sar'ikam'ish depression, there was a permanent *kulan* population while in the K'iz'il-kum desert, they only spent the winter (Bogdanov 1882).

Saiga (*saiga tatarica*)

Saiga antelope are one of the few animals to escape extinction until now. In the past the *saiga* lived in the *Priarali* region where bones found on archaeological sites attest to extensive hunting. The *saiga* favour flat open ground and are not found in hilly regions or areas of broken topography. During migration the *saiga* form huge herds of up to one or two hundred thousand animals. Herds of this size would gather on the Ustiurt plateau in winter.

Gazelle (*gazella subgutturosa*)

Gazelle were once found from the Trans-Caucasus to China. They were regularly sighted in the areas of Irgiz and Chelkar-Irgiz to the north of Ustiurt. In the south, they lived in the Iranian and Afghan deserts. Gazelle are constantly on the move from one grazing area to another. Today, unlike the *kulan* and *saiga*, gazelle do not have regular long distance migration patterns. However, it is possible that in the past they may have moved more widely. Gazelle normally move in small groups of two to five animals, except when migrating when they may form herds of up to twenty animals.

Ustiurt sheep (*ovis ammon arcal*)

The Ustiurt sheep is a sub-species of the mountain sheep. Now almost extinct, they were found in the Ustiurt region in medieval times. Sheep are creatures of habit and use regular paths, routes and shelters. Analysis of the distribution of 'arrow-shaped' structures designed specifically for the hunting of sheep demonstrates that the people who built them were very familiar with the sheep's habits and exploited them carefully.

As was noted above, there are five major groupings within the Ustiurt 'arrow-shaped' structures: (1) the North Ustiurt Group; (2) the Aibuiir-Prisar'ikam'ish Group; (3) the Zhar'inkuduk Group; (4) the Kend'irlisor Group; and (5) the Beineu Group. These groups differ according to their location. It seems possible that this difference could be explained by the different species of wild animals concentrating in specific areas, and also by the different techniques required for hunting each species.

One of the migration routes for *saiga* and *kulan* ran along the eastern cliffs of the Ustiurt plateau. Typical herd behaviour involves the following of linear features in the landscape such as a river bed, the edge of a forest or a pathway (Baskin 1976). This tendency to follow such features may have caused the development of a migration route along the Ustiurt cliffs which was then an obvious location for the construction of 'arrow-shaped' structures using the cliff edge as an integral part of the enclosure. Similarly, the guiding arms functioned as linear features which encouraged the herds to follow them into the enclosures. Since seasonal migration is

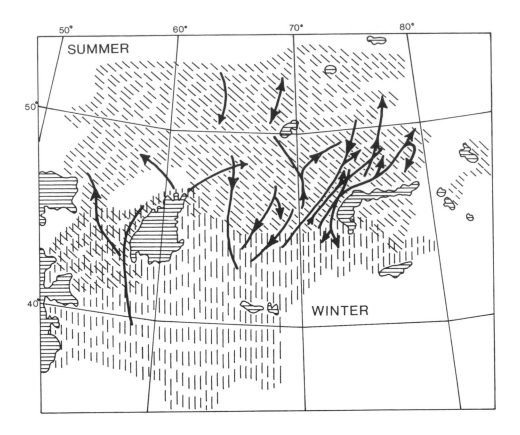

Figure 11.11 Distribution of kulans in Central Asia and Kazakhstan and migration routes in the 18th and 19th centuries (after A.G. Bannikov).

typical only of *saiga* and *kulan*, it seems likely that the North Ustiurt group of structures was built to hunt these two species.

In winter, however, herd sizes are smaller and the animals are not on migration. Winter grazing grounds included the region of the Aibuiir-Prisar'ikam'ish group of structures. Unlike the North Ustiurt group, the Aibuiir-Prisar'ikam'ish group does not form large systems of structures. Today the area coincides with the winter grazing grounds of *kulan*, *saiga* and gazelle. In earlier periods the abundance of water made it possible for animals to live there all year round. At the end of the 19th century Bogdanov (1882) noted that there was a permanent population of *kulan* in the desert near the Sar'ikam'ish lake (today a depression). Orientation of structures within this group varies and is determined by topography rather than by the compass direction. Unlike the North Ustiurt systems where the animals would migrate directly into the enclosures, here the animals would need to be driven within the guiding walls. The Aibuiir-Prisar'ikam'ish group of structures varies also in having most of the triangular enclosures located on hilltops. This can be explained by the fact that herd animals often run to hills or high land to have a clear view of the surrounding landscape. These structures also include 'hides' for hunters lower down the slopes to exploit the tendency of frightened animals to run uphill.

'Arrow-shaped' structures of the Kend'irlisor group are located on gentle slopes and on the edge of deep ravines. Galkin (1988) has suggested that these structures may have been used for the hunting of wild sheep. However, the location of structures within the group suggests that they were used for both active and passive forms of hunting.

Study of the data on 'arrow-shaped' structures confirms the fact that the height and width of fences varies in different parts of the structure. The small enclosures and ring walls were high while banks revetted with stone on the inner face made it hard for the animals to escape. The walls of the large enclosures and guiding 'arms' were usually much lower. Apparently, a good knowledge of animal behaviour enabled builders to select the most appropriate structure requiring the minimum effort to make it work. It would seem that the low walls and ditches that initially guide the animals could easily be jumped, and provided no effective obstacle. However, the walls and banks were built in the knowledge that animals react to the visible obstacle by running along it without attempting to jump over. This kind of behaviour has been recorded in a number of similar cases (Dobie 1952; Baskin 1976).

One question is why the animals did not learn of the danger and avoid it. Studies show that the process of accumulating habits in animals slows after the first year.

As an animal gets older it can survive by copying the behaviour of other animals in the herd. Thus, the larger the herd, the less necessity animals have to learn to avoid danger (Baskin 1976). Such patterns have been observed among North American bison where as long as the herd was large a sense of fear and danger in response to hunters was not built up. However, with the decrease in the bison population, the animals learned to run away from even a small source of danger very rapidly (Baskin 1976). A similar pattern probably occurred in the *saiga* and *kulan* populations in Ustiurt.

It seems likely therefore that there is a direct connection between the distribution and structural form of the enclosures and the specific behaviour patterns of the animals hunted.

Conclusion

Hunting was an important part of the economy of the Ustiurt region up until recent times. Hunting by means of the 'arrow-shaped' structures would have become a commercial activity since the amount of meat, bones and hides would have been too much for the personal use of the hunters. Part of the proceeds of the hunt would have been available for trade. The construction and use of such systems implies a relatively high degree of cooperation among a large group of people. In recent times, the tribes gathered in large groups during the animal migration season. Although there is no direct information on the social structure of nomadic groups in the medieval period or earlier, the traditional nature of the recent economy, limited as it has been by environmental constraints, may be not dissimilar to that of the past. Ethnographic data suggest that the nomads of Ustiurt had a patriarchal tribal system. Archaeological evidence indicates that small economically independent extended family groups lived in small numbers in the Ustiurt region. It is possible that each family owned a single 'arrow-shaped' structure within the North Ustiurt group but since the hunt required cooperation between groups, the tribes united for the period of the hunting season.

The results of the archaeological analysis have shown that 'arrow-shaped' structures can be dated from the second half of the 1st millennium BC up to recent times. However, many of the structures are hard to date with certainty because of the lack of available evidence. The structures are located in certain areas where they are organised in separate groups. The term *aran* was used in connection with the most recent, ethnographically documented, 'arrow-shaped' structures. Comparative analysis of similar systems elsewhere such as the Middle East, northern Europe and North America show that such structures were used for hunting herds of wild game.

Acknowledgements

Archaeological research, particularly that undertaken under the extreme conditions of desert life, depends heavily on a wide range of people. Experts in various related sciences take part in the work, as well as pilots, truck drivers, mechanics, surveyors, architects, labourers and others. The field research could not have been completed without them. Thanks are due also to the archaeologists and scientists E.B. Bizhanov, BC Saipanov, N.U. Iusupov, N.Y. Bagdasarova, S.B. Gubin, and Professor L.M. Baskin.

Notes

1. Department of Archaeology of the Institute of History, Language and Literature of the Uzbek Academy of Sciences, Karakalpak Branch, Republic of Uzbekistan (Nukus)

2. This chapter is based on a translation of Yagodin's publication (1991)

12. Conclusion

A.V.G. Betts

with a contribution by W. Lancaster

Introduction

The *harra* is a special area with regard to its environment and its location in the semi-arid zone between lands of agricultural potential and the true desert. Its rocky landscape provides both barrier and refuge to humans and animals alike. Because of this, the ways in which the region has been used are particularly distinctive. This can be seen as early as the Natufian period where the wadis draining Jebel Druze provided corridors of movement up and down the mountain, probably relating to seasonal changes in climate and natural resources. In the Early Neolithic period, the PPNB, the *harra* was particularly used for hunting, as the evidence from Dhuweila demonstrates. By the Late Neolithic, the first nomadic hunter/herders had moved into the *badia*. Their sites have been found around Burqu' and in the more open sandy parts of the *harra* south of Dhuweila. From the sixth millennium BC to the present day, the *harra* has been used by herders who have adapted their lifestyles to the particular restrictions and advantages of the landscape.

People of the Dhuweila area today and in the recent past (*W. Lancaster*)

The area of the *harra* in which Dhuweila lies is used predominantly by members of a group of tribes known, collectively, as the Ahl al-Jabal. Their name, 'the people of the mountain', is descriptive rather than determin-ative, and refers to the volcanic peak Jebel al-Druze or Jebel al-'Arab in the Syrian Arab Republic, although the terrain used by the tribes stretches into Jordan and, formerly, Saudi Arabia. Indeed, their very name suggests that they are a group who are delineated geographically rather than genealogically. There are three main tribes, al-Masa'id, al-Sharafat and al-Hassan, who are rarely supposed to have been closely related. Little information is currently available about their history but, given the nature of the terrain and the degree of specialist knowledge needed to use it effectively, it seems probable that the present inhabitants have been there for a long time. The Ahl al-Jabal are not one of the great 'noble' tribes; they are primarily sheep-herders, although they possess (or did) camels as well, mostly for transport purposes. There is no tradition that they were

once herding camels elsewhere and were forced to retreat into the *harra* through external pressure. It seems more probable that they were one of those tribes which have always inhabited the desert margin, relying on sheep production for their main livelihood although opportunities for other trade ventures, agriculture, guiding or guarding caravans and other services were never neglected. This use of multiple resources is common to all Arab tribes although the resources available will vary over time and according to the surrounding economic and political climate.

At present, the Ahl al-Jabal herd sheep and goats, run agricultural enterprises and take up paid employment. These separate categories are not mutually exclusive as it is common practice for some members of the family to tend sheep, others to grow grain or vegetables while others are employed by the government (e.g. in the army or civil administration) or are self-employed as traders, transporters or entrepreneurs. Many members of a family switch occupations from time to time, replacing another who has decided to take up yet a different option. Thus their economic activity is closely linked to the towns, villages and the state. This has been the case with all bedu, today and in the past, but especially with sheep-herding groups who inhabit the marginal agricultural areas. In the past fifteen years there has been a readily observable shift in the economic and settlement patterns of the Ahl al-Jabal. In the early 1970s there were few villages between Mafraq and H5 (Safawi) on the Jordan-Iraq road. Now there are not only many more villages but the earlier villages have grown in size and architectural complexity. Where once the housing had been essentially bedouin tents reproduced in concrete blocks, there are now modern 'villas', many of a considerable size and with walled gardens and trees. Agricultural practices have changed also. The pre-modern, predominantly subsistence, grain production has expanded into commercial market-gardening, fruit and olive trees, as well as irrigated wheat and barley fields. It must be emphasised, however, that the population has not shifted. Apart from a general growth in numbers, (largely the result of improved medical facilities), the people now farming the area remain, largely, Ahl al-Jabal. Under modern economic conditions commercial agriculture has become a more viable option than in the past. The fact that many of the members of the tribes have permanent dwellings does not necessarily imply a commitment to settled life; the exchange of personnel and changing occupations mean that most are nomadic for much of the time even though, for administrative purposes or convenience, they have an address. It should be noted that this 'settlement' is nothing new; the archaeological remains which are scattered throughout the more favourable areas show that it is a process which has happened before. The oscillation between settled agriculture and nomadic pastoralism is perfectly normal and appears to be age-old, whether the Ahl al-Jabal were utilising the area or whether it was in the hands of other, unknown tribes. As Hiyari (1975: 510) points out, there are very few environments in the steppe which provide all the year round subsistence every year — a large degree of nomadism is inevitable whatever the basic subsistence may be.

Those members of the tribes who still herd do so in the traditional manner in so far as this is still possible. During winter and spring they move from the *hamad* close to the Iraqi border westward through the *harra* until, by summer, they are near the stubbles around the settlements. Formerly they also moved north onto the slopes of Jebel Druze, but this is no longer politically possible. There is no set pattern as movement depended on the availability of grazing and water, factors which varied greatly from year to year. This is less apparent nowadays as most herders have access to tankers and deep government wells so water can be trucked almost anywhere; but this is only an extension of the old practice of carrying water from wells or natural storage basins to their flocks by means of camels or donkeys, a practice which significantly increased the grazing range (Lancaster and Lancaster 1986, 1991, in press). In the past, wherever they found themselves for the summer the herders had contractual arrangements with the landowners whose stubble they grazed: with the extension of agriculture, however, they are more likely to utilise their own stubbles or those of close relatives. The change is not absolute but more a matter of emphasis.

Under the present economic and political regime it is possible that the nomadic pastoralist element of the tribes rely more heavily than formerly on commercial milk production. At present a good half of the yearly income derived from sheep comes from the sale of milk products, principally cheese, sold to the towns. Although specialist cheese-makers are now usually employed, everyone knows how to make cheese and dried yoghourt, and there is no doubt that these products, along with clarified butter, were used as a medium of exchange during earlier periods. Nowadays the emphasis is on fresh cheese as modern transport is readily available, but dried cheese and yoghourt, as well as clarified butter, all keep well and could, formerly, have been transported by the relatively slower transport of

camel or donkey. Perhaps more likely would be the storage of milk products until the end of the grazing season and their subsequent sale during the summer settlements. The other major source of income from sheep is the sale of fat lamb to the meat market. At present, there is a buoyant demand for meat and ram lambs are sold off whenever cash is needed, although the main sales occur during the early summer as the grazing dries out. It is likely that this was the same in the past though it is probable that more rams were kept because wool was a more valuable commodity than it is today. It should also be remembered that the predominant herd species in the past was probably goats rather than sheep, a factor which may have altered marketing strategies considerably.

The migratory pattern of the tribes has always been variable, depending on political and economic conditions as well as the variability and unpredictability of rainfall. Modern political boundaries have had some effect but these can change depending on upon the often swiftly changing relationships between the various governments. More consistent seems to be the change in the composition of the herding group. Most beduin prefer to migrate and herd in small family groups of two or three tents. With the prevalence of raiding in the past this could rarely be achieved in the eastern gravel *hamad* desert, although given the broken nature of the *harra*, it would have been more possible there. Certainly this is the practice today with single tents being far from uncommon. The major change, however, is the change in composition of the herding household. Basically a single tent is inhabited by a nuclear family, often with the addition of unmarried siblings, a widowed mother or a divorced sister. With the advent of modern transport, wider economic options and especially the need for education, the current household is more likely to be a married man, his wife and his pre-school children. The other members of the family — the unmarried siblings, parents and school-age children — will be living in a village, looking after the farm or in paid employment. In return, although not on a strictly reciprocal basis, the herding son or brother will look after the sheep or goats of the more settled family members. There is no way of knowing whether this type of pattern pertained in the past. Some variation of it probably did if similar economic opportunities existed, but the educational factor is an entirely modern phenomenon.

Until recently, hunting and gathering always made up a proportion of the bedouin subsistence economy and it may have been commercial as well in some degree. Today it is of little significance. The larger wild animals such as gazelle or ibex have all but disappeared and the small animals which remain are unlikely ever to have been important except in times of severe shortage. The gathering of plant foods is now restricted to specialist medicinal or flavouring herbs but only for family consumption. The exception might be the collecting of truffles which have a retail value and which appear in easily gathered quantities, given the right weather conditions. However, the days when hunting and gathering were an essential component of desert subsistence are not entirely forgotten even if the use of 'kites' for capturing gazelle is only remembered as stories related by grand-parents to today's middle-aged generation.

There has been no proper study of the Ahl al-Jabal although much information can be gleaned from Musil (1927), Wetzstein (1860) and Burckhardt (1831), so there is only limited knowledge of their particular herding practices. Available information shows that normally the flocks are grazed during the day and corralled at night, although grazing is usually extended almost to nightfall and, during the summer, sheep especially are rested, preferably in the shade, at midday. For the first few days after birth the lambs remain with their dams, but are then separated and kept near the tent, being suckled morning and evening. Ewes are usually milked only once a day, but this may be related to labour availability as today's flocks are significantly larger than in the past while, as we have seen, the herding family has, under modern conditions, become reduced in size.

An important aspect of flock management is the right of access to grazing and water. This can only be touched on here but, in general, grazing cannot be owned while water can only be reserved by the family responsible for enhancing or creating the supply. Rights to use corrals are undetermined but it is unlikely that strict rules apply as, by and large, 'first come, first served' is the normal bedouin practice. This does not, of course, apply to crops, whether commercial or opportunistic; the sower has absolute rights to the product, either as grain or as grazing, although subsequent rights of access to stubbles can be more complex.

Further study of the Ahl al-Jabal will, undoubtedly, demonstrate that they use the *harra* in other more subtle ways, which may be of considerable importance in understanding the practices of earlier times.

Dhuweila

The site in context

Because Dhuweila is small, it has been possible to excavate a fairly large proportion of the site, and yet even so, it is still difficult to understand all aspects of it. The location, the stone tool repertoire and the faunal remains all indicate that the site saw primary use as a hunting station, although the occupants may have carried out other activities as well. Given the location and the evidence for repeated re-use and re-structuring of the site, it is also most likely that Dhuweila was only occupied on a seasonal basis. The site includes a number of features which may relate to aspects of carcase processing: these include hearths; stone-lined pits; and

piles of fire-cracked stones. Precise identification of the function of these features is not possible from the archaeological record but some clues may be obtained from ethnographic accounts of similar features associated with carcase processing at hunting camps.

Other questions relating to the site include the identity of the people who used it. Were they permanent nomadic hunters or were they groups who moved out from settlements in the verdant areas to hunt occasionally in the *harra*? While gazelle would have been present in the verdant areas, it may only have been in the *harra* that it would have been possible to kill large numbers of animals in a single hunt using the 'kite' systems. Why also does there appear to have been a hiatus of around five hundred years between the two stages of occupation at the site? Stage 1 at Dhuweila, the late PPNB, coincides with a general expansion into the semi-arid areas which has been recorded over much of the southern Levant including the Negev and Sinai. Less is known about the Late Neolithic in the semi-arid regions. With the introduction of nomadic pastoralism around the beginning of the 6th millennium BC, hunter/herder camps and small occupation sites are recorded from most of the North Arabian *badia*; from Jordan, Syria and Iraq. However, the Late Neolithic stage at Dhuweila provides no clear evidence of a herding component in the economic strategy of the occupants of Stage 2 at the site. It may be that the site was used by part of a hunter/herder group in the same way that today the Ahl al-Jabal will divide their subsistence activities among family members in different locations. In identifying relationships between the occupiers of Dhuweila and Neolithic groups whose remains are known from excavated sites elsewhere, it is possible to gain some insight from the objects found at the site which include ornamental items imported from outside the *harra*, some of which have parallels at other Neolithic sites. However, with its rock carvings and its association to the 'kite' systems, Dhuweila still represents an unusual and highly distinctive aspect of the Neolithic of the Levant.

Seasonality

Located as it is, deep within the *harra*, Dhuweila is unlikely to have been a permanent settlement, although it cannot be assumed that conditions were as unfavourable in the sixth and seventh millennia BC as they are today. However, without substantial climatic amelioration, high temperatures and scarcity of water and shade would have made occupation very hard in the summer months. The most likely period of occupation would have been between October and April. Various aspects of the evidence support this suggestion. The main structure is apparently designed for shelter in cold, wet and windy weather. It is semi-subterranean, set into the hillside and most strongly protected from the prevailing westerly winds. In the Late Neolithic period it was paved inside, probably to prevent the occupants from sinking into the debris of previous occupations during wet weather. Successive pavements were laid down as the occupation debris built up on the earlier floors. A similar pattern can be seen at the slightly later cave site of al-Hibr (Betts 1992). With its thick walls, poor ventilation and narrow entrance, such a structure would have been very uncomfortable and impractical in high summer.

The faunal and botanical evidence also provide some indications for winter/spring occupancy. Assuming spring birth peaks for gazelle, there is evidence for hunting in spring/early summer and possibly also in autumn/winter, while three of the birds identified from the site would only be expected to visit the area in the wetter seasons. In the botanical remains, Colledge notes the absence of Chenopod seeds which flower and fruit in late summer/early autumn.

From October, the climate in the *harra* becomes milder. Early autumn dews encourage the growth of annual flowers and grass even before the advent of the winter rains. In winter, the weather is cold, with high winds, sporadic rainstorms and, occasionally, light snowfall. By spring, the weather is warm and sunny, and the ground is covered in fresh new plant growth. From October to April the *harra* would be suitable for herd animals as there would be grazing and standing water in pools after the first rains. In addition, the broken rocky landscape with its hills and deeply incised wadi systems would provide shelter against the winter winds. While it cannot be proven absolutely, it seems likely that Dhuweila was seasonally occupied at some time outside the hot, dry months of summer.

Site function

Ethnographic accounts of hunting systems involving the use of game drives show that there is a particular group of special activity areas associated with the hunt. Apart from the enclosure itself, and its guiding walls, there are also lookout posts, blinds or hides to conceal the hunters, butchering areas and hunting camps. Such ethnographic accounts can be helpful in attempting to reconstruct the pattern of activities revolving around use of the 'kite' systems (e.g. Binford 1978a). Traces of similar activity areas can be identified in the *harra*. Hilltops were used both as lookout posts and knapping stations. Free-standing blinds may have existed near the 'kites' but have not been identified among the large number of stone piles of all periods in the *harra*. However, it is likely that at least some of the stone circles attached to the outer walls of the enclosure were used as blinds. Butchering sites have not been identified in the vicinity of the 'kites'. If they did exist, these would have had mostly ephemeral remains, consisting largely of bio-degradable material which would rapidly

have been dispersed through animal activity and processes of decay, particularly if initial butchering merely consisted of gutting the animals but leaving the carcase whole. Gazelle are small and a man can easily carry one, if not several, carcasses. Nineteenth century accounts describe how gazelle carcases were slit in two along the spine, salted and sun-dried (Betts 1989b). Preserved in this way, the meat could be kept indefinitely. The faunal evidence suggests that whole carcases may have been transported back to the base camp for butchering. Camps such as Dhuweila were in the vicinity of the 'kite' enclosures and a gazelle carcase is more readily transportable whole, particularly if pack animals are not available.

In the ethnographic accounts, the sequence of events in the killing, butchering and processing stages following the hunt depend on a variety of factors. If the animals are large, initial butchering will take place at or close to the point of killing. However, if the killing site is to be re-used within a short time, animals may be frightened by the scent of decay if preliminary butchering is carried out near the traps.

Binford's (1978b) study of the Nunamiut Eskimo is a classic example. One of the prey of the Nunamiut was sheep, killed, prior to the introduction of guns, by using snares or the bow and arrow. They were hunted when they collected at salt licks during summer and early fall. Activities relating to the hunt resulted in a variety of work sites. At the kill site proper, on or near the salt lick, were piles of stones or broken antlers stuck into the ground to act as anchors for the snares. The sheep shot or snared on the lick were never butchered on the lick itself. Their bodies were dragged down to a location on flat ground out of sight of the lick. Remains at the butchering site included meat caches and a hearth area. The area around the licks is treeless and bone had been used as fuel. The third type of site is the observation stand where hunters concealed themselves while watching for sheep approaching the lick. These varied in use depending on the prevailing wind. Hunters would generally bring some unfinished artefact or tool to work on in the stand to relieve the boredom of waiting. As a result, most of the stands yielded flint chips, unfinished tools cached in the rocks around or debris from manufacture. Sometimes there were also bones carried up for food. The final type of associated location is the hunting camp where the expedition hunters ate, slept and processed material for transport back to the residential location. These sites were regularly re-used. Remains at the sites comprised dog weights for tethering, skin weights, meat caches, hearths and tent rings. The skin weights were circles of small stones placed around the edge of a skin laid out to dry. The meat caches consisted of small circles of stream boulders with slightly smaller stones in the centre to raise the meat off the ground. The whole would then be covered in more stones. The hearths consisted of ash and calcined bone, surrounded by a bone scatter formed by the remains of meals. Some were flanked with a few stones. The tent ring was a rough circle of stones used to weigh down a light canvas awning.

Apart from meat caches and hearths, roasting pits are another feature of camp and meat processing sites (e.g. Binford 1983: 166–7; Benedict 1992: 8). These are shallow pits, usually about 50 cm across and 15–20 cm deep. Associated debris includes charcoal and fire-cracked stones. Dhuweila had a number of stone-ringed hearths, some of which were lined with small pebbles, as well as very large quantities of fire-cracked stones and ash. There were also several pits, cut into bedrock and ringed with stones at the lip. The area around the hearths and pits was covered in layers of ash filled with bone and flint fragments, while the faunal evidence suggests that bones from the site may have been splintered for marrow or grease extraction (see Chapter 8). The hearths and pits may have been used for various processing and storage purposes relating to preservation of the meat, preparation of hides, the extraction of marrow or the rendering down of fat.

External contacts

Artefacts other than chipped stone suggest external contacts in both Stages 1 and 2, but not necessarily close cultural relationships with other areas. Items such as stone rings and beads are known from other Jordanian sites. Bead production using Dabba 'marble' was a feature of steppic sites from the Natufian period, but was particularly prevalent in both the Early and Late Neolithic periods (Finlayson and Betts 1990; Baird *et al.* 1992: 24; Wright in Garrard *et al.* 1994b: 91). Beads of various kinds are also found on Neolithic sites in the more verdant areas (e.g. Rollefson *et al.* 1991: 104). The shell beads must have been acquired through trade or exchange networks of some kind. Culturally then, the inhabitants of Dhuweila had contacts with others in and beyond the steppe. The rock engravings, however, are something of an enigma. They appear to be unique to the *harra*, where they are prolific, at least in the vicinity of hunting camps. While animal figurines are found in small numbers on several Neolithic sites, animal engravings in any form have not been recorded from sites beyond the *harra*. The nature of the rock engravings and the motives behind their creation are probably complex. However, it seems unlikely that if the PPNB inhabitants of Dhuweila were hunting parties from settlements in the verdant regions, they would only create engravings in the *harra* and not elsewhere. The carvings show individual animals, probably gazelle, but not the actual hunt in progress. Gazelle were hunted all over the Levant and their remains are found in greater or lesser quantities at almost every PPNB site. The main

distinction at Dhuweila is the method of hunting and the numbers of animals killed. This might suggest that the PPNB Dhuweila hunters were people whose focus of livelihood was the *harra*. This need not necessarily have applied to the people of Stage 2, but it is also possible. Finds from Stage 2 include shell and stone beads but none clearly of Dabba 'marble'. They also include an animal figurine, a fragment of stone ring and six potsherds. While the beads, ring and figurine are indicative of external contacts, the pottery contains basalt inclusions. There is no evidence for pottery firing at Dhuweila so the pottery must have been made at another site somewhere in the *harra*, perhaps one of a less specialised nature.

'Kites'

One important aspect of 'kite' planning has also emerged from this study. While dating of 'kites' is recognised as problematical, the 'kites' or 'kite' systems fall into two distinct groups, the significance of which can be more clearly understood in the light of the Central Asian studies (see 'Arrow-shaped' structures' above). In the *harra* there are chained systems of enclosures, almost always pointing to the west, and individual traps which tend to point in a variety of directions, depending partly on local topography. This is similar to the pattern observed in northern Uzbekistan. Yagodin suggests that chained systems of traps were laid out along the seasonal migration routes of the herds of game. The Central Asian 'kites' of this type have been classified as 'passive', in that the animals would wander along the walls of their own accord, in the course of migration. The hunters would only need to drive them into the enclosures when they drew close to them. In contrast, there are also 'active' systems such as those of the Aibuiir-Prisar'ikam'ish group where the structures do not form large systems, and the orientation of the enclosures varies, being determined by topography rather than by the compass direction. Unlike the North Ustiurt 'passive' systems where the animals would migrate directly into the enclosures, here in the winter grazing grounds of *kulan, saiga* and gazelle, the animals would need to be driven within the guiding walls. This suggests two possible interpretations for the patterning of 'kites' in the *harra*. One is that the varied distribution of chained and single 'kites' relates to some form of seasonal movement. The other, and equally significant, possibility is that, if the chained systems are linked particularly to the earlier prehistoric periods, extensive depredation, and perhaps the spread of settlement on the steppic fringes, may have led to changes in animal behaviour and seasonal movement, resulting in increased use of single 'active' traps in later periods.

Bibliography

Abbes, F.
1991 Les percuteurs de Cheikh Hassan. Paper presented at the Table-Ronde sur la Traitement de la Matière Minérale, Animale et Vegetale au Moyen du Mobilier et des Récipients en Pierre, Institut de Préhistoire Orientale du Centre National du Recherche Scientifique, Jalès, France, February 5–7.

Amick, D. S. and R. P. Mauldin (eds.)
1989 *Experiments in Lithic Technology.* British Archaeological Reports International Series 528. Oxford: British Archaeological Reports.

Anati, E.
1968 *Rock-Art in Central Arabia.* Bibliothèque du Muséon, n. 50, Louvain (Université de Louvain, Institut Orientaliste), Vol. 1.
1972 *Rock-Art in Central Arabia.* Publications de l'Institut Orientaliste de Louvain, n.4, Louvain (Université de Louvain, Institut Orientaliste), Vol. 3.
1979 *L'Art Rupestre. Negev et Sinai.* L'Equerre, Paris. the Rock Engravings, Parts I and II.

Anderson, P. C.
1994 Reflections on the Significance of Two PPN Typological Classes in the Light of Experimentation and Microwear Analysis: Flint 'Sickles' and Obsidian 'Çayönü Tools'. In H.-G. Gebel and S.K. Koslowski (eds.), *Neolithic Chipped Stone Industries of the Fertile Crescent,* 61–82. Berlin: ex oriente.

Arkheologicheskaya karta Kazakhstana
1960 Alma-Ata.

Arkush, B. S.
1986 Aboriginal Exploitation of Pronghorn in the Great Basin. *Journal of Ethnobiology* 6/2: 239–255.

Aston, N., P. Dean and J. McNabb
1991 Flaked flakes: what, where, when and why? *Lithics: The Newsletter of the Lithic Studies Society* 12: 1–11.

Baharav, D.
1974a Notes on the Population Structure and Biomass of the Mountain Gazelle, *Gazella gazella gazella. Israel Journal of Zoology* 23: 39–44.
1974b Food habits of the mountain gazelle in Ramot Yissakhar, Israel. *Israel Journal of Zoology* 23: 218–219.
1981 Food habits of the mountain gazelle in semi -arid habitats of eastern Lower Galilee, Israel. *Journal of Arid Environments* 4: 63–69.
1982 Desert habitat partitioning by the dorcas gazelle. *Journal of Arid Environments* 5: 323–335.
1983a Observation on the ecology of the mountain gazelle in the Upper Galilee, Israel. *Mammalia* 47: 59–69.
1983b Reproductive strategies in female Mountain and Dorcas gazelles (*Gazella gazella gazella* and *Gazella dorcas*). *Journal of Zoology, London* 200: 445–453.

Bailey, C. and A. Danin
1981 Beduin plant utilisation in Sinai and the Negev. *Economic Botany* 35/2: 145–162.

Baird, D.
1989 The significance of a Neolithic sequence in eastern Jordan. Paper presented at the meeting of the British Association for Near Eastern Archaeology, Edinburgh, December 7–9.
1993 Neolithic Chipped Stone assemblages from the Azraq Basin, Jordan and the Significance of the Neolithic of the Arid Zones of the Levant. Unpublished PhD. thesis, University of Edinburgh.
1995 Chipped Stone Raw Material Procurement and Selection in the Neolithic Azraq Basin: Implications for Levantine Neolithic Cultural Developments. In *Studies in the History and Archaeology of Jordan* 5, 505–514. Amman: Department of Antiquities of Jordan.

Baird, D., A. Garrard, L. Martin, and K. Wright
1992 Prehistoric Environment and Settlement in the Azraq Basin: An interim report on the 1989 season. *Levant* 24: 1–31.

Barber, E.
1991 *Prehistoric Textiles.* Princeton, N.J.: Princeton University Press.

Barth, E. K.
1983 Trapping reindeer in South Norway. *Antiquity* 57: 109–115.

Baruch, U. and S. Bottema
1991 Palynological Evidence for Climatic Changes in the Levant c. 17,000–9,000 b.p.. In O. Bar-Yosef and F. Valla (eds.), *The Natufian Culture in the Levant*: 11–20, Michigan: International Monographs in Prehistory, Archaeological Series 1.

Bar-Yosef, O.
1970 The Epi-Paleolithic Cultures of Palestine. PhD Thesis, Hebrew University, Jerusalem.
1981a The Epi-Paleolithic complexes in the southern Levant. In J. Cauvin and P. Sanlaville (eds.), *Préhistoire du Levant*: 389–408, Lyon, Maison de l'Orient: Colloques Internationaux du *Centre National du Recherche Scientifique* No. 598.
1981b The Pre-Pottery Neolithic Period in the Southern Levant. In J. Cauvin and P. Sanlaville (eds.), *Préhistoire du Levant*: 555–569. Lyon, Maison de l'Orient: Colloques Internationaux du *Centre National du Recherche Scientifique* No. 598.
1981c Early nomads in southern Sinai. *National Geographic Society Research Reports 1976 Projects*: 147–159.
1983 The Natufian in the Southern Levant. In T. Cuyler-Young, P. Smith and P. Mortensen (eds.), *The Hilly Flanks and Beyond*: 11–42. Chicago: University of Chicago.
1984 Seasonality among Neolithic hunter-gatherers in southern Sinai. In J. Clutton-Brock and C. Grigson (eds.), *Animals and Archaeology* Vol. 3: 145–160. British Archaeological Reports International Series 202. Oxford: British Archaeological Reports.
1988 Late Pleistocene Adaptations in the Levant. In O. Soffer (ed.), *The Pleistocene Old World. Regional Perspectives*, 219–36, New York and London:

Plenum.

1994 Form, Function and Numbers in Neolithic Lithic Studies. In H.-G. Gebel and S.K. Koslowski (eds.), *Neolithic Chipped Stone Industries of the Fertile Crescent*, 5–14. Berlin: ex oriente.

Bar-Yosef, O and Belfer-Cohen, A.
1992 From Foraging to Farming in the Mediterranean Levant. In A.B. Gebauer and T.D. Price (eds), *Transitions to Agriculture in Prehistory*: 21-48, Madison, Wisconsin: Prehistory Press.

Baskin, L.M.
1976 *Povedenie kop'itn'kh zhivotn'ikh*. Moscow.

Bate, D.M.A.
1937 Description of Faunal Assemblages and their Climatic Inferences. In D.A.E. Garrod and D.M.A. Bate (eds.), *The Stone Age of Mount Carmel*, 139–154. Oxford: Clarendon Press.

Baulmer, M.
n.d. Analytic Comparability Among Flake Measurement Techniques in Lithic Analysis. Paper presented at the 44th Annual Meeting of the Society for American Archaeology, Vancouver, B.C., Canada.

Becker, C.
1991 The Analysis of Mammalian Bones from Basta, A Pre-Pottery Neolithic Site in Jordan: Problems and Potential. *Paléorient* 17: 59–75.

Behrensmeyer, A.K.
1978 Taphonomic and Ecologic Information from Bone Weathering. *Paleobiology* 4: 150–162.

Benedict, J.B.
1992 Footprints in the Snow: High-Altitude Cultural Ecology of the Colorado Front Range, U.S.A. *Arctic and Alpine Research* 24: 1–16.

Bender, F.
1968 *Geologie von Jordanien*. Berlin: Gebruder Bornträger.

Betts, A.
1982 Prehistoric sites at Qa'a Mejalla, Eastern Jordan. *Levant* 14: 1–34.
1983 Black Desert Survey, Jordan: first preliminary report. *Levant* 15: 1–10.
1984 Black Desert Survey, Jordan: second preliminary report. *Levant* 16: 25–34.
1985 Black Desert Survey, Jordan: third preliminary report. *Levant* 17: 29–52.
1986 Prehistory of the Basalt Desert. Unpublished PhD. thesis, University of London.
1987a 1986 Excavations at Dhuweila, Eastern Jordan. A Preliminary Report. *Annual of the Department of Antiquities of Jordan* 31: 121–28.
1987b The Hunter's Perspective: 7th millennium BC rock carvings from eastern Jordan. *World Archaeology* 19: 214–25.
1987c Recent Discoveries Relating to the Neolithic Periods in Eastern Jordan. In A. Hadidi (ed.), *Studies in the History and Archaeology of Jordan* Vol. 3: 225–230. London: Department of Antiquities of Jordan, Amman.
1987d A Preliminary Survey of Late Neolithic settlements at el-Ghirqa Eastern Jordan. *Proceedings of the Prehistoric Society* 53: 327–336.
1988a The Black Desert Survey: prehistoric sites and subsistence strategies in eastern Jordan. In A.N. Garrard and H.G. Gebel (eds.), *The Prehistory of*

Jordan: The State of Research in 1986, 369–391. British Archaeological Reports International Series 396 i, ii. Oxford: British Archaeological Reports.
1988b 1986 Excavations at Dhuweila, eastern Jordan: a preliminary report. *Levant* 20: 7–21.
1989a The Pre-Pottery Neolithic B Period in Eastern Jordan. *Paléorient* 15: 147–153.
1989b The Solubba: Nonpastoral Nomads in Arabia. *Bulletin of the American Schools of Oriental Research* 274: 61–69.
1991 The Late Epipaleolithic in the Black Desert, eastern Jordan. In O. Bar-Yosef and F. Valla (eds.), *The Natufian Culture in the Levant*, 217–234. Ann Arbor: International Monographs in Prehistory.
1992 Tell el-Hibr: A Rock Shelter Occupation of the Fourth Millennium B.C.E. in the Jordanian Badiya. *Bulletin of the American Schools of Oriental Research* 287: 5–23.
1993a The Burqu'/Ruwaysid Project: Preliminary report on the 1991 Field Season. *Levant* 25: 1–11.
1993b The Neolithic Sequence in the east Jordan *badia*. A preliminary overview. *Paléorient* 19: 43–53.
n.d. 'Rock Art of the Middle East' Chapter 18 in *Handbook for Rock Art Research* edited by David Whitley, Alta Mira Press. (in press)

Betts, A.V.G. (ed.)
1991 *Excavations at Jawa 1972–1986. Stratigraphy, Pottery and Other Finds*. Edinburgh: Edinburgh University Press.
1992 *Excavations at Tell Um Hammad 1982–1984. The Early Assemblages (EBI–II)*. Edinburgh: Edinburgh University Press.

Betts, A., Eames, S, Hulka, S., Schroder, M., Rust, J. and McLaren, B.
1996 Studies of Bronze Age Occupation in the Wadi al-'Ajib, Southern Hauran. *Levant* 28: 27-39.

Betts, A., S. Eames, M. Schroder and A. al-Q. Hesan
1995 Archaeological Survey of the Wadi al-'Ajib, Mafraq District. *Annual of the Department of Antiquities of Jordan* 39: 149–168.

Betts, A. and S. Helms
1986 Rock Art in eastern Jordan: 'kite' carvings ? *Paléorient* 12/1:67-72.

Betts, A., van der Borg, K, de Jong, A., McClintock, C. and Strydonck, M.
1987 A Preliminary Survey of Late Neolithic Settlements at el-Ghirqa, Eastern Jordan. *Proceedings of the Prehistoric Society* 53: 327–336.
1994 Early Cotton in North Arabia. *Journal of Archaeological Science* 21: 489-499.

Betts, A., S. Helms, W. Lancaster, E. Jones, A. Lupton, L. Martin and F. Matsaert
1990 The Burqu'/Ruweishid Project: Preliminary Report on the 1988 Field Season. *Levant* 22: 1–20.

Betts, A., S. Helms, W. Lancaster and F. Lancaster
1991 The Burqu'/Ruweishid Project: Preliminary Report on the 1989 Field Season. *Levant* 23: 7–28.

Binford, L.R.
1977 Forty-seven trips: a case study in the character of archaeological formation processes. In R. Wright (ed.), *Stone Tools as Cultural Markers*, 24–36. Canberra: Australian Institute of Aboriginal Studies.

232

1978a Dimensional analysis of behaviour and site structure: learning from an Eskimo hunting stand. *American Antiquity* 43: 330–361.

1978b *Nunamiut Ethnoarchaeology.* Academic Press.

1979 Organisation and formation processes: looking at curated technologies. *Journal of Anthropological Research* 35: 255–273.

1983 *In Pursuit of the Past. Decoding the Archaeological Record.* London: Thames and Hudson

1991 A Corporate Caribou Hunt. Documenting the archaeology of past lifeways. *Expedition* 33: 33–43.

Binford, L.R. and J.B. Bertram

1977 Bone Frequencies and Attritional Processes. In L.R. Binford (ed.), *For Theory Building in Archaeology*: 77–153. New York: Academic Press.

Bisheh, G.

1982 The second season of excavations at Hallabat, 1980. *Annual of the Department of Antiquities of Jordan* 26: 133–43.

Bogdanov, M.N.

1882 *Ocherki perirod'i Kivinskogo oazisa i pust'ini K'iz'ilkum.* Tashkent.

Bordes, F.

1961 *Typologie du Paléolithique, ancien et moyen*, Vols 1, 2. Paris: Centre National du Recherche Scientifique.

Bordes, F. and D. Crabtree

1969 The Corbiac Blade Technique and Other Experiments. *Tebiwa* 12: 1–22.

Braemer, F.

1984 Prospections archéologiques dans le Hawran. *Syria* 61: 219–50.

Brain, C.K.

1981 *The Hunters or the Hunted.* Chicago: University of Chicago Press.

Brézillon, M.

1983 *La Denomination des Objets de Pierre Taillée.* Paris: *Centre National du Recherche Scientifique*, IVe Supplement a Gallia Préhistoire.

Broadbent, N.

1979 *Coastal Resources and Settlement Stability: A Critical Study of a Mesolithic Site Complex in Northern Sweden*, Vol. 3. Uppsala: Societas Archaeologica Upsaliensis.

Brooks, A.C.

1961 *A Study of the Thomson's Gazelle, Gazella thomsonii Gunther, in Tanganyika.* London: Colonial Research Publications No. 25.

Brown, A.G. and M.R. Edmonds

1987 *Lithic Analysis and Later British Prehistory.* British Archaeological Reports, British Series 162. Oxford: British Archaeological Reports.

Burckhardt, J.L.

1831 *Notes on the Beduins and Wahabys.* London.

Butler, B.E., E. Tchernov, H. Hietala and S. Davis

1977 Faunal exploitation during the Late Epipalaeolithic in the Har-Harif. In A.E. Marks (ed.), *Prehistory and Paleoenvironments in the Central Negev, Israel Vol II. The Advat/Aqev area part 2 and the Har Harif*: 327–344. Dallas: SMU Press.

Byrd, B. F.

1988 Late Pleistocene Settlement Diversity in the Azraq Basin. *Paléorient* 14: 257–64.

1989a *The Natufian Encampment at Beidha. Late Pleistocene Adaptation in the Southern Levant.* Aarhus: Jutland Archaeological Society Publications 23/1.

1989b The Natufian: Settlement Variability and Economic Adaptations in the Levant at the End of the Pleistocene. *Journal of World Prehistory* 3: 159–197.

Callahan, E.

1984 I Hate to Bicker, But...: A Study of Microblade Cores With Obtuse Platform Angles. *Lithic Technology* 13: 84–97.

1987 *An Evaluation of the Lithic Technology in Middle Sweden During the Mesolithic and Neolithic*, Vol. 8. Uppsala: Societas Archaeologica Upsaliensis.

Calley, S.

1986a *Technology du Debitage a Mureybet Syrie.* British Archaeological Reports International Series 312, i, ii. Oxford: British Archaeological Reports.

1986b L'Atelier de Qdeir 1 en Syrie: Exploitation des Nucleus Naviformes a la Fin du PPNB, 6e Millenaire. Premiere Approche. *Paléorient* 12: 49–67.

Campana, D.V. and P.J. Crabtree

1990 Communal Hunting in the Natufian of the Southern Levant: The Social and Economic Implications. *Journal of Mediterranean Archaeology* 3: 223–243.

Cauvin, J.

1977 Les fouilles de Mureybat (1971–1974) et leur signification pour les origines de la sedentarisation au Proche–Orient. *Annual of the American Schools of Oriental Research* 44: 19–48.

1982 Nouvelles stations Néolithiques dans la cuvette d'el-Kowm. *Cahiers de l'Euphrate* 3: 79–92.

1990 Les origines préhistoriques du nomadisme pastoral dans les pays du Levant: le cas de l'oasis d'el Kowm (Syrie). In H-P. Francfort (ed.), *Nomades et Sédentaires en Asie Central*, 67–78. Paris: *Centre National du Recherche Scientifique*.

1994 *Naissance des divinités Naissance de l'agriculture.* Paris: *Centre National du Recherche Scientifique*.

Cauvin, M-C.

1974 Une station de tradition natoufienne dans le Hauran (Syrie): Taibé, près de Dera'a. *Annales Archéologiques Arabes Syriennes* 23: 105–110.

1981 L'Epipaléolithic de Syrie d'après les premièrs recherches dans la cuvette d'el -Kowm (1978–1979). In J. Cauvin and P. Sanlaville (eds.), *Prehistoire du Levant*, 375–88. Paris: *Centre National du Recherche Scientifique*.

Chernetsov, V.N.

1971 Naskal'n'ie izobrazheniya Urala. *Svod arkheologicheskikh istochnikov SSSR*: B4–12/2

Clark, G.A., Majchrowicz, D. and Coinman, N.R.

1988 A Typological and technological Study of Upper Palaeolithic Collections from the W.H.S. with observations of Adjacent Time-Stratigraphic Units. In B. MacDonald (ed.), *The Wadi el Hasa Archaeological Survey 1979–1983, West Central Jordan*, 87–127. Ontario: Wilfrid Laurier University Press.

Clutton-Brock, J.

1992 *Horse Power.* London: Natural History Museum Publications.

Clutton-Brock, T.H. and P.H. Harvey
1978 Mammals, resources and reproductive strategies. *Nature* 273: 191–195.

Commenge-Pellerin, C.
1987 *La poterie d'Abou Matar et de l'Ouadi Zoumeli (Beersheva) au IVe millénaire avant l'ère chrétienne.* Cahiers du Centre Rechèrche Français de Jerusalem, Vol. 3. Paris: Association Paléorient.

Compagnoni, B.
1978 The Bone Remains of *Gazella subgutturosa* from Shahr-I-Sokhta. In R.H. Meadow and M.A. Zeder (eds.), *Approaches to Faunal Analysis in the Middle East,* 119–128. Peabody Museum Bulletin 2. Harvard: Peabody Museum.

Cope, C.
1991 Gazelle hunting strategies in the southern Levant. In O. Bar-Yosef and F.R. Valla (eds.), *The Natufian Culture in the Levant,* 341–358. Ann Arbor: International Monographs in Prehistory.

Copeland, L. and F. Hours
1989 *The Hammer on the Rock. Studies in the Early Palaeolithic of Azraq, Jordan.* British Archaeological Reports International Series 540 i, ii. Oxford: British Archaeological Reports.

Crabtree, D. E.
1968 Mesoamerican Polyhedral Cores and Prismatic Blades. *American Antiquity* 33: 446–478.
1972 *An Introduction to Flintworking.* Idaho: Pocatello Idaho State University Museum.

Crabtree, D. and E. Swanson
1968 Edge-ground cobbles and blade-making in the Northwest. *Tebiwa* 11: 50–58.

Crabtree, P.J., D.V. Campana, A. Belfer-Cohen and D.E. Bar-Yosef
1991 First results of the excavations at Salibiya I, lower Jordan Valley. In O. Bar-Yosef and F.R. Valla (eds.), *The Natufian Culture in the Levant,* 161–172. International Monographs in Prehistory 1. Ann Arbor.

Cribb, R.
1982 *The Archaeological Dimensions of Near Eastern Nomadic Pastoralism: towards a spatial model of unstable settlement systems.* Unpublished PhD dissertation, University of Southampton.
1991 *Nomads in Archaeology.* Cambridge: Cambridge University Press.

Crowfoot Payne, J.
1983 The Flint Industries of Jericho. In K. Kenyon and T. Holland (eds.), *Excavations at Jericho,* Appendix C. London: British School of Archaeology in Jerusalem.

Davis, L. B. and B.O.K. Reeves
1990 *Hunters of the Recent Past.* One World Archaeology 15. London: Unwin Hyman.

Davis, S.J.M.
1976 Mammal Bones from the Early Bronze Age City of Arad, Northern Negev: Some Implications Concerning Human Exploitation. *Journal of Archaeological Science* 3: 153–164.
1977 Size Variation of the fox, *Vulpes vulpes* in the palaearctic region today, and in Israel during the late Quaternary. *Journal of Zoology, London* 182: 343–351.
1980a A Note on the Dental and Skeletal Ontogeny of *Gazella. Israel Journal of Zoology* 29: 129–134.
1980b Late Pleistocene and Holocene equid remains from Israel. *Zoological Journal of the Linnean Society* 70: 289–312.
1981 The effects of temperature change and domestication on the body size of Late Pleistocene to Holocene mammals of Israel. *Paleobiology* 7: 101–114.
1983 The Age Profiles of Gazelles Predated by Ancient Man in Israel: Possible Evidence for a Shift From Seasonality to Sedentism in the Natufian. *Paléorient* 9: 55–62.
1985 A preliminary report of the fauna from Hatoula: a Natufian/Khiamian (PPNA) site near Latroun, Israel. In M. Lechevallier and A. Ronen (eds.), *Le site Natoufien-Khiamien de Hatoula, près de Latroun, Israel: fouilles 1980–1982,* 71–98. Jerusalem: Cahiers du CRFJ 1.
1987 *The Archaeology of Animals.* London: Batsford.

Davis, S.J.M., N. Goring-Morris and A. Gopher
1982 Sheep Bones from the Negev Epipalaeolithic. *Paléorient* 8: 87–93.

Dayan, R., E. Tchernov, O. Bar-Yosef and Y. Yom-Tov
1986 Animal Exploitation in Urjat el-Mehed, a Neolithic Site in Southern Sinai. *Paléorient* 12: 105–116.

Desreumaux, A. and J-B. Humbert
1982 Exploration à Khirbet es-Samra: une question pour l'histoire de la Jordanie. In A. Hadidi (ed.), *Studies in the History and Archaeology of Jordan 1,* 239–42. Amman: Department of Antiquities of Jordan.

Dibble, H.
1987 The interpretation of Middle Paleolithic scraper morphology. *American Antiquity* 52: 109–117.

Dibble, H. L. and J.C. Whittaker
1981 New Experimental Evidence on the Relation Between Percussion Flaking and Flake Variation. *Journal of Archaeological Science* 8: 283–296.

Digard, J.-P.
1975 Campements Baxtyari. *Studia Iranica* 4: 117–129.

Dobie, F.T.
1952 *The Mustangs.* Boston.

Dornemann, R. H.
1986 *A Neolithic Village at Tell el-Kowm in the Syrian Desert.* Chicago: Studies in Ancient Oriental Civilization No. 43, The Oriental Institute of Chicago.

Dorrell, P.
1983 Appendix A: Stone Vessels, Tools and Objects. In K. Kenyon and T.A. Holland (eds.), *Jericho,* Volume 5. London: British School of Archaeology in Jerusalem.

Driesch, A. von den
1976 *A Guide to the Measurement of Animal Bones from Archaeological Sites.* Peabody Museum Bulletin 1. Harvard: Peabody Museum.

Driver, J.C.
1990 Meat in due season: the timing of communal hunts. In L.B. Davis and B.O.K. Reeves (eds.), *Hunters of the Recent Past,* 11–33. London: Unwin Hyman.

Echallier, J. and F. Braemer
1995 Nature et Fonctions des 'Desert Kites': données et hypothèses nouvelles. *Paléorient* 21: 35–63.

Edmonds, M.R.
1987 Rocks and Risk: Problems with Lithic Procurement Strategies. In A.G. Brown and M.R. Edmonds (eds.), *Lithic Analysis and Later British Prehistory*: 155–179. British Archaeological Reports, British Series 162. Oxford: British Archaeological Reports.

Edwards, P.C.
1991 More Than One, Less Than Five Hundred: Comments on Campana and Crabtree, and Communal Hunting. *Journal of Mediterranean Archaeology* 4: 109–120.

Eisenmann, V.
1992 Systematic and biostratigraphical interpretation of the equids from Qafzeh, Tabun, Shkul and Kebara. *Archaeozoologia* 5: 43–62.

Estes, R.D.
1967 The Comparative Behavior of Grant's and Thomson's Gazelles. *Journal of Mammalogy* 48: 189–209.

Eversmann, E.
1850 *Estestvennaya istoriya Oreburgskogo kraya*, ch. II. Kazan.

Feinbrun-Dothan, N.
1978 *Flora Palaestina*, Vol. 3. Jerusalem: Israel Academy of Sciences and Humanities.
1986 *Flora Palaestina*, Vol. 4. Jerusalem: Israel Academy of Sciences and Humanities.

Field, H.
1960 *North Arabian Desert Archaeological Survey 1925–1950*. Papers of the Peabody Museum 45/2. Cambridge: Peabody Museum.

Finlayson, W. and A. Betts
1990 Functional Analysis of Chipped Stone Artefacts from the Late Neolithic Site of Gabal Naja, eastern Jordan. *Paléorient* 16: 13–20.

Flannery, K.V.
1972 The origin of the village as a settlement type in Mesoamerica and the Near East: a comparative study. In P. Ucko, R. Tringham and G. Dimbleby (eds.), *Man, Settlement and Urbanism*, 22–53. London: Duckworth.

Flannery, K.V. and M. Winter
1976 Analyzing household activities. In K.V. Flannery (ed.), *The Early Mesoamerican Village*: 34–47. New York: Academic Press.

Frison, G.C.
1978 *Prehistoric Hunters of the High Plains*. London: Academic Press.

Galkin, L.L.
1983 Razvedki i raskopi v severo-vostochnom Priaspii. *Arkheologicheski otkri'tiya* 1981.
1987 Iz'iskaniya v severo-vostochnom Prikaspii. *Arkheologicheskie otkri'tiya* 1985.
1988 Kamenn'ie bat'ir'i Ustiurta. *Nauka i zhizn* 3.

Garfinkel, Y.
1993 The Yarmukian Culture in Israel. *Paléorient* 19/1: 115-134

Garrard, A. N.
1980 Man-Animal-Plant Relationships During The Upper Pleistocene and Early Holocene of the Levant. Unpublished PhD Thesis, University of Cambridge.
1985 The Faunal Remains, Appendix I. In A. Betts 'Black Desert Survey, Jordan: Third Preliminary Report'. *Levant* 17: 39–49.

1991 Natufian settlement in the Azraq Basin, eastern Jordan. In O. Bar-Yosef and F.R. Valla (eds.), *The Natufian Culture in the Levant*, 235–244. International Monographs in Prehistory 1. Ann Arbor.

Garrard, A., N. Stanley Price and L. Copeland
1975 Prehistoric sites in the Azraq Basin, eastern Jordan. *Paléorient* 3: 109–26.

Garrard, A., B. Byrd and A. Betts
1986 Prehistoric environment and settlement in the Azraq Basin: an interim report on the 1984 excavation season. *Levant* 18: 5–24.

Garrard, A., A. Betts, B. Byrd and C. Hunt
1987 Prehistoric Environment and Settlement in the Azraq Basin: an interim report on the 1985 season. *Levant* 19: 5–25.

Garrard, A. N. and H.-G. Gebel (eds.)
1988 *The Prehistory of Jordan: The State of Research in 1986*. British Archaeological Reports International Series 396, i, ii. Oxford: British Archaeological Reports.

Garrard, A., A. Betts, B. Byrd and C. Hunt
1988a Summary of Paleoenvironmental and Prehistoric Investigations in the Azraq Basin. In A. Garrard and H-G. Gebel (eds.), *The Prehistory of Jordan: The State of Research in 1986*, 311–37. British Archaeological Reports International Series 396, i, ii. Oxford: British Archaeological Reports.

Garrard, A.N., S. Colledge, C. Hunt and R. Montague
1988b Environment and subsistence during the Late Pleistocene and Early Holocene in the Azraq Basin. *Paléorient* 14: 40–49.

Garrard, A. N., D. Baird and B. Byrd
1994a The Chronological Basis and Significance of the late Palaeolithic and Neolithic sequence in the Azraq Basin, Jordan. In O. Bar Yosef and R.S. Kra (eds.), *Late Quaternary Chronology and Paleoclimates of the Eastern Mediterranean*, 177–199. Cambridge and Tuscon: American School of Prehistoric Research.

Garrard, A., D. Baird, S. College, L. Martin and K. Wright
1994b Prehistoric Environment and Settlement in the Azraq Basin: an interim report on the 1987 and 1988 excavation seasons. *Levant* 26: 73–109.

Garrard, A., S. Colledge and L. Martin
1996 The emergence of crop cultivation and caprine herding in the 'Marginal Zone' of the southern Levant. In D. Harris (ed.), *The origins and spread of agriculture and pastoralism in Eurasia*, 204–226. London: UCL Press.

Garstang, J.
1935 Jericho: City and Necropolis, Fifth Report. *Annals of Archaeology and Anthropology (Liverpool)* 23: 143–184.

Gebel, H.G.
1988 Late Epipaleolithic — aceramic Neolithic sites in the Petra area. In A.N. Garrard and H-G. Gebel (eds.), *The Prehistory of Jordan: The State of Research in 1986*, 67–100. British Archaeological Reports International Series 396, i, ii. Oxford: British Archaeological Reports.

Gebel, H., M. Muheisen, H. Nissen, N. Qadi and J. Starck
1988 Preliminary report on the first season of excavations at the late aceramic Neolithic site of Basta. In A.N.

Garrard and H-G. Gebel (eds.), *The Prehistory of Jordan: The State of Research in 1986,* 110–134. British Archaeological Reports International Series 396, i, ii. Oxford: British Archaeological Reports.

Gebel, H.-G. and S.K. Koslowski (eds.)
1994   *Neolithic Chipped Stone Industries of the Fertile Crescent.* Berlin: ex oriente.

Geptner, V.G., A.A. Nasimovich and A.G. Bannikov
1961   *Mlekopitaiushchie Sovetskogo Soiuza 1. Parnokopi'itn'ie i neparnokop'itn'ie.* Moscow

Glushkov, I.N.
1900   Cherd'inskie bogul'i. *Etnograficheskoe obozrenie* 14.

Gopher, A.
1989   Neolithic Arrowheads of the Levant: Results and Implications of a Seriation Analysis. *Paléorient* 15: 43–56.

1994   *Arrowheads of the Neolithic Levant.* Winona Lake, Indiana: Eisenbrauns.

Gopher, A., N. Goring-Morris and D. Gordon
1994   Nahal Issaron. The Lithics of the Late PPNB Occupation. In H.-G. Gebel and S.K. Kozlowski (eds.), *Neolithic Chipped Stone Industries of the Fertile Crescent,* 479–494. Berlin: ex oriente.

Goren-Inbar, N.
1988   Too Small To Be True? Reevaluation of Cores On Flakes. In 'Levantine Mousterian Assemblages'. *Lithic Technology* 17: 37–44.

Goring-Morris, N.
1987   *At the Edge: Terminal Pleistocene Hunter - Gatherers in the Negev and Sinai.* British Archaeological Reports, International Series 361. Oxford: British Archaeological Reports.

1993   From Foraging to Herding in the Negev and Sinai: the early to late Neolithic Transition. *Paléorient* 19/1: 65-89.

1994   Aspects of the PPNB Lithic Industry at Kfar Horesh, near Nazareth. In H.-G. Gebel and S.K. Kozlowski (eds.), *Neolithic Chipped Stone Industries of the Fertile Crescent,* 427–444. Berlin: ex oriente.

Goring-Morris, N. and A. Gopher
1983   Nahal Issaron: a Neolithic settlement in the southern Negev. *Israel Exploration Journal* 33: 149–166.

Goring-Morris, N., Y. Goren, L. Horwitz, D. Bar-Yosef and I. Hershkovitz
1995   Investigations at an Early Neolithic Settlement in the Lower Galilee: results of the 1991 season at Kefar HaHoresh. *'Atiqot* 27: 37–62.

Grigson, C.
1993   The Earlist Domestic Horses in the Levant — New Finds from the Fourth Millennium of the Negev. *Journal of Archaeological Science* 20.

Gubin, S.V.
1985   Ochët o pochvenno-arkheologicheskikh issledovanyakh v iugo-vostochnoi chasti plato Ustiurt. Prilozhenie 2 k Otchëtu o rabotakh Ustiurtskoko arkheologicheskogo èkspeditsionnogo otryada 1984 g., *Nauchn'ii arkhif Otdel arkheologii Instituta istorii, yaz'ika i iteratur'i Karakalpakskogo filiala AN UzSSR.*

Gudkova, A.V. and V.N. Yagodin
1963   Arkheologicheskie issledovaniya v Pravoberezhnoi chasti Priaral'skoi del't'i Amudar'i v 1958–1959 gg. *Material'i Khoreezmskoi arkheologo — ètnograf-*

icheskoi èkspeditsii AN SSSR 6.

Guest, E. (ed.)
1966   *Flora of Iraq. Volume One.* Baghdad: Ministry of Agriculture.

Gurvich, I.S.
1977   *Kul'tura severn'ikh yakutov-olenevodov.* Moscow.

Habibi, K., C.R. Thouless and N. Lindsay
1993   Comparative behaviour of sand and mountain gazelles. *Journal of Zoology, London* 229: 41–53.

Haaker, D.
1986   The Determination of Sex and Species in Gazelles with the Use of Stepwise Discriminant Analysis. In Louise H. van Wijngaarden-Bakker (ed.), *Database Management and Zooarchaeology,* 173–181. Strasbourg: PACT Council of Europe.

Hanbury-Tenison, J.
1986   *The Late Chalcolithic to Early Bronze Age I Transition in Palestine and Transjordan.* Oxford: British Archaeological Reports International Series 311.

Hanihara, K. and T. Akazawa (eds.)
1979   *Paleolithic Site of Douara Cave and Paleo-geography of Palmyra Basin in Syria II.* Tokyo: University Museum.

Harding, G.L.
1953   The Cairn of Hani'. *Annual of the Department of Antiquities of Jordan* 2: 8–56.

Harrison, D.L.
1968   *The Mammals of Arabia Vol. 2.* Carnivora. Hyracoidea. Artiodactyla. London: Ernest Benn.

Hayden, B.
1980   Confusion in the Bipolar World: Bashed Pebbles and Splintered Pieces. *Lithic Technology* 9: 2–7.

1987   Manufacture of metates using chipped stone tools. In B. Hayden (ed.), *Lithic Studies Among the Contemporary Highland Maya,* Chapter 3. Tucson: University of Arizona Press.

Hayden, B. and A. Cannon
1983   Where the garbage goes: refuse disposal in the Maya Highlands. *Journal of Anthropological Archaeology* 2: 117–163.

1984   *The Structure of Material Systems: Ethnoarchaeology in the Maya Highlands,* SAA Papers No. 3. Washington DC: Society for American Archaeology.

Helbaek, H.
1966   Pre-Pottery Neolithic farming at Beidha: a preliminary report. In D. Kirkbride, Five seasons at the Pre-Pottery Neolithic village of Beidha. *Palestine Exploration Fund Quarterly* 98: 5–72.

Helmer, D.
1991   Etude de la faune de la phase IA (Natoufien final) de Tell Mureybet (Syrie), fouilles Cauvin. In O. Bar-Yosef and F.R. Valla (eds.), *The Natufian Culture in the Levant,* 359–370. International Monographs in Prehistory. Ann Arbor.

Helms, S. W.
1981   *Jawa: lost city of the black desert.* London: Methuen.

1990   *Early Islamic Architecture of the Desert. A bedouin station in eastern Jordan.* Edinburgh: Edinburgh University Press.

1991   A new architectural survey of Qasr Burqu'. *Antiquaries Journal* 71:216-225.

Helms, S. and A. Betts
1987 The Desert 'Kites' of the Badiyat esh-Sham and North Arabia. *Paléorient* 13: 41–67.

Henry, D.O.
1973 The Natufian of Palestine: its material culture and ecology. PhD thesis, Southern Methodist University. Ann Arbor: University Microfilms.
1981 An analysis of settlement patterns and adaptive strategies of the Natufian. In J. Cauvin and P. Sanlaville (eds.), *Préhistoire du Levant*, 421–32. Paris: *Centre National du Recherche Scientifique*.
1989 *From Foraging to Agriculture.* Philadelphia: Horwitz.

Henry, D.O., A. Leroi-Gourhan and S. Davis
1981 The Excavation of Hayonim Terrace: an Examination of Terminal Pleistocene Climatic and Adaptive Changes. *Journal of Archaeological Science* 8: 33–58.

Henry, D.O. and P.F. Turnbull
1985 Archaeological and faunal evidence from Natufian and Timnian sites in southern Jordan. *Bulletin of the American Schools of Oriental Research* 257: 45–64.
1989 A Reassessment of Caprovine Domestication in the Levantine Neolithic: Old Questions, New Answers. In I. Hershkovitz (ed.), *People and Culture in Change*: 153–181. British Archaeological Reports, International Series 508, i. Oxford: British Archaeological Reports.

Hillman, G. C.
1975 The plant remains from Tell Abu Hureyra: a preliminary report. In A.M.T. Moore, 'The excavation of Tell Abu Hureyra in Syria: a preliminary report'. *Proceedings of the Prehistoric Society* 41: 70–73.
1984a Interpretation of archaeological plant remains: the application of ethnographic models from Turkey. In W. van Zeist and W. Casparie (eds.), *Plants and Ancient Man,* 1–42. Rotterdam and Boston: A.A. Balkema.
1984b Traditional husbandry and processing of archaic cereals in recent times, Part I: the glume wheats. *Bulletin on Sumerian Agriculture* 1: 114–152.
1989 Plant food economy during the Epipaleolithic period at Tell Abu Hureyra, Syria: dietary diversity, seasonality and modes of exploitation. In D. Harris and G. Hillman (eds.), *Foraging and Farming — the evolution of plant exploitation,* 240–268. London: Unwin Hyman.

Hiyari, M.A.
1975 The Origins and Development of the Amirate of the Arabs during the 7th/13th and 8th/14th Centuries. *Bulletin of the School of Oriental and African Studies* 38: 36–42.

Hole, F.
1978 Pastoral nomadism in western Iran. In R. Gould (ed.), *Explorations in Ethnoarchaeology,* 127–167, Albuquerque: University of New Mexico Press.

Hole, F., K.V. Flannery and J. Neely
1969 *Prehistory and Human Ecology of the Deh Luran Plain: an early village sequence from Khuzistan, Iran.* Museum of Anthropology, University of Michigan, Memoirs No. 1. Ann Arbor: University of Michigan.

Horsefield, G. and Glueck, N.
1933 Prehistoric Rock-Drawings in Transjordan. *American Journal of Archaeology* 37: 381-386.

Horwitz, L.K., C. Cope and E. Tchernov
1990 Sexing the Bones of Mountain-Gazelle (*Gazella gazella*) from Prehistoric sites in the Southern Levant. *Paléorient* 16: 1–12.

Hovers, E., L.K. Horwitz, D.E. Bar-Yosef and C. Cope-Miyashiro
1988 The Site of Urkan-E-Rub IIa: A Case Study of Subsistence and Mobility Pattern in the Kebaran Period in the Lower Jordan Valley. *Mitekufat Haeven — Journal of the Israel Prehistoric Society* 21: 20–48.

Ingbar, E., M.L. Larson and B. Bradley
1989 A Nontypological Approach to Debitage Analysis. In D.S. Amick and R. P. Mauldin (eds.), *Experiments in Lithic Technology,* 117–136. British Archaeological Reports International Series 528. Oxford: British Archaeological Reports.

Ingold, T.
1980 *Hunters, pastoralists and ranchers.* Cambridge: Cambridge University Press.

Inizan, M.-L., H. Roche, and J. Tixier
1992 *Technology of Knapped Stone.* Meudon: CREP.

Johnson, J. K. and C.A. Morrow
1987 *The Organization of Core Technology.* Boulder: Westview Press.

Kafafi, Z.
1988 Jebel Abu Thawwab. A Pottery Neolithic Village in Jordan. In A. Garrard and H-G Gebel (eds), *The Prehistory of Jordan: The State of Research in 1986, 451-471.* British Archaeological Reports International Series 396, ii. Oxford: British Archaeological Reports.
1993 The Yarmoukians in Jordan. *Paléorient* 19/1: 101-114

Karelin, G.S.
1883 Puteshestviya G. S. Karelina po Kaspiskomu moriu. *Zapiski Imperatorskoe russkoe geograficheskoe obshchestvo po obshchei geografii* 10.

Kaufman, D.
1986 A Proposed Method for Distinguishing Between Blades and Bladelets. *Lithic Technology* 10: 34–40.

Kelly, C.
1943 Ancient antelope run. *Desert Magazine* 6/5: 31–33.

Kelly, I. T.
1964 *Southern Paiute Ethnography.* University of Utah Anthropological Papers No. 69. Salt Lake City: University of Utah.

Kennedy, D.L., H.I. MacAdam and D.N. Riley
1986 Preliminary report on the southern Hauran Survey, 1985. *Annual of the Department of Antiquities of Jordan* 30: 145–53.

Kenyon, K. and Holland, T.
1982 *Excavations at Jericho. IV.* London: British School of Archaeology in Jerusalem.

King, G.R.D.
1982 Preliminary Report on a Survey of Byzantine and Islamic sites in Jordan, 1980. *Annual of the Department of Antiquities of Jordan* 26: 85–95.

King, G., C. Lenzen and G. Rollefson
1983 Survey of Byzantine and Islamic Sites in Jordan, second season report, 1981. *Annual of the Department of Antiquities of Jordan* 27: 385–436.

Kirkbride, A.S.
1946 Desert 'Kites'. *Journal of the Palestine Oriental Society* 20: 1–5.

Kirkbride, D.
1966 Five seasons at the Pre-Pottery Neolithic village of Beidha in Jordan: a summary. *Palestine Exploration Fund Quarterly*, 8–72.

Klein, R.G. and K. Cruz-Uribe
1984 *The Analysis of Animal Bones from Archeological Sites*. Chicago: University of Chicago Press.

Knight, J.
1991 Technological Analysis of the Anvil Bipolar Technique. *Lithics: The Newsletter of the Lithic Studies Society* 12: 57–87.

Kobayashi, H.
1975 The Experimental Study of Bipolar Flakes. In E. Swanson (ed.), *Lithic Technology: Making and Using Stone Tools*, 115–127. The Hague: Mouton.

Köhler-Rollefson, I.
1989 Changes in Goat Exploitation at 'Ain Ghazal Between the Early and Late Neolithic: a Metrical Analysis. *Paléorient* 15: 141–146.

Köhler-Rollefson, I., W. Gillespie and M. Metzger
1988 The fauna from Neolithic 'Ain Ghazal. In A.N. Garrard and H.-G. Gebel *(eds.)*, *The Prehistory of Jordan: The State of Research in 1986*, 423–430. British Archaeological Reports International Series 396 i, ii. Oxford: British Archaeological Reports.

Kosarev, M. F.
1984 *Zapadnaya Sibir' v drevnosti*. Moscow.

Kramer, C.
1982 *Village Ethnoarchaeology*. New York: Academic Press.

Kraybill, N.
1977 Pre-Agricultural tools for the preparation of foods in the Old World. In C. Reed (ed.), *Origins of Agriculture*, 485–521. The Hague: Mouton.

Krebs, J.R.
1978 Optimal foraging: decision rules for predators. In J.R. Krebs and N.B. Davies (eds.), *Behavioural Ecology*, 23–63. Oxford: Blackwell.

Lamb, H. H.
1972 *Climate: Past, Present and Future*. London: Methuen.

Lancaster, W. and F. Lancaster
1986 Tribe, Community and the Concept of Access to Resources. In A. Rao (ed.), *Mobility and Territoriality*, 127–142. Oxford: Berg.
1991 Limitations on Sheep and Goat Herding in the Eastern Badia of Jordan. *Levant* 23: 125–138.
n.d *People, Land and Water in the Bilad ash-Sham*. Reading: Harwood.

Lange, F. and C. Rydberg
1972 Abandonment and post-abandonment behaviour at a rural central American house site. *American Antiquity* 37: 419–432.

Legge, A.J.
1972 Prehistoric Exploitation of the Gazelle in Palestine. In E.S. Higgs (ed.), *Papers in Economic Prehistory*, 119–124. Cambridge: Cambridge University Press.

Legge, A.J. and P.A. Rowley-Conwy
1987 Gazelle Killing in Stone Age Syria. *Scientific American* 255: 88–95.

Leroi-Gourhan, A. and F. Darmon
1991 Analyses polliniques de stations natoufiennes au Proche-Orient. In O. Bar-Yosef and F. Valla (eds.), *The Natufian Culture in the Levant*, 21–6. International Monographs in Prehistory. Ann Arbor.

Levina, L.M.
1971 Keramika nizhnei i srednei S'irdar'i v I t'isyacheletii n.e. *Trud'i Khorezmskoi arkheologo-ètnograficheskoi èkspeditsii AN SSSR* 7.

Levshin, A.
1832 *Opisanie kirgiz-kazach'ikh ili kirgiz-kaisatskikh ord i stepei*. St Petersburg.

Lewis-Williams, J.D.
1987 A Dream of Eland: an unexplored component of San Shamanism and rock art. *World Archaeology* 19/2: 165-177.

Lomakin, N.O.
1873 O poluostrove Mang'ishlak. *Zapiski Kavkazskogo itdeleniya Imperatorskoe russkoe geograficheskoe obshchestva*, 8.

Lyman, R.L.
1984 Bone Density and Differential Survivorship of Fossil Classes. *Journal of Anthropological Archaeology* 3: 259–299.

MacDonald, B.
1992 *The Southern Ghors and Northeast 'Arabah Archaeological Survey*. Sheffield Archaeological Monographs 5. Sheffield: J.R. Collis Publications.
1988 *The Wadi el Hasa Archaeological Survey 1979–1983, West Central Jordan*. Waterloo, Ontario: Wilfrid Laurier University Press.

Macdonald, M.C.A.
1983 Inscriptions and Rock Art of the Jawa Area, 1982: A Preliminary Report. *Annual of the Department of Antiquities of Jordan* 27: 571–6.

Maitland, R.A.
1927 The Works of the 'Old Men' in Arabia. *Antiquity* 1: 197–203.

Man'ilov, Iu. P.
1978 Srednevekov'ie khorezmiskie pamyatniki Vostochnogo chinka. *Drevnyaya i srednevekovaya kul'tura iugo-vostochnogo Ustiurta*.

Manker, E.
1960 Fangstgropar och stalotomter. Kulturlämningar fran lapsk forntid av Ernst Manker. *Nordiska Museet: Acta Lappinica* 15.

Mardrus, J.C. and P. Mathers
1951 *The Book of the Thousand Nights and One Night*, Vol. 1. London: Routledge and Kegan Paul.

Marean, C.W. and L.M. Spencer
1991 Impact of Carnivore Ravaging on Zooarchaeological Measures of Element Abundance. *American Antiquity* 56: 645–658.

Martin, L.A.
1994 Hunting and herding in a semi-arid region: an archaeozoological and ethological analysis of the faunal remains from the Epipalaeolithic and Neolithic of the eastern Jordanian steppe. Unpublished PhD dissertation, Department of Archaeology and Prehistory, University of Sheffield.

Masson, M.E.
1984   Iz istorii dikikh kulanov v Srednei Azii. *Arkheologiya Priaral'ya 2.*

Mauldin, R. P. and D.S. Amick
1989   Investigating Patterning in Debitage from Experimental Bifacial Core Reduction. In D.S. Amick and R.P. Mauldin (eds.), *Experiments in Lithic Technology*: 67–88. British Archaeological Reports International Series 528. Oxford: British Archaeological Reports.

McCartney, C.J.
1989   Patterns of Variation in Debitage. Unpublished M.A. dissertation, University of Edinburgh.
1992   Preliminary Report of the 1989 Excavations at Site 27 of the Burqu'/Ruweishid Project. *Levant* 24: 33–54.

Meadow, R.H.
1989   Osteological evidence for the process of animal domestication. In J. Clutton-Brock (ed.), *The Walking Larder*, 80–90. London: Unwin Hyman.

Meadow, R.H. and H.-P. Uerpmann
1986   *Equids in the Ancient World.* Wiesbaden: Dr. Ludwig Reichert Verlag.

Medoev, A.G.
1969   Naskal'ni'ie izobrazheniya u gor'i Airakt'i na poluostrove Mang'ishlak, *Kul'tura drevnikh zemledel'tsev i skotovodov Kazakhstana.*

Mendelssohn, H.
1974   The Development of the Populations of Gazelles in Israel and their Behavioural Adaptations. In V. Geist and F. Walther *(eds.), The Behaviour of Ungulates and its Relation to Management*, 722–744. Morges: IUCN Publications.

Meshel, Z.
1974   New Data about the 'Desert Kites'. *Tel Aviv* 1: 129–143.

Miller, R.D.
1975   A Study of Cuts, Grooves, and Other Marks on Recent and Fossil Bone. In E. Swanson (ed.), *Lithic Technology: Making and Using Stone Tools,* 211–226. The Hague: Mouton.

Mitford, E.L.
1884   *A Land March from England to Ceylon Forty Years Ago, though Dalmatia, Montenegro, Turkey, Asia Minor, Syria, Palestine Assyria, Persia, Afghanistan, Seinde, and India,* 2 vols, London: Allen.

Moore, A.M.T.
1973   The Late Neolithic in Palestine. *Levant* 5: 36–68.
1975   The Excavation of Tell Abu Hureyra in Syria: A Preliminary Report. *Proceedings of the Prehistoric Society* 41: 50–77.

Mortensen, P
1983   Patterns of Interaction between Seasonal Settlements and Early Villages in Mesopotamia. In T.Young, P. Smith and P. Mortensen (eds), *The Hilly Flanks and Beyond. Essays on the Prehistory of Southwestern Asia:* 207-230, Chicago: Studies in Ancient Oriental Civilisation 36, Oriental Institute.

Muheisen, M.
1983   *La Préhistoire en Jordanie: Recherches sur l'Epipaléolithique. L'example du gisement de Kharaneh IV.* Unpublished doctoral thesis, Bordeaux.

Muheisen, M., H.-G. Gebel, C. Hannss and R. Neef
1988   Excavations at Ain' Rahub, a final Natufian and Yarmoukian site near Irbid (1985). In A.N. Garrard and H.-G. Gebel *(eds.), The Prehistory of Jordan: The State of Research in 1986,* 473–502. British Archaeological Reports International Series 396, i, ii. Oxford: British Archaeological Reports.

Musil, A.
1927   *Arabia Deserta.* New York: American Geographical Society.
1928   *The Manners and Customs of the Rwala Beduins.* New York: American Geographical Society.

Mylona, D.
1992   *Late Neolithic Economy in Wadi el-Jilat, North-West Jordan.* Unpublished MSc. dissertation, University of Sheffield.

Nelson, B.
1973   *Azraq, Desert Oasis.* London: Allen Lane.

Noy, T., A.J. Legge and E.S. Higgs
1973   Recent excavations at Nahal Oren, Israel. *Proceedings of the Prehistoric Society* 39: 75–99.

Nesheim, A.
1961   Fangstgropar och stalotomter (Trapping Pits and Stalo Sites). *Man* 11.

Nierlé, M.-C.
1983   Mureybet et Cheikh Hassan (Syrie): outillage de mouture et de broyage (9e et 8e millénaires). *Cahiers de l'Euphrate* 3: 177–216.

Nishiaki, Y.
1990   Corner-Thinned Blades: A New Obsidian tool Type from a Pottery Neolithic Mound in the Khabur Basin, Syria. *Bulletin of the American Schools of Oriental Research* 280: 5–14.
1992   Lithic Technology of Neolithic Syria: A Series of Analyses of Flaked Stone Assemblages from Douara Cave II, Tell Damishilyya, Tell Nebi Mend, and Tell Kashkashok II. Unpublished PhD. thesis, University College London, London University.

Nissen, K. M.
1974   The Record of a Hunting Practice at Petroglyph Site NV-LY-1. *Contributions of the University of California Archaeological Research Facility* 20: 53–82.

Nissen, H., M. Muheisen and H. Gebel
1987   Report on the First Two Seasons of Excavation at Basta (1986–1987). *Annual of the Department of Antiquities of Jordan* 31: 79–119.

Noy, T., A. Legge and E.S. Higgs
1973   Recent excavations at Nahal Oren, Israel. *Proceedings of the Prehistoric Society* 39: 75–99.

Ohunma, K. and C. Bergman
1982   Experimental Studies in the Determination of Flaking Mode. *Bulletin of the Institute of Archaeology, University of London* 19: 161–170.

Okladnikov, A.P.
1966   *Petroglif'i Angar'i.* Moscow/Leningrad.

Olzewski, D.
1986   *The North Syrian Late Epipaleolithic: the earliest occupation at Tell Abu Hureyra in the context of the Levantine Late Epipaleolithic.* British Archaeological Reports International Series. Oxford: British Archaeological Reports.

Parr R.E. and M.E. Newman
1992 Immunological Protein Residue Analysis of Projectile Points from the Huntoon Pronghorn Trap Complex, Mineral County, Nevada. Paper presented at the *23rd Great Basin Anthropological Conference*, Boise, Idaho.

Parr, P., Zarins, J., Ibrahim, M., Waechter, J., Garrard, A., Clarke, C., Bidmead, M. and al-Badr, H.
1978 Comprehensive Archeological Survey Program: preliminary report on the second phase of the northern province. *Atlal* 2: 29-50.

Patterson, L.W.
1982 Replication and Classification of Large Size Lithic Debitage. *Lithic Technology* 11: 50–58.
1987 Amorphous Cores and Utilized Flakes: A Commentary. *Lithic Technology* 16: 51–53.

Payne, S.
1973 Kill-Off Patterns in Sheep and Goats: The Mandibles from Asvan Kale. *Anatolian Studies* 23: 281–303.
1983 The Animal Bones from the 1974 Excavations at Douara Cave. In K. Hanihara and T. Akazawa (eds.), *Palaeolithic Site of Douara Cave and Paleogeography of Palmyra Basin in Syria*, 1–108. University Museum Bulletin No. 21. Tokyo: University Museum.

Payne, S. and P.J. Munson
1985 Ruby and How Many Squirrels? The Destruction of Bones by Dogs. In N.R.J. Fieller, D.D. Gilbertson and N.G.A. Ralph (eds.), *Palaeobiological Investigations — research design, methods and data analysis*, 31–39, British Archaeological Reports, International Series 266. Oxford: British Archaeological Reports.

Pendleton, L.S.A. and D. Hurst Thomas
1983 The Fort Sage Drift Fence, Washoe County, Nevada. *Anthropological Papers of the American Museum of Natural History* 58: 1–38.

Perv'ie russkie nauchn'ie issledovaniya Ustiurta
1963 Moscow.

Poidebard, A.
1928 Reconnaissance aérienne au Ledja et au Safa. *Syria* 9: 114–132.
1934 *La Trace du Rome dans le Désert de Syrie.* Paris.

Powell, A.
1992 *An Analysis of the Animal Bones from Area B, Wadi el-Jilat 13, a Late Neolithic Site from Northeast Jordan.* Unpublished MSc. dissertation, University of Sheffield.

Prummel, W. and H.-J. Frisch
1986 A Guide for the Distinction of Species, Sex and Body Side in Bones of Sheep and Goat. *Journal of Archaeological Science* 13: 567–577.

Radlov, V.V.
1893 *Op'it slovarya tiurkiskikh narechii* 1, ch. 1. St Petersburg.

Raymond, A.
1982 Two Historic Aboriginal Game-Drive Enclosures in the Eastern Great Basin. *Journal of California and Great Basin Anthropology* 4: 23–33.

Rees, L. B. W.
1929 The Transjordan Desert. *Antiquity* 3: 389–407.

Reese, D.
1991a Marine Shells in the Levant: Upper Paleolithic, Epipaleolithic, and Neolithic. In O. Bar-Yosef and F. Valla (eds.), *The Natufian Culture in the Levant*, 613–628, International Monographs in Prehistory Archaeological Series 1. Ann Arbor.
1991b The Trade of Indo-Pacific Shells into the Mediterranean Basin and Europe. *Oxford Journal of Archaeology* 10: 159–196.

Rhotert, H.
1938 *Transjordanien, Vorgeschichtliche Forschungen.* Vorlag Strechker und Schroder, Stuttgart.

Rollefson, G.O.
1982 Preliminary Report on the 1980 Excavations at 'Ain al-Assad. *Annual of the Department of Antiquities of Jordan* 26: 5-35.
1986 Neolithic 'Ain Ghazal (Jordan): Ritual and Ceremony, II. *Paléorient* 21: 45–51.
1988 Stratified Burin Classes at 'Ain Ghazal: Implications for the Desert Neolithic of Jordan. In A.N. Garrard and H.-G. Gebel *(eds.), The Prehistory of Jordan: The State of Research in 1986*, 437–447. British Archaeological Reports International Series 396, i, ii. Oxford: British Archaeological Reports.
1989 The Late Aceramic Neolithic of the Levant: A Synthesis. *Paléorient* 15: 168–173.
1990 Neolithic Chipped Stone Technology at Ain' Ghazal, Jordan: The Status of the PPNC Phase. *Paléorient* 16: 119–124.

Rollefson, G. and B. Frölich
1982 A PPNB burin site on Jebel Uweinid, eastern Jordan. *Annual of the Department of Antiquities of Jordan* 26: 189–98.

Rollefson, G., Z. Kaechele and J. Kaechele
1982 A Burin Site in the Umm Utheina district, Jabal Amman. *Annual of the Department of Antiquities of Jordan* 26: 243–48.

Rollefson, G.O. and K. Abu Ghanima
1983 Technological Analysis of Blades and Flakes from 'Ain Ghazal. *Annual of the Department of Antiquities of Jordan* 27: 461–469.

Rollefson, G.O. and A. Simmons
1988a The Neolithic Village of 'Ain Ghazal, Jordan: preliminary report on the 1985 season. *Bulletin of the American Schools of Oriental Research Supplement* 25: 93–106.

Rollefson, G.O. and A. Simmons
1988b The Neolithic settlement at 'Ain Ghazal. In A.N. Garrard and H.G. Gebel (eds.), *The Prehistory of Jordan: The State of Research in 1986*, 393–421. British Archaeological Reports, International Series 396 i, ii. Oxford: British Archaeological Reports.

Rollefson, G.O., Z. Kafafi and A. Simmons
1989 The 1988 season at 'Ain Ghazal: a preliminary report. *Annual of the Department of Antiquities of Jordan* 33: 9–26.

Rollefson, G. O., Z. Kafafi and A.H. Simmons
1991 The Neolithic Village of 'Ain Ghazal, Jordan: Preliminary Report on the 1988 Season. *Bulletin of the American Schools of Oriental Research Supplement* 27: 95–116.

Rollefson, G.O., A.H. Simmons and Z. Kafafi
1992 Neolithic Cultures at 'Ain Ghazal, Jordan. *Journal of Field Archaeology* 19: 443–470.

Rollefson, G.O., M. Forstadt and R. Beck
1994   A Preliminary Typological Analysis of Scrapers, Knives and Borers from 'Ain Ghazal. In H.-G. Gebel and S.K. Kozlowski (eds.), *Neolithic Chipped Stone Industries of the Fertile Crescent*, 445–466. Berlin: ex oriente.

Rubenstein, D.I.
1978   On Predation, Competition, and the Advantages of Group Living. In P.P.G. Bateson and P.H. Klopfer (eds.), *Perspectives in Ethology 3*, 205–231. New York and London: Plenum Press.

1989   Life history and social organization in arid adapted ungulates. *Journal of Arid Environments* 17: 145–156.

Saxon, E.C.
1974   The mobile herding economy of Mt Carmel: an economic analysis of the faunal remains. *Journal of Archaeological Science* 1: 27–45.

Semenov Tyan-Shanskii, O.I.
1977   *Severn'ii olen'*. Moscow.

Servello, F.
1976   Nahal Divshon: a Pre-Pottery Neolithic B hunting camp. In A. Marks (ed.), *Prehistory and Paleoenvironments in the Central Negev, Israel, Vol. 1*, 349–370. Dallas: SMU Press.

Simchenko, Iu. B.
1976   *Kul'tura okhotnikov na olenei Severnoi Evrazii*. Moscow.

Simmons, A.H. and G. Ilany
1977   What Mean These Bones? Behavioural implications of gazelles' remains from archaeological sites. *Paléorient* 3: 269–274.

Simmons, A.H., Z. Kafafi, G.O. Rollefson and K. Moyer
1989   Test Excavations at Wadi Shu'eib, A Major Neolithic Settlement in Central Jordan. *Annual of the Department of Antiquities of Jordan* 33: 27–42.

Simpson, St. J.
1994   Gazelle Hunters and Salt-collectors: A Further Note on the Solubba. *Bulletin of the American Schools of Oriental Research* 293: 79–81.

S'iroechkovskii, E.E.
1986   *Severn'ii olen'*. Moscow.

Sludskii, A.A.
1955   Saigak v Kazakhstane. *Trud'i Instituta zoologii Akademii nauk Kazakhskoi SSR* 4.

Smith, P., O. Bar-Yosef and A. Sillen
1984   Archaeological and skeletal evidence for dietary change during the late Pleistocene -early Holocene in the Levant. In M.N. Cohen and G. Armelagos (eds.), *Paleopathology at the Origins of Agriculture*, 101–136. New York: Academic Press.

Smith, P. and P. Halstead
1989   The Animal Bone from Medieval and Post - Medieval Doncaster. In P.C. Buckland, J.R. Magilton and C. Hayfield (eds.), *The Archaeology of Doncaster 2. The Medieval and Later Town*, 432–446. British Archaeological Reports, British Series 202 ii.. Oxford: British Archaeological Reports.

Solomatin, A.O.
1973   *Kulan*. Moscow.

Solecki, R.S.
1979   Contemporary Kurdish winter-time inhabitants of Shanidar Cave. *World Archaeology* 10: 318–330.

Speiss, A.E.
1979   *Reindeer and Caribou Hunters — An Archaeological Study*. New York and London: Academic Press.

Speth, J.
1972   The mechanical basis of percussion flaking. *American Antiquity* 37: 34–60.

1981   The Role of Platform Angle and Core Size in Hard-Hammer Percussion Flaking. *Lithic Technology* 10: 16–21.

Stahl, A.
1989   Plant-food processing: implications for dietary quality. In D. Harris and G. Hillman (eds.), *Foraging and Farming — the evolution of plant exploitation*, 171–194. London: Unwin Hyman.

Starck, J.M.
1988   Comparative Analysis of Stone-Ring Artefacts from Baga and Basta. In A. Garrard and H-G Gebel (eds), *The Prehistory of Jordan: The State of Research in 1986, 137-174*. British Archaeological Reports International Series 396, ii. Oxford: British Archaeological Reports.

Stekelis, M.
1950–51 A New Neolithic Industry: The Yarmukian of Palestine. *Israel Exploration Journal* 1: 1–19.

Stekelis, M. and T. Yizraely
1963   Excavations at Nahal Oren, Preliminary Report. *Israel Exploration Journal* 13: 1–12.

Stordeur, D.
1993   Sédentaires et nomades du PPNB final dans le désert du Palmyre (Syrie). *Paléorient* 19/11: 187–204.

Steward, J.H.
1943   Culture Element Distributions 23: Northern and Gosiute Shoshoni. *University of California Anthropological Records* 8/3.

Swanson, E.
1975   *Lithic Technology: Making and Using Stone Tools*. The Hague: Mouton.

Tappen, N.C.
1969   The Relationship of Weathering Cracks to Split-line Orientation in Bone. *American Journal of Physical Anthropology* 31: 191–198.

Tappen, N.C. and G.R. Peske
1970   Weathering Cracks and Split-Line Patterns in Archaeological Bone. *American Antiquity* 35: 383–386.

Tchernov, E. and O. Bar-Yosef
1982   Animal exploitation in the Pre-Pottery Neolithic B period at Wadi Tbeik, Southern Sinai. *Paléorient* 8: 17–37.

Tchernov, E., T. Dayan and Y. Yom-Tov
1986/87 The Paleogeography of *Gazella gazella* and *Gazella dorcas* during the Holocene of the Southern Levant. *Israel Journal of Zoology* 34: 51–59.

Teltser, P. A.
1991   Generalized Core Technology and Tool Use: A Mississippian Example. *Journal of Field Archaeology* 18: 363–375.

Teploukhov, A.F.
1880   O doislamicheskikh zhertvenn'oikh mestakh na Ural'skikh gorakh. *Zapiski Ural'skogo otdeleniya, Obshchestva liubitelei estestvoznaniya* VI. 1.

Terenozhkin, A.I.
1940   O drevnem goncharstve v Khorezme. *Izvestiya Uzbekskogo filiala AN SSSR 6.*

Tolstov, S.P.
1947   Goroda guzov (Istoriko-ètnograficheskie ètiud'i). *Sovetskaya ètnografiya 3.*
1948   *Drevnii Khorezm. Op'it istoriko -arkheologicheskogo issledovaniya.* Moscow.
1958   Rabot'i Khorezmskoi arkheologo-ètnograficheskoi èkspeditsii AN SSSR v 1949-1953 gg. *Trud'i Khorezmskoi arkheologi-ètnograficheskoi èkspeditsii AN SSSR 11.*

Tomka, S.A.
1989   Differentiating Lithic Reduction Techniques: An Experimental Approach. In D.S. Amick and R.P. Mauldin (eds.), *Experiments in Lithic Technology*: 137–161, Oxford: British Archaeological Reports International Series 528.

Torrence, R. (ed.)
1989   *Time, Energy and Stone Tools.* Cambridge: Cambridge University Press.

Tresguerres, J. F.
1991   Grabos Sobre Roca en la Zona de Khirbet es -Samra (Jordania). *III Simposio Biblico Espanol,* 53–63. Valencia-Lisboa: Fundacion Biblica Espanola.

Tret'yakov, P.N.
1934   Pervob'itnaya okhota v Severnoi Azii. *Izvestiya gos. Akademii istorii material'noi kul'tur'i 106.*

Trud'i Orenburgskoi uchenoi arkhivnoi komissii
1906   16, Protokol No. 14 ot 17/XII 1904 g. Orenburg.

Uerpmann, H.-P.
1979   *Probleme der Neolithisierung des Mittelmeerraums. Beihefte zum Tubinger Atlas des Vorderen Orients Reihe B (Geisteswissenschaften) Nr. 28.* Wiesbaden: Dr. Ludwig Reichert Verlag.
1982   Faunal Remains from Shams ed-Din Tannira, a Halafian Site in Northern Syria. *Berytus 30:* 3–52.
1987   *The Ancient Distribution of Ungulate Mammals in the Middle East.* Wiesbaden: Dr. Ludwig Reichert Verlag.

UNDP
1966   United Nations Development Programme (1966) *General Report on the groundwater investigations of the Azraq Basin.* New York: United Nations.

Vainshtein, S.I.
1961   *Tuvints'i-Todzhist'i. Istoriko-ètnograficheskie ocherki.* Moscow.

Valikhanov, Ch.
1904   *Zapiski otdeleniya ètnografii IRGO,* 29. St Petersburg.

Vanderwal, R.L.
1977   The 'fabricator' in Australia and New Guinea. In R.V.S. Wright (ed.), *Stone Tools as Cultural Markers,* 380–390. Australian Institute of Aboriginal Studies, Prehistory and Material Culture Series, 12. Canberra: Australian Institute of Aboriginal Studies.

Vasilievich, G.M.
1969   *Evenki. Istoriko-ètnograficheskie ocherki (18 – nachalo 20 vv.).* Leningrad.

Viktorov, S.V.
1971   *Pust'iniya Ustiurt i vopros'i ee osvoeniya.* Moscow.

Vries, B. de
1981   The Umm el-Jimal Project, 1972–1977. *Bulletin of the American Schools of Oriental Research* 241: 53–72.

Waechter, J. d'A and V. Seton Williams
1938   The Excavations at Wadi Dhobai 1937–1938 and the Dhobaian Industry. *Journal of the Palestine Oriental Society* 18: 1–23.

Walther, F.R.
1972   Social Grouping in Grant's Gazelle (*Gazella granti Brooke* 1827) in the Serengeti National Park. *Tierpsychol* 31: 348–403.

Wetzstein, W.G.
1860   *Reisebericht über Hauran und die Trachonen.* Berlin.

White, P.J.
1968   Fabricators, outils 'ecailles or scalar cores? *Mankind* 6: 658–666.

Wright, K.I.
1990   Grain milling and household economies in early Near Eastern villages. Paper presented at the 1990 Meeting of the British Association for Near Eastern Archaeology, University of Birmingham, November 10–11.
1991   The origins and development of ground stone assemblages in Late Pleistocene Southwest Asia. *Paléorient* 17/1: 19-45.
1992   Ground Stone Assemblage Variation in the Late Pleistocene and Early Holocene of the Levant. Unpublished PhD thesis, Department of Anthropology, Yale University.
n.d.   Grinding tools, food processing and agricultural origins in southwest Asia. Ms.

Wright, K.I., N. Qadi, K. Ibrahim and H. Mustafa
n.d.   Tell Abu Hamid 1986–87: Ground Stone Artifacts. In G. Dollfus and Z. Kafafi (eds.), *Excavations at Tell Abu Hamid, Jordan.* Paris: Editions Recherche sur les Civilisations.

Wright, W.
1895   *Palmyra and Zenobia.* London: Nelson.

Yagodin, V.N.
1963   Marshrutn'ie arkheologicheskie issledovaniya v leboberzhnoi chasti Priaral'skoi delt'i r. Amudar'i. *Material'i Khorezmskoi arkhèologo-ètnograficheskoi èkspeditsii AN SSSR 7.*
1978   Pamyatniki kochev'ikh plemen drevnosti i srednevekov'ya, *Drevnyaya i srednevekoaya kul'tura Iugo-Vostochnogo Ustiurta.*
1981   Khaivan-kala — rannesredneveokov'ii Kerder. *Arkheologicheskie issledovaniya v Karakalpakii.*
1991   *Strelovidn'ie planirovki Ustiurta (Op'it istoriko - kul'turnoi interpretatsii).* Tashkent.

Yagodin, V.N., E.B. Bizhanov and Iu. P. Man'ilov
1975   Otchët ob arkheologo-topografiicheskikh issledovaniyakh na plato Ustiurt v 1974 godu. *Nauchn'ii arkhiv Otdel arkheologii Instituta istorii, yaz'ika i literatur'i Karakalpakskogo filiala AN UzSSR.*

Zarins, J.
1990   Early Pastoral Nomadism and the Settlement of Lower Mesopotamia. *Bulletin of the American Schools of Oriental Research* 280: 31-65.

Zarins, J., Whalen, N., Ibrahim, M. Mursi, al-J. and Khan, M.
1980 Comprehensive Archaeological Survey Program: Preliminary Report on the Central and Southwestern Provinces Survey. *Atlal* 4:9-36.

Zeist, W. van and J. Bakker-Heeres
1982 Archaeobotanical studies in the Levant 1: Neolithic sites in the Damascus Basin: Aswad Ghoraifé, Ramad. *Palaeohistoria* 24: 165–256.
1984 Archaeobotanical studies in the Levant 3: Late Paleolithic Mureybit. *Palaeohistoria* 26: 171–199.

Zeist, W. van and H. Woldring
1980 Holocene vegetation and climate of Northwestern Syria. *Palaeohistoria* 22: 111–125.

Zeuner, F., D. Kirkbride and B. Park
1957 Stone Age Exploration in Jordan, I. *Palestine Exploration Fund Quarterly*: 17–54.

Zohary, D.
1971 Origin of South-West Asiatic Cereals: wheats Barley, Oats and Rye. In P. Davis, P. Harper and I. Hedge (eds.), *Plant Life of South-West Asia,* 235–263. Edinburgh: The Botanical Society of Edinburgh.
1989 Domestication of the South-West Asian Neolithic crop assemblages of cereals, pulses and flax: evidence from the living plants. In D. Harris and G. Hillman (eds.), *Foraging and Farming — the evolution of plant exploitation,* 358–373. London: Unwin Hyman.

Zohary, D. and M. Hopf
1988 *Domestication of Plants in the Old World.* Oxford: Clarendon Press.

Zohary, M.
1962 *Plant Life of Palestine.* New York: Roland Press.
1966 *Flora Palaestina,* Vol. 1. Jerusalem: Israel Academy of Sciences.
1972 *Flora Palaestina,* Vol. 2. Jerusalem: Israel Academy of Sciences.

Plates

Plate 2   Dhuweila: pit P17, showing broken pebbles and ash of phase 5.

Plate 1   Dhuweila: squares 2200, 2100, looking west in final stages of excavation.

Plate 3   Dhuweila: wall AM after partial excavation.

Plate 4   Dhuweila: feature AL.

Plate 6   Dhuweila: feature BH.

Plate 5   Dhuweila: squares 4200, 4100, general view of
pavement at base of Stage 2.

247

Plate 7   A. Fabric impressed plaster; B. Cotton fibres embedded in plaster (x300).

Plate 8   Rock carving: Dhuweila, series of horned animals facing right, incised on cobble.

Plate 9   Rock carving: Dhuweila, two horned animals facing right, incised on cobble.

Plate 10   Rock carving: Abu Masiade esh-Sharqi, three horned animals facing right, one suckling (?), incised on cobble.

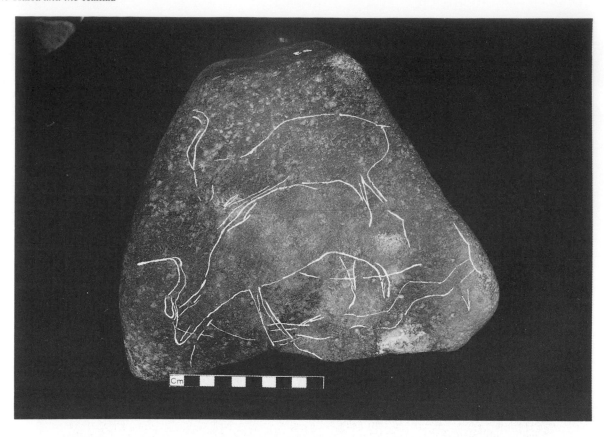

Plate 11   Rock carving: Abu Masiade esh-Sharqi, two horned animals facing left, wavy parallel lines below, incised on cobble.

Plate 12   Rock carving: Abu Masiade al-Gharbi, horned animal facing right, incised on cobble.

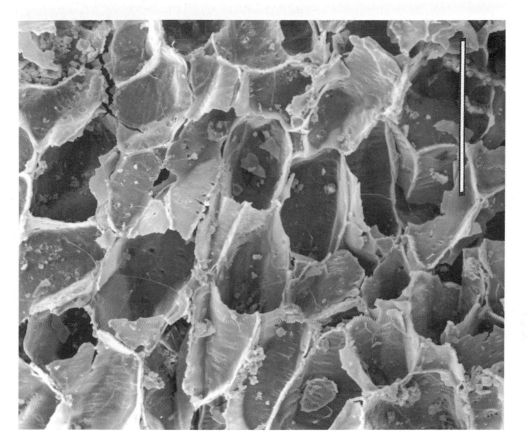

Plate 14   Archaeological Cistanche tubulosa (Orobancheaceae): parenchymatous cells.

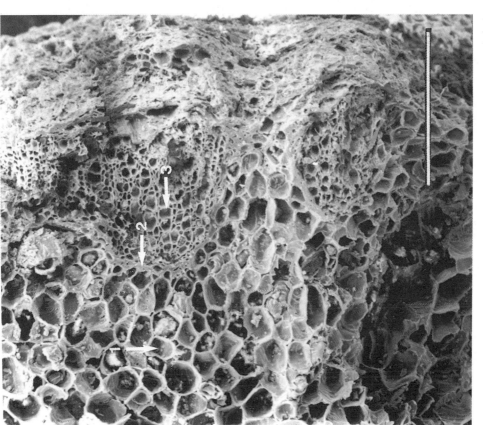

Plate 13   Archaeological Cistanche tubulosa (Orobancheaceae): parenchymatous tissues of the swollen stem showing vascular bundle. 1 parenchymatous cells; 2 deteriorated phloem; 3 xylem vessels.

Plate 15   Harra: typical landscape with recent corrals located on ancient flint scatters along a small wadi.

Plate 16   Isolated basalt-capped limestone peak, flint outcrops on slope, knapping sites on summit and 'kite' walls running across base of hill.